UNIVERSITY LEADERSHIP IN URBAN SCHOOL RENEWAL

UNIVERSITY LEADERSHIP IN URBAN SCHOOL RENEWAL

Edited by Nancy L. Zimpher
and
Kenneth R. Howey

Foreword by Michael Baer
Foreword by Gregory M. St. L. O'Brien

AMERICAN COUNCIL ON EDUCATION
PRAEGER
Series on Higher Education

Library of Congress Cataloging-in-Publication Data

University leadership in urban school renewal /
    edited by Nancy L. Zimpher and Kenneth R. Howey ; foreword by
    Michael Baer ; foreword by Gregory M. St. L. O'Brien.
    p. cm.—(ACE/Praeger series on higher education)
  Includes bibliographical references and index.
  ISBN 0–275–98095–2 (alk. paper)
  1. College-school cooperation—United States. 2. Urban schools—
United States. I. Nancy L. Zimpher II. Kenneth R. Howey III. Series

LB2331.53.U53   2004
378.1'03—dc 22   2004047972

British Library Cataloguing in Publication Data is available.

Library of Congress Catalog Card Number: 2004047972
ISBN: 0–275–98095–2

First published in 2004

Praeger Publishers, 88 Post Road West, Westport, CT 06881

An imprint of Greenwood Publishing Group, Inc.
www.praeger.com

Printed in the United States of America

The paper used in this book complies with the
Permanent Paper Standard issued by the National
Information Standards Organization (Z39.48–1984).

10 9 8 7 6 5 4 3 2 1

The editors and publisher gratefully acknowledge permission to reprint passages from
the following:

"The Quantum Jump" by Julius Stulman as published by the World Institute Council,
Inc., in *Fields Within Fields . . . Within Fields*, 1972. Reprinted with the permission of the
Estate of Julius Stulman.

Contents

Foreword

It is difficult to imagine themes that might resonate more closely with the values of the American Council on Education (ACE) than the ideas that are presented in this book: leadership, change, community partnership, and the importance of teacher education and learning. In its major report, "To Touch the Future," issued in October 1999 by the ACE Presidents' Task Force on Teacher Education, the leadership of institutional presidents was cited as critical to addressing the issue of providing the American K–12 educational system with an adequate number of well-prepared teachers. That report noted the research identifying the quality of classroom teachers as being the single most important variable in the preparation and success of students. The panel writing the report, in their more than one year of deliberation, concluded that the involvement of the entire institution was crucial to the preparation of teachers and that only in response to strong leadership from institutional presidents and chancellors was that involvement likely to occur.

The timing for this book, frankly, could not be better. With higher education facing increasing financial constraints and our nation's systems of public education under continued strain, it is imperative that we dedicate our efforts to strengthening the partnership of higher education with K–12 education and with the community to ensure the success of education at all levels. This book features examples of university leaders who took a personal interest in and led their institutions' efforts to improve the quality of teacher preparation and develop partnerships with school systems to ensure that more future teachers were recruited, prepared, and provided with an excellent transition into their teaching role. These leaders used their influential positions to communicate with their campus communities and to partner beyond their institutions with school systems and the broader communities in which they are located.

This book features the stories of several presidents and chancellors of our urban institutions, whose communities, like many others, face enormous challenges and who have taken on tremendous responsibility for the future of our youth. These individuals—whom you will meet through their candid stories in the chapters of this book—understand that the economic and social futures of our metropolitan areas are dependent on educated men and women. The teachers their universities prepare today will shape tomorrow's leaders.

The stakes are high, and the need for informed, creative, and strategic leadership is great. In this regard, this book offers important lessons, not only for leaders of large public institutions but also for leaders of institutions of all kinds, for the authors of these chapters have numerous practical and useful things to say about setting a vision, mobilizing teams, and perhaps most important, about collaborating amid the complex realities of twenty-first century America. If there is one thing that higher education is increasingly learning, it is that there is a vital need to partner—with business, with neighbors, with other institutions and organizations, and with the communities we serve. The triumphs—and the struggles—outlined in this book are both informative and inspiring.

They are also a call to action. As these chapters make plain, active presidential leadership on behalf of teacher education reform and school renewal reflects the responsibilities of higher education to be an active participant in the continuum of learning that is vital to our nation's future. And yet it is not only the responsibility of higher education. Ensuring caring, competent teachers and learning environments in which all our youth can thrive is the shared responsibility of presidents and chancellors, their colleges and universities, and the communities in which we live—it is *our* shared responsibility. As this book makes clear, committed individuals within and without our colleges and universities must work together to improve education for all. The 14 institutions profiled here have answered this call and provided a roadmap for others. The time is right to follow their lead.

Michael Baer
Senior Vice President, Programs and Analysis
American Council on Education

Foreword

Play ball!

The connection between our national pastime and the 19 institutions that make up the Great Cities' Universities coalition (GCU) is both historical and metaphoric. Historical in that the roots of our now-incorporated coalition go back four decades to the time when leaders from 13 public research-oriented universities—which just happened to be located in cities with professional baseball teams—joined together to advance the interests of their institutions. What seemed a quirky organizing principle, however, soon proved to be an apt metaphor for the goals and aspirations for the GCU. GCU represents the alliance of public research-oriented institutions that were both located in and engaged in shaping the future of America's "big league" cities. For the universities that comprised that original Urban 13, as it was known then, and for the 19 institutions that make up the GCU now, stepping up to the plate in a leadership role in our nation's metropolitan centers is central to each institution's mission. Not to belabor the metaphor, but the presidents and chancellors of the GCU believe that the public urban research universities we lead are and will continue to be the "heavy hitters" shaping our nation's future for years to come. Why? Because it is our rapidly growing urban centers that are driving our economic, cultural, and political future, and it is the public institutions in those centers that are the engines behind that growth. Our institutions, through our strong community partnerships, and the almost 350,000 diverse students we serve, are uniquely able to provide the creativity, innovation and research-based strategies to address challenges in urban education, criminal justice, workforce development, urban transportation, and biomedical and health care delivery.

Foremost among the challenges facing our urban universities is the issue of public education and school renewal. The GCU institutions are especially qualified to address these issues; although we represent less than 1 percent of the nation's colleges and universities, we prepare more than 20 percent of the nation's teachers. We have a responsibility to the youth of America through the teachers we educate, and we take that charge seriously. In 1997 the Great Cities' Universities was officially incorporated with a mandate to focus on collaborative initiatives among our institutions to enhance our collective capacity to make a significant impact on our metropolitan centers. Our first federally funded collaboration was the Urban Teacher Educator Corps, a partnership to find innovative ways to attract, train, retain, and support large numbers of new certified teachers for our most-challenged urban schools.

This book provides an overview of the myriad ways in which GCU member institutions are making a difference in preparing qualified and exemplary teachers for the classrooms that need them most. But this book is more than a compendium of innovative ideas. It is also a thoughtful examination of what lies behind K–16 renewal and the leadership efforts that will be required if we are to accomplish change.

While the 14 GCU presidents and chancellors who have contributed to this book would be the first to tell you that their jobs—like baseball— are team efforts, it is nonetheless certain that the complex challenges that face our urban schools and cities also require dedicated and accomplished leadership. And so this book also presents a thoughtful look at the kinds of leadership that will be necessary to forge public-private collaborations, unite communities in support of our children, and advance the missions of our urban universities to serve, to teach, and to discover.

As president of the GCU—and a former urban university president of more than 15 years—I welcome this book for two reasons. First, it has important ideas to share regarding the leadership strategies and philosophies that enable individuals to contribute in significant ways within a complex urban environment. While the job of an urban university president presents unique challenges—as I can attest—the thoughtful analysis of the authors of these chapters also offers valuable insights into leadership in general and is an important addition to the literature of leadership of public institutions. Second, this book provides a clarion call to action for higher education to make teacher education and school renewal an all-university priority. Our colleges and universities—of all kinds—affect the education of America's youth through the students we prepare, the research we engage in, and the connections we can provide. To paraphrase the African proverb, it takes a university—not just a School of Education—to raise a teacher, and this book demonstrates not only why that is so but how that responsibility can be fulfilled.

I want to thank Nancy Zimpher and Kenneth Howey, the editors of this collection, for their leadership in convening these presidents and encouraging them to tell their stories of personal and institutional leadership in changing the face of urban education in America. The stories described in this volume are the narratives of real individuals and of their failures as well as successes. Most important, as you'll hear in the first-person voice of the president or chancellor narrator, these are stories of hope and excitement in the future of our urban institutions and in the schools they touch.

Gregory M. St. L. O'Brien, May 2003
President, Great Cities' Universities Coalition

Great Cities' Universities Member Institutions

- City University of New York
- Cleveland State University
- Georgia State University
- Florida International University
- Indiana University–Purdue University Indianapolis
- Portland State University
- University of Alabama at Birmingham
- University of Cincinnati
- University of Colorado at Denver
- University of Houston
- University of Illinois at Chicago
- University of Massachusetts Boston
- University of Memphis
- University of Missouri–Kansas City

- University of Missouri–St. Louis
- University of New Orleans
- University of Wisconsin–Milwaukee
- Virginia Commonwealth University
- Wayne State University

Acknowledgments

If the nature of presidential leadership at public universities can be characterized by one word, it would be *collaborative*, and nothing illustrates this spirit so well as the compilation of this book. We are indebted to our colleagues at the Great Cities' Universities, not only for their thoughtful contributions to this volume but also for their mutual support, innovative perspectives, and continuing professional guidance. Participation in the GCU is a unique professional privilege.

While the stories and ideas expressed herein are very much those of each chancellor and president, they also reflect the contributions of a team of colleagues who helped to compile data, interview participants, consult with other members of the Great Cities' Universities, and shape the writing of the chapters across several months of highly interactive discussions and meetings around the themes that are explored here. We acknowledge with gratitude the work of the GCU documenters who have assisted the presidents and chancellors in helping us to explore the ways in which university leaders and their communities are partnering for school renewal.

GCU Documenters

Marty Alberg, University of Memphis
Donna Bergh, Portland State University
John Cleek, University of Missouri–Kansas City

Marie Colombo, Wayne State University

Melanie Haimes-Bartolf, Virginia Commonwealth University

Jennier Hill, University of Missouri–Kansas City

Rachel Kincaid, University of New Orleans

Neva Nahan, Wayne State University

Charu Malik, University of Wisconsin–Milwaukee

Monica Medina, Indiana University–Purdue University Indianapolis

Flint Mitchell, University of New Orleans

Fran Peterman, Cleveland State University

Stephanie Harting Rockette, University of Missouri–St. Louis

Ralph Tucker, University of Massachusetts Boston

Carolyn Vander Schee, Georgia State University

Nelson Vincent, University of Cincinnati

Susan Vivano, University of Missouri–St. Louis

Susan Wienstein, University of Illinois at Chicago

We also want to add personal thanks to Charu Malik, whose attention to a thousand details and extraordinary organizational talent were essential to the success not only of this written work but also to the meetings and discussions that sparked the ideas it explores. Thanks also to M. J. Brukardt for her editorial assistance.

While the strengths of this volume are the result of the combined efforts of our authors and contributors, any omissions are those of its editors. It is our hope that these chapters will inspire others—as they have us—to a renewed commitment to educational excellence in our urban schools.

Nancy L. Zimpher
Kenneth R. Howey

CHAPTER 1

Engagement in Urban School Renewal

Kenneth R. Howey and Nancy L. Zimpher

The fundamental warrant for the broad and sustained engagement of universities in assisting with the success of urban youth in their elementary and secondary schooling is made on moral grounds: all children have an educational birthright to competent and caring teachers and high-quality schools.... The presidents writing in this volume believe that universities share in the responsibility for ensuring that this birthright is fulfilled.

At a time when the challenges facing higher education and its leaders have never been greater, we dare to ask urban university presidents and chancellors to do more. While we recognize the pressing and legitimate presidential concerns for institutional growth, academic and research rigor, equality of access, secure funding streams, technology integration, and increased community engagement, we would add another priority: urban school renewal. The reasons for this are based on convictions both altruistic and self-interested: They are altruistic in that the future of our nation rests on how well we educate all our children; today, millions of young people are struggling, thanks to failing public schools. As educators, we cannot stand by and refuse to act. These convictions are self-interested in that students in our cities' elementary and high schools today will be students at our universities tomorrow. If our institutions are to succeed, our future students must be prepared for what we can offer. Increasingly they are not.

Fortunately this call to community partnership is already being answered. In countless institutions across the country, leaders in higher education are becoming more actively involved in urban school renewal. This book provides firsthand accounts of how 14 urban university presidents are providing leadership in addressing the problems attached to the education of youth in large urban centers. It is designed both to inspire like-minded efforts and to provide an assessment of the leadership strategies such efforts will demand.

The presidents and chancellors and their universities profiled here are members of the Great Cities' Universities Coalition (GCU), a coalition of 19 public urban research universities that are collaborating to address pressing challenges within their urban communities. These GCU universities are located in urban, metropolitan areas whose public schools collectively serve almost 2.7 million pupils. The 19 GCU universities together enroll almost 350,000 full- and part-time college students, and they annually prepare almost 25,000 teachers.

To put the efforts of the GCU presidents and chancellors in context, this chapter will outline the challenges and opportunities that face our public schools, their teachers, and the universities that train those teachers. It will examine the ways in which university presidents and chancellors can exert leadership in meeting these opportunities, both within the university and with their partnering communities. The chapters that follow build on this framework by examining specific programs that are being developed at urban institutions across the country and by analyzing the leadership strategies employed to support those programs.

THE RATIONALE FOR ACTION

The rationale for university presidents to assume a leadership role in advancing precollege education is fourfold. First, the problems in P–12 urban schools are deeply rooted, pervasive, and long-standing. Urban school districts by themselves have not been able to stem the tide of failure, and resources across the broader community need to be mobilized better to address these problems. The respect typically accorded presidents in urban universities provides them with a convening power to help coalesce various community leaders and agencies toward resolving problems attendant to urban schools.

Second, university presidents are educators, and as such, they bring their understanding of educational issues to the particular problems of urban P–12 education, especially in partnership with their elementary and secondary educational counterparts.

Third, the universities in which presidents and chancellors serve—as is clearly demonstrated throughout the chapters that follow—afford a wealth of resources to help redress these problems.

And fourth, presidents understand that their universities, although not on the front lines in instructing precollege youth, nonetheless have some liability for the academic successes and failures of these youngsters. There is growing empirical evidence that high-quality teaching is essential to high student achievement. Because urban universities prepare large numbers of teachers for urban schools, and because the role of universities in recruiting, preparing, supporting, and further educating teachers over time is central to quality teaching and pupil learning, universities bear responsibility for the level of educational success in our urban centers.

How critical are high-quality teachers to student success? In Tennessee, millions of K–12 students' standardized test scores have been compiled over the years. Sanders and Rivers (1998) studied these data to examine the impact of teachers on their students. They ranked both the top and bottom 20 percent of teachers in terms of their ability to improve their pupils' scores in various content areas, including mathematics. Since students are generally assigned annually to teachers on an arbitrary basis, over time Tennessee students encountered teachers ranked in effectiveness in varying degrees from high to low. The Sanders and Rivers study contrasted students who were similar in achievement at the end of the second grade. Children assigned for three years in a row (grades 3, 4, and 5) to teachers in the top 20 percent now placed on average in the 83rd percentile, while those assigned to teachers in the lowest 20 percent now scored below the 30th percentile. There was an astonishing 54-point difference between the two groups of students, who three years before had scored alike.

Based on this research, improved teacher preparation is understandably and increasingly a focal point in policy deliberations. In 1996, for example, the National Commission on Teaching and America's Future (NCTAF) concluded that recruiting, preparing, and retaining good teachers was the central strategy for improving our schools. The NCTAF reporxt underscored the fact that school reform will not succeed unless it focuses on assuring a "caring, competent, and qualified teacher for every child" (p. 10).

THE MAGNITUDE OF THE PROBLEM

While many factors militate against achieving this bold and challenging goal, two stand out. The first is the sheer magnitude of the number of new teachers that will be needed in the short term. The NCTAF's recent summary report (2003), titled *No Dream Denied: A Pledge to America's Children*, graphically portrayed the teaching force in the United States as a revolving-door profession. It reported that more than 1 million teachers enter or leave teaching annually—roughly a third of all teachers (p. 11). Daunting as these numbers are, they mask a second, greater problem. The teacher shortage is greatest in high-need or high-poverty schools—many of which are located in urban centers—precisely where talented teachers are least likely to be found. For example, Lankford, Loeb, and Wyckoff (2002) analyzed 15 years of administrative records in the state of New York. They examined teacher quality through a composite index of teacher degree, experience, in- or out-of-field assignment, the ranking of the university the teacher attended, and scores on state certification examinations. They concluded that the teachers who teach poor, minority students in *urban* areas are substantially less qualified than other teachers. Jepsen and Rivkin (2002), in a study of class size in California, reported that minority students in high-poverty schools were six times more likely *not* to have a qualified teacher than white students in low-poverty schools. The NCTAF concluded that across the country we have the least-qualified teachers precisely where the most-qualified teachers are needed (1996).

Contemporary American schools remain sharply segregated by race and social class. Unfortunately these factors are often highly correlated. For example, Orfield, Bachmeier, and Eitle (1997) reported that only 5 percent of segregated white schools face conditions of concentrated poverty, contrasted with an astounding 80 percent of segregated black and Latino schools. It should further be noted that between 1980 and 1992, Caucasian student enrollment in this country's largest cities declined by 20 percent (Council of the Great City Schools, 1994). Hypersegregation of African American and Hispanic students has become commonplace. Urban teachers, Weiner reports, "were less likely to work with White students and more likely to be teaching immigrants and when teaching African-American and Hispanic students might well be working in schools that were not racially diverse" (2000, p. 388).

Urban education is often a bleak landscape, but it is not without hope. There are qualitative differences from school to school and classroom to classroom in our urban centers, and there are thousands of successful urban schools and urban teachers. Even in high-poverty schools the majority of students graduate (66%) and are likely to be employed or attending school full time (73%) several years after graduating (*The State of the Cities*, 1997). Nonetheless, the present situation simply cannot be excused. Our most precious resource, our very future, is the youth who attend these schools.

Data from the 1996 National Center for Education Statistics (NCES) publication *Urban Schools: The Challenge of Location and Poverty* reveal that more low-income students attend urban schools—44 percent, contrasted with 23 percent of suburban and 30 percent of rural youth. Urban students are also more likely to live with a single parent, to have less-educated or unemployed parent(s), to have handicapping conditions or learning disabilities, to be homeless, and to have difficulty speaking English. Further, they are more likely than their suburban and rural counterparts to have more than one of the above attributes.

High-poverty schools are defined by the U.S. Department of Education as schools where more than 40 percent of students receive free or reduced-cost lunch. There are growing pockets of the underclass in most urban settings where high-poverty schools are located. Youngsters in high-poverty schools are routinely exposed to safety and health risks, have limited access to regular medical care, have changed schools frequently, and are more prone to risk-taking behavior resulting in conditions such as teen pregnancy.

Given schools with limited resources and large numbers of teachers with provisional licenses or teaching out of field in urban settings, is it any wonder that the NCES study reports that students in urban public schools compared less favorably than students in suburban schools on *all* educational outcomes and less favorably than their rural counterparts on approximately half of the indicators of academic achievement, including 8th-grade achievement and high school completion (1996).

Conditions in these schools and school communities characterized by economic impoverishment also often serve as *disincentives* when teachers consider where they will teach. For example, the eight-year Research About Teacher Education (RATE) Study sponsored by the American Association of Colleges for Teacher Education (AACTE, 1990) consistently revealed that the majority of prospective teachers (more than 85%) preferred to teach in contexts other than urban neighborhood schools, where they often differ from their students in terms of culture, language, race, and class. Further, up to half of the novice teachers who do begin teaching in urban schools leave within three years. For universities to prepare teachers to teach effectively in a challenging urban school is not enough. They must work in partnership to ensure conditions are such that teachers will stay and continue to develop professionally.

In the face of urban poverty, segregation, and failing academic achievement, the need for high-quality urban teachers has never been greater nor in greater jeopardy. The presidents writing in this volume believe that universities share in the responsibility for ensuring that the educational birthright to competent and caring teachers and high-quality schools is fulfilled for all children. And they are taking action on several fronts, as this volume will demonstrate, to improve the quality of schooling and teaching in urban settings.

In this regard we have identified 15 programmatic priorities where presidents and chancellors can exert leadership. Organized into three distinct areas of focus, the first group of priorities targets *programmatic change*. The second five strategies focus on *organizational change* within the university, and the final five activities involve *leadership and partnering* outside the university. Not all priorities will apply equally to every institution, but together they form a comprehensive outline of the range of opportunities available to university leaders who seek to partner for school reform.

PRESIDENTS AND PROGRAMMATIC PRIORITIES WITHIN THE UNIVERSITY

Five priorities for presidential leadership are presented here:

1. Strengthen general and liberal education for prospective urban teachers.
2. Ensure that diversity is value-added.
3. Improve and extend leadership preparation for urban schools.
4. Promote interprofessional preparation for comprehensive urban schools.
5. Develop distinctive urban teacher preparation programs.

1. Strengthen General and Liberal Education for Prospective Urban Teachers

That prospective teachers need breadth and depth of study in the subject matter or content areas they teach is hardly debatable. In a recent review of the research on teacher preparation prepared for the U.S. Department of Education by Wilson, Floden, and Ferrini-Mundy (2001), the obvious was underscored: "consistent with common belief, several studies showed a positive connection between teachers' subject matter preparation and both higher student achievement and higher teacher performance on evaluations, particularly in mathematics, science, and reading" (p.7). These are the very core areas in which so many urban youth are failing and where presidents, along with provosts, deans, and faculty, can make meaningful inroads by building bridges and programmatic coherence between professional studies and prerequisite study in general and liberal education.

As she describes in her chapter, President Shirley Raines, of the University of Memphis, began her tenure with a "simple act with a strong message"—she asked the dean of the College of Education to meet with the Arts and Science faculty and the dean of Arts and Science to meet with the Education faculty. The scaffolding for sustained cooperation was quickly put in place, and the two faculties have since jointly formulated an Institute for Excellence in Teaching and Learning in order to develop a comprehensive approach to improving and sustaining the highest levels of teaching and learning in the Memphis schools. Martha Gilliland, chancellor at the University of Missouri–Kansas City, writes, "teacher and principal preparation cannot be the responsibility of the School of Education alone." She hired a provost who agreed with this commitment, and she is supporting him as he changes the reward system so that faculty will be reinforced in their efforts to participate in this important activity.

The strengthened linkages between professional and general study, however, need to extend beyond the subject matter taught by P–12 teachers to include a study of the urban experience and culture as well. The culture shock felt by so many novice teachers who take a teaching position in high-poverty urban schools is well documented. A deep chasm often exists between the teacher's social status, cultural norms, and language and language patterns and those of the students. Given that the pipeline of prospective teachers is still composed primarily of individuals who are of European descent, middle class, and monolingual and who have grown up in the suburbs or a rural area (Zimpher, 1989), the problem deserves the attention of the university at large.

Teaching is a highly interpersonal and moral enterprise, and a rich understanding of youngsters and the context in which they live is an essential aspect of good pedagogy. It is also abundantly clear that for many teachers, especially those who will teach in high-poverty schools, the understandings and appreciation of the students they will teach and the settings in which they live cannot be acquired in abbreviated preparation programs. As a direct response to this problem, universities in urban settings should prepare all of their students—especially prospective teachers—to understand more fully the nature of urban communities and the multiple cultures typically found within them. General education courses, with a focus on urban contexts, can explore diverse urban perspectives through such lenses as those provided by the historian, the sociologist, the cultural anthropologist, the political scientist, and the urban geographer, assisting all students in acquiring multiple interpretations and richer understandings of urban communities and cultures. Examples of this general education urban focus at Portland State University and the University of Wisconsin–Milwaukee are described in chapters that follow.

Working relationships between faculty members in professional schools of education and those in the arts, sciences, and humanities are fraught with challenges related to mission, professional identity, time, rewards, and incentives. It is unrealistic to expect faculty members in the arts, sciences, and humanities to forsake their disciplinary scholarship or departmental mission to become deeply engaged in teacher education. It is not unreasonable, however, for several of these faculty members in urban universities to have an urban focus in one or more of their course offerings, whether their specialty is anthropology or political science. They can collaborate on developing a thematic program of study that can serve not only prospective teachers but also the student body as a whole. Urban university presidents can encourage such program development.

2. Ensure That Diversity Is Value-Added

The rich diversity that exists across the faculty and student body in most urban universities should also contribute to students' appreciation of and ability to flourish in urban schools and urban communities. Gurin (2000), in her testimony in support of the affirmative action undertaken at the University of Michigan Law School, delineated three types of diversity and the long-term positive benefits for students who had the opportunity to engage extensively in each. She defined the *structural diversity* of an institution primarily in terms of the racial and ethnic composition of the student body. The incorporation of knowledge about diversity in the curriculum she labeled *classroom diversity*. Equally important, she argued, is informal *interactional diversity* in the host of social, cultural, entertainment, and athletic events available in university settings. We would add a fourth dimension, *instructional diversity*, found in faculty members who have the pedagogical or instructional expertise to draw positively upon the diversity in their classroom interactions. As Gurin notes, "a racially and ethnically diverse university student body has far-ranging and significant benefits for all students, non-minorities and minorities alike. Students learn better in a diverse educational environment, and they are better prepared to become active participants in our pluralistic, democratic society once they leave such a setting" (p. 1).

Knowing how to capitalize on diversity is critical to the success of teachers in urban contexts. There is a range of activities that university leaders can pursue to promote diversity and emphasize its beneficial effects, including aggressively recruiting diverse faculty and students; designing curriculum that explicitly addresses multiple dimensions of diversity; linking, in a variety of ways, the formal curriculum to a host of cultural events, activities, and agencies on campus; and finally, promoting instructional strategies in which diverse viewpoints are value-added. Daniel Bernstine, president at Portland State University, has made diversity a pervasive priority for the university. As he describes in his chapter, he initiated a Diversity Action Council and academic units have developed diversity plans that address matters of recruitment, structural changes, and resource allocation focused on diversity.

3. Improve and Extend Leadership Preparation for Urban Schools

The impact of strong leadership in every context—including education—is well documented in multiple literatures. Conversely it is a common lack of instructional leadership in urban schools that contributes to many of the shortcomings that exist. Resnick and Glennan (2002) state the problem:

> The diffused control of professional development resources, coupled with frequently inept preparation and recruitment of new teachers, leads to inadequate development of professional competencies and cultures (Ball and Cohen, 1999; Miles and Guiney, 2000; NCTAF, 1996). Meanwhile, district administrators, from principals to central office staff, spend relatively little time in classrooms and even less time in analyzing instruction with teachers. They may arrange time for teachers' meetings and professional development, but they rarely provide intellectual leadership for growth in teaching skill (Fink and Resnick, 2001). The structure of large school districts makes it difficult for administrators to provide instructional leadership. (p. 4)

There are two readily apparent all-university strategies that can address this problem. The first is to go beyond the School or College of Education and draw on the broader resources of the university in preparing principals, superintendents, and other key administrators, ideally in partnership with urban districts and the broader community. Resources in social work, business, law, and medicine all can be brought to bear on preparing leaders to deal with the complex problems and the coordination of social services attendant to many urban schools. At the University of Illinois at Chicago (UIC), for example, Chancellor Sylvia Manning has had an impact on the large Chicago Public Schools district by encouraging the UIC Center for School Leadership Development to administer the Chicago Principals Assessment Center. At the University of Massachusetts in Boston, the distance-learning dean partnered with the Massachusetts Association of School Principals to launch a Web-based Superintendents Academy that provides modules and graduate credit courses statewide.

A second bold direction would be, again in partnership, to develop leadership teams at every school level. The challenges of urban schools require shared leadership, involving such individuals as lead teachers, social workers, media technologists, school psychologists, and others working closely together at the school site. The Milwaukee Partnership Academy, described by Nancy Zimpher, former Chancellor of the University of Wisconsin–Milwaukee, is doing this by establishing learning or leadership teams in every one of the 165 schools in the Milwaukee Public Schools.

4. Promote Interprofessional Preparation for Comprehensive Urban Schools

A corollary to training leadership teams is the design of *interprofessional programs*, or agency-based interdisciplinary training programs that enable urban P–12 schools, especially in high-poverty settings, also to provide direct links to social services, family, medical, and legal support as needed. As Davies, the founder of the Institute for Responsive Education and a leader in school/family/community partnerships, writes, "school success and community success are linked.... Linking school and community development is important because we know that educational progress for the have-nots requires progress in the areas of access to affordable housing, good health care, jobs, transportation, safe streets, and reduction of alcohol and drug abuse" (2002, p. 392).

Gerald Bepko, during his tenure as chancellor at Indiana University–Purdue University Indianapolis (IUPUI), helped to mobilize prospective teachers, student nurses, and those completing master's degrees in social work to design an interdisciplinary curriculum, in conjunction with community professionals. Grants also supported community renewal in neighborhoods adjoining the IUPUI campus. At Virginia Commonwealth University, President Eugene Trani encouraged a formal partnership between the Carver neighborhood, a predominately African American community, and more than 30 academic and administrative units for school and community renewal activities.

5. Develop Distinctive Urban Teacher Preparation Programs

Professional preparation programs designed specifically for urban teachers is a fifth opportunity that requires presidential leadership. Our long history with teacher preparation and urban teacher preparation has demonstrated that placing teachers for a short time in an urban school is simply not enough preparation for them to succeed in these schools. More professional programs are needed that explicitly acknowledge the urban context throughout the curriculum. A model program mission statement for such an urban focus might look like this:

> The purpose of the [Urban/Multicultural Teacher Education Program] is to prepare highly qualified teachers to work in schools in urban/multicultural settings with children who come primarily from impoverished families. [It] is framed in the disciplines of social foundations, particularly sociology and

anthropology of education. The politics of schooling are examined through a sociological analysis of school structures. They examine the ways in which political and social structures impact teachers' work lives in urban school bureaucracies. The traditional "methods" of language arts, science, math, and social studies are framed as part of the elementary school curriculum but within the *sociocultural context of children's lives*. The methods portion of our program is also grounded in transformative school practices based on the premise that traditional schooling has not been successful in urban/ multicultural communities and that teachers must have a wide repertoire of pedagogical and curricular practices that engage students from diverse communities. (Howey, 1996, p. 21)

From such urban mission statements, specific urban themes can be derived that can run throughout the preparation program so that in a recursive manner prospective teachers can acquire needed abilities and understandings to succeed in an urban context. The need to centrally involve experienced, expert teachers from urban schools cannot be emphasized strongly enough. The experience and craft wisdom of urban teachers and administrators is needed in rethinking all aspects of urban teacher preparation. This is not to suggest that university presidents should be engaged in the actual design of professional education programs. They can, however, take leadership in underscoring the need for programs designed specifically to recruit and prepare teachers for urban schools where major shortages of qualified teachers exist.

Joseph Steger, now retired from the University of Cincinnati, exhibited strong leadership toward ensuring that the Cincinnati Initiative for Teacher Education (CITE) program would be put in place to prepare teachers for urban schools. This distinctive partnership between the University, the Cincinnati Public Schools, and the teachers' union places prospective teachers with master teachers who supervise them in yearlong paid internships.

Several of the chapters that follow describe how presidents have been active in supporting rigorous alternative preparation programs. Blanche Touhill, as chancellor at the University of Missouri–St. Louis, assigned one of her endowed professors to work half time with the St. Louis Public Schools to develop a joint, standards-based program for midcareer transition teachers. As a result, in the 2000–2001 school year, there were no middle or high school teachers in the St. Louis Public Schools who did not hold an appropriate specialized teaching credential.

Our brief review of five programmatic leadership opportunities within the university is provided to illustrate the range of areas where presidents and chancellors can exert their power and expertise to help redress the multiple problems attached to the education of precollege youth. We are well aware that curricular changes, instructional innovations, and the design of new programs lie primarily within the purview of faculty and under the aegis of departmental chairs, deans, and the provost. Nonetheless, presidents, as the accountable leaders of their institutions, also bear responsibility for core functions internally in addition to the fund raising, statesmanship, and political involvement they are responsible for externally. Building on these five strategies, presidents can concurrently work toward more broad-based organizational change, as outlined in the section that follows.

LEADERSHIP AND ORGANIZATIONAL CHANGE WITHIN THE ACADEMY

While presidential leadership is the cornerstone of this volume—particularly in relationship to internal institutional conditions that affect teacher education and efforts to support K–12 school renewal—presidents cannot lead alone. They must, by necessity, set in motion the ways and means of building a broader base of institutional support for university-wide engagement. Over time, as will be evident in the chapters that follow, university presidents find their own distinctive ways of encouraging institutional change and participation. Here we direct attention to five strategies that particularly support institutional engagement in teacher education reform and urban school renewal:

1. Structure initiatives to ensure cross-disciplinary participation.
2. Broaden leadership involvement.
3. Encourage the development of institution-wide clinical faculty roles.
4. Ensure that rewards and incentives support institutional initiatives.
5. Utilize the convening power of the presidency to mobilize others.

1. Structure Initiatives to Ensure Cross-disciplinary Participation

For most of the past century, American universities have been organized after the Germanic model of the modern university, with disciplines arranged within larger units called schools and colleges. We gain in this organizational pattern an integration of related disciplinary study that strengthens intellectual thought and programmatic power. But with this time-honored structure we also lose the integration of thought and the interdisciplinary properties of most professions; we segregate the range of disciplines that can inform the practice of each academic and professional pursuit. Nowhere is this truer, perhaps, than in the education of teachers, an endeavor historically under the purview of schools and colleges of education.

Far too often teacher *general* knowledge (usually embedded in the liberal studies curriculum), *content* knowledge (typically housed in colleges of the arts and sciences) and *pedagogical* knowledge (typically pursued in schools and colleges of education) are not well connected to one another, either intellectually or in terms of thoughtful curriculum organization. Presidents who aspire to lead reform initiatives in teacher education as all-university activities have to find ways to overcome the silo effect of these largely independent but nonetheless historically important organizational divisions. There are numerous accounts throughout this book of ways in which universities, such as the University of Memphis, are encouraging cross-disciplinary networks.

One way to break down institutional silos is by creating some variation of a matrix organization. If departments and schools are viewed as "vertical" structures within the university, "horizontal" structures that cut across academic units provide the "matrix" character, "giving staff freedom and flexibility. It is designed to create a little disequilibrium in the academy" (Zimpher, Percy, & Brukardt, 2002, p. 178). It can also eliminate, to some degree, the silos and turf battles that often accompany institutional change. James Duderstadt, president emeritus of the University of Michigan, refers to this image as a divisionless university, "a web of structures" (2000, p. B6) that integrates disciplines and colleges both horizontally and vertically. However executed, presidents need to think in terms of fluid organizational structures that break down institutional barriers and constraining reward structures that could squelch any bona fide all-university effort to reform teacher education. This has been promulgated at the University of Wisconsin–Milwaukee through a Milwaukee Idea office that coordinates a campuswide community engagement effort and funds a range of interdisciplinary activities to promote partnerships with the community.

2. Broaden Leadership Participation

Sylvia Manning refers in her chapter to "distributed leadership"—which the president can implement in many ways, including the appointment of one or more deans to work horizontally across schools and colleges on an institutional priority, such as building all-university/community partnerships. These individuals typically have a special designation that signals responsibility and authority for a given priority that cuts across academic units. For example, a dean can simultaneously assume vertical authority for his or her school or college while at the same time taking on some specific responsibilities horizontally for all-university priorities. This horizontal leadership could be assumed by a central-office administrator, but by having deans take on different priorities, a more collaborative culture among these leaders is fostered.

We have also had experience with deans' councils, wherein a specific cross-institutional project is lead by a team of deans with one dean selected for leadership of the team. Whatever organizational structure is pursued, simply asking the dean of education to broaden the curricular base for teacher education likely will not bring about needed programmatic changes, nor does this signal that the president truly intends to bring about significant institutional change in the design and delivery of university-wide teacher education.

3. Encourage the Development of Institution-wide Clinical Faculty Roles

Since the reforms in medical education in the early 1920s, the notion of teaching hospitals with clinical faculty has been a staple of the medical profession and, more recently, of an array of the health sciences (Flexner, 1910). In fact, in a number of institutions, the designation of clinical faculty was restricted for use only in the medical professions. Increasingly, however, a broader array of professions is concluding that official clinical faculty designations can serve their programmatic interests and general mission. Different terminologies are applied depending on the professional field, but from pharmacy to business programs and from journalism and mass communications to engineering, the practice of sending students to the field to achieve firsthand practical experience has been a central tenet.

In education, supervising staff that resides at the school site is typically referred to as *cooperating teachers;* university professors who supervise in the school site are called *university supervisors*. Neither category carries with it much distinction. Cooperating teachers are generally paid nominal honoraria for student-teaching supervision, and full-time university supervisors are often not only at the lower end of the salary schedule but they also are typically persons without full faculty status. To complicate matters, neither party has access to the design and implementation of the other aspects of the program—cooperating teachers may help out at the school site but typically are not involved in on-campus curriculum design or instruction; university supervisors, in turn, have little authority over the nature and quality of the experiences provided for the student interns at the school sites.

Presidents can assume leadership in their institutions by addressing the quality of clinical personnel, their status within their institutions, and the scope of their responsibilities. Reexamining campus rules and regulations governing access to and application of the clinical faculty title and working with school districts to embed the university supervisor more effectively in monitoring the internships at the school sites are good examples of where all-university oversight and ownership of teacher education can be advanced. Further, the new and improved clinical assignments can be the means for universities to assume an expanded partnership role in needed school renewal.

4. Ensure That Rewards and Incentives Support Institutional Initiatives

Executing any institutional change is difficult without making patently clear that the new work will not only be encouraged but also formally recognized in a variety of ways, as is the case, for example, at the University of Missouri–St. Louis through its endowed professorships. As institutions increasingly consider ways to more fully engage themselves with their local, highly complex, and problem-rich urban communities, presidential encouragement of individual and collective engagement will be critical. Presidents also must be clear about the principles that guide their engagement: "By engagement, we refer to institutions that have redesigned their teaching, research and extension and service functions to become even more sympathetically and productively involved with their communities" (Kellogg Commission, 1999, p. vii). Universities are not social service agencies and cannot be all things to all people; engagement must derive from the core mission of teaching, research, and service. Thus, presidents have to articulate their particular vision of engagement, as Chancellor Gilliland at the University of Missouri–Kansas City illustrates in her chapter. Like her, presidents have to live and breathe engagement. The president of the National Association of State Universities and Land-Grant Colleges (NASULGC), C. Peter Magrath, observes that it can't be an "add-on" or just another "nice thing to do," but rather it should be a mainstream activity and a readaptation of a philosophy that is "both the right thing for our society's interest and a very smart thing for America's universities" (Magrath, 1999). Chancellor Gora notes in her chapter that such community/university collaboration is critical to the future of her institution.

And finally, presidents have to be willing to provide money—not just rhetoric. They must ensure that schools, colleges, departments, and divisions understand that the reward structures support the engagement mission and that the tenure and promotion criteria align with it. Just as importantly, the president's duties include generating resources—venture capital, grants and contracts, gifts, and state and federal investments—in support of engagement strategies, specifically those affecting university-wide teacher education initiatives. While this responsibility does not fall solely on the president or chancellor, it will require a significant amount of her or his attention.

5. Utilize the Convening Power of the Presidency to Mobilize Others

As is demonstrated in the chapters that follow, presidents of urban universities are key players in the urban landscape and exert considerable influence in their communities. Presidents can claim a degree of neutrality typically not assigned to political leaders or even to corporate heads. They can also bring the rich resources of their institution to bear on significant challenges, and they appear to be adept at coalescing others in their urban communities, as this book illustrates. In order to do this, however, there are some significant prerequisites. Presidents should be

- Interested in and knowledgeable about their university's assets and needs of the community in order to bring appropriate resources to bear on the right priorities at the right time
- Personally committed to addressing the challenge, whether it be educational, environmental, or economic in scope
- Charismatic or persuasive, traits that undoubtedly derive from strong personal commitment to the belief in their university's responsibility for contributing in major ways to the renewal of the community in which it is located
- Visible, accessible, and persistent—change requires sustained effort, as Gregory O'Brien, former Chancellor of the University of New Orleans, makes clear in his chapter's reflections on leadership

Embracing these values will allow presidents to use their convening power internally within their institutions and in the larger community. That said, it must be recognized that convening power, while necessary to any renewal endeavor, is not sufficient. In the final analysis, initiatives will rise or fall on the extent of the urban challenge they seek to address, on the strength of the ideas that animate the initiatives, and on the power of the partnerships to put the ideas into action. Commitment to teacher education reform and school renewal has to start somewhere and we believe it begins with the president.

EXTERNAL PARTNERING AND MOBILIZATION STRATEGIES

Just as we identified five potential priorities internally through which university presidents can exert leadership, we have identified five priorities for partnering externally:

1. Institute more inclusive and stronger urban P–16 partnerships.
2. Pursue joint teacher recruitment activities (especially for underrepresented populations).
3. Influence the policy arena in support of teacher education and retention.
4. Provide training and support for veteran teachers.
5. Contribute to the resource base for urban districts and school renewal.

1. Institute More Inclusive and Stronger Urban P–16 Partnerships

As suggested earlier, so-called reforms in teacher education over the last two decades have focused largely on forging partnerships between schools of education and individual P–12 schools. Faculty members in schools of education often spend considerable time in one or more of these partnership schools, organized to accommodate and educate novice teachers. Commonly referred to as *Partner* or *Professional Development Schools*, these partnering arrangements tend to be ad hoc and transient in nature. While they often represent improvements in the quality of teacher preparation, they nonetheless operate at a boutique level. Such efforts are often not able to go to scale because they do not address districtwide policy and practice. Chancellor Gora, at University of Massachusetts Boston, is working to change that. The university has developed a prototype Professional Development School, in this instance in partnership with Dorchester High School, a high-poverty, diverse inner-city school comprised primarily of minority students. Chancellor Gora's approach is to experiment with a variety of interventions to improve student learning at one site and carefully study and document what works before expanding the university's limited resources elsewhere.

True reform requires bold, ambitious partnerships that are interinstitutional in nature. Such relationships are often organized around P–16 councils, much like those described at the University of Cincinnati and the University of Wisconsin–Milwaukee. What distinguishes successful P–16 councils is the active participation and commitment by the leaders of major stakeholder groups. Together, they work collaboratively and in a sustained manner to address long-standing and complex problems. Because such councils bring together community leadership, they can have both the will and resources to put in place personnel and support structures in *every* school in order to advance quality teaching and learning for all children.

Perhaps the most unique partnership arrangement in the chapters that follow is represented in the large number of endowed professorships that Blanche Touhill, as chancellor at University of Missouri–St. Louis, put in place with the support of philanthropist Desmond Lee. Each of the more than 30 eminent scholars recruited to these endowed professorships has a joint appointment with another major community agency or arts institution in the greater St. Louis area. Additionally, some of these professors work in partnership at the highest levels of the St. Louis Public Schools.

President Irvin Reid, at Wayne State University, holds the firm belief that "both the City of Detroit's and Wayne State University's long-term success depends upon the success of the Detroit Public Schools." He has worked aggressively to form a strong partnership with the CEO of the Detroit Public Schools. The two of them held joint summit meetings of their cabinets to explore how they could best work together in a strong and sustained manner in order to address core challenges in the Detroit Public Schools. President Reid also established a close working relationship with the state secretary of education to move this agenda forward.

2. Pursue Joint Teacher Recruitment Activities

The looming national shortage of teachers—especially teachers of color—cannot be adequately addressed solely by our colleges of education, no matter how committed to recruitment. It will require new approaches and robust partnerships, not only with urban school districts but also with sister institutions of higher education, the business community, and nonprofit sectors as well. Helping to forge these partnerships is an important presidential task. Eugene Trani, for example, helped to organize members of the Richmond Renaissance—an association of business leaders focused on economic development—to help recruit high-quality prospective teachers to the Richmond Public Schools at job fairs across the country. The result of his leadership and this partnership endeavor is more than 800 recruited teachers over three years.

In a similarly impressive effort at Wayne State, President Reid, working closely with the state secretary of education and leaders in the Detroit Public Schools, put in place in a very short time A Limited License to Instruct program to address the major teacher shortage in the Detroit Public Schools. More than 1,200 applications were received and nearly 700 new teachers-to-be were enrolled over a two-year period in a dramatic, rapid response to a critical need.

One strategy for expanding teacher recruitment to nontraditional candidates is by developing career lattices for aides and paraprofessionals who assist licensed teachers in urban classrooms. A large percentage of these individuals are from minority populations and are often single mothers who live in their school's immediate neighborhood. Recruiting the most able of these paraprofessionals into a teaching career calls for a more viable pipeline so that they can complete a college education, gain a teaching license, and teach in the community in which they reside and where their children go to school.

This is no small challenge. While prototype programs are in place at many universities, they must be expanded. In order to develop such an enlarged and stronger pipeline, coordinated action is called for, including further curriculum articulation between the technical colleges—where many of these paraprofessionals will begin their work toward teacher licensure—and the universities where they will complete it. Negotiations are necessary between the school board and the teachers' union so that these aides can find ways to pursue their teacher education while retaining their employment as paraprofessionals. Business leaders and workforce development boards will need to assist in providing scholarships and fellowships. And a curriculum designed for these nontraditional students will involve participation by the dean of Education and the deans of Arts, and Letters and Science, as well as, of course, the president or chancellor of the university.

In short, effective recruitment efforts cannot easily be accomplished alone—whether undertaken by the district, the union, the community at large, the community college, or the university. Throughout the chapters that follow, illustrations are provided of university presidents assuming a strong leadership role in addressing teacher shortages in their urban districts through a range of partnership activities.

3. Influence the Policy Arena in Support of Teacher Education and Retention

Just as recruiting and preparing more and better prepared teachers for urban schools is a priority in most urban communities, so too is their retention and continuing education and support. Programs designed specifically for beginning teachers are typically referred to as induction, entry-year, or transitional. Such programs can reasonably be seen as the responsibility of P–16 councils, described earlier. They should be both an extension of the preservice program (traditionally the purview of universities) and the forerunner of continuing professional development (historically the responsibility of the school district). Instituting such programs represents an opportunity for university presidents to exert leadership through the influence they can bring to bear on public opinion and state and federal legislators.

Why are such induction programs so important and why must they be defended? Simplistic views of teaching and how one learns to teach unfortunately remain pervasive and, in turn, limit measures of student learning. Far too many politicians and taxpayers alike view teaching—even teaching in challenging urban classrooms—as basically the efficient transmission of information. Preparation for such teaching is similarly viewed as a rather straightforward and uncomplicated endeavor, with knowledge of the subject matter the primary precondition for teaching success. In fact, preparation in professional schools of education is viewed by many as unnecessary.

These "antieducationist" (Lagemann, 2000) sentiments are gaining strength today, especially among conservatives. For example, the Thomas B. Fordham Foundation recently published a manifesto, *The Teachers We Need and How to Get More of Them* (1999). The proposals in this document would eliminate *all* requirements for the licensure of teachers except for criminal background checks, examinations of content knowledge, and a required major in the subject to be taught. The report promotes access to teaching by means other than professional schools of education. This position, we believe, would only further contribute to having the least pedagogically competent teachers in the very schools where considerable competence is most needed.

Collectively, and in a sustained manner, the challenges and complexity of teaching in general, and especially in urban, high-poverty schools, need to be more fully and forcefully communicated to policy makers and the general public. Michael Schwartz, president of Cleveland State University, takes seriously his responsibility as a "public intellectual" to contribute directly to the well-being and prosperity of the community. Upon his appointment as president he visited every single Cleveland Municipal High School. He also invited principals, counselors, and members of the United Pastors in Mission into his home to discuss educational issues. Perhaps the most vivid example of how he participates in policy making to advance improvements in urban education is through his role with the Cleveland Municipal School District school board. President Schwartz attends all meetings as an ex officio member and influential educator and leader.

University presidents can also assume a lead role in support of expanded, multiyear induction programs. At present, induction is rarely programmatic, is typically the purview of the district, is disconnected from university preparation, and is focused primarily on a limited form of assessment rather than the needed continuing education of the novice teacher. For too long, we in higher education have looked the other way when it comes to the depth and brevity of education for teachers. Induction programming should be viewed as an extension of preservice preparation and should be a multiyear endeavor. A more graduated entry into full-time teaching for beginning teachers can serve multiple purposes, not the least of which is assuring greater accountability for the quality of instruction for the youngsters in those urban classrooms where beginning teachers are assigned. From the perspective of the university president, there are multiple policy issues to be addressed, including: determination of funding sources for such programs, the negotiation of roles and responsibilities of all partners, the assignment of novice teachers, and the preparation and credentialing of consulting or mentor teachers.

Among the many innovative programs and projects that President Joseph Steger championed while at the University of Cincinnati (UC), in partnership with other educational stakeholders, is the Standards in Practice (SIP) program. This is a mentoring and coaching program, which assures that UC graduates receive assistance through their preparation programs and upon graduation from mentor teachers who can provide guidance in terms of standards-based curriculum and high-stakes testing.

Carl Patton, the president at Georgia State, has had a distinguished career not only at the university but also in a variety of leadership roles in the Atlanta community. Among the several innovations he has promoted is the Georgia State University Quality Assurance Guarantee for Educators policy, a program that underscores the university's effectiveness in teaching students from diverse populations. Since 1999 this unique policy has guaranteed the effectiveness of any individual graduating from a teacher licensure program at Georgia State for the first two years after graduation. If problems exist, retraining that involves an individualized improvement plan is provided. The warranty is undergirded by the two-year Teacher Education Graduate Induction Program, which provides a range of educative support and assessment services and underscores the critical need for continued support and intervention in the challenging first years of teaching in an urban classroom.

At UIC Chancellor Manning has been highly supportive of the innovative Mentoring and Induction of New Teachers (MINT) program initiated in the late 1990s at UIC in collaboration with the Chicago Public Schools Teachers' Academy for Professional Development, the Chicago Teachers Union Quest Center, and the Chicago Principal and Administrators Association. UIC provided leadership initially based upon research and then facilitated the transition of new policies and practices into the school district and the union, who were strong partners from the beginning of this endeavor.

4. Provide Training and Support for Veteran Teachers

Historically universities have provided advanced programs and graduate degrees as well as targeted workshops and courses for veteran teachers and administrators. But we can do more. Teachers benefit when they leave the confines of their schools and interact with other professionals around the corpus of knowledge derived from recent research and development initiatives. Such ongoing training is especially relevant in light of the growing number of teachers in urban contexts who are lacking in content and pedagogical qualifications. Universities can also assume an expanded leadership role by improving and expanding opportunities for teacher growth on the job, in a variety of didactic and expositional settings.

Attributes of *embedded* teacher professional development include structured activities for learning on the job, buttressed with demonstration. Research has shown that teachers should have practice in repeated trials in order to acquire complex teaching strategies. If guided practice or coaching in the teacher's classroom is provided, teacher performance is further strengthened. Finally, if impact on student learning is the goal, then examining the effects of that teaching on pupil learning should be incorporated in this rigorous form of "clinical" training (Showers, Joyce, & Bennett, 1987).

Embedded professional development activities such as these, to the extent they have been instituted, typically have been the purview of schools and school districts. Even though we know the critical elements of potent professional development, urban schools and school districts typically do not have the instructional leadership or the resources to put them in place. Our position is that universities have the research and development capability to help institute these more powerful forms of embedded professional development—in partnership with schools. Moving from periodic expository workshops to guided practice in the classroom and ultimately to critical examination of the effects of teaching on student learning is both challenging and costly. However, as the key to improved teaching is this very form of embedded professional development, universities must assume more of a leadership role in making this mission a reality. The research and training arm of the university should work in partnership with school districts and unions to put in place more rigorous continuing professional development; presidents should push for this, as improved teaching will not occur without their support.

5. Contribute to the Resource Base for Urban Districts and School Renewal

Title I of the 2001 reauthorization of the Elementary and Secondary Education Act (ESEA), referred to as "No Child Left Behind" by the Bush administration, focuses squarely on improving academic achievement in high-poverty schools. Among the requirements of this law are that all students make adequate yearly progress (AYP) and reach a state-defined proficiency level on math and reading assessments within 12 years.

The high-stakes nature of Title I can be seen in the consequences for schools that do not make this AYP for five consecutive years. In these instances the district has to make "significant" plans to change the school governance structure, which may include state takeovers, the hiring of a private management contractor, major staff restructuring, or converting the school to a charter school. In partnership with urban districts and through vehicles like urban P–16 councils, universities could focus some of their resources specifically on those schools that have the worst records of student achievement, most likely located in high-poverty urban areas. The university could, for example, concentrate faculty resources, tutors from the larger student body, and clusters of prospective teachers to these schools. If prospective teachers were assigned there, then highly qualified district personnel would also need to be assigned to work with these novices as well. Different partners would contribute resources of different types. Focusing on these schools would underscore the commitment of the university to ensuring success for *all* youngsters, as is richly illustrated throughout this book. For example, at IUPUI, Gerald Bepko was centrally involved in collaborative efforts to institute full-service schools in the Indianapolis district and in a project to foster experimentation through charter schools wherein IUPUI offered technical assistance and policy advice in their development. He and his institution were also centrally engaged in reopening schools in depressed areas adjoining the campus where schools had been closed and youngsters bused long distances.

Martha Gilliland has been a forceful leader in developing a proposal titled *A Partnership for the Educational Future of Kansas City*. She is seeking support for this ambitious partnership that includes a Teacher Preparation Academy working with a network of local urban schools. These schools will have an innovative staffing pattern including clinical professors, master teachers, teaching fellows, and teaching interns working in teams. This is an excellent illustration of integrating reform in teacher preparation with reform in P–12 schools.

Gregory O'Brien, in another major venture, planned a Partnerships Zone—a "district within a district" concept—to assist with urban district and school renewal. As part of the New Millennium Schools Initiative, as it is called, the University of New Orleans would take over the operation of five partnership zone schools in close proximity to the campus. Although encountering resistance, Chancellor O'Brien nevertheless renewed his efforts to promote improved schooling by working closely with the new superintendent in New Orleans and other local university presidents and seeking legislative support at the state level as well.

THE ESSENTIAL ROLE OF THE UNIVERSITY PRESIDENT

In summary, just as there are ample opportunities for presidents to lead internally, in support of educational and organizational change, so also similar opportunities exist to work externally with leaders in urban school districts and the larger community. We advocate developing partnerships involving interinstitutional linkages where the leaders of each of the partners are engaged. By *leaders* we mean individuals who are in a position to allocate resources from their institution to a shared agenda.

In this chapter we have attempted to paint a portrait of the problems and opportunities of urban education. We have argued that it is a moral imperative for universities to be directly and deeply involved in addressing the failure to learn of tens of thousands of youngsters in our nation's major cities.

Suggesting that schools or colleges of Education strengthen their professional programs and focus more directly on preparing teachers for urban high-poverty schools is not enough to overcome the long-standing and deep-rooted problems in urban districts. Resources across the university need to be coalesced to institute a much bolder scheme of teacher preparation, taking into account general and liberal education, preprofessional education, professional and clinical education, and finally, induction programming. At times this preparation will intersect with school and community renewal.

We believe that the convening power of the university president and chancellor can, over time, mobilize needed resources both within the university and in the broader community to ensure improved learning for *all* youngsters. We call on university presidents to assume leadership for multiple actions that can be taken both within their institutions and also outside their institutions in partnership with urban districts and other community leaders.

A CLOSER LOOK AT LEADERSHIP

The call to presidential leadership in service to urban school renewal has not gone unanswered. The chapters that follow amply illustrate the range of creative presidential leadership in regard to the strategic priorities we have described in this opening chapter. More importantly, they provide a much-needed look at the nature of leadership at our urban public institutions of higher education.

There is a large and diverse literature on leadership and change generally; however, the literature on presidential leadership in universities is relatively sparse. There have been a number of single-campus accounts or portraits and a growing but smaller number of empirical studies. Arthur's (1995) history of the New College in Florida presents an example of the former, and the American Council on Education (ACE) Project on Leadership and Institutional Transformation (Eckel, Hill, Green, & Mallon, 1998) represents inroads made in the latter regard. In this book we hope to bridge theoretically and empirically supported propositions about leadership and change with firsthand biographical accounts. To that end, we asked each of these 14 presidents of urban universities to make as explicit as possible their leadership actions and change strategies within the context of how they have worked to improve the quality of education for urban youth. This follows the sage advice of Michael Fullan, the change theorist, when he wrote:

> I define change agentry as being *self-conscious* about the nature of change and the change process. Those skilled in change are appreciative of its semi-unpredictable and volatile character, and they are explicitly concerned with the pursuit of ideas and competencies for coping with and influencing more and more aspects of the process toward some desired set of ends. They are open, moreover, to discovering new ends as the journey unfolds. (1993, p. 12)

The journey to urban school change and renewal unfolds in the chapters that follow. Within them you will meet 14 urban university presidents who perform at a high level in the complex and challenging environment of urban higher education. We hope their evolving theories about leadership and change and their innovative actions in support of urban school renewal will inform and inspire your own understanding of the nature of change and those who lead it.

Kenneth R. Howey *is a research professor in the College of Education, Criminal Justice and Human Services at the University of Cincinnati. Previously he held faculty and administrative appointments at the University of Minnesota, The Ohio State University, and the University of Wisconsin–Madison and the University of Wisconsin–Milwaukee. He was the principle investigator for the longest-running study of teacher education in the United States and for several years directed the national reform consortium, the Urban Network to Improve Teacher Education, UNITE. He is the author of several books and articles on teacher education. Dr. Howey is the recipient of the American Association of Colleges for Teacher Education's highest award for distinguished contributions to teacher education throughout a career.*

Nancy L. Zimpher *became the twenty-fifth president of the University of Cincinnati in 2003 and its first woman president. She previously served as the chancellor of the University of Wisconsin–Milwaukee. A teacher and educator, she also served as Dean of the College of Education and executive dean of the Professional Colleges at The Ohio State University in Columbus, Ohio. She was president of the Holmes Partnership from 1996-2001 and co-coordinator in 2000 of the U.S. Secretary of Education's National Summit on Teacher Quality. She is the recipient of the American Association of Colleges for Teacher Education's Edward C. Pomeroy Award for Outstanding Contributions to Teacher Education.*

BIBLIOGRAPHY

ABT Associates. (1993). *Prospects: The congressionally mandated study of educational growth and opportunity.* Washington, DC: U.S. Department of Education.

American Association of Colleges for Teacher Education. (1990). *Teaching teachers: Facts and figures (RATE VI).* Washington, DC: AACTE.

Arthur, F.C. (1995). *New college: The first three decades.* Sarasota, FL: New College Foundation.

Ball, D.L., & Cohen, D.K. (1999). Developing practice, developing practitioners: Towards a practice-based theory of professional education. In L. Darling-Hammond & G. Sykes (Eds.), *Teaching as a learning profession* (pp. 3–31). San Francisco: Jossey-Bass.

Council of the Great City Schools. (1994). *National urban education goals: 1992–93 indicators report.* Washington, DC: Council of the Great City Schools.

Davies, D. (2002). The 10th school revisited: Are school/family/community partnerships on the reform agenda now? *Phi Delta Kappan, 33*(5), 388–392.

Duderstadt, J. (2000, February 4). A choice of transformations for the 21st century university. *Chronicle of Higher Education,* Arts and Opinion, B6.

Eckel, P., Hill, B., Green, M., & Mallon, B. (1998, 1999). *On change.*, Occasional Paper Series of the ACE Project on Leadership and Institutional Transformation. Washington, DC: American Council on Education.

Fideler, E. F., & Haselkorn, D. (1999). *Learning the ropes: Urban teacher induction programs and practices in the United States.* Boston, MA: Recruiting New Teachers.

Fink, E., & Resnick, L. B. (2001). Developing principals as instructional leaders. *Phi Delta Kappan, 82,* 578–606.

Flexner, A. (1910). *Medical education in the United States and Canada.* New York: Carnegie Foundation for the Advancement of Teaching.

Fullan, M. (1993). *Change Forces.* New York: Falmer.

Gideonse, H. D. (1986). Guiding images for teaching and teacher education. In T. L. Lasely (Ed.), *The dynamics of change in teacher education.* Washington, DC: American Association of Colleges for Teacher Education.

Greenwald, R., Hedges, L. V., & Laine, R. D. (1996, Fall). The effect of school resources on student achievement. *Review of Educational Research, 66,* 361–396.

Gurin, P. (2000). Expert report of Patricia Gurin: Gratz, et al. v. Bollinger, et al., No. 97–75321 (E.D. Mich). Retrieved March 31, 2003, from http://www.umich.edu/~urel/admissions/legal/expert/gurintoc.html.

Howey, K. R. (1996). *The Urban Network to Improve Teacher Education: A final report. Preparing teachers for inner city schools.* Columbus, OH: Urban Network to Improve Teacher Education.

Jepsen, C., & Rivkin, S. (2002). *Class size reduction, teacher quality, and academic achievement in California public elementary schools.* San Francisco: Public Policy Institute of California.

Kellogg Commission on the Future of State and Land-Grant Universities. (1999). *The engaged institution: Returning to our roots.* Washington, DC: National Association of State Universities and Land-Grant Colleges.

Lagemann, E. C. (2000). *An elusive science: The troubling history of education research.* Chicago: University of Chicago Press.

Lankford, H., Loeb, S., & Wyckoff, J. (2002). Teacher sorting and the plight of public schools: A descriptive analysis. *Educational Evaluation and Policy Analysis, 24,* 37–62.

Magrath, P. (1999, March). The engaged university: It integrates teaching, research and outreach. An address at University Engagement in the Community: A Vision of the 21st Century, a conference held at the University of Wisconsin–Milwaukee.

Miles, K. H., & Guiney, E. (2000, June 14). School districts' new role. *Education Week.*

National Center for Education Statistics (NCES). (1996). *Urban schools: The challenge of location and poverty.* Washington, DC: U.S. Department of Education, Office of Educational Research and Improvement.

National Commission on Teaching and America's Future (NCTAF). (2003). *No dream denied: A pledge to America's children.* New York: NCTAF.

No Child Left Behind Act of 2001: Reauthorization of the Elementary and Secondary Education Act (ESEA). Retrieved March 31, 2003, from http://www.ed.gov/legislation/ESEA02/.

Orfield, G., Bachmeier, M., James, D., & Eitle, T. (1997). *Deepening segregation in American public schools.* Cambridge, MA: Civil Rights Project, Harvard Graduate School of Education.

Resnick, L. B., & Glennan, T. K. (2002). Leadership for learning: A theory of action for urban school districts. In A. Hightower, M. McLaughlin, M. Knapp, & J. Marsh (Eds.), *School districts and instructional renewal.* Critical Issues in Educational Leadership, 8. New York: Teachers College Press.

Sanders, W. L., & Rivers, J. C. (1998). *Cumulative and residual effects of teachers on future students' academic achievement.* Knoxville, TN: University of Tennessee Press.

Showers, B., Joyce, B., & Bennett, B. (1987). Synthesis of research on staff development: A framework for future study and state-of-the-art analysis. *Educational Leadership, 45*(3), 77–87.

The state of the cities. (1997). Washington, DC: U.S. Department of Housing and Urban Development.

Thomas B. Fordham Foundation (TBFF). (1999). The teachers we need and how to get more of them. In M. Kanstoroom & C. Finn (Eds.), *Better teachers, better schools* (pp. 1–18). Washington, DC: TBFF.

Weiner, L. (2000). Research in the 90s: Implications for urban teacher preparation. *Review of Educational Research, 70*(3), 369–406.

Wilson, S., Floden, R., & Ferrini-Mundy, J. (2001). *Teacher preparation research: Current knowledge, gaps, and recommendations.* Seattle: Center for the Study of Teaching and Policy, University of Washington.

Zimpher, N. L. (1989). The RATE project: A profile of teacher education students. *Journal of Teacher Education, 40*(6), 27–30.

Zimpher, N. L., Percy, S. L., & Brukardt, M. J. (2002). *A time for boldness: A story of institutional change.* Bolton, MA: Anker.

CHAPTER 2

A New Chancellor Sets the Stage

Jo Ann M. Gora

I chose to focus on the university-school collaboration because it is a microcosm of the university-community collaboration so critical to our future as a public urban institution. It is also the most visible place for the university to demonstrate its expertise and commitment to the social good.

I joined University of Massachusetts Boston (UMass Boston) as chancellor in August 2001 after having served nine years as provost of an urban doctoral university, Old Dominion University, in Virginia. As a sociologist, I recognized that culture and context define perceptions and influence actions. As a new chancellor, I realized that all eyes would be on me my first year. How and where I spent my time and whom I focused on in the community—both within and outside the university—would identify my priorities more clearly than any words I spoke.

I knew I needed first to learn the university, to learn the culture of the institution, its history, its hopes, its regrets. I met face-to-face with the entire university faculty. I walked the halls and talked continuously to faculty and staff. I realized, too, that I needed to learn the wider community—the leaders, the history, and the issues. I needed to learn how the university was perceived. Only then would I move to establish a detailed agenda, one that built on our institutional strengths and responded forcefully to the community's needs.

I resolved to get to know the most influential community leaders. By spending time with Boston's entrepreneurs and opinion makers, I learned how the city worked and what its leaders valued. I also spoke with them about university priorities and how they fit with city needs. By year's end, I had met and talked at length and in private with 215 of the most influential people in Boston—legislators, state and city officials, corporate executives, foundation presidents, school superintendents and principals, and representatives of the media. From them I learned about the problems the city faced and determined that the university needed to be a recognized force contributing to the solutions of those problems.

From the start, I realized the university had a great story to tell that it wasn't telling well. Boston is a city dominated by private universities. Harvard and MIT head the list, but there are more than 30 others, not to mention the 12 public institutions, all vying for attention and support from the media, the foundations, and the politicians. To be seen as a force, to be heard above the din, the story must be told well. Moreover, communicating our role in the community is all-important in defining our value to our funding sources.

And the University of Massachusetts Boston is a force. With 13,350 students and 467 full-time faculty, it is the largest public doctoral university in the Greater Boston area. Like most urban universities, we play a major role in educating the entrepreneurs and workforce of the community. Our students reflect the makeup of the city and return to the city as graduates. The university is truly engaged in the community through the public policy research of its 26 institutes and centers and, importantly, through the efforts of the dean and faculty of its Graduate College of Education (GCE), where we are engaged with the social institution dominating the life of the city—the K–12 public school system.

The university's entry into teacher education, work with the schools, and educational policy began in 1982, with our merger with Boston State College. Boston State's beginnings go back to the mid-nineteenth century, when it began as a teacher training school, so it has a long history with the city and state. Over the years, our Graduate College of Education had developed a clear focus on an urban agenda, training teachers for the urban schools, building professional development schools (PDSs) in partnership with three school superintendents, and researching what impacts student achievement. To help them as much as possible, to focus a spotlight on their activities, and to encourage new initiatives, I needed to understand the history and culture of the Boston Public Schools (BPS).

BOSTON PUBLIC SCHOOLS

Boston faces many of the same problems with its urban schools as do other cities, among them poverty, racial imbalance, high dropout rates, and the challenges of a multitude of new ethnic and linguistic minorities.

The numbers are dramatically clear. Boston Public Schools are over-whelmingly nonwhite. By 1999–2000, in approximate numbers, half of the students were black, a quarter Hispanic, 10 percent Asian, and 15 per-cent white. These numbers reflect the number of youths under the age of 18 in the overall population of Boston, although with some differences: while blacks comprise half the school population, they are only 37 per-cent of the overall population under 18; and although whites are only 15 percent of the school population, they are 25 percent of the overall pop-ulation under 18.

This degree of nonwhite concentration in the city's schools is a rela-tively recent phenomenon. In 1973, a year before the Boston school de-segregation decision, 60 percent were white. Seven years later, this was down to 35 percent. By 1987, the figure was 26 percent, and by 1999–2000, many of the remaining 15 percent were concentrated in the city's exam schools, especially at the high school level (Check, 2002).

In the 1980s and 1990s, increasing numbers of non-English-speaking students from Latin America, the Caribbean, Asia, and Africa changed Boston schools from a biracial system to a multiethnic, multilingual one attended primarily by poor children of many backgrounds. We see this re-flected in language instruction offered in the schools:

> During the 2000–2001 school year more than a third of all Boston students needed second language services. In 1990–2000, bilingual programs were of-fered to 9,300 students (15% of all students) in nine languages—Cape Verdean, Chinese (both Mandarin and Cantonese), Greek, Haitian Creole, Somali, Spanish, Portuguese, and Vietnamese. Spanish-speakers made up 61% of the total bilingual population. In addition, a "multilingual" program provided En-glish as a Second Language instruction (but no native language instruction), to low-incidence language populations such as Korean, Indonesian, Laotian, Portuguese, Russian, and Polish. Thousands of additional English Language Learners were in regular education classes. (Check, 2002, p. 187)

At the same time, Boston schools, like others across the country, face an unprecedented challenge to find more good teachers (and the oppor-tunity to bring a fresh perspective to the schools if the teachers can be found). A December 2001 report sponsored by the mayor and the super-intendent's office began by stating, "Over half of Boston's teachers will leave within the next five years, creating the need for more than 2,500 new teachers. The challenge is both to attract talented candidates to replace these teachers and to effectively induct and retain them. Recent trends suggest that nearly half of all new teachers will leave the classroom within their first three to five years" (Murray, 2001, p. 3).

Moreover, Massachusetts, like the rest of the country, has many core secondary classes taught by out-of-field teachers—19 percent. This is somewhat better than the 24 percent nationally, but in a comparison study over a recent six-year period, the out-of-field rate for schools with high minority enrollment rose from 15 percent to 32 percent, with Massachusetts second only to Illinois in having the largest gap between all schools and high-minority schools (Jerald, 2002).

In part as a result of facts like these and in part as a result of community and political conflict over the schools, Boston experienced high turnover in its superintendents—six in the 12 years between 1983 and 1995—and frequent changes in direction (Check, 2002). The turnover was sometimes associated with about-face changes in instructional policies, with one result that teachers who have been in the system a certain length of time can be reluctant to commit quickly or wholeheartedly to new educational approaches, believing they may be asked to change again in a few years.

There has been stability, however, since October 1995, when Thomas Payzant, a career educator and former head of the San Diego public schools and assistant U.S. secretary of education, was appointed Boston superintendent of schools. A tenure of this length is unusual among urban school superintendents today, and the ensuing stability for the system has been one key to the sustained effort needed to make progress on school reform.

A major factor behind Payzant's staying power has been a change in the way the Boston School Committee is chosen. An elected committee since its beginnings in the mid-nineteenth century, it was often at odds with the mayor and superintendent. Then in 1992, following a referendum and home-rule petition, the elected committee was replaced by one appointed by the mayor. When the term of the incumbent ran out in 1995, Payzant became the first superintendent appointed under the new system.

More recently, the state adopted the Massachusetts Comprehensive Assessment System (MCAS) as the primary measure of success and the sole criterion for graduation beginning in 2003. MCAS became the touchstone for much criticism, as test results in the 2000–2001 school year showed as many as two-thirds of Boston's high school students risked not graduating under this requirement (Check, 2002). By November 2002, there was some improvement, but 40 percent of high school seniors had yet to pass both the English and math parts of the exam, and a number that large gave rise to accelerating public concern as the end of the school year loomed on the horizon.

Payzant's major task in the years since 1999 has been to implement a systemwide reform plan adopted by the school committee to improve teaching and learning so that all students can achieve high levels of performance. This work has been supported by $20 million from the Annenberg Foundation, $15 million from the private sector, $8 million from the Carnegie Corporation of New York, and $10 million in public funds. Some of the additional priorities directed by the plan include restructuring high schools, a focus on literacy so that all students are reading at grade level by grade 3, and improving instructional practice through schoolwide professional development (Check, 2002).

Small learning communities (SLCs) are currently implemented as a core strategy both for combating alienation and for improving instruction. Among the criteria that define a small learning community, students should take at least 75 percent of their courses within the SLC, and teachers assigned to the SLC should teach at least 75 percent of their courses within it. There is flexibility in how SLCs can be organized into the school, via clusters, houses, or pathways.

The second major change concerns instruction. In an August 2002 open letter, Superintendent Payzant announced that, in order to move more thoroughly away from information transmission as the classroom focus and instead to promote students' learning to learn—more ownership, independence, engagement, and motivation on the part of students—Readers' Workshop would become the core method of instruction at all levels. Elementary, middle, and high school language teachers were to implement it by September 2003, and science, social studies and other areas will begin to use it based on the experience gained in language arts.

In workshop instruction the larger part of class time, 60 percent, is spent in independent reading or writing. This is preceded by the teacher presenting and modeling a specific teaching point and followed by sharing, response, and clarification by the teacher. Writers' Workshop has already been introduced throughout the Boston Public Schools, and workshop instruction is also used in selected math, history, and other segments of the curriculum.

A NEW CHANCELLOR

The setting I have described is what I discovered when I arrived at the University of Massachusetts Boston in August 2001—a school system with a strategy, a university with a commitment to public service, and a Graduate College of Education with a commitment to urban schools. It was a school system still a long distance from the results it wanted to achieve, with schools and university alike straining against budget limitations as they nevertheless took measures to move forward.

I came with strong convictions that K–12 education is critically important to the city and that playing a significant role in the community is what the urban university is all about. Nowhere is that community role more important than it is with the schools, so I was enthusiastic to learn of the support for education by Boston Mayor Tom Menino and the success of Boston Superintendent of Schools Thomas Payzant. What I saw left me hopeful for progress in the schools because I found that the main players, including the mayor, the superintendent, and the dean of the UMass Boston Graduate College of Education, were marching to the same drummer. We all agreed on the importance of the public schools in the life of the city. We agreed on the importance of university-school collaboration to promote change. We agreed on the importance of recruiting the best and brightest to teaching and providing extensive mentoring to new teachers, a key to retaining them.

When I met with Mayor Menino, I found that education was high on his list of municipal priorities. He has taken important steps to improve education, especially in the area of technology in the schools. The mayor, an alumnus of UMass Boston, was clearly proud of increasing the number of computers in the schools from one for every 63 students in 1995 to one for every 5 in 2001, and his goal is to make that one for every 4, with replacement of obsolete computers.

After I arrived at UMass Boston, I was asked to join the mayor's board of directors for his Boston Public School Technology Initiative. At my first meeting of this group, I realized what a powerful advocate for school-university collaboration our mayor was. I didn't have to fight to get to the table: my place setting was already engraved. Clearly, the university could play a pivotal role in training the teachers to use new instructional technologies.

When I met, early on, with Superintendent Payzant, I discovered that he knew many of our Graduate College of Education faculty by name and was familiar with the research they did on student achievement. He liked the work we did and valued us. What a contrast with my experience in other cities!

When I met with the dean of our Graduate College of Education, I discovered that we agreed with the agenda of recruiting better students to become teachers and training better teachers. We shared a focus on mentoring new teachers. I urged her to expand our recruitment strategies and alternative certification programs as a part of the recruiting/training strategy. Importantly, she had already lined up many of the faculty behind her professional development school strategy and awakened the university to the importance of curricular improvements in teacher education.

Because the major actors were in agreement, I was able to move more strongly ahead to confirm publicly my commitment to teacher education and to working with the schools and was able to take concrete steps that underlined that commitment. Initially, I deduced that I could be most helpful to the dean internally by reducing roadblocks within the provost's office, ensuring the funding of new faculty positions, protecting the college from budget cuts, and publicly declaring to the university community the important role the college was playing in the school community. Since the college's faculty represents only 10 percent of the university faculty, I knew I was paying disproportionate attention to them, but they were critical to my strategy to raise the profile of the university as a whole in the community. When budget cuts are necessary, too often the professional schools lose out to the older, more politically dominant faculty in the arts and sciences. I was determined not to let this happen and to awaken the entire faculty to the important role the education faculty were playing in the commonwealth, bringing visibility and recognition to the university.

Raising the profile of the university and its college of education is no easy task in a city well-known for its dominant private (and rich) universities. However, UMass Boston as a whole does more, much more, for the state, the city, and neighboring communities than is commonly known, so correcting that has been a major goal, and there was logic in my emphasizing the GCE. In the GCE I had a well-oiled team with clear direction and strong support from the existing political infrastructure. I wanted to encourage the college to expand, coordinate, and focus its partnership with K–12.

NEW INITIATIVES

The education faculty and dean had carved a meaningful role for the university in an environment where, for the most part, there was a strong school leadership, clear agreement on goals within the political structure, and commitment by funding agencies and the media. In addition to reducing roadblocks and taking specific actions on faculty lines and budget, my role has been to provide encouragement for larger initiatives and to emphasize the commitment of my office to GCE goals.

I affirmed the importance of our connection with the city a month after my arrival in my first convocation speech, quoting the first chancellor of the university, John Ryan, who said at the founding convocation in 1966, that "the urban university should be closely integrated with the society in which it exists and for which it teaches, studies, experiments, and communicates." I praised the focus of our centers and institutes on public policy, our particular excellence in public policy research and collaboration with off-campus organizations, and the importance of extending this work.

My long meetings with Superintendent Payzant were another beginning point of my public commitment. There were also meetings with other Boston Public School officials and with the senior education advisor in the governor's office. These were followed by a joint meeting with superintendents, mayors' representatives, and other players from Boston, Cambridge, and Somerville. UMass Boston people at the meeting included College of Arts and Sciences (CAS) faculty who were active with the schools, as well as GCE personnel. At the meeting I was able to mark our commitment to K–12 education by announcing a new scholarship initiative for students who agreed to teach in those schools after graduation. This was part of our strategy to recruit the best and the brightest to the teaching profession to help address the teacher shortage plaguing our city. I also discussed our intensified work with additional high schools so that we now have professional development school arrangements with four schools. And I began the process of increasing our focus on alternative certification programs.

Here, in part, is what I said to the group:

> For the past several months I have been gathering information on the K–12 education reform agenda in Massachusetts from sources both internal and external to the university. I have reviewed the Graduate College of Education's professional educational program graduates' performance data on the Massachusetts Educator Licensure Test. I have conferred with the Chairman of the Board of Education and the State Commissioner of Education to glean their perspective on the quality of K–12 education in the state. I welcome this opportunity to meet with you this evening with the hope to create a chancellor-superintendent-mayor linkage and other school administrator-to-administrator linkages among UMass Boston and the public school districts. The purpose is to foster a dialogue on programs needed for effective professional development as well as new teacher training. Obtaining data from you, the education leadership and governmental leadership in our immediate cities, will position me to take concrete actions on campus in policy and in practice to demonstrate a university-wide commitment to teacher education.

PIPELINE SCHOLARSHIPS

To increase the number of high-performing high school students pursuing a teaching career, I worked with the GCE to develop a scholarship initiative for high-achieving students that would provide a free ride for undergraduate and graduate education leading to a career teaching in the urban schools. UMass Boston has begun the Urban Teacher Educator Corps (U-TEC) pipeline as a teacher recruitment, preparation, and retention program for students who will become career teachers in the public urban schools. Generically the components of the program are familiar provisions for enhancing student recruiting and success in an urban university, but we have combined them here with an unusual degree of collaboration among many parties and with a focus on mentoring in the first three years.

The program is supported financially by both the state and the university. The university has committed funds for 20 students annually in the master's U-TEC program. High school students with a minimum 3.3 grade point average receive remission of both undergraduate and graduate tuition and fees in return for their commitment to three years teaching in Boston, Cambridge, or Somerville schools upon graduation. The state, in its Tomorrow's Teachers initiative, is committing to full scholarships for four years of undergraduate work for students who agree to teach four years anywhere within the state. The university waives tuition and fees for the graduate program and has received funding from the Great Cities' Universities' Urban Education Corps to create a mentoring program for three years.

Although using scholarship support is not a unique approach to recruiting academically talented students, providing postemployment mentoring support is not so common and is the key new element of this program. Professional support for new teacher graduates of the program is based on a monthly seminar taught by a UMass Boston faculty member and a mentor teacher from the school system, and this will continue for at least three years. The university will also develop a Web site exclusively for new teachers in Boston, Cambridge, and Somerville, where they can communicate with faculty and program colleagues about challenges they are facing on the job. We expect that the Web site will become a model tool for use by all our teacher education alumni.

The program was developed in cooperation with human resource personnel from the Boston Public School system and is collaborative in many ways in addition to financial aid. A special admissions group made up of UMass Boston GCE faculty and personnel from the BPS reviews U-TEC applications. Recruiting is focused on students who want to teach math, science, English as a second language, and special education. The Boston Public School system has agreed to give all graduates of the U-TEC pipeline program high priority in hiring.

There are also special provisions for support of undergraduates. UMass Boston undergraduates do not enroll in the teacher education program until they are juniors. However, all undergraduates in the U-TEC program will receive advising from GCE faculty from the beginning of their freshman year. They also will be placed in special classes in the College of Arts and Sciences selected to enhance subject matter knowledge for prospective teachers. CAS faculty who have expressed a particular interest in preparing teachers for urban schools will teach these courses. U-TEC undergraduates who slip below the required 3.3 grade point average in their course work will receive extra tutoring and academic support from this same CAS group of teachers, as long as they demonstrate strong motivation to succeed.

In their teacher prep work within the GCE, U-TEC students will take the same courses as regularly admitted students. But they will need to commit to doing their prepracticum and their student teaching in urban settings. The U-TEC graduates will be followed as they move into their careers, in order to collect data on their lasting commitment to urban education and to provide data to improve the program.

COLLABORATION WITH ARTS AND SCIENCES

I have urged the GCE to focus on improving the curriculum and the mentoring of first-year teachers, and I have emphasized the role of the Arts and Sciences faculty in shaping the teacher education curriculum. Making teacher education a university priority helped cement the interest of CAS faculty in working with education faculty. While pursuing these initiatives, the college was involved in preparation for a visit from the National Council for the Accreditation of Teacher Education (NCATE), where the commitment of CAS faculty would be especially critical.

CAS faculty serves with GCE faculty on a coordinating council with overall responsibility for teacher preparation programs. Many members of the CAS faculty are on other GCE committees as well. They attend seminars for assessing student outcomes. Many supervise student teachers. They have done presentations around diversity to GCE faculty and in classes. Some also have worked directly in the Boston Public Schools, where, for example, three history professors taught American history to Boston Public Schools faculty under a grant-funded project for the enhancement of teaching history; further collaborations by this group with the schools and GCE are in the works. Several math professors have voluntarily elected to take their sabbaticals in the Boston Public Schools to work with school faculty on content knowledge. In addition, Hispanic Studies and Classics each have had approved a series of advanced-level courses for public school teachers. I have publicly applauded these actions to reward those involved and to stimulate others to follow suit.

Another area of participation by CAS faculty with significant impact began during 2000–2001, when the Graduate College of Education, with the support of a Title II Teacher Quality Grant, established discipline-based teams with GCE and CAS faculty and personnel from the Boston Public Schools. These teams were charged with the task of reviewing and revising all programs leading to initial licensure in mathematics, science, social studies, and literacy. The teams began by reviewing the results of BPS students' scores on the MCAS and the program graduates' performance on the Massachusetts Educator Certification Test from 1998–2001, the new Massachusetts Regulations for Teacher Licensure, and other national guidelines.

Participation by science faculty has been slower in coming, but it is growing. With my appointment of a new provost with a science research background and an interest in science education in the schools and community, we should continue to see this grow.

THE MASS/UMASS BOSTON SUPERINTENDENTS' ACADEMY

As I sought to engage more and more elements of the university in support of the school systems, I realized I had a willing and entrepreneurial ally in our distance-learning dean. He reached out to the head of the Massachusetts Association of School Superintendents (MASS) to launch a Web-based Superintendents' Academy in fall 2002. The academy delivers noncredit professional development modules and graduate education credit courses to all Massachusetts superintendents and designees. Development module topic areas include school finance, the Education Reform Act, special education issues, legal issues, and technology for administrators and teachers.

When I met with the principals in this initiative, I realized that there was energy and enthusiasm for going forward immediately. Therefore, several modules were tested in fall 2002, and the full program for all superintendents began in the spring of 2003.

The MASS/UMass Boston Superintendents' Academy includes every school district in the state as a member. Each district pays annual dues that entitle the superintendent to enroll along with any number of designees during the year. Web-based instruction relying heavily on video streaming and videoconferencing is supplemented with regional meetings throughout the state at the five University of Massachusetts campuses.

Once again, all the pieces were in place for an important new initiative in support of the school systems: the director of MASS and his colleagues were eager for the program, our distance-learning dean was able to produce the needed modules, and I provided the encouragement and seed money for the launch of the program.

TROOPS TO TEACHERS AND ALTERNATIVE CERTIFICATION

The potential exists for an alternative certification program to play a major role in filling the overwhelming demand for teachers in the next five years. With the soft economy in Boston, unemployed dot-com workers would make natural candidates for an alternative certification program because of their math and science expertise, a priority item for the schools. Currently employed unlicensed teachers, of whom there are many in the schools, are a source of candidates, as are the increasing number of retirees, older but still energetic and ambitious to work. Another source of candidates is retiring military personnel, and a program already exists to facilitate their move into alternative certification and teaching.

Troops to Teachers (TTT) is a program of the U.S. Departments of Defense and Education to assist retiring or retired military personnel to become teachers in schools that serve low-income families. TTT helps relieve teacher shortages, especially in math, science, special education, and other high-need subject areas. Stipends of up to $5,000 are available to reimburse costs associated with becoming certified to teach for recipients who agree to teach three years in a high-need school district and bonuses of $10,000 to those who teach for three years in a school that serves a high percentage of students from low-income families.

In my previous position in Virginia, I oversaw a precursor of the federally funded Troops to Teachers program, entitled the Military Career Transition Program, which took advantage of the large military bases in Norfolk. Teachers with a military background come with certain valuable assets—they are frequently well prepared in math and science, they do not feel uncomfortable with the discipline challenges that urban classrooms can present, and they are often mature males, an advantage in working toward a more gender-balanced corps of teachers. Moreover, they are eager for a second career, and teaching is an attractive profession because of the training orientation of the military.

We are pursuing the possibility of a TTT program at UMass Boston. Although Massachusetts military bases have been closed, new language in the TTT program has extended services to National Guard and Reserve officers, which creates a sizable population of servicemen and -women with a potential interest in a TTT effort in Boston.

The university is well positioned to develop such a program. Many courses and some full programs within the GCE already exist on-line, and their number is steadily increasing as part of a plan to make on-line versions of most GCE courses available. The Teach Next Year (TNY) program within the GCE gives us experience with intensive, site-focused education for students who are often older and, like retiring military, come with considerable life experience. In addition, since 1982, when we established the Joiner Center for the Study of War and Social Consequences, we have developed expertise in a variety of veterans' issues, and we currently have about seven hundred to eight hundred veterans in our student body.

In most states, the TTT programs are run by their respective state departments of education. Massachusetts has not yet set up an oversight structure for the TTT program, so these opportunities have been ignored. However, my conversations with Senator Kennedy's office revealed that such a structure is not necessary to secure federal funds. Our congressional liaison is now pointing the way to this additional source of support for alternative certification programs.

THE TECHNOLOGY INITIATIVE

In the last three years Boston Mayor Menino and the Boston Public Schools have intensified their efforts to bring technology into the schools. These have included a new program to bring computers to 4th graders and their parents, a Boston Public Schools Web portal, a new technology academy (Tech Boston), and initiatives toward larger projects for the future. UMass Boston has been a central participant in several of them.

Technology Goes Home at School (TGH@School) is a program to teach basic computer skills to parents and their children together and to put computers in their homes. The pilot program is being delivered to 4th graders in six schools—65 students and parents—with free computers, software, Internet access, and tech support provided upon successful completion. Access to the Web portal gives parents an additional means to participate in their child's education and follow their child's progress. UMass Boston has trained the teachers and, through its Center for Social Policy, evaluated and redesigned the curriculum. By the fall of 2004, 1,600 students and parents will have passed through the program.

The Boston Area Advanced Technological Education Connections (BATEC) is a consortium of UMass Boston, three community colleges, the Metropolitan School to Career Partnership (which represents nine school systems in the Greater Boston area and UMass Boston), and Tech Boston/BPS. During the summer of 2002, with National Science Foundation (NSF) support, BATEC prepared a multimillion dollar proposal to NSF to establish an advanced technological education center at UMass Boston. Its purpose is to coordinate course offerings, provide a coherent roadmap for technology education from high school through the community colleges and the university, and support a wide array of instructional technology degree and certificate programs offered by the partners.

Also, at the request of the Boston Public Schools Office of Instructional Technology, we have been working together to create a Certificate in Instructional Technology for Educators. Planning for the certificate is moving along well, and one course in the program is already running.

PROMOTING EVALUATION RESEARCH

I have been working to give greater emphasis and recognition to our own faculty's efforts to identify what works in improving K–12 student achievement. Our involvement with the professional development schools has been a focus for evaluation research. Sabbaticals have been provided, funds dedicated, and media attention drawn to our evaluation of the different initiatives introduced in the PDSs. As a social scientist, I am eager to use our involvement with one PDS as a springboard for change in other schools. To identify and understand the factors that influence student achievement will enable us to replicate them in other schools. Our goal is systemic change.

In my conversations with GCE faculty, I continuously asked for the research that would evaluate and subsequently focus our efforts in the PDSs. I emphasized that the major impediment to our emerging as a national model in university-school collaboration is that we don't yet know as much as we need to about what works in improving student achievement. We have had our successes, but our knowledge of the key factors is still too impressionistic. Like cities and researchers nationally, we are just beginning to focus on which measures have impact, which ones give us leverage, which ones are truly the key to making a difference to changing the culture in schools. Once we have a better grasp of that, we will look to expand the scope and pace of our efforts, and then we will see whether and how much budgetary limits and the natural inertia of organizations are impediments.

COLLABORATION WITH K–12 SCHOOLS: DORCHESTER HIGH AND TEACH NEXT YEAR

The GCE has extensive collaborative arrangements with area schools, ranging from internships for individual teachers in training to established partnerships with many schools, including four professional development schools—three in Boston and another in the nearby city of Somerville. The school with which, by far, we have the most extensive collaborative relationship is Dorchester High School (DHS).

DHS is a comprehensive high school serving one thousand students. It is a high-poverty, diverse, inner-city school, approximately 65 percent Haitian or African American, a quarter Latino, and the remaining few students white or Asian. At the time of our beginning a PDS relationship with the school in 1998, it was among the city's worst in terms of test results, violence, and dropout rates.

Some of our work with DHS goes back many years. Since the early 1980s, UMass Boston has provided programs of academic support, which are described below—Urban Scholars, Upward Bound, and GEAR UP among them. Our more extensive work with DHS has come in the last four years and was triggered by $1,887,000 in gifts to support work in the schools, including more than $1,150,000 for work at DHS from an alumna, an educational philanthropist who funds multiple reform efforts in Boston. The core gift for DHS was made in 1998, $1 million to be spread over four years.

Our work with DHS now spans many activities. Chief among them is Teach Next Year, a site-based program for preparing master's-level students to teach in urban schools. An internship program with strong mentoring, TNY has been particularly successful in attracting minority students and in their staying on to teach at DHS or other city schools after graduation. Each year, $100,000 of the grant money has gone to support TNY interns: $10,000 is provided each intern, and the university also provides a tuition waiver and fee reduction. Our interns do have choices as to where they do their internships, and the $10,000—now provided by the BPS system—has been a huge incentive for them to choose DHS. It is not the only reason TNY is attractive to them, however: the TNY program provides a support network of peers and mentors, the DHS setting is a challenging place to work, and interns, who are screened for a commitment to underserved students and urban education, come with that orientation. Prior to the TNY program, DHS was not a place at which UMass Boston students wanted to intern or teach; now it is.

TNY interns assist a veteran mentor teacher for 10 to 20 hours a week during the first term and then teach two classes independently during the second, plus an additional cotaught class, typically English as a second language or special education. Interns also tutor for one period each day, in science, social studies, or English, especially MCAS prep.

The TNY program follows a cohort model in that all interns take all courses together except those covering subject matter content. They are enrolled in a one-year, 36-credit master's degree/secondary education certification program that runs from July through June. Their coursework mirrors that of the regular GCE curriculum, except that there are no electives. Of the normal nine elective credits, three are used to increase the practicum, three to increase clinical teaching, and three for a course in action research during the clinical. In addition, the focus of some courses is clearly urban.

During the spring semester, interns take a course on research in which they each focus on some element of their practice and student learning, an activity that also contributes to an atmosphere of inquiry among teaching staff. Recent examples of interns' research projects include exploring test-taking strategies, reality-based feedback, and science misconceptions. Additionally, each intern spearheads an after-school project—known as a Legacy project—with students. Projects of the first-year cohort included a business club, school newspaper, media-TV projection club, a social action group, an adventure club, and math tutoring for advanced students. Legacy projects the second year have a stronger emphasis on family/community outreach and involvement.

Additional measures support both the interns and collaborating DHS faculty. Some UMass Boston courses for TNY interns—developmental psychology and the research course—are offered on site at DHS to accommodate interns' schedules. Also, mentor teachers are released from two classes to pursue self-designed, self-directed professional development projects to allow for better communication with students' families during the school day and to observe and mentor their intern.

Comments by the first-year graduates confirm a positive view of the program. In response to the question, "Are you glad you participated in TNY?" typical comments of the first year's group were

"Yes, this year has been a life-shaping experience never to be forgotten."

"Yes, financially and professionally I could not have made a better choice."

"Yes, this has been one of the hardest years of my life, but I have learned and experienced an incredible amount of life."

TNY graduates have been successful at continuing to teach in urban schools. Of the first-year cohort of nine interns, six stayed on at DHS, two worked in other Boston public high schools, and one went on to another Massachusetts urban setting at Brockton High School. Altogether, more than 10 percent of the DHS teachers are now TNY graduates. They are taking leadership positions in the school, and their number is already large enough to have an impact.

TNY is by no means the only program at DHS for fostering student achievement. There are approximately 20 others that provide face-to-face support, serving more than 800 students in the areas of academics, college preparation, student empowerment, and career planning and job placement. A description of measures focused on curriculum and instruction would go to several pages. A number of university faculty and staff persons teach, advise, mentor, and otherwise interact with school staff. Likewise, several DHS teachers and administrators teach and advise at the university. A university staff person coordinates partnership work. A steering committee composed of teachers, administrators, parent/community members, students, interns, corporate and nonprofit partners, and college/university personnel meets after school on alternating months.

RESTRUCTURING

At the same time, and with UMass Boston support, DHS has restructured around small learning communities. The SLCs took longer to put in place—two years' planning rather than one for many of the other programs at DHS—in order to make sure there was strong participation and buy-in by DHS faculty, and also because institutional support from the BPS was required. The nature and themes of particular SLCs have changed some in the short time they have been in existence. For the 2001–2002 and 2002–2003 school years, they included these seven:

- The Academy of Public Service. Social science oriented, it provides internships and job shadowing in areas related to community and public service.
- The Entrepreneurship SLC. For students interested in going into business or working in corporate life.
- The Technology SLC. Computers, computer-aided design, and other applications.
- The Accelerated Academy. A diploma-plus model that appeals to quite varied groups of students: those who have not yet found the success their potential indicates, dual-enrollment students taking some courses at community colleges or other postsecondary institutions, and job-sharing students who need extra flexibility in their schedules.
- The Freshman Academy. For 9th graders, to make the transition to high school smoother. It provides intensive work in English and math—twice as much as in subsequent years.
- The LAB cluster. For special education students with a vocational orientation.
- Bilingual. Not strictly an SLC, but it provides a common place for those whose language classes are separate from the rest.

Within the Boston Public School system, DHS has been a pioneer in small learning communities, and the experience at DHS has been one guide to the policy of SLCs now adopted for the entire system.

EVALUATION

Everyone agrees that the atmosphere at DHS is greatly improved in the few years since we began the partnership work in 1998. Some call it a different place, and this includes independent outside evaluators. There is a high level of engagement among high school faculty and TNY interns. Most faculty want interns. One of our liaison staff observed that we spent the first couple of years establishing trust between university and school personnel. The level of trust is now high, not only among university/school people but among teachers at DHS and among teachers and administrators at the school.

Still, there is a distance to go to create a culture of achievement in the school. The report on the first year notes that there is little peer support or pressure for high student achievement, particularly in the lower grades. Discipline is still a challenge, and opportunities for improving communication keep appearing.

The framework for evaluation was developed by UMass Boston in collaboration with BPS and with Tufts and Simmons, the two other universities with PDSs in Boston. The main goal of PDSs adopted by the BPS is the institutionalization of organizational structures that will ultimately lead to high levels of student achievement. The evaluation model calls for four elements: student achievement and a culture of achievement, curriculum and instructional practices, using data for continuous improvement, and teacher preparation programs at the college and university level.

This 2002–2003 evaluation of the partnership between UMass Boston and DHS focuses on the first element, student achievement, because we found that although there were many strategies in place at DHS for fostering student achievement, the majority of students were not achieving at expected levels in their individual classes or on the state's high-stakes MCAS exam.

The analysis is based in part on extensive interviews with 23 students and 108 teachers, conducted 20 hours a week over a four-month period. Transcripts of selected portions of the interviews are not short of laudatory comments—the teacher who "performed magic in front of the class," the intern for whom the program was a perfect match and who "could sing its praises all day." There is also the everyday stuff of running programs: teachers or interns who don't fit well with the person they're matched with and those who are a match made in heaven; interns learning that commitment and creativity are not enough; interns who discover that they have to "really work on their assumptions, but that's huge, huge, huge." The anecdotal is useful in building up a picture of what happens, and if there is enough of this kind of material, well organized, it can even serve as a component of a how-to manual.

Yet, even if everyone likes TNY and the other PDS program elements, as things stand they have not been enough to change the culture of the school to nearly the extent needed. I hope the interview approach will afford insight as to what the next steps should be. Beyond that, much more is required, relating systemic actions to quantitative indicators of progress. If we can be successful in one urban high school posing the greatest challenges, we will have learned much. If we can simultaneously pinpoint the key elements in that success, we will have gone a long way toward discovering a strategy that can be replicated in other schools.

Understanding the key factors in improving the schools, increasing the focus of GCE and university programs and curricula, and corralling funding to support school and university programs are all closely related. As chancellor, I am constantly on the lookout for ways to combine people, money, and key programmatic initiatives to make things happen. The process entails taking advantage of the unique access to information across the university that the chancellor's role gives me and giving enough attention to the goal of improving the schools that I can see the potential connections. The process is both planned and fortuitous, and it relies heavily on a similar and collaborative effort by faculty and our partners outside the university.

CONCLUDING OBSERVATIONS

I regard the task of improving K–12 education as a large puzzle with many pieces and many small changes that need to be put in place. Given the scope and variety of what is needed, my task as a university chancellor is to establish priorities, put good people in senior positions, connect people with common interests, and cultivate buy-in among a range of influential players. Change takes time; changing a school or university culture can take many years, with luck.

The power of the presidency lies in identifying priorities and allocating resources, both time and money. Supporting the dean of the Graduate College of Education, both in programs and budget, has sent a strong message internally and externally. Externally, my active participation in the Boston Higher Education Partnership and the mayor's Technology Initiative, and the development of new public relations materials highlighting our role in the community, have clearly signaled my commitment to the urban education agenda. Internally, I have encouraged the college to pursue significant new programs—the scholarship initiative and alternative certification among them—and supported in concrete ways our work at our professional development schools, at our new Superintendents' Academy, and in delivering educational technology programs to the schools.

For the future, I look for quantitative evidence on those particular changes in policy and practice that make a difference and have some leverage, particularly those changes that can be replicated in other schools. We are looking in depth at one urban high school, Dorchester High, and we are also implementing and studying programs beyond DHS that affect large numbers, including the Superintendents' Academy and alternative certification programs. Covering the ground this way, I am hopeful that we will discover ways to be effective in achieving quality urban education for all.

In one year, one can only hope to set the stage for future progress. However, there is no year quite as visible as the first year of a presidency, so it has been an ideal time to signal my concern for and commitment to urban education. I was fortunate to find so many important pieces in place—an energetic and thoughtful dean, a progressive and dedicated mayor, and an experienced and wise school superintendent. Quickly, I was able to identify several new initiatives that were aligned with previous efforts and supportive of the school system's needs.

I chose to focus on the university-school collaboration because it is a microcosm of the university community collaboration so critical to our future as a public urban institution. It is also the most visible place for the university to demonstrate its expertise and commitment to the social good. Much leadership is based on building on institutional strengths and identifying where small increments can make a big difference. Not always is a new chancellor or president fortunate enough to find coherence between institutional strengths and political realities. Amidst budget setbacks, community concerns about our plans for new construction, and collective bargaining issues, deciding to focus attention and resources on the university's partnership with its urban school neighbors was—as the kids like to say— a "no brainer." The fact that the community political infrastructure facilitated this commitment was almost too good to be true. Rarely are all the stars so clearly aligned!

Jo Ann M. Gora's more-than-20 year career in higher education administration included service at Old Dominion University in Norfolk, Virginia, as provost and vice president for academic affairs before she was named chancellor of the

University of Massachusetts Boston in 2001. During her tenure at Old Dominion she led the institution through two strategic planning processes resulting in the creation of an undergraduate guaranteed internship program called the Career Advantage and the establishment of a Career Management Center. She also directed the development of TELETECHNET, Old Dominion's statewide distance-learning program offering 30 degree programs to 60 sites across Virginia and six other states. Responding to economic development needs, she was responsible for the development of the Virginia Commercial Space Flight Authority, the introduction of the Virginia Modeling, Analysis and Simulation Center, and the operation of the NASA Full Scale Wind Tunnel. At UMass Boston she has raised admission standards, increased community outreach, improved the instructional technology infrastructure, and worked to develop academic centers of excellence in the environmental sciences and public policy. Chancellor Gora holds master's and doctoral degrees in sociology from Rutgers University and received her bachelor's degree from Vassar College.

BIBLIOGRAPHY

Check, J. W. (2002). *Politics, language, and culture: A critical look at urban school reform.* Westport, CT: Praeger. *Author's note:* Check provides excellent background on the Boston Public Schools and his discussion of school reform is a valuable addition to the perspectives of this volume.

Jerald, C. D. (2002). *All talk, no action: Putting an end to out-of-field teaching.* Retrieved March 31, 2003, from the Education Trust, http://www.edtrust.org/main/main/reports.asp.

Murray, J. (2001, December). *Boston's next generation of teachers: Recommendations for recruiting, inducting and retaining new teachers for the Boston Public Schools.* Report commissioned by the Mayor's Office, City of Boston and the Office of the Superintendent, Boston Public Schools. Cambridge, MA: distributed by the Harvard Children's Initiative.

CHAPTER 3

Taking the Long View

Gerald L. Bepko

Universities cannot be all things to all people, and they should not promise more than they reasonably can achieve. The principal purpose of universities is to create optimal conditions for learning for their relevant student populations. Nor should the work of our faculty be wholly local in nature, provincial, or pedestrian. It should be competitive in intellectual terms with any public university faculty. Nevertheless, despite our commitment to these general norms of university life, urban campuses have a special opportunity to serve in important ways and to be enriched by the challenge of connecting their academic work with the practical needs of their regions.

This chapter is a reflection of my nearly 17 years of increasing consciousness and support for issues of community-university engagement and the increasingly wide range of efforts to address them. It reflects the assumption that leadership for me in this arena is found less in bold, single actions directed from university administration and more in the setting of broad priorities and expectations, facilitating the efforts of those who have been enlisted in the cause, serving in ways both highly visible and inconspicuous to support their efforts, and rewarding people in various ways for their commitment. My observations are based on the assumption that urban universities should try wherever and whenever feasible to contribute to an improved community educational system by better teacher preparation, by support for teachers in practice, by engagement with the larger communities in ways that promote education, and by supporting experimentation in our communities. This chapter describes some examples in each of these categories.

THE COMMUNITY CONTEXT

The city of Indianapolis, in which our university resides, is the seat of state government and the state's largest and most diverse population center. Also known as the Crossroads of America, Indianapolis is the convergence point of more interstate highways than any other city in the country; half the nation's population is within a day's drive.

The nation's 12th-largest city and, according to the Office of Management and Budget (1993), the 29th-largest Metropolitan Statistical Area, our city has undergone a dramatic renewal in the past 10 years. Added to the many amateur and professional sports attractions for which it had been well-known are many more cultural amenities and a revitalized downtown area. Since 1960, the population in Marion County has increased by nearly 24 percent, while the nearest surrounding counties have increased their populations by an average of more than 40 percent (Indiana Business Research Center, 2000).

Indianapolis Public Schools

Most of the attention on education reform in our city has been focused on the largest school district—the Indianapolis Public Schools (IPS). Although it is the state's largest school system, it is only one of 11 school districts in Marion County. It serves students within the old city boundaries that were expanded to be coterminous with the county at about the same time that Indiana University–Purdue University Indianapolis (IUPUI) was organized. The incorporation of wealthier suburbs into the old city broadened the tax base for most city services, but relief for the poor and public schools were excluded from the financial benefits of this broader consolidation.

Most of the enrollment in Indianapolis Public Schools comes from neighborhoods within the old city boundaries, much of which now is known as Center Township. IPS has five traditional high schools, 17 middle schools, and 56 elementary schools. More than 62 percent of the students are eligible for free lunch, and two-thirds are minority students. The average college attendance rate is 46 percent, compared with the overall state average of 64 percent. Within the last five years, IPS has enrolled a significant number of immigrant students, and many schools now are scrambling to find bilingual teachers, resources, and support.

Challenges like these have an impact on programs for teacher preparation but are not unlike those faced by other urban schools systems in America. According to the National Center for Education Statistics, there is a dramatic need for more urban teachers nationwide. The center's data suggest that one of every three students in elementary and secondary public schools currently is a member of a minority group. By the year 2035, it is expected that a majority of all K–12 students will be from minority groups. The number of language-minority students is also expected to rise dramatically largely because of immigration trends (Chapa and Valencia, 1993).

Indiana University–Purdue University Indianapolis

IUPUI is situated along the east bank of the White River in downtown Indianapolis. It is adjacent to an exceptional urban park—the White River State Park—which contains the Indianapolis Zoo, the NCAA Headquarters with its museum-like Hall of Champions, the Eiteljorg Museum of Indian and Western Art, and the new Indiana State Museum. Also adjoining are the Indiana Historical Society, the Indiana state capitol complex, and the Indianapolis central business district. Under construction is a retrofitted new home for the Indiana University (IU) Herron School of Art at IUPUI, a century-old studio art school with galleries and exhibition space in the arts and culture corridor south of campus. In this setting, the IUPUI campus has been energized and enveloped by a growing, bustling, exciting center-city environment.

Almost equidistant from Indiana University Bloomington to the south and Purdue University West Lafayette to the north, IUPUI is the state's third-largest campus in terms of student enrollment. Created in 1969, IUPUI is a unique partnership between Indiana's two major state universities, where students receive degrees from Indiana University or Purdue University. While it bears the names of both Indiana University and Purdue University, IUPUI is part of Indiana University. All faculty and staff are employees of IU, and all students are registered within IU. Drawing on the traditional strengths of each institution, IUPUI brings together in downtown Indianapolis the most comprehensive range of degree programs anywhere in the state.

More than 29,000 students enroll annually in some 180 academic programs from associate to doctoral/professional. Purdue University oversees academic programs in science, engineering, and technology, while Indiana University assumes responsibility for programs in allied health, art, business, dentistry, education, journalism, law, liberal arts, medicine, nursing, optometry, physical education and tourism management, public and environmental affairs, and social work. Each year about 4,700 earn IU or Purdue degrees upon completing their studies at IUPUI. More than 60 percent of the undergraduate students at IUPUI are the first in their families to attend college.

Indiana University has eight campuses in the state, the largest of which are in Bloomington (with more than 38,000 students) and Indianapolis. Although each of these two large campuses has academic units or schools based wholly on that campus, some schools (e.g., the IU Schools of Business, Education, Informatics, Journalism, Music, Public and Environmental Affairs, Nursing, and Social Work) are based jointly in Bloomington/ Indianapolis, with the dean's primary reporting line being either to the chancellor of the Bloomington campus or of the Indianapolis campus. For example, the dean of the IU School of Education is based in Bloomington, and an executive associate dean is in place to manage the programs at IUPUI. This arrangement, which requires consultation and teamwork, has allowed both for intercampus collaboration and for the IUPUI campus to take on a particular community-responsive focus or flavor while maintaining linkages to the stature of the IU School of Education in the recruitment and promotion of faculty, conferral of degrees, and other matters.

Although the profile of the general student body at IUPUI is coming closer to reflecting the community's diversity, the education students at IUPUI are more white, female, English speaking, and middle class than their fellow students and than the students in the urban classrooms in which they are likely to teach (Darling-Hammond, 1990; Grant and Secada, 1990). Currently, 10 percent of the teacher candidates are minority, and 8 percent are African American; three-fourths are female. Mirroring the national figures, a significant number of Indianapolis's prospective teachers come from backgrounds that provide little or no experience with minority children. These trends have caused the IU School of Education at IUPUI to focus on issues specifically related to teacher preparation in urban schools.

The Neighborhoods Surrounding IUPUI

In addition to the bustling downtown, IUPUI also sits near two low-income communities that are both struggling to meet education, health, and social services needs. Both communities have had uneven and sometimes awkward relationships with IU and its IUPUI campus. Over the years, as the campus expanded, more land was acquired, in the process displacing many residents of the community and resulting in some ill feeling.

Bordering the north side of the campus is one of those communities—the United Northwest Area (UNWA), a poor neighborhood with an aging population and deteriorating housing stock, only recently revived with some community development investments in new, moderately priced housing. To the west of IUPUI, across the White River, there is another community, with three subdivisions known as Haughville, Hawthorne, and Stringtown, which spread out in a series of residential neighborhoods, old commercial areas, and a few remaining manufacturing centers. Within the last five years, the demographics of this tripartite community have changed, reflecting the 295 percent increase in the number of Latino residents who live in the region. While this westside community was once primarily populated with working-class citizens of Eastern European origins, it has become culturally and racially diverse, with many African American and Hispanic American residents.

Bridging these two communities and moving north from the IUPUI campus is a new institutional phenomenon known as Clarian Health Partners, which is the entity born of the 1997 consolidation of Indiana University's hospitals—an adult hospital and Riley Hospital for Children—located on the IUPUI campus and the Methodist Hospitals of Indiana, located about two miles north of campus in the UNWA neighborhood. Although Clarian is an independent, not-for-profit organization, it is closely allied with the university. Members of the Indiana University family serve on the board of Clarian Health Partners, and most of the physicians who serve in the Clarian system are university faculty. Because of these close associations, Clarian and IUPUI have joined in various community causes, including the commitment to make the northwest sector of Indianapolis the best urban environment in the nation.

Our Neighborhood Schools

The UNWA neighborhood has four elementary schools; two of them are among the lowest-performing schools in the Indianapolis Public Schools system. Crispus Attucks Middle School, an African American historical landmark, is the only middle school in the community. In the post–World War II era, when it was a high school, Crispus Attucks was the school at which Oscar Robertson played basketball. As a middle school, it now has a good magnet program and support from alumni as well as private-sector groups. For high school, however, students who live in the neighborhood are bused to the south side of the city.

To the west, in Haughville, Hawthorne, and Stringtown, there is a powerful neighborhood association named the Westside Cooperative Organization, or WESCO. In 2001, the George Washington Community School (GWCS) was reopened as a middle school (with the first two years of high school added soon thereafter), a reopening based on the collaborative work of WESCO and the IUPUI campus. In 1995, this only remaining neighborhood school had been closed to cut costs at a time when IPS enrollments were at an all-time low, but the neighborhood's population grew rapidly and changed dramatically since that time, creating pressure for the reopening.

To plan the reopening, a community advisory committee composed of community members, parents, service providers, business leaders, and education partners (including IU School of Education faculty from IUPUI) met monthly for more than two years. The neighborhood enthusiastically supported the reconstruction of the building, once a thriving high school. This was a huge victory for the struggling community. Unfortunately, because there remain no elementary schools in the neighborhood, many younger children still must be bused to schools in other parts of the city.

Because of the changing demographics, as one might expect, these adjoining neighborhoods (UNWA and WESCO) now have a growing number of children. If these are to be among the best urban areas in the nation, it is essential for these children to have a broad range of high-quality educational opportunities and for the university community to take a special interest in their welfare and development.

A CALL TO ENGAGEMENT

The history, geography, adjoining institutions and communities, and changing demographics, have all had an impact on the IUPUI university family and its leadership. They certainly have had an impact on me, a former IU Law School dean drawn into the university administration as chancellor in 1986. Law schools tend to be self-contained, like medical schools, so my contacts with the rest of the campus were limited, and my involvement with the community focused mostly on the legal profession. Like most others who have been recruited into the administration of IUPUI, however, I was soon influenced by conditions in the communities surrounding the campus and the plight of the adjoining neighborhoods— UNWA, Haughville, Hawthorne, and Stringtown—inevitably draw one's attentions and shape thoughts about how universities function in the community.

It is not unusual for the president or chancellor of an urban university campus to be involved in the local chamber of commerce, boards of business entities important to the economic development of the region, boards of charitable organizations seeking to improve urban quality-of-life conditions, and interinstitutional educational partnerships to improve the intellectual and cultural life of the city. And so it was with me. I have chaired the local United Way Campaign and been chair of the board of directors for the United Way of Central Indiana. In 2001, I was president of the Indianapolis Economic Club, whose monthly speakers' program attracts an average of 1,000 participants.

This community involvement has been a precipitating factor in the creation of university programs of various purposes, shapes, and kinds. Programs have developed with my encouragement either indirectly, based on the tone that I have tried to set, or directly, by virtue of my active participation. One of the most important among these is the series of efforts that have been made to support improvements in K–12 education.

HOLDING INSTITUTIONAL VALUES IN TRUST

The desire to make our adjoining communities part of the best urban environment in the nation and to assist with the development of schools is part of a larger set of values that has pervaded IUPUI and that I have sought to encourage. These are based on the assumption that urban campuses should be thoroughly engaged, accepting the agenda of the larger community as part of their own research and teaching agenda, and taking it for granted that the success of the region and state are part of the responsibility of the university.

Universities cannot be all things to all people, and they should not promise more than they reasonably can achieve. The principal purpose of universities is to create optimal conditions for learning for their relevant student populations. Nor should the work of our faculty be wholly local in nature, provincial, or pedestrian. It should be competitive in intellectual terms with any public university faculty. Nevertheless, despite our commitment to these general norms of university life, urban campuses have a special opportunity to serve in important ways and to be enriched by the challenge of connecting their academic work with the practical needs of their regions. This university engagement, which it sometimes is called today, is often of great benefit to the larger community and also is supportive of the contemporary movement to cultivate social capital, civic responsibility, and a commitment to service and philanthropy that are valuable to community members and students alike.

How should the university respond to the various educational challenges in the larger community of which we are a part? The best response is likely to be tied to the overall commitment of urban campuses to exemplary civic engagement. This engagement is a part of the institutional culture that is grounded in our campus's history of practice-based education in the caring professions and informed by professional standards that guide many of our community-responsive research agendas. For example, with my encouragement, and the encouragement of many others, our entire campus community took pride in the leadership provided by the IU School of Medicine faculty in the Campaign for Healthy Babies, initiated to address a too-high infant mortality rate in Marion County. Patricia A. Keener, M.D., of our medical faculty, who participated in that program and many others, won the 2002 American Association for Higher Education Ernest A. Lynton Award for Faculty Professional Service and Academic Outreach.

This engagement also is based on the intense interest in voluntary action for the public good that emanates from centers and projects that I've played a role in launching or supporting, such as the IU Center on Philanthropy—a multidisciplinary academic center devoted to studying the history, economics, philosophy, sociology, and practices of the charitable world. Our culture is also influenced by the Center for Service and Learning, founded in 1993, which is a focal point for service learning course development and student voluntarism, and by the Polis Center, which engages in a wide variety of research projects on urban culture, including maintaining the Social Assets and Vulnerabilities Indicators for the region, launched in 1995. IUPUI also has the IU Center for Urban Policy and the Environment, begun in 1992, which focuses on issues of interest to policy makers and urban planners.

FACILITATING THE WORK OF FACULTY

The story of IUPUI's connections to the community, its schools, and educational opportunity in general also reflects the approach to management that I have found to be effective in a higher education environment. It derives from insights offered by the late Herman B. Wells, the long-serving president and patriarch of Indiana University, who argued that the way to success for universities is to recruit the best people available, to make every effort to provide them with the resources they need to carry out their work, to give them moral support, guidance, and encouragement, and to carefully stay out of or smooth their way. The role of university leaders is to steer, not row; to be the keepers of the vision and values of an institution; and to bring talented people into the cause who are empowered to make the institution great, consistent with its vision and values. This type of thinking may not be likely to produce immediate or short-term results, but then most issues in education are not short term or resolvable through immediate remedies.

My partner in campus administration, particularly in academic matters, was IUPUI Executive Vice Chancellor and Dean of the Faculties William M. Plater. He described the academic administrator's role in engagement in an essay titled "Habits of Living: Engaging the Campus as Citizen One Scholar at a Time":

> Academic leaders must be able to relate their academic communities to their social communities, to serve as translators in making the language of the corporate and academic worlds comprehensible and tolerable to each other.... They can, in effect, embody the concept of citizenship by their own personal and individual engagement in bringing the two communities in a defined, rational relationship. They can do what the engaged scholar does best: they can teach. (1999, p. 142)

Plater's excellent work has been of fundamental importance in areas of engagement as in all other academic matters, and he played a significant role in launching the curriculum reform in our School of Education that is described in this chapter.

For faculty to do their best work, departmental and school leadership must be recruited with utmost care. In July 2000, I enthusiastically supported the appointment by then-IU President Myles Brand of Gerardo Gonzalez, the first Latino to serve as dean of the IU School of Education, based at IU Bloomington. It was clear that in the selection of Dean Gonzalez, whose experience included serving as interim dean of the College of Education at the University of Florida, we would have leadership committed to education reform and the problems associated with poverty in inner-city schools.

The faculty members of the IU School of Education at IUPUI have devoted years to developing key partnerships and are invested in the development of IPS schools that serve as professional development sites. Several faculty members have been recognized locally and nationally for effectively researching and exploring new ways to prepare teachers for urban schools. Three IPS elementary schools—the Key School, the Center for Inquiry, and Cold Springs Academy—have received national recognition because of the efforts of the IUPUI-based faculty, and all have a long tradition of being professional development sites for the elementary teacher education program.

In July 2001, Barbara Wilcox retired from the position of executive associate dean for Indianapolis programs in the IU School of Education. Dean Gonzalez—in concert with, and with the support of, the campus administration—appointed Khaula Murtadha, the first African American woman to serve as the executive associate dean for education at the IUPUI campus. Dean Murtadha, an internal candidate, had served as the principal investigator for the Strategic Directions Interagency Collaboration for Urban School Professional Development and Research and was responsible for the School of Education's relationship with the United Way of Central Indiana's Bridges to Success (BTS) program, about which more will be said later.

Because of Dean Murtadha's community experiences, she values a strong relationship among the university, community, and schools. Her commitment to urban schools, in particular, supports Dean Gonzalez's assertion that "everything we do is focused on preparing teachers and other education professionals to address education and human development problems...[and] because some of those problems are so highly concentrated in the urban settings, we have focused a great deal of our research on the unique characteristics of urban populations" (Jenlink, 2002, p. 107).

With the leadership of Barbara Wilcox, later advanced by her successor, Khaula Murtadha, the IU School of Education faculty at IUPUI developed a new approach to urban teacher education known as the Learning to Teach/Teaching to Learn program (LT/TL). This program successfully integrates the academic rigor of education theory with the development of creative and practical teaching skills. What makes LT/TL unique is the trinity of university faculty, urban public school teachers, and community members who worked together to design, maintain, and assess this program that prepares teacher candidates and teachers-in-practice to act as change agents in their schools and communities.

LT/TL is a four-semester block-sequencing curriculum that includes a team of three to four faculty who jointly teach a cohort of 25 to 30 students each semester. Each cohort is assigned to an urban professional development school site and completes the four semesters of professional education coursework together.

The instructional approach in LT/TL is based on social constructivist theories of learning that require teacher candidates to be keenly involved in their own learning. Through exposure to early field experiences, students reflect on how learning occurs for them personally as well as on how the children they teach develop their concepts, skills, and beliefs. The program incorporates group collaboration and individual dialogue so that faculty can actively engage students in ways that help expand the borders of their own knowledge. As students learn to collaborate with their peers, they become more competent in interacting with the diversity of students, faculty, administrators, and parents at the professional development schools. Through dialogue, faculty, mentor teachers, and students jointly become reflective practitioners, diagnosticians, and planners as they con-

sider the social, cultural, and academic variables that influence their no-
tions of urban schools. As students learn about the broader, complex truths
related to urban schools and theories related to teaching, they begin to define their roles as teachers in a working context.

IUPUI collaborates with 20 professional development schools that reflect the rich cultural and language diversity of the metropolitan area.
Teacher candidates are based in one of these professional development
school sites for the three semesters before student teaching, all in all completing a total of 120 hours of supervised field experience. The fieldwork
is closely associated with coursework, carefully integrated with the overall
curriculum, and supervised jointly by course instructors and mentor teachers. Typically, teacher education courses are taught on location at the
school site. Unlike the IU Bloomington teacher education program, IUPUI
students and faculty spend most of their time in the schools that serve as
professional development sites.

Although many students experience discomfort or culture shock in their
early field experiences in urban schools, their faculty and mentor teachers—who, through research and observation, are prepared to address students' difficulties—help students begin to critically examine their belief
systems in the context of their future role as teachers and come to see themselves as professionals who are lifelong learners, learning to teach and
teaching to learn. In 1997, the Association for Teacher Educators recognized LT/TL at the IUPUI campus as one of three Distinguished Programs
in Teacher Education.

The collaboration of university faculty and teachers in urban schools affirms a shared vision of what it means to be a teacher in an urban school.
It was essential to the development of the LT/TL program and forms the
underpinnings for ongoing professional development for teachers in these
schools, which also is an essential part of the School of Education's and
the university's mission. Each summer, for example, teachers are invited to
enroll in the IUPUI Summer in the City series of courses, where they can
take advantage of minicourses that range from a single day to two weeks
and cover subjects that include how to create a Web site and how to use
drama in the classroom to explore different cultures.

Other intensive professional development seminars provide teachers,
counselors, and administrators with opportunities to construct new ways
to advance their teaching or approach emerging issues. The School of Education at IUPUI has hosted the Indiana Urban Superintendents Association and the Indiana Essential Schools Network. Both organizations support ongoing professional development and serve as advocates for urban
schools. Recently, IUPUI education faculty designed a Web-based profes-

sional development module for educators as part of the Virtual Curriculum Project sponsored by the Great Cities' Universities. The module was developed in partnership with the Indiana Essential Schools Network.

Strong leadership has been important to the LT/TL program and the continuing professional development programs, and a succession of faculty leaders and administrators sustained the effort with my encouragement. The programs maintain a life of their own, however, because they have deep roots in the work of the faculty and their ongoing collaboration with community partners. At the same time, recruiting new leadership for the school allowed me the opportunity to reaffirm the university's commitment to urban teacher preparation by communicating to stakeholders the importance of this continuing focus. I also was able to set the expectation that persons recruited to conduct the management of the School of Education would have the inclination and experience to support faculty in carrying forward these successful reforms.

SERVING AS A SPOKESPERSON IN THE COMMUNITY

The schools in our communities have been the subject of continuing commentary for all of the nearly 17 years that I served as chancellor of IUPUI. From faculty complaints about poorly prepared university-level students to public outcries over disappointing results on the expanding standardized tests of K–12 achievement to expressions of fear about the deplorable dropout rates in many urban school districts, we have heard a drumbeat of concern that students and schools are not meeting expectations.

I have never been completely certain of the origins or causes of the circumstances that provoke these continuing laments. Whatever the underlying problems may be, it seems that these conditions are less a matter of shortcomings on the part of any one of the many people and institutions that participate in the educational process and more the result of complicated social, organizational, and cultural forces that are not susceptible to easy descriptions or facile solutions. The nature of IUPUI's engagement with schools has been influenced by this understanding of the complexity of the origins of school problems.

My belief that educational outcomes are improved in the long term through broad-gauged efforts is related to the idea that community emphasis on education and learning is of fundamental importance. If parents and others in the community place an emphasis on learning, and create an optimal environment for learning, schoolwork will probably improve. Students will be more likely to come to school ready to learn and will devote themselves more enthusiastically to their studies. With this thought in mind, we have encouraged a variety of community-based efforts to raise consciousness of the importance of learning and high expectations for the educational process.

In addition to the efforts made by the School of Education, several IUPUI units have developed key teacher support and education partnership programs. For many years, I played a leadership role in convening informal meetings over breakfast or lunch of the six chancellors or presidents of the colleges and universities in the Indianapolis metropolitan area. These meetings were to discuss areas of mutual concern and potential collaboration. In one such meeting, the broad concept of Project SEAM[1] emerged. The overall goal of Project SEAM is to review the curriculum in K–12 and provide a seamless transition between high school and college math, language arts, and the sciences. The chancellors and presidents, or their representatives, contributed to the broad conception of the program, although IUPUI personnel played a leading role. Phase one of the project has already identified gaps in the precollege curriculum and the needs of central Indiana area teachers for additional professional development in their content area.

Scott Evenbeck, the dean of IUPUI's University College, has provided the energy and leadership in bringing together the partners, coordinating the community-wide initiative, and securing the enabling external grants. Faculty from IUPUI programs in biology, chemistry, physics, mathematics, and writing meet with colleagues from other campuses and with teachers in those disciplines. IPS is one of 15 school districts participating in this program along with 5 area colleges and universities. Now in phase two, the initiative provides financial and logistical support for professional development opportunities and support for the continuation of the interinstitutional cooperation efforts. This program not only plays a seminal role in addressing curriculum disparities among the schools but also identifies the resources needed by practicing teachers. It has attracted nearly $13 million in grant support, counting the matching amounts provided by the public school districts.

Several IUPUI initiatives have developed into long-term engagement with the community, sometimes with support from me behind the scenes and sometimes with my more direct involvement. An example of this is the IUPUI Office of Neighborhood Resources (ONR). ONR was created, at least in part, to provide a university home for the U.S. Department of Housing and Urban Development (HUD) Community Outreach Partnership Center (COPC) project grants.

The first three-year COPC grant, received in January 1998, was dependent on demonstrable engagement between IUPUI and the community being served—the three westside neighborhoods represented in the WESCO partnership. Although dedicated, involved, well-meaning, and knowledgeable people from both IUPUI and the community had all the right ideas in place and the makings of a structure for accomplishing them, there was initial community skepticism as well as the lingering resentment, mentioned earlier, of IUPUI's physical expansion. I was asked, and agreed, to convene the university-community partners. Although I did not have to continue hands-on involvement, the evidence of high-level commitment from IUPUI and the creation of ONR were as reassuring to the community partners as they were important to HUD, our funding agency. The COPC grant initiatives have involved other IUPUI departments and offices, such as the Center for Service and Learning, the Small Business Development Center, the School of Nursing Institute for Action Research in Community Health, and the School of Public and Environmental Affairs.

Earning the trust of WESCO leaders helped pave the way for the involvement of IUPUI's education faculty in the reopening of the Washington Community School. The new Washington Community School, reopened in the fall of 2000, became a professional development site for the School of Education, and cohorts of 28 preservice teachers regularly complete six-week field experiences there. In September 2002, the Washington School celebrated its 75th anniversary, and I was privileged to attend the celebratory reception.

DEVELOPING SUPPORT FOR EXPERIMENTATION

Our School of Education faculty members were considered essential participants in the development of the Washington Community School, not only because of their involvement with WESCO but also because of their involvement as founding partners of IUPUI's Better Together collaboration for full-service schools in Indianapolis.

Full-service schools also address the critical need for parents and others in the community to place an emphasis on learning and to create an optimal environment for learning. These innovative experiments in urban education recognize that schools anchor neighborhoods. Full-service schools offer education, nutrition, health services, counseling, tutoring, mentoring, recreation, and social skill development. They endeavor to connect families, schools, and the community in ambitious efforts to address a broad range of quality-of-life issues that influence learning.

In 1994, Barbara Wilcox, then-executive associate dean of the IU School of Education; Angela McBride, the dean of the IU School of Nursing; and Roberta Greene, the dean of the IU School of Social Work were awarded a Strategic Directions grant to create an infrastructure for inter-professional collaboration among their schools and the direct teaching, research, and service activities that address the expressed needs of the community and five IPS schools. Strategic Directions grants were intra-university financial incentives provided by then-Indiana University President Myles Brand to encourage initiatives in support of IU's long-range plan titled *The Strategic Directions Charter: Becoming America's New Public University*. As IU vice president for long-range planning, I coordinated the development of the *Strategic Directions Charter* and played a role in the Strategic Directions grant-making process. The Better Together collaboration was attractive to those of us evaluating the grant proposals because it simultaneously addressed two key strategic initiatives: community engagement and interdisciplinary collaboration among academic units.

The team of faculty from each of the schools developed the Better Together program on the assumption that a major factor influencing the quality of K–12 education is the combination of teaching, health, and social services that are available to students. The Better Together program was grounded in the urban collaborative mission of IUPUI and in the need to address the multitude of problems that plagued IPS. The deans also saw Better Together as an opportunity to deepen a collaborative relationship with a program that already existed: the Bridges to Success program. BTS, supported by the United Way of Central Indiana, is a forerunner of the full-service schools movement in Indianapolis. According to its mission statement, BTS aims to increase "the educational success of students by better meeting the non-academic needs of children and their families through the partnership of our education, human, and community service delivery systems with a long-range vision of establishing schools as 'life-long learning centers' and focal points of their communities" (Bridges to Success Web site). As chair of the board of directors for United Way of Central Indiana, I was able to support these developments both as chancellor and as a voice within United Way.

From 1992 until 1995, three of the five schools in the UNWA neighborhood had served as pilot sites for BTS. Several IUPUI faculty members were involved in the development of these individual BTS school sites, but there were few, if any, programmatic links between the pilot sites and university schools, including the IU School of Education. There was little coordination with the training of future professionals in education, health, or social services, and there was too little input from the community about the way we prepared professionals in those fields. The partnerships that did exist between the faculty at IUPUI and the UNWA schools were not directly supported with university resources and were not integrated into the curricula of the professional schools. The Better Together program, and the working group among the schools that developed it, assumed that IUPUI is uniquely situated to build from the BTS initiatives in ways that enhance learning at IPS and the professional education missions of the schools.

In the first three years of the program, the schools developed service-learning opportunities for IUPUI students in each of the UNWA schools. Preservice teachers assisted in-service teachers and provided individual tutoring to students in all five schools. Student nurses offered first aid health services for 10 hours a week at four of the schools. Social workers completing their master's degrees guided group therapy for students in two of the schools. During the first year, IUPUI students placed in UNWA met with IUPUI faculty, teachers, and community leaders to discuss issues and to learn how to approach them in an interdisciplinary manner.

After the first year, the faculty designed an undergraduate/graduate seminar to prepare students from each of the schools to work collaboratively. The seminar engaged the students in a critical analysis of contemporary issues by viewing various theoretical approaches and practices. The overall goal of the course was for students to become interprofessional practitioners who can integrate their experiences and expertise with human service providers. The faculty, believing that no one professional can know enough to meet all the needs of the children or families he or she faces, designed the seminar to help practitioners develop the expertise and ability to work together in creative and innovative ways.

Unfortunately, Strategic Directions funding for the Better Together program ended in 1999, but the interdisciplinary course is still offered by the three schools, and the community initiatives remain a critical element of the new elementary and secondary teacher education program. Preservice teachers are now offered an "early field experience" in schools located in UNWA or WESCO neighborhoods. Nursing and social work students also still have field experiences based on the community collaborations established under Better Together.

The Better Together faculty, in many ways, gained encouragement from the mission, vision, and values of IUPUI as a public urban campus with a commitment to engage with the community on its needs. Moreover, by virtue of IU and IUPUI campus resources—particularly in health-related fields—our university family has been able to place faculty resources so as to create a catalyst and transform BTS into the Better Together full-service schools.

The continuing development, evolution, and improvement of educational opportunities, however, are not likely to come from within public schools and universities alone. There are many voices in our communities, and to complete our engagement with the community with respect to education, it has seemed important to connect with emerging agents for change outside of academe. The most significant, and recent, of the efforts in which I have become personally involved as a board member is an organization named Project E. Project E was founded by an Indianapolis philanthropist named Christel DeHaan, who is devoted to children and raising educational levels. She has sometimes been controversial among educators because her efforts to enlist public support for education have been seen as based on a critical attitude toward current performance levels or as disparaging of education leaders. Nevertheless, it has become apparent, in my view, that private resources and voices such as Christel DeHaan's are extremely valuable ingredients in the renewal and improvement of education.

Project E has made an effort to have educational achievement become the subject of political debate in Indiana by purchasing commercial television and radio time to highlight educational achievement issues. It has also funded awards for excellence in teaching in K–12. Each year Project E gives 10 teachers $10,000 each as part of their awards for excellence program as well as giving $1,000 awards to each of 10 runners-up.

Project E also is engaged in advocacy for experimentation in education through charter schools and was a factor in the enactment of charter school-enabling legislation in Indiana, which permitted charter schools to open in 2002. This, too, has been controversial among those committed to public education, but the public seems supportive of the charter experimentation, especially since some of the new charter schools have taken on the most challenging cohorts of students. We have been carefully supportive of these developments by offering technical and policy advice, although Indiana University, which is authorized under the charter law to issue charters, along with all other public universities in the state, has not yet set up a mechanism to receive proposals for the issuance of charters. The mayor of Indianapolis—a supporter of charter schools—is one of the designated issuers and has set up a commission to review applications. In consultation with us, the mayor appointed Professor Jose Rosario of the IU School of Education at IUPUI as a member of the commission. One of the charters issued by the mayor on the recommendation of the commission was to the Christel House Academy in Indianapolis, founded by Christel DeHaan.

The Christel House in Indianapolis is operated in parallel to Christel Houses that have been created in Mexico, India, Venezuela, and South Africa to help the poorest children gain a first-rate education. My wife,

Jean, and I visited the Christel House in Cape Town, South Africa, and wrote an article about it that appeared in the *Indianapolis Business Journal*. Christel House provides health care, nutrition, structure, hope, and opportunity to children who would otherwise be forgotten. After visiting the Christel House in Cape Town, it seemed to us even more important to encourage private philanthropic support, such as that provided by Christel DeHaan, and set standards for leaders of the business community to devote themselves and their resources to the advancement of children. In our retirement, we plan to be volunteers in this and other related educational causes.

TAKING THE LONGER VIEW

The values of an urban institution such as IUPUI should include university engagement. Among the many areas of engagement possible, the most important are likely to be those that are focused on precollege education and all the various institutions, dynamics, and people who must work together to make it succeed. As university officers, we should be advocates for university engagement with the schools.

My approach to explaining how university chancellors and presidents can make a difference in the schools is probably influenced by the length of my service as chancellor and my recent retirement. At this time, however, it seems to me that the relationships between universities and the schools in their states may best be viewed in terms of how they will be shaped and formed over long periods of time, with many experiments, with many efforts by many people, and with accumulated experience. Others represented in this book have cited valuable university projects and events that have contributed to the advancement of education. My contribution to this compilation is to suggest that a longer view can also be important.

The role of the president or chancellor is often to be the shaper and keeper of institutional values. It is to be an advocate, a facilitator who convenes the appropriate persons and puts precious resources in place to serve as a catalyst for action. It is to shape and reinforce the vision and values of a university community so that over time people will embrace them and be energized to apply their creative talents. It is to facilitate and support the work of faculty and others who reflect the vision and values of the institution. It is to serve as a spokesperson in the larger community, to develop support for good projects, to ensure that the larger community understands the role of the university, and to encourage experimentation. It is to be a champion for the value of university engagement, and it is to urge that among the most important areas of engagement is education—

engagement that not only addresses issues currently of importance to our communities, that not only enriches and informs our teaching and research, but that also improves our own students' learning. By improving the education of young people and the preparation of their teachers, those universities that draw heavily from enrollments in their own regions will ultimately reap the rewards of continuing engagement with their community's schools.

NOTE

1. The Central Indiana Educational Service Center received a $6.6 million grant from the Lilly Endowment for the Project SEAM initiative.

Gerald L. Bepko *completed his term as interim president of Indiana University in Bloomington, Indiana, following 16 years as chancellor of Indiana University–Purdue University Indianapolis. During his tenure at IUPUI, enrollment increased by 22 percent and annual research grants rose from $38 million to more than $200 million a year. He led a renewed emphasis on undergraduate education, culminating in the establishment of the University College in 1997. Before his academic career, Chancellor Bepko practiced law in Chicago and was a special agent for the Federal Bureau of Investigation. He joined the Indiana University faculty of the School of Law–Indianapolis in 1972 and served as associate dean for academic affairs and dean of the law school. He has been a visiting professor at the University of Illinois, The Ohio State University, and Indiana University Bloomington. He is a member of the National Conference of Commissioners on Uniform State Laws and the permanent editorial board of the Uniform Commercial Code. He currently serves as vice chair of the Great Cities' Universities.*

BIBLIOGRAPHY

Bridges to Success. Retrieved March 31, 2003, from http://www.bridgestosuccess. org.

Chapa, J., & Valencia, R. (1993). Latino population growth, demographic characteristics, and educational stagnation: An examination of recent trends. *Hispanic Journal of Behavioral Sciences, 15*(2), 165–187.

Darling-Hammond, L. (1990). Teachers and teaching: Signs of a changing profession. In W. R. Houston (Ed.), *Handbook of research on teacher education* (pp. 267–290). New York: Macmillan.

Grant, C., & Secada, W. G. (1990). Preparing teachers for diversity. In W. R. Houston (Ed.), *Handbook of research on teacher education* (pp. 403–422). New York: Macmillan.

Indiana Business Research Center Kelly School of Business. (2000). *Population change in Indiana Counties 1960 to 2000 and 1970 to 2000*. Retrieved March 31, 2003, from http://www.ibrc.indiana.edu/cor/popchange.htm.

Jenlink, P. M. (2002, Spring/Summer). The challenges of Urban Education: A conversation with Gerardo Gonzalez, University Dean of the School of Education at Indiana University. *Teacher Education and Practice, 15*(1/2), 107.

Office of Management and Budget. (1993). *Metropolitan areas definition*. Retrieved March 31, 2003, from http://quickfacts.census.gov/qfd/meta/long_metro.htm.

Plater, W. (1999). Habits of living: Engaging the campus citizen one scholar at a time. In R. Bringle, E. Malloy, & R. Games (Eds.), *Colleges and universities as citizens* (pp. 141–172). Needham Heights, MA: Allyn and Bacon.

CHAPTER

The University of Illinois at Chicago: Distributed Leadership

Sylvia Manning

For UIC's College of Education the problem is not to get in the door, not to find acceptance for its programs, but to avoid being scattered among too many projects, to manage wisely the continuous process of triage required by the myriad demands upon its limited human and financial resources. The principles it uses are local need, wide effect, and above all, leverage. The college seeks to focus its efforts at the key points where effects may multiply.

The qualities of good leadership are slippery. They are different in different contexts to the point of inconsistency, they resist description, and when articulated their descriptions tend toward generalities that are difficult to translate into specific action. Nonetheless, leadership must be nurtured at all levels of education if our urban schools are to serve their students well. At the universities that prepare our teachers and school principals, leadership in addressing the challenges of high-need urban schools must in some degree include the president or chancellor, if only to empower the leaders in the College of Education and persuade the leaders in the arts and sciences. For this kind of leadership, I believe that there are a few basic requirements:

- A self-conscious examination of the context, an understanding of the individuals within that context, and a willingness to suit one's leadership to that context and those individuals
- An appreciation of difference and tension as part of the change process; an openness, therefore, to others' perspectives
- An understanding of leadership as a role that requires a desire to be of service to those one leads
- A recognition of leadership in a large, complex university as necessarily a distributed or shared role

CONTEXT: UNIVERSITY OF ILLINOIS AT CHICAGO

The University of Illinois at Chicago (UIC) emerged from a sequence of changes in location, mission, and name that are germane to its current understanding of itself and its purpose. In 1946 a two-year branch of the University of Illinois was opened at Navy Pier in Chicago to accommodate the influx of students created by the GI bill. Affectionately called Harvard on the Rocks, it was understood as a lower-division outpost of the University of Illinois, from which students would usually continue to *the* university, downstate in Champaign-Urbana. By the late 1950s, however, agitation began for a four-year campus to serve the higher education needs of the youth of Chicago, and in 1965 an entirely new campus was opened at the intersection of the two major expressways serving downtown Chicago. It was named the University of Illinois at Chicago Circle. Significant, at least symbolically, to the campus's current role in the city is the fact that leadership in the drive to create this campus and locate it at the urban center came, from its earliest conception through its completion, from the late mayor Richard J. Daley, father of today's mayor, Richard M. Daley.

But the story does not end there. Dating in parts back to the nineteenth century, about three-quarters of a mile due west of Chicago Circle stood the University of Illinois Health Sciences campus. In 1982, that campus was merged with the Circle campus to create the University of Illinois at Chicago; the two halves would become known as the east and west sides of UIC. UIC was classified by the Carnegie Foundation for the Advancement of Teaching as a Research I university, with growing numbers of doctoral programs on both the east and west sides and substantial external research support.

CONTEXT: THE GREAT CITIES COMMITMENT

By the early nineties, UIC very much needed to clarify its mission beyond the obvious fact that it housed the health sciences colleges of the University of Illinois while the Urbana-Champaign campus had agriculture, veterinary medicine, and law. A strategic planning process inaugurated by UIC Chancellor James J. Stukel, now president of the University of Illinois, led to the inception in December 1993, of UIC's Great Cities Initiative. The initiative was marked by a number of developments, including the establishment of its signature College of Urban Planning and Public Affairs and its multidisciplinary think tank the Great Cities Institute, but its most powerful effect may have been to define a distinct role for UIC.

There was often some confusion as people assumed that the initiative was a specific program or set of programs. The Great Cities Initiative was more of an umbrella, or a banner, highlighting and encouraging the numerous efforts across the campus that constituted UIC's relationship with its own city and others. Under this banner, resources were pooled, disciplinary barriers were breached, and community-building events were institutionalized. For the past several years, for example, UIC has hosted the opening reception for Chicago's Unity Month, a community-wide celebration designed to increase sensitivity to issues of gender, ethnicity, race, sexual orientation, and ability/disability.

In 2001, we changed the name from the Great Cities Initiative to the Great Cities Commitment. After Jim Stukel left the campus in 1995 to become the university president, the initiative had been moved somewhat out of the UIC spotlight—although its programs had continued to flourish and grow. As chancellor (I was appointed in 2000 after serving as interim chancellor for a year), I wanted a word that would signal long-term continuity and a guiding principle for the campus rather than a specific set of programs. We arrived at *commitment*. We define it to indicate an *intentional* engagement, that we are a university eager to turn our expertise and research capability to the challenges confronting great cities. To an extraordinary degree, we partner with communities, civic groups, governmental bodies, foundations, corporations, and others to work together to define the problems and seek solutions.

The Great Cities Commitment brings together the research focus of the present-day campus with its heritage of community betterment, a heritage made visible in its stewardship of the remaining structures of Jane Addams's Hull House settlement. At the same time, it is important that we emphasize that we are not a settlement house. Our engagement is research-based, and our projects often involve students; that is how the engagement is continuous with our missions of research and teaching. The Great Cities Commitment is not separate from research and teaching but a hallmark of our practice. Examples include the outreach from our hospital and clinics, the many community-based programs of our School of Public Health, housing and transportation studies from our School of Architecture and our College of Urban Planning and Public Affairs, the Center for Urban Economic Development, and a multifaceted Neighborhood Initiative with our adjacent communities of Pilsen and Chicago's Near West. Our focus on urban education and the partnerships between our College of Education and other Chicago organizations are part of this larger commitment to the community.

I do not wish to pretend that we experience no tension between world-class research and community engagement. UIC has set high standards for itself: the level and quantity of research we perform put us arguably among the top 50 to 60 universities in the country. The level and quantity of civic engagement we demonstrate across the disciplines, although very high, is also not unique: there are probably 50 or 60 other universities that can claim that, too. It is in the combination of our level and quantity of research with our level and quantity of engagement that we may well be attempting something unprecedented.

Nothing removes the tensions inherent in this kind of endeavor, since they are created not by the conjoining of intense research with intense engagement but by the limitations of seven 24-hour days in a week. Engaged scholarship inevitably takes time away from professors' other academic responsibilities. To work with a system of the magnitude of the Chicago Public Schools (CPS), for example, is to put oneself at the logistical mercy of the district. Eventually, such demand cramps everything else that a professor wants to do, in research and in teaching and mentoring students. Furthermore, engaged scholarship may manifest itself more in action than in publication, making it far less amenable than traditional research to peer review and evaluation, to replication and citation, and to contribution to a systematic body of knowledge.

We compound the challenge of combining high-intensity research and high-intensity engagement with our commitment to continuing to serve the students we have traditionally served. Seventy-five percent of our 26,000 students are from the Chicago area, approximately 43 percent self-identify as ethnic/racial minorities, more than 30 percent are nonnative speakers of English, many are recent immigrants, and many are from families of modest means and are the first in their families to attend a university. Can this combination of research, engagement, and commitment to local students be sustained? We don't know. Right now, we seem to be doing it; the faculty accepts my renewed foregrounding of the Great Cities Commitment, continues to work on a document that would guide the recognition of relevant public service in promotion decisions, and sustains a steady, above-average growth in research output.

When asked recently by the president of the Chicago Urban League whether UIC was going to become an elite university or stick to its urban mission, I found myself answering, "Yes." I do not see it as either necessary or just that we hold separate the notion of a university that conducts extensive, first-quality research and graduate training from the notion of a university that provides access to undergraduates from weaker school systems and with limited mobility. The environment provided undergraduates at a major research university is a special opportunity, and it should not be restricted to students from the best high schools who can afford to leave home for college. But as we raise the expectations of our students, UIC must recognize a compelling obligation to work with the public schools to ensure that their students can meet those expectations. In this way, UIC's rapid rise as a research university over the past decade does not lessen but rather intensifies its duty to its community, its city, and its region. And the duty carries a fortifying load of self-interest as well: the urban teachers and school leaders we train and the urban schools we partner with are the teachers and leaders and schools that educate many of the students we enroll.

A related issue that grows out of the campus's development into what was formerly called a Research I institution is that, at such institutions, Colleges of Education historically have not had the same prestige within the university as the hard sciences or the humanities. Yet we could not describe ourselves as having a commitment to the city without making education a significant area of research and practical engagement. Teacher education must be central to UIC's mission, and the kinds of initiatives in which our Education faculty is engaged cannot go forward without full campus backing. As we ascend the ladder of academic prestige derived from extensive and notable scholarship and sponsored research, we must ensure that our College of Education keeps pace.

One key to our current success in balancing scholarship and community work may be the way in which we define our engagement, both for the purposes of faculty promotion as we are working to count it and in how we explain publicly the connections among our missions. We choose modes of engagement that arise from our research and scholarship or that provide valuable and usually unique opportunities for the education of our students, or both. As I noted above with regard to our Jane Addams's legacy, we are not a social service agency. We do not engage in partnerships for their own sake but rather when doing so allows us thereby to enhance our research or pursue our educational mission. To take an example from outside of Education: when a class of students in Architecture works with public housing residents to design a new public housing complex, the project makes sense because our students learn how to deal with clients, our faculty further their research into affordable housing, and the residents learn how to make their needs and preferences known. The boundaries between research and teaching and engagement are fuzzy in a way we find most desirable.

Urban education is not my personal mission but UIC's mission, and it is not one I would necessarily emphasize at an institution in a different setting. When I took the position of chancellor, I found a campus broadly engaged with the urban challenges surrounding it and a College of Education deeply committed to the city's schools and students and already significantly involved in school reform. It would be misleading, to say the least, to credit the many university/school projects that have been and are being developed at UIC to my leadership. To do so would grossly underemphasize the work of our faculty and deans, and at any rate, many of the initiatives addressed here are the result of long-term efforts that began before I arrived.

Nevertheless, it is true that I do believe strongly in the centrality of education research and reform to the UIC mission, because of both its land-grant status and its urban location, and I think people know that. UIC and I are close to meeting the call of the American Council on Education that "presidents must respond [to the need for more effective teacher training] by putting teacher education front and center on their personal and institutional agendas" (1999, p. 4), albeit that teacher education is not the sole occupant of that position. For me as a leader, it was not a matter of changing things in the College of Education. It was a matter of advancing something that was already strong, through renewed foregrounding of our Great Cities Commitment, emphasis on the compatibility of our aspirations in research and scholarship with genuine civic engagement, and assurance that faculty engaged in the preparation of teachers do not feel like poor cousins within the academy.

CONTEXT: THE CHICAGO PUBLIC SCHOOLS

The problems of urban schooling that Howey and Zimpher identify in the chapter that begins this collection are also the problems of the Chicago Public Schools. The approximately 400,000 P–12 students in these schools reflect the racial and economic makeup that Zimpher and Howey discuss as powerful codeterminants of academic achievement. CPS students are 52 percent African American, 35 percent Latino, 9.6 percent white, and 3.2 percent Asian/Pacific Islander. Fourteen percent of these students have limited English proficiency. An overwhelming majority (85.6%) comes from low-income households. While there is a relative balance between the numbers of African American students and African American teachers in the schools (52% and 42%), students of other ethnicities are far less likely to see their backgrounds reflected in their instructors. Forty-five percent of CPS teachers are white, and only 11 percent are Latino; these numbers almost reverse the representation in the student population (CPS at a Glance, 2001).

UIC's involvement in public school reform has been influenced by the circumstance that in Chicago the challenge of P–12 education has been publicly debated, particularly in the last decade. To say that our favorite preoccupations are the Sox, the Cubs, the Bulls, the Bears, and School Reform may sound flippant or cynical, but it is also a sign of widespread, real concern. The urgency of the need for significant change is palpable. One statistic tells the city what it needs to know: In *School Kids/Street Kids*, UIC sociology professor Nilda Flores-Gonzalez examined the graduating class of 1993 at a high school in Chicago that has an overwhelmingly Latino student population (83%). "For the class of 1993, I calculated that 39% graduated in June 1993, 47% had dropped out, and 14% were still in school. These rates exclude the students who transferred in and out of the school" (2002, p. 3).

The city's schools have had a turbulent recent history. Caught between teacher strikes and enormous deficits, the schools were performing so poorly in the early 1990s that in 1995 Mayor Richard M. Daley created a management team to take over the board of education. Here is one lively description of what the team did: "Daley's team found hoarded supplies in a warehouse. They fired scores of well-paid but indolent bureaucrats from the central office, took over schools at will, balanced the budget in one year, dumped union tradesmen who held cushy jobs, and privatized some services. And then they began flunking kids" (Martinez, 2000).

The reason that they began flunking kids is that the new CPS team, headed by CEO Paul Vallas and Board President Gery Chico, instituted criteria for promotion to the next grade based exclusively on standardized test scores. These criteria seemed modest at first: "In 1997, for example, for a student to enter seventh grade, he or she had to perform at the level of a fifth grader in his third month of school" (Martinez, 2000). The standards were raised each year, so that by 2000, the student would have to score at the level of a beginning 6th grader. The ultimate goal, according to Vallas, was to raise standards to the national norm, which is the level of the approaching grade. Board President Chico, meanwhile, suggested that the strict focus on test scores would eventually broaden to include other criteria for promotion, such as classroom performance.

While test scores did climb steadily upward during the first few years of the new policies, as increasing numbers of students were held back or required to improve their scores through a board-implemented summer Bridge program, voices of dissent were raised. The *Chicago Tribune* reported on a "threatened federal civil rights inquiry into whether the Chicago school system's reliance on nationally standardized tests to determine promotion discriminates against African-American and Latino students" (Martinez, 2000). (Recall that 87% of CPS students are either African American or Latino.)

Still, the improvement in test scores in the late 1990s led some to dub the standards-based reforms the Chicago Miracle. The rate at which scores rose became steadily less miraculous, however, until by 2001, reading scores for 3rd graders and high school students had actually declined from the year before. Mayor Daley publicly expressed his disappointment with those results, and by June of that year, both Board President Chico and CEO Vallas had resigned. A new team began to modify policies and to intensify the curricular emphasis on reading.

In 2002, talk in Chicago about public schooling was as likely to be about failures as about successes. Although Mayor Daley exuberantly announced improved test scores at the end of the 2001–2002 school year, troublesome issues continued to be raised, many of them again related to race. While Latino growth has significantly increased the overall diversity of the city's population, Chicago's neighborhoods remain strikingly segregated. According to one analysis, more than 60 percent of Chicago communities have 75 percent or more of their population from a single race (Mendell, 2001, p. 4). This means that the schools are strikingly segregated as well, and such segregation makes the concentration of school failure in particular neighborhoods hard to ignore.

A 2002 *Chicago Tribune* article reported that "178 of the 179 schools on the failing list have predominantly black or Hispanic enrollments and are concentrated on the West and South sides" (Martinez, 2002). Some blame this on bad teaching or the resistance of the teachers' union or bad parenting, while others see it as yet more evidence of the powerful combined effect of minority status and poverty in the United States. Whatever the reasons, for the schools not much has changed: "A visual survey of Chicago's failing schools evokes déjà vu. Twenty years after a consent decree meant to desegregate schools, 13 years after school reform became a mantra, seven years after Mayor Richard Daley took control of the city's schools, observers say the failing schools remain clustered in the same neighborhoods as before reforms began" (Martinez, 2000).

That Chicago still struggles is neither astonishing nor scandalous, given the magnitude and complexity of the problem. Despite the gloom of the picture painted by Martinez, there are some alignments on the side of progress. The business community is genuinely engaged, although there may be some real differences between what it is eager to support and the best judgment of many educators. The CPS leadership continues to be dedicated and bold while it champions more nuanced analysis and measures. There are pockets of achievement that hold great promise. And the mayor sustains a focus on P–12 education that some think of as almost an obsession.

The mayor also asserts publicly that the best contribution his father made was the founding of UIC—and we find it natural to connect those two dots.

LEADERSHIP IN CONTEXT: THE UNIVERSITY SYSTEM

Before my appointment as chancellor at UIC, I served as vice president for academic affairs for the University of Illinois (a three-campus system: Chicago, Springfield, and Urbana-Champaign). Much of the work of this position faces outward from the university—toward the trustees, the legislature, the state coordinating board, and others—and includes assembly of the annual budget request to the state. It was easy to see the political and economic value that can come from situating three campuses within a system rather than independently, but any academic value was less clear. It seemed to me that eliciting such value would depend upon our figuring out how to do together things that would be harder or not as good or impossible for any campus to do alone.

This conviction led to several efforts on my part. One was to establish a small seed fund for collaborations between counterpart departments or colleges on the campuses. Another was to create the University of Illinois Online as a consortium of the three campuses. And in my final year in the job, one effort was to examine whether our Colleges of Education could have more effect, or could be positioned to gain more effect, in the real world of Illinois P–12 education if they joined forces. Everyone admits that P–12 in Illinois is broken, and one question was whether the University of Illinois as a whole was doing all it could or should to help. But we really had only a very general idea of what, collectively, we were doing. I established a working group, chaired by a highly regarded Education professor from UIC, to examine what was already happening, figure out what we should be doing, and then identify any gap between those two and recommend accordingly.

This working group eventually led to my successor's formation of the University of Illinois Task Force on P–16 Education, which operates at the system level, is publicly endorsed by the president of the university, and is chaired by University of Illinois President Emeritus Stanley O. Ikenberry, a brilliant leader with a deep commitment to teacher education. The task force set itself the job of creating the circumstances under which the University of Illinois can meet the following challenge:

> The University should apply research, teaching, and public service resources to identify and address those areas of lifelong education that can most benefit from university collaboration with others in the public and private sectors. By following this path, the University of Illinois can be a national leader in demonstrating how a public research institution shares responsibility for supporting the greatest possible academic development of students from diverse backgrounds at all levels of the system. (A 2020 Vision, 2000, p. 8)

The task force brought together two colleges and a Department of Education that reside on three very different campuses with the usual centrifugal instincts of system campuses. Together, they identified a series of initiatives:

- Expand partnerships between the university and community colleges to recruit more students into the teaching profession, expand teacher preparation opportunities and increase current teacher quality and retention.
- Develop school leadership and development curricula.
- Extend model teacher mentoring and induction programs statewide to strengthen teacher quality and improve retention.
- Create additional professional development opportunities for teachers, including online options.
- Inform policy making through research and data collection on teacher quality and retention (*To Ensure a High-Quality Education*, 2002).

The task force garnered business and corporate support statewide in ways that can make a palpable difference to what the university can accomplish. And then it reached out to education leaders at all levels across the state for a P–16 Leadership Summit. The work of UIC faculty in a troubled urban school district, along with the local, national, and international recognition these engaged scholars are garnering, make UIC an essential partner in this project. I went to considerable length—including disrupting the schedule of a major renovation—to ensure that the summit, held in December 2002, was convened on the UIC campus. This had nothing to do with my role during the earliest beginnings of the task force. It had everything to do with positioning UIC, internally as well as externally, in its commitment to partnership with urban schools. I wanted us at the literal center of the University of Illinois effort; my opportunity as host to open the meeting was an opportunity to send a signal of support to our faculty and to the Chicago community. It is also an example of how I approach my own leadership role.

LEADERSHIP IN CONTEXT: LARGE, COMPLEX INSTITUTIONS

[Moral leadership] emphasizes bringing diverse people into a common cause by making the school a covenantal community. Covenantal communities have at their center shared ideas, principles, and purposes that provide a powerful source of authority for leadership practice. In covenantal communities the purpose of leadership is to create a shared followership. Leaders in covenantal communities function as head followers.... For many, *follow-ership* is a pejorative term that embodies hierarchy and implies subordination. This is only true if followership is linked interpersonally to following another person. But when followership is linked to ideas it takes on intellectual and spiritual qualities ... [In this model] leadership is based on goals, purposes, values, commitments, and other ideas that provide the basis for followership.   (Sergiovanni, 2000, pp. 167–168)

The president of a university is much like the groundskeeper of a cemetery. There are a lot of people under him, but not many are listening.
(Old joke for an after-dinner speech)

The phrase *covenantal community* may be a bit elevated for what we have achieved at UIC, but Sergiovanni's concept of leadership as based not in personality but in shared ideas, principles, and purposes suits both our efforts under the Great Cities Commitment and my own belief in the necessity of distributed leadership in a large, complex, academic organization.

One role that falls particularly to the president or chancellor is to demonstrate campus support for education initiatives to foundations and other external sources of support, to the school district, to various partners, and to other interested parties. A donor or agency that is considering investing in a new program usually wants assurance that the program is and will continue to be supported by the administration—that the faculty involved will have the time and flexibility they need, that the campus sees the program as integral to its mission, and that we are and will be committed to fulfilling the university's responsibilities regarding matching funds, support services, or whatever else is required. The assurance can come from a number of quarters, but this is a circumstance in which I believe that allowing the college to deliver the chancellor, as it were, is well worth the time expended. It provides strong moral support to the faculty's entrepreneurship and contributes directly to their success in winning external financial support.

In other situations, the interested party may initiate contact with the chancellor, and for the chancellor it is the better part of wisdom to deliver the dean. An alderman of the city of Chicago whose district included a portion of the UIC campus, troubled by the performance of his elementary schools in a recent report of the Chicago Public Schools, suggested that he would like to talk with me. I invited him to campus, but I also told him that he needed to talk with those who really understood the issues, and I brought the dean of the College of Education to the meeting. The discussion that ensued was successful, in large part because I did not lead it: like the hostess of a fine dinner party, I furnished the table and then sat back to let my guests discover their mutual interests. Leadership sometimes means simply bringing the right people together and then getting out of their way.

One place for leadership on campus on the part of the chancellor is in the perennial challenge, especially at research universities, of getting the faculty in arts and sciences to share with the faculty in education the responsibility for teacher preparation. The American Council on Education (1999) urges each of us to create a structure to do just that.

Across American universities, scholars in these two schools have traditionally viewed each other with complementary suspicions: the Education faculty members suspect that faculty members in the liberal arts disciplines do not respect or understand what they do, and faculty in the liberal arts suspect that students in Education are being trained not in the substance of the disciplines they will teach but exclusively in pedagogical technique. To transcend these barriers, we need faculty in the disciplines who both are dedicated to producing more and better teachers for the schools and can gain the respect and approval of their colleagues. To achieve that, we need department heads or chairs who are sympathetic to this effort and are willing to demand that education faculty in the arts and sciences departments be hired specifically because their disciplinary and pedagogical interests will inform each other and, once hired, that they not be marginalized. Teacher educators in the arts and sciences departments must also be serious teacher education researchers and clinical teacher educators need to be assured of appropriate, nontraditional criteria in the review of their work.

A continuum of committed leadership is required. The liberal arts departments are more inclined to be concerned with teacher education if they are led by chairs or heads so inclined. Chairs or heads are able to act on their commitments to education only to the extent that their dean will support them. During a recent budget rescission at UIC that resulted in a cutback of hiring in the College of Liberal Arts and Sciences (LAS), one set of positions that the dean retained was the set of appointments in education (science education, etc.). That choice is one that a chancellor could direct a dean to make, but it is surely preferable when, as in our case, it is a decision the dean makes out of his own values and perception of needs. We are fortunate to have a dean of LAS for whom the LAS-Education partnership makes both educational and political sense, and a dean of Education who thinks the same. We also have a number of such department heads, and therefore a good start on appointing discipline-based teacher education researchers in LAS—especially in Chemistry and Mathematics. We have either committed faculty or a tradition of involvement with teacher training, or both, in Environmental Sciences, in the Department of Spanish, Italian, French, and Portuguese, in English, and in History. We are seeking faculty members in all the relevant departments who think of teacher education as central to their life's work.

Despite these assets, we must still describe our efforts to bring faculty from LAS and Education together as having met with only mixed success. We continue to work to further a productive relationship, but it will take time. UIC is heir to all the typical barriers to multidisciplinary efforts in higher education, as well as to the specific unease between colleges of Education and the liberal arts. We do have in place a Council on Teacher Education, made up of faculty from LAS, Education, and Art and Architecture, but its real progress had been hampered in at least two ways. First, one dimension of the unease between Education and the liberal arts is that research or scholarship in the liberal arts has been and continues to be understood within the disciplines as not having education in the discipline anywhere near the center. Faculty in the liberal arts does research in its disciplines and rarely in the teaching of those disciplines. Furthermore, the work of a council of this sort is usually not about the application of knowledge based on research; it is about program design and curriculum.

A second hindrance to progress on the part of our Council on Teacher Education arises from the circumstance that the Illinois State Board of Education has been converting to standards-based curricular requirements in a manner for which no detail appears too small to account. The result has been a flood of lengthy and elaborate matrices by which programs must be reviewed and a council that has, in consequence, been overwhelmed by such paperwork.

Nevertheless, the council does exist, and that is something more than a start: it is also a statement of institutional intent. It might be useful as well to have someone in the chancellor's or provost's office who would oversee the council and coordinate all the efforts across the campus that connect with the public schools. Such a position would, of course, create new tensions, but unfortunately a compelling reason at present for not establishing one is budgetary constraint. Nor am I persuaded that the position is essential: I continue to believe that while the leadership of the chancellor in this regard may be a necessary condition for change, it is far from sufficient. Without my opposition but also without my advocacy, the department heads and deans could do it; without their leadership, I would not stand a chance.

LEADERSHIP IN CONTEXT: UIC IN CHICAGO

The challenges to be met in the Chicago Public Schools for all children to be well educated call for work far beyond the capacity of any one College of Education. In any school district, there are areas where a college can and cannot be most effective. UIC has developed a general framework for education initiatives that grows largely out of the convictions of the Great Cities Commitment about the need for strategic engagement that can affect an extended area:

- Research should be grounded in local needs; UIC initiatives develop in response to the specific needs of CPS. Of course, since these do mirror the needs of many other urban school districts, UIC initiatives have the long-range potential for much broader impact.

- UIC has limited resources, and CPS is big; we have to insert ourselves at a point that will spread.

- Education initiatives should target a substantial population. Dean Victoria Chou discourages what she calls "boutique" projects, in which a faculty member engages with a single school, in favor of systemwide, or at least regionwide, endeavors (CPS used to be divided into six regions and is now divided into a larger number of "areas" with about 24 schools in each; UIC focuses on high-poverty, predominantly minority westside Chicago public schools). School-based reforms are limited in their potential for success because the school must at the same time continue to conform to the requirements of the very school district against whose policies the reform efforts have been developed. "For changes to be meaningful and lasting," Flores-Gonzalez observes, "they must happen systemwide" (2002, p. 158).

For UIC's College of Education the problem is not to get in the door, not to find acceptance for its programs, but to avoid being scattered among too many projects, to manage wisely the continuous process of triage required by the myriad demands upon its limited human and financial resources. The principles it uses are local need, wide effect, and above all, leverage. The college seeks to focus its efforts at the key points where effects may multiply.

This section presents two programs—the Chicago Principals Assessment Center and a mentoring and induction program for new teachers—that illustrate these three principles. They are also programs in which the university has offered transitional leadership resources until such time as the school system can take on the responsibilities. And they are programs that seek to implement a practice of distributed leadership similar to what we advocate for the university. All three aspects are key: to move beyond individual partnerships with individual schools to effect significant changes that are felt at the district level; to assist the school district by providing leadership as it builds internal capacity; and to develop strategic leadership in the schools as at the university campus. The continuum of leadership that is critical to the university must extend as well through the schools if we are to make changes that matter. Just as we need leadership from the campus as part of a state university system and as part of an urban community, and leadership within and between the Colleges of Education and of Liberal Arts and Sciences, we also need leadership in the school districts, leadership by principals, and leadership by experienced teachers in the schools.

There are a number of other programs and faculty activities that could have been elaborated here as well. UIC's Small Schools Workshop has been successful in assisting the staff of some of the large public schools in the city as they attempt to reformulate those institutions into several smaller, independent entities where students can get more attention from teachers and where particular foci can be developed that address the specific experiences and histories of the students' communities. Professor Timothy Shanahan was recruited in 2001 by new CPS Superintendent Arne Duncan to overhaul the district's reading program. In consequence, there are now reading specialists in all struggling CPS schools to advise teachers and to monitor and contribute to student achievement. UIC's College of Education has also begun an advanced reading development demonstration project with 10 elementary schools, funded by the CPS and the Chicago Community Trust. Both of these examples, like those that will be discussed in detail below, reflect the College of Education's commitment to engage with the public school system in order to create large-scale change from within.

UIC Center for School Leadership Development and the Chicago Principals Assessment Center

There are persuasive research findings to support the claim that good school leadership creates good schools. Such leadership "embraces unconventional and innovative practices, recruits good teachers who share a similar educational vision, and invests resources in whatever can help teachers reach their goals" (Flores-Gonzalez, 2002, p. 157). Look behind a high-performing school that should be failing based on its students' socioeconomic status—the so-called Golden Spike schools (*Chicago Sun-Times*, 2001)—and you will find a talented principal. Through their own work in Chicago schools, UIC Education faculty have seen firsthand the importance of skilled, committed principals. The Center for School Leadership Development is being developed in response to this need.

Work on the leadership center began during the 2001–2002 academic year. It has been established as a distinct entity within the College of Education, with its director reporting directly to the dean but holding as well a joint appointment in the program in Policy Studies. The center will house an Ed.D. program in school administration and ongoing leadership training programs for principals, teachers, and community and family members. The creation of this multifaceted leadership program reflects the engaged, research-driven, large-scale initiatives that are becoming representative of UIC, as well as a belief in the centrality of dedicated leadership.

The origin of the center can be traced to the confluence of several factors. First, members of the Policy Studies faculty were dissatisfied with their existing program for principal certification. In part through their work in local public schools, they had become increasingly aware that the quality of school leadership is critical to school success, particularly in low-income neighborhoods. In the absence of strong school leadership, they observed, it is difficult for the school as an organization to create the kind of environment for teachers and students that is needed for students to learn. They suspected that many of their graduates, despite their completion of all state requirements, could not meet that standard of leadership. Thus while program members were unsure that they were doing as well at principal preparation as they could, it was becoming clear that principal preparation might be the single most important contribution the college could make to the Chicago Public Schools. At the same time, a consensus was building in both the professional literature and the public media that school leadership is central to student success.[1] With the funding community starting to pay attention to such findings, UIC educators realized that it was time to redesign their program. An initial grant from the MacArthur Foundation provided the resources to begin the development of the UIC Center for School Leadership Development.

Even in its early stages, the center was able to make a direct contribution to the quality of public education in Chicago by taking over administration of the Chicago Principals Assessment Center (CPAC). CPAC had been developed by the Financial Resource Advisory Committee of the Civic Committee of Chicago's Commercial Club, a voluntary organization of the city's major corporate and professional leaders. The center was fully functional, but the civic committee believed that its role was to initiate innovation, not to manage ongoing programs. It sought an entity to which it could entrust the operation of the top-notch assessment center it had developed, and it called upon UIC. (Incidentally, this approach created an occasion for practical assistance from the chancellor. Trusting UIC meant, among other things, confidence that the chancellor was genuinely committed to the support of the education of teachers and principals.)

The assessment center provided additional resources and a mandate for research into successful training programs—to investigate the practices of principals whose schools perform well above what socioeconomic status indicators would predict—and to assess and redesign the existing program. UIC took over administration of the assessment center in January of 2002 and accepted the mandate that anyone wishing to apply for a school principal position in CPS would have to go through the CPAC assessment. Our College of Education helped build the credibility of the process among candidates and showed that the assessment provides significant differentiation among candidates' assessed performances.

The next phase of the relationship is now being planned, and it will be a transition in which the assessment center moves away from UIC and toward incorporation into a new approach to principal recruitment and preparation for CPS, an approach that will require a one-year internship followed by a CPAC assessment and that will accommodate such innovative approaches as the foundations-funded New Leaders for New Schools Program. UIC is entirely comfortable with this development as appropriate to our supportive role: we provided leadership to the CPAC while CPS revamped its principal hiring process to include the CPAC in a new place in that process.

Other facets of the Center for School Leadership Development are in the planning stages. To create maximally effective programs in leadership training, professional development, and doctoral studies, the center's staff is currently engaged in research on several fronts. One project involves looking at critiques of existing principal preparation programs and at responses to those critiques by schools of education and school districts. In another, the center's staff is conducting focus groups of principals of high-performing schools in order to incorporate their insights into the program's development.

UIC staff involved in this project have been talking to CPS about its needs and where the center might fit in, especially on Chicago's west side, where UIC is located and which is one of the poorest-performing districts in the system. This region will be a special, although not exclusive, focus of the center, providing access to high-minority, high-poverty communities in order to determine what kinds of schools such communities need and what kinds of principals can make such schools flourish. In part this special focus reflects the university's overall, ongoing commitment to serving the people of the area. At the same time, the college has concluded that training in the context of practice is important and, working closely with these schools, will provide a venue for educating UIC students who want to be researchers, teachers, or principals. Finally, and significantly for the perceived validity of any findings that grow out of the center's programs, the region is large enough, encompassing approximately one hundred schools, to support claims that what is accomplished there is of potentially widespread significance, that it is more than a showcase operation of the sort that might not be reproducible in other contexts.

Teachers as Leaders: The MINT Program

In 1997, UIC initiated MINT (Mentoring and Induction of New Teachers) in collaboration with the CPS Teachers Academy for Professional Development and the Chicago Teachers Union Quest Center and assisted by the Chicago Principals and Administrators Association. New teacher retention has been a severe problem in Chicago, as it is nationally. The MINT program responded to that problem by creating a structure of onsite support for new teachers. All new teachers are connected to an experienced, skilled instructor with whom they meet regularly, whom they observe in the classroom, who observes them, and who helps them.

While new teacher retention is the stated and central goal of MINT, it is significant that the program aims to achieve this goal through the development and support of teacher-leaders in the schools. Prospective mentor teachers are identified by the school principal based on a list of standards provided by MINT and are then asked to complete an application indicating their interest in participating. Those who commit themselves to the program go through an initial training session as well as periodic full-day in-service seminars throughout the year; they receive a stipend for their service. In 2000, MINT was named by the U.S. Department of Education as one of six exemplary programs in the nation in new teacher support.

For its first four years, the program was funded by the MacArthur Foundation and the McDougal Family Foundation. In the fifth year, it was funded almost entirely by the CPS, and now the CPS is responsible for the program, integrating it into a new system of professional development for its teachers. It has renamed the program GOLDEN (Guidance, Orientation, and Leadership Development Empowering New) Teachers. The erstwhile MINT is, in our opinion, an outstanding example of the university providing leadership based on its research but stepping back from long-term management of established functions.

LEADERSHIP: THE PARADE GROUND AND THE PULPIT

William Bennett, as drug czar for the United States, popularized the notion of a *bully pulpit*: a podium from which a leader might cajole, harangue, or otherwise persuade the people to do what is right, or what the leader thinks is right. The idea was that such a pulpit, occupied by a well-chosen speaker, might be more effective than a bundle of laws and regulations and, at any rate, would be needed to create support for those laws and regulations. It is not at all clear whether the strategy was successful for the war on drugs, but I am close to certain that it cannot work for a university.

Certainly there is a place and a role for the president or chancellor as speaker. The chancellor articulates the vision of the campus, for the world around it and for the campus itself. The chancellor receives, and can seek, innumerable occasions for strategic statements of purpose, values, and commitments. Leadership may often consist of telling people what you have learned from them. I tell UIC that it has become a major research university and that it will soon be a great one; that it lives up to an extraordinary commitment to engage in the partnerships we call Great Cities; and that it serves undergraduates who, in part because many of them are underprepared, give us the daily gratification of teaching students who are hungry for what we have to offer and who are demanding and ambitious. I know all that because I have learned it from the faculty, students, and staff.

But in the exercise of such leadership, the chancellor must start a cascade. In teacher education and partnerships with the schools, the cascade I see is of leadership from the chancellor to the provost and deans, from the deans to the department heads and faculty, from the faculty to the Chicago Public Schools and to the principals and mentor teachers in those schools. The sheer numbers of people involved—and needed—require us to listen with care to groups and to the individuals that constitute those groups, to accept difference, and to keep our eyes firmly on our mutual, ultimate goals.

That is why it seems to me that a parade ground might be a more apt metaphor than a pulpit. The leader walks at the front of the parade, carries the banner, and may wear a fine uniform. But she is the leader of the parade, not the parade itself. A large, multifaceted parade along a complicated route requires extensive preparation, and that leadership, the leadership that actually makes it happen, must be distributed.

Distributed leadership requires trust. I trust the judgment of our dean of the College of Education and of the other deans whose colleges participate in the preparation of teachers. I rely on their ability to lead their faculty and on the faculty's professional acumen. In return, I weave their efforts tightly into the mantle that at once positions and distinguishes UIC among its peers.

NOTE

1. Fullan, for example, argues that "the process of tacit knowledge conversion [converting the 'skills and beliefs which are below the level of awareness' into explicit knowledge and thus into action] makes middle managers, like principals, crucial...Middle managers can help mediate external and internal forces toward purposeful knowledge by attacking incoherence resulting from overloaded and fragmented situations." (1999, p. 16).

Sylvia Manning *was named interim chancellor of the University of Illinois at Chicago in 1999 and appointed permanent chancellor in 2000. Before becoming chancellor, she served for five years as vice president for academic affairs for the University of Illinois system. As chancellor she has reorganized the campus's administrative structure so that offices engaging with external stakeholders can serve UIC and its community, city, and state more effectively. A native of Montreal, Canada, and a naturalized citizen, Chancellor Manning was an honors graduate of McGill University before going to Yale for her doctorate degree in English language and literature. A former Woodrow Wilson Fellow and Danforth Teaching Fellow, she held faculty and administrative positions at the University of Southern California and California State University, Hayward. She serves on the executive committee of the board of directors of the Chicagoland Chamber of Commerce and on the boards of Chicago United, the Noble Street Charter School, the Chicago Metro History Education Committee, the Chicago Central Area Committee, and the Chicago Area Committee.*

BIBLIOGRAPHY

American Council on Education. (1999). *To touch the future: Transforming the way teachers are taught—An action agenda for college and university presidents.* Washington, DC: ACE.

CPS at a glance. (2001, May). Chicago: Chicago Public Schools. Retrieved March 31, 2003, from http://www.cps.edu/CPS at a Glance/cps at a glance.html.

Chicago Sun-Times. (2001). [Golden spikes chart]. Retrieved March 31, 2003, from http://www.suntimes.com/includes/golden_spike0621.html.

Clowes, G. (2001, August). Chicago schools' CEO Paul Vallas resigns. *School Reform News.* Retrieved March 31, 2003, from http://www.heartland.org/Article.cfm?artId=9463.

Flores-Gonzalez, N. (2002). *School kids/street kids: Identity development in Latino students.* New York: Teachers College Press.

Fullan, M. (1999). *Change forces: The sequel.* London: Falmer.

Martinez, M. (2000, October 22). When the goals of reform collide raising standards may have a high price. *Chicago Tribune*. Retrieved March 31, 2002, from http://pqasb.pqarchiver.com/chicagotribune/index.html?ts= 1049926613.

Martinez, M., Banchero, S., & Little, D. (2002, July 21). Race, poverty define failing schools. *Chicago Tribune*. Retrieved March 31, 2003, from http://pqasb.pqarchiver.com/chicagotribune/index.html?ts = 1049926613.

Mendell, D. (2001, August 12). New numbers add up to decade of diversity. *Chicago Tribune*, sec.1, pp.1, 14–15.

Sergiovanni, T. J. (2000). *The lifeworld of leadership: Creating culture, community, and personal meaning in our schools*. San Francisco: Jossey-Bass.

To ensure a high-quality education for every Illinois child. (2002). Internal document, University of Illinois Task Force on P–16 Education.

A 2020 vision for a University of Illinois initiative: P–16 and beyond. (2000). Internal document, University of Illinois Task Force on P–16 Education.

CHAPTER

The New Millennium Schools Partnership or 45 Days That Changed My Life

Gregory M. St. L. O'Brien

Each of us has a few experiences that change the course of our professional or personal lives. Being asked to serve as New Orleans interim superintendent of schools in 1998 was one of those life-changing experiences. The following narrative traces a series of innovations and attempted innovations on the part of the University of New Orleans that have occurred since that time, in large measure because of that experience.

THE NEW ORLEANS SCHOOLS REFORM MOVEMENT

The New Orleans community, like many other major urban centers, has a failed school system. In the face of a strong, competing, parochial school system (whose roots go back to the first New Orleans convent school in 1727) and middle-class flight to the suburbs, its 125 schools struggle to serve more than 75,000 students, the majority of whom are students of color and from impoverished homes. It is a struggle the schools are losing. In 2003, 21 New Orleans public schools were performing so poorly the state Legislature threatened to take them over, with another 40 schools in line for the same fate (McGill, 2003).

In 1997, after the termination of another unsuccessful superintendent, the election of another failed school board, and further deterioration of children's scores on standardized, high-stakes tests, groups of business, civic, and faith-based organization leaders joined forces with the mayor to figure out what to do with our failed school system. From that meeting emerged the Greater New Orleans Education Foundation (GNOEF), a broad-based community group that would insist on school reform in New Orleans. A Commitment to Reform agreement was crafted and more or less forced upon the school board members at the time. When the failed superintendent was removed, an acting superintendent was appointed and the GNOEF took an aggressive leadership role in the search for the next superintendent. That is when this story begins.

A CALL FROM NEW ORLEANS

I was in Washington, D.C., with then-New Orleans Mayor Marc Morial (who was chair-elect of the U.S. Conference of Mayors) and several other Great Cities' Universities (GCU) presidents, to present the concept of a partnership between GCU and the U.S. Conference of Mayors. I had been active in the Urban 13 (a predecessor group to the GCU) and am currently president of the Great Cities' Universities.

Prior to our presentation I received a call from Alden McDonald, a business leader involved with GNOEF, informing me that the acting superintendent of New Orleans Public Schools had suddenly resigned. The school board, in an agreement with GNOEF, had decided to appoint me as interim superintendent until the search for a permanent superintendent was completed, approximately two months hence. I protested that I already had a day job that took all my time: chancellor of New Orleans University, Louisiana's second-largest university, serving more than 17,000 students and 1,500 faculty and staff. In addition, I protested that I was white, while more than 90 percent of the Orleans Parish public school system were African American, as were the last three school superintendents, and that my governing board, the Louisiana State University (LSU) System Board of Supervisors, would most likely oppose the move. My excuses fell on deaf ears. The School Board had decided to appoint me because I was the only person on whom they could all agree. The School Board and GNOEF would let me or my governing board decline their call to serve, but nonetheless, they would make the appointment that night, while the mayor and I were in Washington.

In all candor, I was deeply touched and honored by the "draft," and was intrigued by the challenge. I called the president of the LSU System, who told me "No!" My provost, a former dean of our college of education, told me "no," and that I was crazy to think about it. Several other colleagues warned me that I was risking the credibility of the University of New Orleans (UNO) and my own reputation if I tried to do both jobs at once. Nevertheless, I agreed to serve and the LSU Board gave me 45 days to serve as both chancellor and interim superintendent of schools while a permanent superintendent could be identified.

I had led national organizations, been a major university president for more than 10 years, and consulted on large-scale governmental reorganizations, but nothing had prepared me for the organizational complexity and dysfunctionality of a large, urban, public school system. While I was able to accomplish a few things, such as a (more or less) mandatory summer school for children who would face the state's new high-stakes tests the following spring, it became clear to me during my 45-day tenure that the public school bureaucracy, in its current state of disarray, would stifle my, or any other leader's, initiatives.

Over those weeks as interim superintendent, it also became clear to me that it was extremely difficult to link our university resources, or those of the seven other metropolitan New Orleans colleges and universities, to affect school reform amid the current circumstances. The system was dedicated not to change or reform, but to the comfortable, ineffective ways it currently enjoyed. Change would have to come from other directions.

A CALL TO ACTION

One of my important on-campus activities at the UNO during those weeks was giving several awards at our annual Martin Luther King, Jr. celebration. During what were to be pro forma remarks prior to the awards, I became emotional in recounting the challenges inner-city kids face, particularly the fact that they could never realize Dr. King's dream for them if they could not read by the third grade. Clearly, my days as interim superintendent were fundamentally reordering my priorities. I asked each student present to volunteer to help a third grader in New Orleans Public Schools to learn to read. More than 100 students volunteered and a new student organization, Pre-Service Teachers in Action (PSTA), was formed in the College of Education to marshal the new volunteers.

We issued a call to faculty, staff, and anyone else with an interest in this area, to meet and talk about how we could lend our energy and expertise to improving the public schools. More than 100 faculty and staff volunteered to help, principally in the five schools nearest the campus. These schools held potential to be models for others in the Orleans parish because they were in an area of rapid redevelopment. Under my leadership, the University of New Orleans had initiated a successful 70-acre Research and Technology Park some years earlier, adjacent to the campus. The Park now hosts, and is building, facilities for 55 high-technology companies and university research centers that work with an additional 40 firms, including the Naval Information Technology Center, the Advanced Technology Center, and the Center for Energy and Resources Management. To date, the Park has attracted more than 2,000 jobs to an area now being called the Silicon Bayou. Recruiting bright, well-paid, young professionals to the city of New Orleans is difficult, however, due to the quality of the city's public schools. Our efforts in the schools near the University and the Technology Park could help to make the city more attractive to young families.

THE PARTNERSHIP ZONE

With the implementation of the volunteer PSTA effort, the University of New Orleans initiated contact with the principals of the five public schools nearest the campus, and we agreed to a fundamental partnership that would touch on curriculum reform, volunteer tutoring assistance, and physical plant help, among other efforts. I participated in the meetings with the principals because it was important for them to know the level of the commitment of our institution. We met with the schools, not as experts coming to tell them how to change, but as partners eager to work together to address the challenges they identified.

Our 100-plus volunteers immediately started working with these schools in what we called the Partnership Zone. A professor of education serving as assistant to the chancellor, Bob Eason, and a former area school superintendent and attorney, Barbara Ferguson, took the lead in coordinating the Partnership Zone effort.

As our conversations continued, we began to envision a deeply articulated relationship between the elementary and middle schools in the Zone, its high school, and the University of New Orleans. In fact, we began to think of the Partnership Zone as a district within the district. Our goal for this new university/school partnership was to guarantee academic gains for all students by developing a support structure to insulate schools from the political and bureaucratic distractors plaguing large, urban school districts. And that is when the resistance started to form on all sides, both inside and outside of the university.

About this time, UNO appointed a new dean in the College of Education, Jim Meza, who himself had served as interim statewide superintendent of public instruction. Our College of Education serves more than 3,500 students and is the largest graduate college of education in Louisiana. Our faculty and staff work with more than 60 schools both locally and statewide.

When the new dean and I met with several of his faculty leaders to discuss the idea of a university-based school district, several of them argued that the university could not take responsibility for the educational outcomes of children because the students' learning was impacted by so many factors beyond our control—parental unemployment, lack of health care, unsafe living conditions. Realistically, UNO should only be responsible for the preparation of our graduates. The new dean took the lead at that point. He led discussions with his faculty for several weeks then returned to inform me that his faculty had agreed to the concept of a university-based "district within a district" for which they (or some of them, at least) would be responsible. I am grateful to Dean Meza and his faculty for their faith, and their willingness to take on the tremendous challenge of school reform efforts for which there is no guarantee of success.

THE EXPLOSION

And so we began quiet conversations with principals in the Partnership Zone about what autonomy we would need for successful reform and articulation in these five schools as a "district within the district." The local newspaper heard about our project and published an article about it, despite our pleas to the contrary. The timing was unfortunate—we had not yet met with school board members about the idea because it was in the formative stages. Big mistake! School board members immediately declared their opposition to any "university takeover" and questioned our failure to consult with them and our presumption that the school board needed university help. The board maintained it was progressing well in its own efforts to reform the schools, pointing to its recent appointment of *another* new superintendent, a former marine colonel. At the same time, other area universities questioned whether we were trying to preempt them from their involvements with the schools. Our effort had become big news whether we liked it or not. We didn't like it.

Despite the controversy, public support for our effort was overwhelming. The media, business community, Louisiana's Board of Elementary and Secondary Education, the Governor, and even the LSU System encouraged us in our "district within a district" effort. And so we moved forward—talking about the idea, sharing ideas, and learning from others. Dean Jim Meza, Professor Peggy Kirby, a school reform expert on our faculty, and Alden McDonald, a reform-minded business leader (the one who asked me to serve as interim superintendent), joined me in a myriad of meetings with school board members, church leaders, and teachers' union representatives.

NEGOTIATION AND COMPROMISE

We named the project the New Millennium Schools Initiative, and at first proposed a multiple charter school initiative in which UNO would take over the operation of the five Partnership Zone schools. Seeing public support, some school board members tentatively began to discuss the possibility with us. They asked us not to use the word "charter" as they didn't like charter schools, so we agreed to use the term "management contract" for the five schools. With the encouragement of U.S. Senator Mary Landrieu, UNO received a $1 million grant to support a center of excellence in school and teacher education reform that could support some of the transition costs for the New Millennium Schools project.

Some argued we should take on only the five worst performing public schools in the city, not the five closest to us. Here, I resisted. A fundamental part of our initial logic was to improve the poor schools surrounding UNO so the young middle-class people who were moving to our area to take jobs in the UNO Research and Technology Park could buy homes in the city, near the campus, rather than moving to the suburbs. The five Partnership Zone schools were a critical ingredient to that success. In a spirit of compromise that was, in hindsight, naïve, we agreed to take on 10 schools—the five Partnership Zone schools and five schools of the School Board's choice. We finally settled on a total of six schools—the five Partnership Zone Schools and a nearby elementary school that served a public housing community. With the strong support of Mayor-elect Ray Nagin, UNO approached the school board with a proposal to allow these six schools to vote (with 75% faculty support required) to join UNO in the New Millennium Schools Initiative.

UNION RESISTANCE

We then met with the president of the local teachers' union to discuss the New Millennium School Initiative. We promised to maintain all salary and leave provisions of the existing union contract, but would transfer teachers from the adopted schools to become University of New Orleans employees, on leave from the school system. As UNO did not collectively bargain, we indicated we would consult, but not bargain, with the union.

Publicly, the union leadership said they supported the New Millennium School Initiative, but privately, they aggressively resisted the concept. In one negotiation the union clause limiting the length of faculty meetings arose. The union leadership team indicated that if the New Millennium School faculty wanted to have a longer-than-provided-for faculty meeting to discuss how to change the school's educational program, they could write the union executive committee, who then would consider their request on a meeting-by-meeting basis, and in all likelihood inform them, after the union executive committee meeting, that they had permission to meet longer than the specified time. In response, the UNO team indicated that the type of school reform we wanted to initiate required the school's faculty to be unconstrained by such specifics while they, and the university-based school reform team, redesigned the school.

AN APPARENT, BUT UNREAL COMPROMISE

Newspapers and television media, civic groups, business organizations, faith-based institutions, and parental groups all endorsed the proposal for the six schools. The union, however, urged the entire faculty to reject the proposal resoundingly. While the majority of faculty members in most of the six schools voted to join New Millennium Schools, faculty in only one school—the one serving the public housing community—met our preestablished criterion that at least 75 percent of the faculty choose to participate in order for the school to be included. We agreed to work with that one school as a prototype for the New Millennium Schools Initiative and UNO proceeded to negotiate a contract. Union resistance and legal maneuvering continued for several weeks while the public thought the school board actually had agreed to UNO's management takeover and reform proposal. Meanwhile, the school year began. Yet, the school board was still negotiating, unofficially, on behalf of the union about UNO abiding by the board's union contract for the faculty in the school who wanted to become part of the New Millennium Schools Initiative.

Four weeks into the school year I announced it was educationally unsound to change school governance so late in the school year. I cut off negotiation with the school system for that academic year, while expressing our desire to negotiate for the 2003–2004 year well in advance. The blame game ensued, with several union leaders saying we never really wanted to take on any schools. UNO stalwartly continued to work with the superintendent of schools (who was fired), the deputy superintendent who was made interim superintendent (until she left the system), and with selected school board members.

AN ALTERNATIVE APPROACH TO THE NEW MILLENNIUM PARTNERSHIP

Meanwhile, calls for state takeover of the school board, state takeover of failed schools, and for more school choice, dominated the press throughout 2002 and 2003. We at the UNO have tried to craft our approach for the coming year in light of this myriad of proposals and in partnership with several other institutions. The Orleans Parish School Board hired a truly outstanding new superintendent, Anthony Amato, formerly of New York City and Hartford, Connecticut. Our goal is to make sure that our approaches to the New Millennium Schools project and urban school reform in the Partnership Zone support his efforts, so that we can move forward despite the varied forces impinging on the school system.

We currently are seeking two legislative actions to move the New Millennium Schools initiative forward in ways that can, if necessary, work around the local union and the anti-reform members of the school board. (We think it will be necessary.)

THE SOUTHEAST LOUISIANA CHARTERING AUTHORITY

Success in any fundamental reform initiative—especially if that initiative has been controversial—often cannot succeed if one university or one person is seen as the epicenter of the initiative. At the suggestion of Dean Meza and Professor Kirby, we are drafting legislation to permit a group of five local university presidents to form a regional chartering authority. Groups of parents who want to convert their local public school to a charter school could go to this authority for permission to do so or to obtain assistance by one or more of the local universities. The Southeast Louisiana Chartering Authority (SELCA) would cover multiple parishes (counties) in the New Orleans metropolitan area, but would include, and perhaps be most used in, New Orleans itself.

The SELCA would help parental groups avoid current local school board control which can stop chartering initiatives for months, forcing parental interest and leadership to turn its attention to other alternatives. It would be more agile than the annual review process by the statewide Board of Elementary and Secondary Education. It would also provide local universities offering teacher education programs accredited by the National Council for Accreditation of Teacher Education (NCATE) the opportunity to help these parental groups, to the extent their institutional resources or external funds permit. At the same time, any university/school partnership would not be perceived as a university takeover because it would be evaluated by a consortium of institutions. Candidly, by the nature of our state's charter school legislation, SELCA also circumvents the ability of the teachers' union or the local school boards to impede parental desires for school reform. Schools initially eligible to participate would include, we hope, the five schools who initially joined us in the Partnership Zone and other schools who have failed academically and whose parents want to bring about fundamental change for their children.

THE UNO LAB SCHOOL: A NATIONAL MODEL MIDDLE SCHOOL

The University of New Orleans also is proposing to create, on its east campus, a model middle school under university laboratory school legislative precedents. This school would serve the children of Orleans Parish residents who work at the University of New Orleans or the UNO Research and Technology Park, as well as children from the nearby public housing development, most of whom now attend the elementary school that last year overwhelmingly voted to join the New Millennium Schools Initiative. This lab school will give the young professionals who are being attracted to the Park an incentive to become residents of the city of New Orleans by providing a public school of excellence for their children. This will be done in an atmosphere rich in economic, racial, and social diversity, which is the mark of every great city.

The University remains committed to supporting New Orleans Public Schools and especially its superintendent. In the two weeks prior to the writing of this chapter, First Lady Laura Bush visited the campus to endorse the Orleans Parish Teaching Fellows, a program that is attracting certified teachers to teach in our city's most challenged schools. The First Lady spoke to UNO's education majors about the importance of staying in the New Orleans Public School system. The University also has its own recently launched teacher recruitment program, Teach Greater New Orleans (TGNO) recognized this week by the National Council on Teacher Quality for its success in bringing professionals experienced in other fields—especially math and science—to teaching. TGNO provides intensive summer preservice training to individuals who have a B.A. degree, followed by yearlong support from the university, district, and school for the practitioner teacher that includes a peer mentor, university-based advisor, and practitioner cohort classes. The $4,000 tuition is underwritten by federal grants for students who agree to teach for three years in local urban schools. The majority of the TGNO teachers will teach in the New Orleans Public School system, but the program participants also serve surrounding school districts in the metro area. Response to the launch of TGNO in the spring of 2003 was enthusiastic with 200 applicants vying for the 100 slots.

Both programs are in partnership with The New Teacher Project, a national nonprofit specializing in the recruitment of new teachers in hard-to-staff school districts. Meanwhile, UNO's participation in the Great Cities' Universities' Urban Educator Corps initiative is providing urban-focused content to our teachers in training about the opportunities and challenges of teaching in America's inner-city schools.

So, there is progress in some areas such as teacher preparation. UNO continues to find alternative paths to fundamental school reform for city schools, despite continued resistance. Most of all, UNO continues to find ways to marshal the university's power, as one of America's great urban research institutions, to change the educational outcomes for the children of the city and, ultimately, for their children. Those 45 days as interim superintendent of schools changed my life. I am committed to finding creative ways to renew our urban schools and to enhance teacher education, and I know UNO's university's partnership efforts can help effect lasting change in the lives of the children and families of the community. To do so, the university will need to take to heart some of the lessons I learned during my 45 days and beyond.

SIX LESSONS LEARNED—WELL AND NOT SO WELL

While life-changing in its impact on me professionally and personally, my experiences as interim superintendent of schools, of attempting small, systemwide school reform through the mandated summer school for at-risk third and seventh graders, and of leading the effort to create New Millennium Schools, all brought home to me several points about leadership and change in complex systems that I hope may be of interest. Like Steven Covey's "Seven Habits" some of these lessons need to be learned over and over again.

1. Remember, We Are Partners Not Just Leaders

It is difficult when one is trying to bring about visionary change to remember that the leader can have the vision, but if he or she cannot engage others into that shared vision, the proposal, no matter how popular with the general public, is doomed to failure in the small details where resistance can be most effective. While universities do have responsibilities for student outcomes in our schools, we cannot succeed without many partners, including parents and teachers. This is especially true when dramatic change from the status quo is proposed, even in a visibly failed school system.

2. Successful Partners Share Success, Unsuccessful Partners Are Often Alone

It is too easy when an idea runs into difficulty to cite the inadequacy of the proposal and the proposer. It is wiser to make sure there are a number of partners who are invested in the whole strategy from the beginning, so that when rough times are encountered others are ready to take up the effort to overcome resistance or to change tactics in order to succeed. Our faculty are now partnering with many others to ensure that these new New Millennium proposals are successful.

3. Without Vision There Will Be No Dramatic Change— With It There May Be

There is a sense we can change things for the better in New Orleans. Despite decades of failure and a virtual meltdown of our school system's governance and management during the past few years, that cautious optimism stems in part from the fundamental proposals for change put forth by the UNO and other institutions of higher education. We can make a difference as leaders if we envision *and articulate* what can be, even while we work hard to see that it *will* be.

4. Sometimes It Is Necessary to Say No, Rather Than Compromise Essential Principles

This may have been the hardest lesson to learn, and to relearn, and to re-relearn. Cutting off negotiations with the school board for management of the one school was embarrassing to me, to UNO, and to the school board, yet it was the only way I could see for us to obtain the autonomy needed to undertake true reform. Many inside and outside of the university and broader communities thought UNO would never give up. We had to stop that tactic in order to find one that would work for the schools themselves, the university, and the children we wanted to serve.

5. While the Specifics of a Vision May Change, Commitment to That Vision Must Never Change

Most people thought UNO had given up after the first resistance by school board members and officials to the "district within a district" idea in 2001. The New Millennium Schools Initiative, the management contract proposal, the faculty votes, the union resistance, and even the canceling of negotiations to take responsibility for one school in midfall 2002 were initiatives to keep the strategic vision alive and find circumstances that would permit the vision to come to successful fruition in another form.

6. What We Do Is Really Important

This is so obvious I almost didn't want to mention it, but this is perhaps the most important message and lesson of all. As leaders we can and do make a difference. Our roles as college and university presidents give us an unmatchable bully pulpit to encourage our faculty, staff, students, and communities to do what is right and good for our future. We, as college leaders, may have become a bit too careful and consensus oriented during the last decade or two.

My 45 days as interim superintendent of New Orleans Public Schools and my 16 years as a university president remind me constantly that we *can* change the course of people's lives and communities' futures by our actions, or, in contrast, by our inactions.

Gregory M. St. L. O'Brien *served as chancellor of the University of New Orleans from 1987 to 2003. Before his tenure at UNO he served on the faculty of Harvard Medical School, Case Western Reserve University, and the University of Wisconsin–Milwaukee. He also served as provost of the University of Michigan–Flint and the University of South Florida. During his tenure at UNO he oversaw more than 50 new building and renovation projects in collaboration with a variety of community partners, including the development of the New Orleans Research and Technology Park, the rebirth of historic Lee Circle around the university's Ogden Museum of Southern Art, and the university-affiliated National D-Day Museum. O'Brien is currently chair of the Great Cities' Universities; he has also served as the first urban-research university chair of the National Association of State Universities and Land Grant Colleges, chair of the Sun Belt Athletic conference, and chair of the NCAA Presidents' Commission. In 1999 he was named Gambit Weekly's* New Orleanian of the Year.

BIBLIOGRAPHY

McGill, K. (2003, April 2). Troubled New Orleans schools get new boss. Associated Press. Retrieved March 31, 2003, from http://www.newsday.com/news/nationworld/nation/wire/sns-ap-new-orleans-schools,0,499428.story?coll=sns-ap-nation-headlines.

CHAPTER

System-to-System Reform of Teacher Education and School Renewal

Nancy L. Zimpher

The Milwaukee Partnership Academy has allowed many stakeholders and key constituents to come together to help make the changes that will ensure student success in our educational system. The breadth and range of this constantly growing partnership indicates the increasing public awareness that reform in education is a collective responsibility and that this change must be systemic.

INTRODUCTION: THE CHALLENGE

WANTED: Large urban research university, committed to research, teaching and service, located in lovely residential neighborhood, seeks chancellor to help correct university's intermittent mission drift, threats of invisibility within a culturally diverse urban nexus, and to turn urban giant in a direction that will reap long-term gains for students, faculty, staff, and society at large.

This ad is fictional, of course, and is a far cry from the one initially posted in *The Chronicle of Higher Education* when the University of Wisconsin–Milwaukee (UWM) initiated its search for a new chancellor in the fall of 1997. Still, it conveys the early lessons learned in the first six months of my tenure as chancellor. After numerous interviews, conversations, meetings, and focus groups, after pouring over the historical accounts of UWM's evolution, and after learning more about the campus's longtime history of community engagement, I better understood UWM's strengths—and its shortcomings.

This chapter tells, in three parts, the story of UWM's move from a well-kept secret to a widely visible institution: its historical roots and emergence as an engaged urban university; teacher education redesign and urban school renewal as a centerpiece of that engagement; and lessons learned about system-to-system reform of teacher education and school renewal.

AN URBAN UNIVERSITY EMERGES

The University of Wisconsin–Milwaukee began in 1885 when its predecessor institution, the Milwaukee Normal School, was founded. At its roots, UWM is a teachers' school and for more than 60 years this antecedent (renamed Milwaukee State Teachers College in 1927 and finally Wisconsin State College in 1951) produced high-quality teachers for the greater Milwaukee region and state. It became the University of Wisconsin–Milwaukee in 1956, and in 1971 joined what are now 26 two- and four-year institutions that make up the University of Wisconsin System (UW–System). UWM has grown from a small teachers' college of about 5,000 students to a research university of more than 25,000 students that offers 100 bachelor degrees, 32 masters, and 18 doctoral programs. The enrollment target for 2006 is set at 30,000, and UWM currently serves more than 45,000 students in adult and continuing education courses annually. As a member of the two-campus doctoral cluster, which includes Madison and Milwaukee, its charge is reflected in what the UW–System refers to as a select mission:

> To fulfill its mission as a major urban doctoral university and to meet the diverse needs of Wisconsin's largest metropolitan area, the University of Wisconsin–Milwaukee must provide a wide array of degree programs, a balanced program of applied and basic research, and a faculty who are active in public service. (University of Wisconsin System, 1999, online).

To the extent that UWM has been able to move forward academically and in the eyes of local and national audiences, such growth fundamentally rests on its unique mission in the UW constellation as Wisconsin's *urban* university.

A REVITALIZED MISSION AND VISION IN THE "MILWAUKEE IDEA"

Like Saul on the road to Damascus, I had a life-changing experience soon after my arrival at UWM in August of 1998. I was invited, as were all the UW chancellors, to attend a UW–Madison celebration of the sesquicentennial founding of the state. It was a beautiful morning, and listening to then-Governor Tommy Thompson extol the value of the UW–System, I was struck by the story he was telling. It was all about the Wisconsin Idea, "that the boundaries of the university are the boundaries of the state," (Stark, 1995, p. 101) and how this riveting philosophy, articulated 150 years ago, had served as the comprehensive mission of all the campuses lo these many years.

On the 90-mile drive back to Milwaukee from Madison, a trip I later made about twice a week, I began to ponder where Milwaukee (and UWM) fit into this grand Wisconsin Idea tradition. The answer came days later when I attended my first-ever retreat of the UWM's Academic Deans Council, wherein we were doing a collective *think* on the revitalization of UWM's mission and vision. The conversations were provocative and focused on how UWM could stem the two problems identified earlier of "intermittent mission drift" and "threats of invisibility." It is difficult to recall who said it first, but it seemed to resonate with everyone in attendance; the answer could be our own "Milwaukee Idea," to expand our boundaries to the boundaries of the community and beyond.

In many respects, the rest is history. During that two-day discussion, we began to talk about a Milwaukee Idea that would reflect the connections our institution already had in place with our community and that could reshape our ambition to become a premier urban public research university. We set in motion a series of activities that led to our understanding that The Milwaukee Idea is at once an institutional attitude, a set of strategic community-based activities, and also the banner under which we successfully bid for the state, federal, and private resources needed to grow UWM into premier institutional status.

A Time for Boldness (Zimpher, Percy, and Brukardt, 2002) provides a full description of how the university joined with our neighbors and the greater metropolitan Milwaukee community to frame a set of goals and activities that now define our university-wide engagement agenda. The process included bringing together "100 people for 100 days" to produce a framework, or scaffolding, for reinventing Wisconsin's nineteenth-century idea into one that would more closely speak to our evolving twenty-first-century world. Predictably, the 100 people grew to about 250 participants, and the 100 days stretched to three months. Idea development involved plenary sessions, affinity group discussions, planning documents, strategic activities, and ultimately the launch of more than 15 distinct first ideas, representing UWM's commitment to education and the arts, environment and health, and economic development. In short, our planning was directed at using the triadic mission of teaching, research, and outreach, as Clark Kerr implores, "in service to society" (1998, p. 11). We used the occasion of my Inaugural in 1999 to announce the vision of what The Milwaukee Idea could mean for UWM and the community.

A MILWAUKEE IDEA: THE EDUCATION PARTNERSHIP

Enhancing UWM's already strong engagement in K–12 education was an important focus of The Milwaukee Idea and one in which I had a keen interest. I arrived in Milwaukee with considerable background in school/university relations. In Columbus, Ohio, as part of my responsibilities as dean of the College of Education and executive dean of the Professional Colleges, I worked with the Columbus Public Schools, the Columbus Education Association, and the school board. I also served on the executive board of a statewide initiative to improve Ohio's schools, called Ohio's BEST: Building Excellent Schools for Tomorrow. I further served as president of the Holmes Partnership, a national effort to provide support and inspiration to the evolving school/university partnerships of 75 major university initiatives to reform teacher education and stimulate school renewal. I am no stranger to the systemic problems that face urban schools and school/university partnerships focused on P–16 (pre-kindergarten through undergraduate) reform. What remained, then, was how I would eventually apply this background to my new setting and new responsibilities.

Milwaukee required a transition far beyond a decanal role, or even my executive dean role. I had to remain conscious of the fact that as a university chancellor, I needed to attend to the full array of academic demands. Still, I had promised myself that should the chancellorship provide a platform for advocating an all-university approach to teacher education and school renewal, I would seize that opportunity. But first, I needed to understand better the ways in which Milwaukee was a very different educational scene than Columbus. When I arrived, the Governor and the legislature had just mandated the authority of UWM to grant charters to public and private schools. It was not an optional activity. We were told to help Milwaukee create these alternative choice models, and the politics surrounding this edict were causing UWM no small amount of trouble.

In the early months of my tenure, the then-superintendent of the Milwaukee Public Schools (MPS) and the head of the Milwaukee Teachers' Education Association (MTEA) made it obvious that if UWM supported the creation of charter schools, we were no friend of theirs. I met personally with these two leaders over several months, trying to assure them that all my educational history was witness to my personal and professional commitment to urban public education, but they rejected my advances. Since I was deeply engaged in the formatting of the visioning process of The Milwaukee Idea, I had little time to contemplate how we were going to dig out of this political quagmire.

But fortunes change quickly in urban public education. An off-cycle school board election ousted a number of board members previously supported by the teachers' union, an election strategy masterminded by the mayor and the Association of Commerce. The new board was sworn in and promptly dismissed the current superintendent. As a consequence, political alliances shifted and within weeks I was at the table with a friendly collaborator, the new superintendent, Spence Korté. His interest and the shifts in power brought the union back to the table, and the decks were cleared for better collaboration between UWM and MPS than had been possible in the recent past. Further, The Milwaukee Idea was maturing simultaneously. One of the early identified first ideas of that initiative was a more systemic partnership with MPS and the community, initially referred to as the Education Partnership, which ultimately became what is called today the Milwaukee Partnership Academy (MPA).

THE EDUCATION PARTNERSHIP GIVES WAY TO THE MPA

In common with other urban P–16 councils formed throughout the nation to enhance quality teaching and learning, the creation of the Milwaukee Partnership Academy was driven by two ideas that had the force of necessity and inevitability behind them: the need to mobilize resources through collaboration *and* the opportunity to position ourselves for competitive federal dollars. What sets the MPA apart, however, in both these common motives is that: (1) the MPA includes business and industry groups and the clear engagement on campus of the arts and sciences, in addition to the more usual partnerships between schools of education and large urban school districts; and, (2) this *inter-institutional* partnership allows various institutions to address long-standing and deep-seated problems on a sustained basis, made possible by collectively generated federal resources.

A quick overview of the funding history of the MPA will perhaps better demonstrate this point. It all started with a proposal, initiated by UWM, to develop a broad, community-based partnership to achieve the overarching goal of developing a comprehensive teacher education prototype preparing K–8 teachers for high-need schools. This proposal was submitted to the U.S. Department of Education in 1999, for funds from the Title II grant. This prototype would draw from best practices, enable policies across a national network of urban partnerships, and leverage various program components and high-quality teacher education materials back across selected sites in a redesign process. Teacher preparation, as, necessarily, both a partnership and an all-university endeavor, would intersect with school and community renewal. The prototype called for major changes in the university's teacher education program, aligning changes in the arts and sciences, professional preparation, and entry into the profession so that the outcome would be a more coherent, protracted, and potent form of teacher preparation.

In the summer of 1999, as a result of this collaboration, UWM and our partners were awarded an $8.4 million, five-year Title II Partnership Grant for Improving Teacher Quality. The partnership envisioned in our Title II proposal called for a broad array of partners representing key constituencies: the University of Wisconsin-Milwaukee, the Milwaukee Public Schools and its Board of Directors, the Milwaukee Teachers' Education Association, the Milwaukee Area Technical College (MATC), the Private Industry Council (PIC), and the Metropolitan Milwaukee Association of Commerce (MMAC).

The formation of such a partnership then provided an umbrella under which to unite various other major grants and programs: federal funds awarded to both UWM and MPS under GEAR-UP (Gaining Early Awareness and Readiness for Undergraduate Programs); two PT3 (Preparing Teachers for Technology) federal grants; and a teacher recruitment grant. In a six-week period in the summer of 1999, the Department of Education awarded UWM and its partners more than $26 million.

I must admit that a clear portrait of the partnership we had proposed was not immediately evident at its creation. Our original Milwaukee Idea of an education partnership morphed into the Title II partnership. Within that context, I was recruited to sketch out the partnership concept, complete with a proposed board structure and governance procedures. I was also designated as the convener of this new board and, when we received funding, it was my task to see to it that the board became operational. Only on hindsight is it clear to me that throughout the years of my tenure at UWM, I was often called upon to play this convening role—in economic development, diversity training, and in the area of population health, to name but a few. It just happened that this early opportunity to convene key stakeholders was in an area where I held considerable familiarity. But it continues to be my strong belief that achieving teacher quality necessitates an all-university approach to program design and school renewal, so I was more than willing to lead the charge.

Of course, once funded, the promises made in the Title II proposal had to be honored. Only when we finally convened the board for its initial meeting did we begin to imagine the potential for what we had created. As our monthly meetings progressed, we began to see that we needed to focus on commitments related not only to the grant but also to other pressing educational issues. It became increasingly clear that it was no longer adequate to think of this partnership as solely a means of managing the grants. What helped us to identify a new, more active path for the MPA were the hard facts and limited success of Milwaukee's public schools.

COLLECTIVE RESPONSIBILITY FOR MILWAUKEE SCHOOLS

Milwaukee's urban profile is overwhelmingly consonant with the challenges recorded in other "frost belt cities" in the Midwest. Among the students served by MPS, more than 80 percent are students of color, with three quarters on free or reduced lunches. The current graduation rate for Milwaukee is 53 percent and the district has experienced significant declines in grade-level performance as students move to higher-level classes (Milwaukee Public Schools, 2001). Interestingly, and not without significance relative to the figures above, per-pupil support for MPS students is $500 less than the state average, and $1,200 less than neighboring suburban schools (Peterson, 2001). As national studies have confirmed, students with the greatest learning deficiencies are taught in school districts with typically the lowest investment in financial support. According to Kati Haycock, director of The Education Trust, "In too many states, we see yet again that the very students who need the most, get the least. At a time when schools, districts and states are rightly focusing on closing the achievement gap separating low-income and minority students from other students, states can and must do more to close those funding gaps" (2002, para. 2, online).

Generalizing from demographic data on metropolitan Milwaukee, more than half of the city's residents are people of color, with ninety-six percent of all persons of color living within the city limits. Forty-six percent of the city's residents live in poverty, while 4 out of 10 of these residents of color have not completed high school, have no job, or work only part time (Bracey, 2000; Levine & Callaghan, 1998). Parents who struggle to maintain an hourly wage that can support their families are also often challenged in providing adequate home support for schooling activities, as well as sufficient nutrition and overall care to ensure their children a fair start in school. The picture that emerges when the above figures are put together graphically portrays the layered complexity of the problems facing urban education and points to the *multilayered, systemic,* and *university-wide* approach required to address these issues.

When looking closely at students served by MPS and their parents, it is also important to consider the professional teaching staff that serves the district. Seventy percent of the teachers are of Anglo descent, in contrast to the 85 percent of MPS students who are of color (Pruitt, 2003). In the teacher pipeline nationally, barely 12 percent of the prospective teacher candidates are trainees of color, and a disproportionate number of teacher candidates come from small town or rural settings. Rarely do they specify an interest in teaching in an urban district, or even in an experimental instructional environment. As noted in national studies, the highest misplacement of teachers occurs in urban settings—particularly in the subjects of science and mathematics—and the attrition rate both nationally and locally continues to be troubling (National Commission on Teaching and America's Future, 1996). In MPS, about 40 percent of newly hired teachers leave within five years.

These findings help explain why the Milwaukee Partnership Academy began to shift its focus from initial grant management to a sense of *collective responsibility* for the significant learning gaps in the district. More specifically, since a large number of the professionals serving on the educational staff of MPS had received one degree or more, or a certificate for continuing education from UWM or its sister two-year college, the Milwaukee Area Technical College, ours was not just a case of community responsibility. More directly, the situation is clearly a case of institutional obligation to improve the ways in which UWM prepares teachers, provides them to MPS, and supports their continuing professional development and retention.

This reality set the MPA on a path to remedy instructional inequalities, and to unite all partners in an effort to ensure quality teachers for quality learning. After much discussion and planning among the partners, we decided on an overall goal of having every child in MPS at or above grade level in reading, writing and math. With the support of the recently hired superintendent of MPS, this goal likely will be transfigured, yet again, into actions making clear that *increased graduation rates* is the culminating reality statistic. As the partnership grows and conditions change, the goal is adjusted as well.

It is also true that the new ESEA legislation "No Child Left Behind" (NCLB), has put a lot of pressure on the MPA, both to implement its rules and regulations properly and effectively, and also to find ways to view NCLB as an opportunity, not a burden. Our collective approach to teacher education and school renewal was based on our belief about best practices relative to balanced literacy, and evolved before we had a clear picture of what NCLB would entail. While we saw these two initiatives as related in many ways, we did not want our strategies compromised by political or ideological stances taken by NCLB. Rather, we wanted these strategies to reinforce each other. We have been enabled in connecting the MPA initiative to NCLB by Wisconsin's Department of Public Instruction, and are grateful for that close connection to this complex federal legislation.

The Partnership also determined that to accomplish our goal—basic and ambitious at the same time—we needed to define a set of action steps or breakthrough strategies, signaling to the broader community that we knew what our collective goal was, *and* that we knew how to get there. These breakthrough strategies, were based on what we have discovered as successes in other urban districts, were approaches to teaching and learning that have been well documented in the research literature, and have been successfully implemented in some MPS buildings as well. Our goal was nothing less than to take these successes to scale district-wide.

It seems easy now in hindsight to view the emergence of a clear vision and a set of strategies as a direct and consistent evolution of collaborative thought. Au contraire! There were many missteps. Recall that I was tasked by the Title II grant with responsibility for creating a fully functioning partnership board. With my executive assistant handling the logistics, I began by devising guidelines, assigning responsibilities, convening and leading the meetings, and lobbying for a summer, daylong retreat. There were internal and external political sensitivities to attend to as well. In the initial drafting of the Title II proposal, we were committed to the concept of university-wide engagement. This required the full cooperation of at least the School of Education, the College of Letters and Science, and the School of the Arts, their deans, and their faculty. In short, we wrote them all into the grant, but specifically targeted the dean of the School of Education for a key leadership role.

I have often observed that as a chancellor who was also an informed educator, I was either a dean of education's worst nightmare, or a dream come true. To deflect the former image and to build a good working relationship with the dean—and in keeping with my desire to create a more horizontal management structure for the university—I asked the dean of education to carry the additional responsibility of chancellor's deputy for educational partnerships. This approach was also congruent with two other recently appointed chancellor's deputies—one to direct university-wide initiatives under The Milwaukee Idea and the other to lead campus-community urban design initiatives. More specifically, the additional role provided the dean of education with clear responsibility for convening other deans, faculty, and staff to work on the cross-curricular redesign of teacher education and to work directly with instructional leaders in MPS and the MTEA. The duality of these roles, mine as the convening chancellor and the dean as program implementer, allowed us to work well together.

Meanwhile, in terms of external politics, Superintendent Korté was not just sitting on his hands waiting for the partnership to mature. He had his own well-defined leadership team, a national consultant who was advising him on key literacy issues, principal training, and accountability issues, and he had sponsored site visits literally around the country to assess successful instructional strategies in other urban districts that might be adapted in MPS. The work of the various federal grants moved forward as well, such that changes in the preprofessional program at UWM and its teacher education program were evolving, as was the role of 20 teachers-in-residence, who were released for two years from MPS to assist in all aspects of the redesign of the teacher education program and the early induction years in MPS.

How then to align these complex and somewhat disparate political and programmatic interests, while constantly taking the pulse of key constituencies to make sure they were still on board? And how to move tactically from grants monitoring, to major changes in the performance profile of district teachers and students? When in doubt, plan a retreat. After a year of operation the original partners really needed to spend focused time together to rearticulate our collective mission, to expand on the breakthrough strategies, and to build a broader base of ownership for our work. I convened the retreat, a decision that paid off in shared vision, collaborative support, and mutual respect.

As I look back, it is both remarkable and encouraging how this collaboration has grown to include representatives from local private colleges, the Milwaukee Public Museum, the Milwaukee Public Library, parents, principals, faith-based and health and human service organizations. It has won the support of the state's governor, lieutenant governor, superintendent of public instruction, the mayor, and other elected officials. The MPA has not only allowed many stakeholders and key constituents to come together to help make the changes that will ensure student success in our educational system, but also, by institutionalizing this collaborative relationship, has compelled a consistent commitment and accountability from these various partners. The breadth and range of this constantly growing partnership indicates the increasing public awareness that reform in education is a collective responsibility and that this change must be systemic. As such, all participating partners have begun to realize their important role in contributing to school success.

The three primary goals of the MPA also reflect this understanding.

1. Increase student achievement at all education levels
2. Improve the quality of teaching and learning
3. Address systemic issues across educational institutions.

The MPA's actual work may be described as connecting the dots among these ultimately interdependent goals. And what allows the MPA to carry out this work is that as a collaborative it provides a forum for *collective leadership and responsibility*, with an almost parliamentary structure of shared governance, work, accountability, and success. A forum like the MPA is uniquely positioned to coalesce the power of the local leadership, while at the same time dissolving individual vested interests in the service of a larger, broad-based goal. By sharing the vision, responsibility, and authority of educating children, the MPA champions the cause of "Sharing in Student Success" (S^3), the name given to the May 2002 public launch of our agenda.

THE MPA BOARD AND IMPLEMENTATION TEAM

The MPA board is composed of 20 members with voting rights, drawn from the seven executive partners noted previously; issues are typically resolved by consensus. The Board also includes nonvoting members, including a dozen affiliates who are community representatives and who have a vested interest in supporting the work of the MPA. Early on, two significant elected officials joined our conversations monthly—Wisconsin's lieutenant governor and the state superintendent of public instruction.

The MPA Board meets monthly and the executive committee sets the board's agenda. Two-hour monthly meetings focus on the progress of the MPA in achieving its strategic breakthrough strategies. The MPA board is chaired in rotation by the superintendent of MPS, the executive director of MTEA, and the chancellor of UW–Milwaukee. It is staffed by a team of support professionals funded through the Title II grant, and augmented by the efforts of staff members from across the partner organizations.

The board also includes representatives from a structure called the Implementation Team. Critical to the success of the MPA, the Implementation Team in 2001–2002 was composed chiefly of members of the professional instructional staff of MPS as well as representatives from the MTEA, UWM, and MATC. Initially, the team was led by the deputy superintendent of the MPS and staffed by an assistant in the superintendent's office. Today, the Implementation Team is led by an executive director. The Implementation Team meets weekly for approximately one-half day, and logs countless hours in between. The team is organized into work groups, headed by cochairs from the respective partners. I was able to contribute to the team by making strategic UWM appointments of individuals I knew could help move the group forward. It was the Implementation Team and its work groups that developed what we termed *breakthrough strategies*: drawing from visits to other urban districts to learn about best practices; sharing ideas that were working well at other partnership sites and in selected MPS buildings; and scouring the research literature in support of promising programs. In addition, the Implementation Team planned the summer retreat referenced earlier and executed the MPA's action plans. The Implementation Team is undoubtedly the most crucial element of the MPA, as it is comprised of instructional leaders across the partner organizations. Without its efforts, there would be no MPA. Actualizing the goals of the partnership through the creation of the representative Implementation Team and its work groups has made it possible for all the partners to share responsibility for the success of students in MPS and for teacher-candidates in the pipeline.

FIVE BREAKTHROUGH STRATEGIES

As one of its first tasks after the goal-setting activity, the Partnership identified five breakthrough strategies to support and forward the MPS's agenda of quality teaching and learning:

Strategy 1: District-Wide Implementation of the Balanced Literary Framework

In order to meet the ambitious goal of moving every child to grade level or above in reading, writing, and math, we chose to approach this omnibus learning goal through a Balanced Literacy Framework (BLF). Building upon already existing literacy programs in individual schools, this framework serves as a guide for teaching and learning literacy across all subject areas and grade levels in every Milwaukee Public School and provides a balance of skill development and literacy-rich activities. At this time, MPA has fully launched the reading/writing agenda, has laid the groundwork for the launch of the math initiative, and is now beginning to turn its attention to science.

The key element of the BLF is the creation of the position designated as "the literacy coach," a select set of first-rate teacher professionals who operate in each of the district's 165 buildings. The primary tasks of the literacy coach include building-wide assistance in literacy development through the creation of key professional development opportunities, materials preparation and availability, networking, and generally setting the pace for the effective implementation of successful literacy strategies throughout the building.

Strategy 2: Learning Teams

In order to meet the literacy needs of the entire district, the MPA agreed to the creation and sustained maintenance of learning teams in every building. These teams possess the expertise to provide support and training for all staff in all schools. These collaborative teams are composed of individuals from the school community who are selected and prepared to collect and interpret data relevant to the school's education or action plan, provide support to teachers, enable professional development embedded at the school site for all personnel in the school, and help create positive conditions in the school context for teachers as well as pupil learning. Each team is composed of the principal, the literacy coach, additional teacher leaders, parents, and others as chosen by the building staff. The MPA regards the learning teams as key to developing greater instructional capacity at the school level and, thus, to continuing school improvement.

Strategy 3: Professional Development

Our goal in professional development was to have all adults in the schools and across the district participate in continuous learning as members of a community of learners that focuses on results, improved student learning, and utilization of the BLF across all content areas. A natural progression from the first two priorities and necessary for their long-term success, this strategy is focused on providing ongoing, comprehensive professional development for staff at the building level, in order to ensure student success. The professional development opportunities increasingly being provided through literacy specialists, literacy coaches, learning teams, and principals—as well as the more traditional route of district-level support staff— promise to replace the random and often uncoordinated manner in which thousands of dollars in expenditures have been outsourced over the years. They also promise to ensure that more embedded professional development will be orchestrated by the learning teams at each school site in order to meet the unique literacy and leadership needs of their staffs.

Strategy 4: Assessing, Monitoring, and Developing Strategies to Improve Student Achievement

The MPA plan includes the development of a system to monitor and report the progress of students at the individual, classroom, and district levels. The main purpose of developing a plan to collect, assess, monitor, and report student progress was to make results available for use by classroom teachers, schools, and MPS families to advance balanced literacy through a user-friendly reporting format, now referred to as the MPA Report Card. The development of this reporting system was the result of aggressive activity on the part of technology professionals in the school district who carefully studied data monitoring systems elsewhere in the country for adoption in MPS. Sharing data on a regular basis with key constituencies is the cornerstone of the MPA's accountability system. It also supports the district's commitment to take the process of value-added assessment from the existing classroom and school level to the individual pupil level.

Strategy 5: Tutoring and Family Literacy

Tutoring and adult/family education programs acknowledge the critical role played by family and community in improving student achievement and are designed to train and involve families and the larger community in ensuring that all students are at or above grade level. Recognizing the vital importance of this strategy to our overall goals, I designated a vice chancellor from my administrative staff to serve on the Implementation Team. This priority's plan includes curriculum development, volunteer recruitment and training, and parent literacy activities. Three major strategies were employed to put this plan into action: (1) provide a tutor from the community for every student in need of academic support; (2) provide resources for parents/guardians to assist students; and, (3) provide tutors, students, and parents with the technology skills needed to support these efforts.

CHALLENGES AND OPPORTUNITIES

The Milwaukee Partnership Academy is increasingly coming into focus. On May 13, 2002, the MPA was publicly introduced to the community as part of a sweeping "Call to Action," and implementation of its various goals went into effect immediately. The theme for the launch was "Sharing in Student Success" and the presence of various members and leaders of education, business, labor, political, faith-based, civic, and community organizations underscored the significance of this growing partnership. Their support was a visible demonstration of how a broad-based set of key community groups could collectively assume responsibility and hold themselves accountable for achieving quality teaching and learning in our urban school district.

Perhaps the most important sign of the MPA's organic growth is that we learned to think and work as a team. This did not just magically happen. It required my involvement in countless meetings, active participation in decision making, and willingness to provide people and resources as needed. But the results were gratifying. As partners we learned to be attentive to the interdependence of our work, which led us to negotiate constructively between commitment to our vested and mutual interests. We learned to make the time to sit down together frequently, troubleshooting when implementation ran into a snag, bringing along local foundations' interest and commitment, inviting elected officials to the table, working to combine forces with a broad array of community groups with already operational tutoring programs, periodically briefing the local press, and, most importantly, spreading the word and taking the long view.

This chapter has certainly provided me the opportunity to reflect on my involvement in this systemic partnership. While I have worked closely for years within the context of urban school-university partnership, the MPA goes beyond anything I had ever been involved in previously. It is so rare when all the key partners can be garnered simultaneously; and beyond that, that we would be able to craft a common agenda and stick with it. Even more extraordinary is that this partnership successfully navigated changes in leadership in the school board and in the superintendent and UWM chancellor positions.

While there is no question that my convening role as a university chancellor helped move this effort along, my participation had been driven by the desire to position UWM as a critical part of the solution. I have also used my convening role to implore other key leaders to stay involved. Together, I think we all saw the transformation of urban public education as a moral imperative, to provide equality of educational opportunity to the children and youth of our urban core.

In all of this, it was clear how crucial the convening powers of a university president can be, not only to call meetings, but also to make sure other key leaders find time in their busy schedules to attend and contribute to the agenda. I played a significant role, too, in making sure the agenda was worth their time and energy, and, more importantly, that it would yield results. From the university's perspective, the three deans of the arts, education, and letters and science played key roles, as did the chancellor's deputy for The Milwaukee Idea. Their leadership was necessary, but not sufficient. Someone at the head of the organization must be engaged, too, and that someone needed to be the chancellor. This is the same line I gave early on to the superintendent, the head of the union, the CEO of the Chamber, and other partners. But, over time, I did not have to give that lecture any longer. Everyone understood, and everyone was consistently at the table. Nonetheless, we had a long way to go in delivering measurable results, and in the final analysis, early successes were the only way we would ultimately bring the community to the table to do as we originally envisioned, namely to share in student success.

The pitfalls were numerous, even daunting. This was high-maintenance work; I had to repeatedly limit the number and level of battles that I chose to wage personally. As problems were reported to me, I tried to send others to resolve them, using my intervention only as a last resort. I am troubled when people miss meetings—not so much because of out-of-town travel, but because they make other local choices in their daily schedule. I know what it takes to hold a calendar date as sacrosanct and I expect others to do the same. Getting people to stay on message is also difficult; they have their own organizations' visions as a top priority. Getting leaders to nest their agenda within a mutual vision is truly a challenge. There is also the issue of local corporate and philanthropic investment. We had more success from the federal and national foundations than from our own Milwaukee donors. But we continued to overcome the skepticism of the past. What kept me going was the knowledge that our work was critical to the economic viability of the state, and that we could be a national prototype for urban school reform.

TEN PARTNERSHIP DESIGN ELEMENTS

To the extent that these MPA strategies unfold successfully, and ultimately renew teaching and learning—both in the public schools and in how teachers are prepared—several key factors will have made the difference. Many of the same attributes necessary to fostering university/community engagement also fit well in a framework of supporting emerging P–16 partnerships. Some address process; others are more substantive in nature. Together they are posed as a list of partnership design elements that suggest ways in which system-to-system P–16 partnerships can work most effectively.

Design Element #1: Partnership Participation Is Mission-Driven

The Milwaukee Idea and the Milwaukee Partnership Academy are both driven by "audacious goals" as defined in *Built to Last: Successful Habits of Visionary Companies* (1994). What authors James Collins and Jerry Porras concluded in their study of 18 successful companies was that visionary companies were not guided by charismatic men and women as much as by a strong set of ideas; these companies were not so much focusing on reengineering as on vision. Moreover, these companies preserved their core values while simultaneously stimulating forward progress. For UWM, The Milwaukee Idea exemplifies such a vision of the university extending to the boundaries of the community and beyond.

In the same sense, the ambitious teaching and learning agenda of the MPA has to resonate with MPS as the district articulates its vision of pupil performance, and to various local publics as well. Undoubtedly the commitment to every student being at or above grade level in reading, writing, and math, and MPA's ambitious intent to increase graduation rates substantially will translate locally to "No Child Left Behind," the epitome of the audacious goal. This cannot happen, however, unless the superintendent and all the key partners continue to stay focused for the long haul. Teachers and community leaders have to be assured of the sustainability of the goals and strategies that undergird this work. I would be less than forthright if I did not say that coherence and constancy of message across such a diverse and complex cast of partners is challenging and demands more time and energy than I had anticipated.

Design Element #2: Partnerships Reflect Scalability

When I arrived at UWM in 1998 and began to pursue school-university relationships, I discovered UWM already had more than 144 existing and active partnership projects with the MPS. Activities spanned departments and disciplines and included faculty, staff, and students from a host of schools and colleges, as well as numerous partners from the teaching and professional staff of MPS. Faculty and staff from the School of Nursing, for example, were working with community health centers and local school building staffs. What was not in place, however, was a *systemic* effort. Consequently, there did not seem to be much momentum for going to scale and ushering in more systemic change efforts.

Too many school-university partnerships remain boutique in nature, dependent on the enthusiasm and interests of isolated faculty or departments. The MPA is not in the business of curtailing boutique efforts. Rather, it seeks to create momentum for broad change and to mobilize individual collaborations in ways that will have long-term payoff for both the university and the schools.

Design Element #3: Partnerships Depend on University-Wide Capacity

The continuing success of the MPA will partly depend upon how well UWM is able to make teacher education an all-university concern and commitment. Interestingly, the MPA partnership itself has created precisely the impetus and context that the university needed to position teacher preparation as a central and shared responsibility. As chancellor, I personally took specific steps to make teacher education an all-university agenda—appointing a chancellor's deputy for education partnerships and using this as a vehicle to bring together the arts and science interests with those of the School of Education. In addition, the Title II grant allowed UWM to initiate a program for recruiting teachers-in-residence (TIRs) who also serve as clinical faculty and boundary spanners among UWM, MPS, and other partners.

I consistently supported the action of a more robust clinical faculty, across all professional programs. The TIRs are a prototype for this strategy and a building block for eventually creating a compatible faculty-in-residence initiative for professors to serve in related field settings. Additionally, I was instrumental in the early design discussions that resulted in The Milwaukee Idea initiative called Cultures and Communities—redefining our general education curriculum to make it more meaningful to prospective teacher candidates. A great deal of my time also was spent advocating for increased state funding of our Investment Plan through which, in the 2001–2003 biennium, we received significant funding from the governor and the legislature to increase the number of teacher-candidates in our baccalaureate program. What must follow are appropriate institutional supports in budgeting and personnel action that reflect the commitment to teacher education as an all-university responsibility— from the chancellor and the deans, to department chairs, faculty, and staff. It helps as well to increase the understanding by our partners that this signals a fundamental change by UWM, which requires support and encouragement on their part.

Design Element #4: Partnerships Are Constructed Based on Leadership and Inclusiveness

Upon reflection of the leadership role of universities in moving forward with teacher education reform and school renewal, I am convinced of one thing. University presidents, in particular, are vested with a unique kind of convening power that allows them to influence problem solving in positive and productive ways. Since urban environments are often problem rich, there is a lot of room for leadership of this kind in our cities. Others can exercise convening power, but it appears presidents are well-suited to this role because of the general credibility assigned to them, their political neutrality, and the kind of capacity the institutions they lead are able to bring to the table. This is exactly the *modus operandi* at work with the MPA. I served as the primary convener of the MPA, in large part because UWM had the Title II funding resources that others did not. Once at the table, however, the partners themselves were able to seize upon similar funding opportunities.

Coupled with the convening power of a president is the ability to get the right people to the right table at the right time over the right issues. The burning bush for us was, strictly speaking, the crisis in urban public education. Other significant players saw it and agreed to seek solutions— and there was something in the solution that spoke to the individual interests of almost all the players. So, a key condition of successful partnerships is getting people to stay at the table long enough to determine that together they will be eminently more successful than staying in their own institutional boxes.

Design Element #5: Partnership Goals Result in Strategic Action

As with the design of The Milwaukee Idea, rhetoric alone will not carry the day. To move a community toward confidence and, ultimately, support, we had to show Milwaukee that we, as professional educators, knew how to fix the problem of descending test scores and low graduation rates. Since this is not a process where you can count on speed, we had to rely on a limited number of well-articulated strategies that were research-based and, in most instances, successfully modeled in other districts. Further, we claimed—and I think rightly so—that these strategies were breakthroughs or departures from business as usual. Thus, over a protracted period of time we were able to coalesce around five breakthrough strategies. This technique conforms relatively closely to the Goldilocks theory: "not too many, not too few." These are a set of strategies that all can regularly recite and will, if focused on over the long haul, bring fundamental change to the way teachers are prepared. Improved teacher training will have positive consequences on learning, performance, and, ultimately, graduation rates.

Design Element #6: Partnership Credibility Is Driven by Public Accountability

If one end of the continuum of the process of transformational change is vision, then the other end is outcomes; we need to keep our eye on both—preferably at the same time. The MPA has to make sure that its vision of quality teaching and learning, with the initial priority to have every student at or above grade level, translates into actual gains in the growth of literacy rates for students and retention figures for teachers.

Coincident to the evolution of the MPA, the Metropolitan Milwaukee Chamber of Commerce commenced a strategic planning process that resulted in a public presentation of the *Blueprint for Economic Prosperity* (2002) endorsed by the MMAC Board. The Blueprint outlines a set of strategies that the MMAC believed would "empower metro Milwaukee to compete successfully with other regional economies" (MMAC, 2002, para. 1, online). These stategies would help to create more jobs, more capital investment, more business starts, and better quality of life for more citizens. Since, understandably, education was to be one of the anchor planks in the MMAC's platform, the MPA was invited to help shape the goals and benchmarks to be proposed in that area. All but one of the seven items ultimately put forward was framed by the constituent members of the MPA, including increased targets for graduation rates, proficiency test performance, teacher retention, a reduction in necessary remediation for MPS grads who find their way to postsecondary education, and improved college graduation rates. All this went public to about 1,400 participants at the MMAC's 2002 annual meeting. It was with great pride that at that very public meeting, the *only* group recognized as the lead team for any of the five planks put forward was the MPA. For once, education was ahead of the curve!

Design Element #7: System-to-System Partnerships Require a Commitment to Institutional Change at All Levels

Clearly, if change is to be systemic, dynamic, and ongoing, then collaborating and partnering cannot be considered optional. But, collaboration, on campus or with the community, is both critical and difficult. Within institutions, a major challenge to achieving well-rounded quality teaching and learning can be our own institutional separatism. Schools of education often assume responsibility for preparing teachers without adequate interaction or engagement with the disciplines in the arts and sciences. Furthermore, classroom teachers who supervise teacher candidates are often active only at the school site, not in the design and development of the entire teacher education program.

Institutional cultures can also impede collaborations. K–12 school leaders, often controlled by conditions outside the classroom, such as getting students to school on time, feeding them on schedule, and moving them from class to class, can find it difficult to plan and act outside these constraints. Universities face their own limitations, especially with regard to course schedules, load assignments, and managing time for their triadic role of teaching, scholarship, and service. Finding quality time in schools is often a luxury, not a necessity. Challenging the bureaucratic tendencies in the daily lives of our partner institutions is perhaps the hardest work of all. Penetrating distinctly different cultures, regularized hierarchies, patterns of behavior, rules and regulations, indigenous governing boards— all are pitfalls of abandoned partnerships. The cure is obvious but costly. Thousands of hours are logged in creating more and better communication vehicles, and oh, the meetings! My schedule alone included biweekly MPA executive meetings, a monthly board meeting, and numerous calls and meetings in between. While it is perhaps too early to declare victory on this aspect of the MPA, at least we saw the enemy, and knew it was we, ourselves.

Design Element #8: Partnership Strategies Must Be Responsible for the Entire Continuum of Teacher Development

Inherent in the MPA design is the assumption that learning to teach is highly developmental. Therefore, the effects of teacher preparation must be felt at all levels of what is often referred to as "the teacher development continuum:" who we recruit to teaching; what preprofessional and professional experiences temper their process of learning to teach; which novice and veteran professionals are involved and how they are engaged in the critical early years of teaching; and what are the most effective learning and leadership experiences for veteran teachers. Further, the MPA is committed to the challenge of recruiting a high-quality and *diverse* cohort of prospective students into careers in teaching.

As noted earlier, our best opportunity to counter the cultural insularity of the majority of our teacher candidates is in the preprofessional program of general studies. Redesigning our general education curriculum provides a set of foundational courses that broadens the intellectual horizons of prospective teachers and at the same time builds an important intellectual foundation and appreciation for diversity and cultural competence among these candidates.

The professional preparation component that is evolving through the MPA is an increasingly blended curriculum that builds on cultural understanding and balances content and pedagogy. This approach includes the formation of local design teams across the arts and sciences, education, and the district to achieve better integration of disciplinary knowledge with pedagogical knowledge. Relatedly, placement of prospective teachers in urban classrooms throughout the professional program and through internships at key partnership sites solidifies the interdependency of theory and practice. Once hired by the district, the MPA concept of the learning team, established in each building in the district, provides a new teacher with the support of a team of key professionals focused on enabling success in the entry years of teaching.

Design Element #9: Partnerships Are Built on a Shared Conception of Quality Teaching and Learning

We know that quality teaching is vital to learner outcomes. Studies conducted at the University of Tennessee (Sanders & Rivers, 1996), and replicated in large urban school districts, demonstrate that students who have access to high-quality teachers considerably outperform those students who have less competent teachers. When factors such as motivation, work habits, socioeconomic status, and parental influence are controlled, the defining factor for student learning is the quality of the teacher.

What makes a good teacher? Some believe they are born, not made—and if you're a woman, you have a nurturing advantage. Others believe a firm basis in pedagogy is the key. Or, perhaps, the secret is in the science of the discipline: if you know your subject, you'll be able to teach it. Yet another group—mostly veteran teachers—believes that only on-the-job, in-the-classroom training will do. Universities add complication to complexity by denying the relevance of pedagogy in our doctoral programs, choosing instead to focus on issues of research methodology. In short, commonplace assumptions about teaching tend to deny the science of teaching over teaching as an art. This makes the science of teaching everybody's—and, ultimately, nobody's—work.

The question is not whether we need improved instruction in *either* content *or* pedagogy or whether we need more research *or* classroom experience, but rather how we can provide *all* of these for our teachers-to-be. And to provide it all, especially the content-specific pedagogical understandings necessary for successful teaching, our schools and colleges of education cannot go it alone. Our colleges of arts and science, humanities, and professions are essential partners, working collaboratively with their education colleagues to produce high-quality teachers. This collaboration is a centerpiece of the MPA.

Design Element #10: Partnerships Flourish Based on a Consistent and Shared Message

Being *on* message has been key to the evolution of the MPA. Mastering message depends first on a clear goal that can be recited easily: Every child at or above grade level in reading, writing and mathematics. By sticking to the mantra, spokespersons give the clear message that everyone is involved at all times with all children to realize this ambitious goal.

The question is whether the MPA has reached the "tipping point." According to Gladwell, "ideas, behavior, messages, and products often spread like outbreaks of infectious disease." In fairness, I would say MPA has not reached that point, "that one dramatic moment in an epidemic when everything can change all at once...the Tipping Point" (2000, p. 9). It is still seeking that point in time when the message is so compelling that everyone gets it and no one has to be reminded. The MPA is working with its public relations staff across the partners, with the local media, with the corporate, nonprofit, and philanthropic sectors of the community, and within its own organizations to (a) stay focused on the goal, and (b) to sustain the key breakthrough strategies that someday will make the MPA transparent and success a reality in the complex, urban environment.

CONCLUSION

UWM's Milwaukee Idea grew out of a powerful process of rethinking the boundaries so that the different constituencies of the community do not remain isolated, but rather, work as extensions of each other. Inherent to this idea is the equally compelling assumption that a merging of boundaries brings with it a sharing of results and responsibilities. The Milwaukee Partnership Academy builds on this tradition, creating a forum that invites all citizens to work toward an education system without walls and boundaries for all. Are there still many questions that need to be addressed, problems that need to be resolved, snags to be overcome, and lots of work to be done? Yes to all these questions. But the best answer is that which we already have underway—a system-to-system partnership that grows into its goals and evolves with them. Since the MPA is larger than any one entity or person, its very unity equips it well to face the many challenges of teacher education reform and school renewal that lie ahead.

Nancy L. Zimpher *became the president of the University of Cincinnati in 2003, after serving for five years as chancellor of the University of Wisconsin–Milwaukee. Her career also includes the deanship of the College of Education and executive deanship of the Professional Colleges at The Ohio State University in Columbus, Ohio. An author and editor of books on higher education and teacher education, she served as president of the Holmes Partnership from 1996–2001 and as a member of the Executive Board of the National Council for Accreditation of Teacher Education. She was co-chair of the Milwaukee Partnership Academy: an urban P–16 Council for Quality Teaching and Learning. She currently chairs the Commission on International Programs for the National Association of State Universities and Land-Grant Colleges, and has served as a member of the American Council on Education's Leadership and Institutional Effectiveness Commission. Chancellor Zimpher is a recipient of numerous awards, including the Distinguished Research Award from the Association of Teacher Educators, Wisconsin Department of Public Instruction State Superintendent's Friend of Education Award and she is in the Ohio Women's Hall of Fame.*

BIBLIOGRAPHY

Bracey, G. (2000, January). A comparison of the performance of the Milwaukee Public Schools and school systems in selected other cities. *Education Policy Project*, CERAI-00–03.

Collins, J. & Porras, J. (1994). *Built to last: Successful habits of visionary companies.* New York: Harpers Business.

The Education Trust. (2002, August 8). The funding gap: students who need the most get the least. News Release. Retrieved March 31, 2003, from http://www.edtrust.org/main/news/08_08_02_fundgap.asp

Gladwell, M. (2000). *The tipping point.* New York: Little, Brown and Company.

Kerr, C. (1998, January/February). Clark Kerr's perspective on leadership challenges. *Change 30*(1), 11.

Levine, M. & Callaghan, S. (1998, May). *The economic state of Milwaukee: The city and the region* (Policy Research Report Abstract). Milwaukee, WI: University of Wisconsin–Milwaukee Center for Economic Development. Retrieved on March 31, 2003, from http://www.uwm.edu/Dept/CED/ publications/milw98.html.

Metropolitan Milwaukee Association of Commerce. (2002). *MMAC's Blueprint for economic prosperity*. Retrieved February 13, 2004 from http://www. mmac.org.

Milwaukee Public Schools. (2001). *2000–2001 Accountability report for the Milwaukee Public Schools*. Milwaukee, WI: Office of Research and Assessment. Retrieved March 31, 2003, from http://www2.milwaukee.k12/wi/us/acc-trep/.

National Commission on Teaching and America's Future. (1996). *What matters most: Teaching for America's future*. New York: NCTAF.

Peterson, B. (2001, Spring). Public schools: Back to separate and unequal? *Freedom Road 1*(1). Retrieved March 31, 2003, from http://www.freedom-road.org/fr/01/publicschools.html.

Pruitt, C. (2003, January 10). MPS alternative teacher training aims for equity. *Milwaukee Times Weekly*. Retrieved March 31, 2003, from http://www.life-timeofservice.org.

Sanders, W. L. & Rivers, J. C. (1996, November). *Research progress report: Cumulative and residual effects of teachers on future student academic achievement*. Knoxville, TN: University of Tennessee Value-Added Research and Assessment Center.

Stark, J. (1995). The Wisconsin Idea: The university's service to the state. In *State of Wisconsin 1995–1996 Blue Book*. Madison, WI: Department of Administration.

University of Wisconsin System. (1999, revised August) Select mission of the University of Wisconsin–Milwaukee. *Mission of the University of Wisconsin System*. Retrieved March 31, 2003, from http://www.uwm.edu /Dept/Chancellor/uwm_mission.htm.

Zimpher, N. L., Percy, S. L., & Brukardt, M. J. (2002). *A time for boldness: A story of institutional change*. Bolton, MA: Anker Publishing Company, Inc.

CHAPTER 7

You Can't Teach without Teachers: The Wayne State University and Detroit Public Schools Partnership

Irvin D. Reid

I have made mutually beneficial partnerships the model for our engagement. To be sustainable, it is necessary that partnerships truly benefit both parties. The possibilities are endless, but the challenge is specific—Detroit Public Schools needs the resources Wayne State University creates. In turn, Wayne State University needs the resources Detroit Public Schools offers.

This is a story of complicated and mutually beneficial partnerships—leadership partnerships, institutional partnerships, and teacher partnerships. These partnerships involve the work of dozens of individuals and I seek to represent them in the pages that follow. Thus, you will hear the collective voice of Wayne State University (WSU), as well as my voice as Wayne State University's president, as I attempt to convey the importance of a university effort in developing relationships.

I joined Wayne State University in the fall of 1997 as its ninth president. My background as president of Montclair State University in New Jersey and academic specialization in business and marketing convinced me of the necessity of clear communication—to the campus and the community. I immediately identified a set of challenges for the university to address and I articulated a message that continues today: American cities are once again centers of change and engines of personal and social growth.

As an urban university, we draw our strength from our metropolitan experience. This is not simply our mission or our decision, it is our definition and our destiny. Wayne State has four pillars that undergird everything we do—the strength of our urban mission; the importance of our global presence; the implementation of new technology in fulfilling our roles in teaching, research, and public service; and a commitment to diversity. I took this message to many audiences, primarily in the community and including the public schools. From my arrival, it was apparent to me that Wayne State had an obligation to contribute across a broad range of urban challenges, but particularly to P–12 education, to teacher education, and, specifically, to the Detroit Public Schools.

Wayne State has a long history of contributing to the scholarship and innovation in P–12 education. The College of Education is Wayne State's second oldest unit (founded in 1881) and it graduates more than 1,000 students a year. Wayne State's future is tied to enhancing the quality of public education in the city that is both its home and in which it serves as the city's only public university.

As I began my transition period of establishing a leadership team and building momentum for change, it remained clear that Wayne State must play a key role in the enhancement of teacher education in Southeast Michigan but especially in partnership with the Detroit Public Schools (DPS). This commitment led to the Limited License to Instruct (LLI) project that is the heart of this story. The LLI project is not simply a commitment to improving partnering efforts with our schools; it is also a significant leadership step toward helping to meet the growing shortage of highly qualified teachers in Michigan. Even as I write these words the project already involves almost 700 students and teachers in developing the expertise for success in urban schools. The LLI brought great change through a partnership and provides an important career opportunity for hundreds of individuals who aspire to teach.

But I am letting my passion for the story get ahead of setting the stage.

DETROIT: A CITY OF SURPRISES

To begin, Detroit is a place of many surprises. Detroit's scale surprises most. It is the sixth largest metropolitan area in the United States ranging across six counties. Metropolitan Detroit has a population of about 4.5 million. Detroit's long history surprises some; it is much older than most U.S. cities, having celebrated its 300th anniversary in 2001. The city's population change and composition may also be surprising. At the center of the metropolitan area, the city of Detroit has declined in population over 50 years to just under 1 million residents, which still makes Detroit the 10th largest city in the United States.

The Detroit metropolitan area is culturally diverse with a population that is 23 percent African American, 2 percent Asian American, and 3 percent Hispanic; it has the largest Arab American population outside the Middle East, estimated to be more than 300,000. The turbulent history of race relations in Detroit is well-documented elsewhere (Sugrue, 1996) and accounts for the dramatic differences in the ethnic makeup of Detroit and its suburbs (82% of Detroit is African American, compared with the suburbs which are 5.3% African American). As a destination for employment, metropolitan Detroit has been a magnet for international and national immigration for a century—hundreds of thousands of Poles, West Virginians, Bangladeshi, Alabamans, Iraqis, South Carolinians, and others came to Detroit to manufacture stoves, automobiles, electronics, and innumerable other products. Detroit has spent the last third of its history accommodating the tides of immigration, housing movement, and industrial change. And within that sea of change has been the challenge of educating the next generation.

WAYNE STATE UNIVERSITY

Wayne State University has for more than a century played the key role as the higher education opportunity for first-generation students. As a traditional urban university, Wayne State began as a series of independent units. The Detroit College of Medicine, a private institution was founded in 1868; in 1881 the Detroit Board of Education founded the Detroit Normal Training School (later to become the Detroit Teachers College), and the College of Pharmacy and City Law School opened its doors in the 1920s. Along with the development of these colleges, David Mackenzie, a DPS high school principal, in 1904 began to offer informal post-secondary classes at the high school to encourage able but economically disadvantaged high school graduates to go on to college. Mackenzie was able to negotiate successfully the transfer of course credit for these students to institutions such as the University of Michigan. Over the course of the next 20 years this program grew into first, the Detroit Junior College and later, the four-year College of the City of Detroit. In 1933 the Detroit Board of Education combined City College with the three professional colleges and the name Wayne University was adopted, after Wayne County in which we reside and after the Revolutionary War general Anthony Wayne who routed the British from Detroit. Not until 1956 did the State of Michigan create Wayne State University as a constitutionally established and constitutionally autonomous university.

These historical steps are important to the story of teacher education for two critical reasons: first, the roots of teacher education at Wayne State University go deep in our history—more than 120 years. Second, the creation of the Wayne State University entity was part of the Detroit Public Schools. Legally, operationally, and very practically, from 1933 to 1956 it was part of one of the largest public school districts in the United States. That legacy certainly means Wayne State has a joint family history with DPS. Of course, family legacies are complicated and fraught with forces that push one out of the family, as well as pull one in.

Today Wayne State University is a national urban research university with more than 31,000 students, 80 percent of whom come from the tri-county area and 11 percent from outside the United States. We have the largest single campus medical school in the United States, the fourth largest college of education in the United States, research expenditures in excess of $150 million, and libraries that are technological leaders, investing a greater percentage of acquisitions in online resources than any other research library in the country. Wayne State's 13 schools and colleges enroll more than 13,000 graduate and professional students, which distinguishes Wayne as having one of the largest graduate/professional enrollments in the nation; we are ranked seventh in the nation in the number of doctoral degrees awarded to African Americans.

OUR PARTNER, THE DETROIT PUBLIC SCHOOLS

The Detroit Public School District not only shares a common history with Wayne State, it is also a longtime neighbor. For more than 40 years, the headquarters has been next door to the university. The DPS district is large (154,648 students in 2000); sprawling (268 schools and more than 8,000 classrooms); and challenged by aging facilities (average age: 66 years), social context (70% of students qualify for free or reduced-price lunch), and personnel needs (in 2000–2001 more than 1,300 unlicensed teachers were employed and some projections suggest that by 2008 more than half of the teachers in Wayne County, of which Detroit is a part, may retire) (*DPS District Data*, 2001).

Detroit Public Schools has also experienced significant structural change in the past five years. By action of the Michigan State legislature, then-Governor John Engler effectively gained control of the Detroit Public School Board in 1999. By law, a new school board was created, to which the mayor of Detroit appointed six members and the governor appointed one member—the latter of whom holds a veto on the appointment of the chief executive officer. The new board asked Wayne State University President Emeritus David Adamany (WSU president from 1982–97 and, since 2000, president of Temple University) to serve as interim CEO while a national search was conducted. After a difficult and public search—where one candidate was vetoed by the governor's representative—Dr. Kenneth Stephen Burnley, former superintendent of Colorado Springs School District, was selected as CEO in May 2000. Burnley started July 1, 2000 with a four-year contract and the knowledge that in 2004 the voters of Detroit will vote to continue with the new school board structure or return to the previous board model. Effectively, Burnley is on a fast track with a tight timeline to change a large and challenged district.

I hope the complexity of the setting for Wayne State and DPS is apparent in these few paragraphs—Wayne was part of DPS and DPS shaped aspects of Wayne. By action of the State of Michigan, Wayne State was separated from DPS and made constitutionally autonomous, and, also by action of the State of Michigan, DPS's board was replaced. The new board appointed Wayne State's immediate past president as interim CEO; I joined Wayne State shortly before the board change and Burnley joined immediately thereafter. At a minimum, Wayne State University and Detroit Public Schools have intertwined histories, intertwined structures, state interventions, and new leadership. And, of course, during this intertwined history, Wayne State's College of Education has continued to produce tens of thousands of teachers and administrators who serve DPS.

A MIXED PARTNERSHIP RECORD

Even before the administrative changes within the Detroit Public Schools of the past five years, and my tenure here, Wayne State's relationship with DPS has ebbed and flowed. In the early 1990s, like many other urban universities, Wayne State came under increasing pressure from school districts, teachers, parents, and state legislators to use its expertise more directly in public school systems. As that conversation developed in Michigan, Wayne State's then-President Adamany proposed that WSU take a major role in the operation of six feeder schools and one high school in its neighborhood. The resultant proposal—that Wayne State manage the seven schools—generated significant controversy and was opposed by vocal members of the community. While I do not know exactly what the DPS position was on the proposal, it did not appear to be supportive—and the concept of Wayne State managing part of the DPS district faded away.

Shortly thereafter, President Adamany was approached by Governor Engler and the Senate Majority Leader with the suggestion that Wayne State play a role in the yet-to-emerge charter school movement in Michigan. In

1991, the legislature passed, and Governor Engler signed into law, a bill appropriating funds to study and initiate a middle school to be operated by Wayne State. While the history of the University Public School is longer than space permits, from its 1994 opening to the present it has successfully retained middle school students and improved academic achievement, even as it has struggled to improve state-mandated test scores. Its future role in our research university is uncertain.

What does appear certain is that the process of establishing the University Public School damaged—for many reasons—the relationship between DPS and Wayne State. As late as 1997 stories circulated that DPS did not welcome grant proposals that involved cosponsorship with Wayne State. The Comer Schools and Families Project provides a dramatic example. This major proposal for collaborative school-based educational reform, in partnership with the Yale Child Study Center School Development Program and national funders, was developed as the University Public School was being formed. DPS rejected Wayne State as a potential partner and brought in Eastern Michigan University, located in Ypsilanti, 35 miles away. It seems clear that the foray into school operation by Wayne State—perceived by some to be similar to a charter school relationship in a district where charter schools are controversial—appears to have blunted major districtwide partnerships rather than advanced them. Partnerships between Wayne State and DPS that have developed since 1991 were more specifically linked to individual program areas, such as mathematics and science education or special education, than to joint institutional initiatives.

As I review this history, I would say that the decade of the 1990s was a period in which operational level partnerships could be formed, but the interplay of leadership between DPS and WSU did not systematically create a larger partnership framework. The stage was set for change.

A NEW ERA OF PARTNERSHIP

In the spring of 1999 events and efforts initiated an accelerated change in Wayne State's relationship with the Detroit schools. That summer, David Adamany took the newly created position of DPS CEO on an interim basis (1999–2000), while the new school board searched for a permanent CEO. Once again, Wayne State and DPS were closely linked. By that time, I had two years of personal experience in Detroit. I had successfully helped the university begin to establish community partnerships to create a research and technology park and to develop a facility master plan. The campus and community leaders knew that I was committed to partnering as an integral part of the way the university and I interact with the community. By this time I also believed firmly that the long-term success of both the city of Detroit and Wayne State University depended upon the success of the Detroit schools. In fact, ideas for incorporating educational initiatives into our technology park were built into our planning efforts from the beginning.

I knew the person who replaced Adamany in the CEO position would face an extremely challenging task but also inherit major assets—a long-term contract, more than $1.4 billion in approved construction bonding, and support from the governor, mayor, and community leadership. Wayne State could offer another asset to support the CEO—a partnership.

As soon as Ken Burnley was selected as CEO, I wrote him offering support. I suggested that as soon as possible leaders of DPS and WSU should meet to develop relationships that would advance both institutions and support the education of Detroit students. This commitment to developing mutually beneficial partnerships is fundamental to Wayne State's long-term strategy. In fact, I have made the "Engaged University" one of Wayne State's five strategic directions, in addition to improving the learning experience, the quality of campus life, our preeminence in research and scholarship, and continuing educational opportunities.

The model through which our engagement will succeed is mutually beneficial partnerships. To be sustainable it is necessary that partnerships truly benefit both parties. In building a partnership with the Detroit schools, the opportunity for mutual benefit is apparent: our student teachers, their students; our curriculum for teachers, their hiring of our graduates; our curriculum for administrators, their administrators who take our programs; our research on learning, their teachers applying that research. The possibilities are endless, but the challenge is specific: Detroit Public Schools needs the resources Wayne State University creates—teachers, better educated administrators, research findings, and educational opportunities for high school graduates. In turn, Wayne State University needs the resources Detroit Public Schools offers: student teaching opportunities, high school graduates, opportunities for research, and onsite mutual learning projects.

Following his arrival, Ken Burnley responded "yes" to the suggestion of a meeting of our respective cabinets. With amazing speed, given the number and level of individuals involved, the senior leadership of both institutions gathered for an all-day retreat in July 2000. By meeting in the first hectic month after CEO Burnley took over the nation's 12th largest city or county school district, the signal was clear: DPS and Wayne State had entered a new era. This was the first such meeting in the 44 years since Wayne was part of DPS. The meeting's prompt scheduling signaled the value both CEO Burnley and I placed on a new relationship. The symbolism was significant—new leadership for DPS plus new leadership for WSU equaled a new opportunity for partnership. The opportunity was clear when, at that July meeting on the Wayne State University campus, the two teams also agreed to a reciprocal meeting hosted by Detroit Public Schools at a DPS location.

Even as that second summit was being scheduled events began unfolding leading to the most significant partnership between Wayne State and DPS since 1956: the Limited License to Instruct (LLI) project.

LIMITED LICENSE TO INSTRUCT

Like other urban school districts, Detroit faces the perpetual challenge of securing enough qualified and certified teachers. As the chapters in this volume make clear, the job of a P–12 teacher in the urban United States is extraordinarily challenging. Further, teaching as a profession has been under attack either directly or indirectly as criticism of schools has mounted over the past 20 years. Finally, college graduates, particularly women (who make up an increasingly large proportion of the university's graduates) have other career options, many of which are more financially rewarding. Hence, Detroit shares with other school districts, particularly those in urban centers, the challenge of a teacher shortage. In Detroit, that challenge is quantifiable: in June 2001, DPS was short 1,300 certified teachers—or roughly one-eighth of its teaching staff. To compound the pressure of this number, the age distribution of Detroit teachers means many more of them are, or soon will be, eligible for retirement under the Michigan Teacher Retirement plan. A teacher shortage is not a problem that a school district can ignore.

There have been efforts to address teacher shortages in the past. DPS partnered with WSU in the early 1990s, for example, on Alternative Pathways to Teaching (APT). Growing out of a model at the Bank Street College, APT recruited from employees within the Detroit district, focusing on noncertified substitute teachers, technicians, paraprofessionals, and others. While this was a small program—there were only 175 participants over its seven years from 1993–2000—APT was important as a pilot project. It taught us the necessary elements of a teacher preparation program that involved transitioning employees to certified teachers. In a school district the size of Detroit, however, 25 new teachers a year was grossly insufficient. The crisis required a systematic solution.

With our first summit setting a new tone, conversations at DPS in the spring of 2001 turned to a plan to provide certified teachers by upgrading those individuals already working in DPS. Dr. Burnley and Michigan's Assistant Secretary for Education convened senior staff from DPS and the Michigan Department of Education (MDOE) to explore what MDOE could do to support Detroit schools. At that meeting, the announcement that 1,000 noncertified emergency substitutes were teaching in Detroit schools galvanized attention. As a result, the director of professional preparation at MDOE, Carolyn Logan, and DPS Executive Director of Human Resources, Beverly Schneider, quickly met and discussed possible solutions. Logan suggested a model developed in the mid-1980s to prepare individuals coming out of industry or the military as teachers. It gained strong support from the new superintendent of the MDOE, Tom Watkins, who, having worked at Wayne State during the 1990s, brings a thorough understanding of Detroit, Wayne State, and its College of Education to the position.

Watkins arrived May 1, 2001—even as these discussions were beginning—and brought strong leadership to the state's involvement in meeting the teacher shortage. Watkins hit the ground running and published a report "Thirty Ideas in 30 Days" at the completion of his first month, which included everything from asking the media to report on three educational success stories for every negative report to facilitating "recruitment of nontraditional educators to allay the teacher shortage" (Watkins, 2001, online).

Given Wayne State's role in piloting the earlier APT project, both Logan and Schneider felt Wayne State University was the best partner to take the lead in implementing a new program in the State. Within the renewed context of cooperation between DPS and WSU, the Limited License to Instruct (LLI) program was born. Its key element is that the partnership model that Burnley and I championed became the model for the LLI. The program has two codirectors: Inez Dejesus, DPS executive director for human resources, and Sharon Elliott, WSU assistant dean for teacher education. As Wayne State's leader for teacher education, Elliott is a proven, get-it-done person and deeply committed to urban teaching. Further, the codirectors worked with the assertive support of Paula Wood, dean of the College of Education, Lavon Sheffield, chief of staff of DPS, and Keith Johnson, director of operations, Detroit Federation of Teachers. Thus, cooperation existed throughout the two institutions and encompassed the vital partnership of the Detroit Federation of Teachers.

The strength of the partnership is evidenced by member commitment to weekly steering committee meetings that are held to troubleshoot and develop procedures. Leadership support is manifested in how well members of the steering committee work together. As one member recently commented, the committee was able to focus on decision-making rather than bogging down over what it could or could not do.

As LLI got underway, Burnley and I held our second summit in May 2001 at Golightly Technical School, a new facility on Detroit's east side which houses programs directed at workforce preparation. At that summit, our DPS partners provided information on their extensive strategic planning effort which had taken place since the first WSU-DPS meeting, the scope of facilities needs, and the plan for using the $1.4 billion bond already available (as well as the need for another substantial bond). The scale of Detroit's challenges—a multibillion dollar deferred maintenance effort—and the commitment to change demonstrated DPS's determined strategy: change fundamentally and change fast.

The second summit again symbolized a significant commitment of time by senior leadership—a critical component in its success—and reinforced a new era of cooperation. This era of cooperation was marked by the speed with which the LLI project was brought to life—from discussions in April to an agreement among DPS, WSU, and MDOE in June!

As the implementation of the LLI program proceeded throughout the summer, WSU Provost Charles Bantz strongly endorsed Dean Wood's strategy and sought to support the academic needs of such a transformational program. As important as my presidential leadership was to supporting the partnership, successful collaborations must also involve a broad range of participants; the commitment of the provost and dean was essential.

The LLI approach built on lessons learned in adult reentry education: use cohorts, provide intensive short courses, provide anytime learning where possible, offer onsite mentoring support for students, and provide tuition assistance. This model created enormous challenges for both DPS and Wayne State. It meant finding ways to process the more than 1,200 applications that were received for the first LLI class. The applications had to be supported by DPS and reviewed by Wayne State much more rapidly than the usual admittance process. And, at the same time as the applications were being reviewed, the two-year curriculum needed to be designed (based on research, student needs, district needs, and certification requirements). Even as students were being selected and curriculum developed, staffing of courses and subsequent development of web-based modules began. The LLI project demanded both simultaneous and sequential activity by dozens of individuals in two large institutions that were renewed partners. Such commitment would not have been possible without my presidential leadership in helping to establish the partnership, set the priorities, and assure institutional support for LLI. Early and often in my tenure I have asked my academic colleagues to partner with a spirit of openness and compromise, a spirit I have endeavored to model. They have responded with creativity and enthusiasm, as the LLI story illustrates.

It was with great pride, therefore, that the first cohort of LLI students began in the fall of 2001—not in the traditional semester format, but with an extensive orientation, transitional online modules to bring the cohorts up to a baseline, and a series of cohort group meetings. It was a cohort designed to make a dent in Detroit's teacher shortage. Whereas the APT had 175 participants between 1993 and 2000, in one dramatic step the LLI program enrolled its first cohort of 500 teachers-to-be. With a two-year curriculum and financial and academic support in place, the partnership provided the dramatic possibility of rapidly addressing Detroit's teacher shortage.

Now, as we enter only the second year of the LLI, nearly 500 students are continuing in the first cohort. Wayne State has admitted a second cohort of 200 students, and the program is expanding to several other universities in the state for broader dissemination. The Michigan Department of Education and its superintendent, Tom Watkins, have been key partners in facilitating the LLI—both in terms of program design, funding, and by providing the new credential: the limited license to instruct.

CONCLUSION

Like most great dramas, this story continues. The struggle to train effectively sufficient numbers of teachers who will be committed to urban education cannot let up with the initial success of the Limited License to Instruct project. Even though almost 700 prospective teachers are involved, that number still meets less than half the current shortage. Teachers will retire, some teachers will be drawn to less demanding teaching situations, and other teachers will be drawn to other careers—particularly as the economy improves. We cannot step back from our commitment to recruit, educate, and support teachers.

In sharing this story, I hope it is apparent that the participation of dozens of individuals at Detroit Public Schools and Wayne State University was absolutely necessary. The partnership of the Michigan Department of Education and the then-brand new Superintendent, Tom Watkins, was also highly critical. To create the concept of a Limited License to Instruct required the support and creativity of the Michigan Department of Education.

Also in sharing this story, I hope I have signaled the vital role the presidency can play in identifying partnership opportunities, convening leadership around a shared vision, and encouraging partnerships among the university, its College of Education, and the public schools. Our story shows how, with the commitment of leadership and in partnership with colleagues, it is possible to enhance teacher education and meet community needs.

NOTE

My thanks to Paula Wood, Charles Bantz, and the staff of the Center for Urban Studies.

Irvin D. Reid was sworn in as Wayne State University's ninth president in 1997, after serving as president of Montclair State University and in leadership positions at the University of Tennessee at Chattanooga. He also served as associate professor at Howard University and senior specialist for NASA. Active in community service organizations, Dr. Reid is on the boards of the Life Sciences Corridor, the Michigan Economic Development Corporation, the Detroit Economic Growth Corporation, the Detroit Urban League, the Economic Club of Detroit, and the Detroit Regional Chamber of Commerce. In 2000 he was named one of 20 Michiganders of the year by the Detroit News and in 1999 he received the Distinguished Postgraduate Achievement Award in Education and Administration from Howard University. In 1995 President Reid became the first recipient of the Austrian-American Medal, awarded by the Austrian-American Council of North America, for service in promoting global education and international understanding.

BIBLIOGRAPHY

Detroit Public Schools District Data. (2001). Detroit, MI: Office of Student Information, Detroit Public Schools. Retrieved March 31, 2003, from http://www.detroitk12.org/data/index.htm.

Reid, I. (1998, September 18). *Vision for Wayne State* Inaugural Address. Retrieved March 31, 2003, from http://www.president.wayne.edu.

Sugrue, T. J. (1996). *The origins of the urban crisis: Race and inequality in postwar Detroit.* Princeton, NJ: Princeton University Press.

Watkins, T. (2001). *Thirty Ideas in 30 Days.* Lansing, MI: Michigan Department of Education. Retrieved March 31, 2003, from http://www.michigan.gov/documents/053101ideas_8401_7.pdf.

CHAPTER 8

Many Voices, One Future: Creating New Standards— The Gold Line Future at UMKC

Martha W. Gilliland

Leadership at its best is an opportunity to access the collective wisdom of others and move it to action for social progress.

THE QUANTUM JUMP

We stand
At civilization's impasse
Groping for direction
Crossed to the word
Seeking unheard symbols
To consciousness

We stand
In relational constructs
Echoes of blinding pages
School-tool designed
Education—no education
Security seeking—insecurity
Fact—no fact
Calling for additive steps
A pathway to wisdom
While survival begs
A quantum jump
Toward wholeness

No longer
Can singular to multiple
Thinkwise
Or otherwise
Can multiple to singular
Survive us
Only a total commitment
Resonating integrity
In multiple to multiple relationships
Unified fields…within fields…within fields
Through a methodology of pattern
In metamorphical change
Can man-mankind
Continue emergence

(Stulman, 1972, p. 3–6).

When I became chancellor of the University of Missouri-Kansas City (UMKC) in 2000, I was convinced that public research universities had to conduct a serious self-examination of the standards to which they held themselves accountable, that our self-examination had to be inclusive (accessing the wisdom of faculty, staff, students, and constituent), that the pedagogy of self-examination had to be creative dialogue (not solely intellectual debate), and that the results had to be new standards and new ways of measuring ourselves. I wanted to have a dialogue about possibilities, emerging accomplishments that are greater in a quantum way than in the past, and new standards, new measures, to which we are holding ourselves accountable. Since our school colors are blue and gold—and gold has the ring of top-of-the-line—that future has been termed the "Gold Line Future," as opposed to the blue line future of incremental change.

When I arrived in Kansas City, the public K–12 environment was also seeking quantum change. As I will describe in more detail later in this chapter, Kansas City's landmark desegregation case of long-standing had seriously eroded the effectiveness of the local K–12 schools. Our university—the city's public research and professional training university—was mired in traditional bureaucratic standards that inhibited response to a swiftly changing economic marketplace and the corresponding educational demands of our students. As the newcomer in town, expectations of me were high: produce a radically different leadership outcome for higher education, and, hopefully, have some productive impact on our public K–12 counterparts.

The basic mission of a public research university is to educate mainstream America and enhance the economic and social well-being of a region and state. In my role as chancellor, it was clear to me that placing our university as a central resource for both economic development and the personal development of our citizens was a top priority—and an incredibly complex challenge.

My first duty was to listen. I met with leaders around the community, from both the public and private sectors, and listened to their concerns regarding educational opportunity in Kansas City, the purported failure of public school education, and wide-ranging perceptions of their hometown university. These civic leaders were firm in their belief in education as necessary for social progress and for successful living. They were well-grounded in the advantages gained by a metropolitan area that offered access to high-quality educational systems and their naturally aligned by-products—thriving cultural organizations, intellectual capital to fuel new business development, and a skilled workforce that can sustain growth and lead through change. These same voices were quick to caution me, however, that UMKC—my new home and professional focus—was seen in both the civic arena and the public school debate as a modest player at best, and an ineffectual partner at worst.

The challenges were now clearly focused, and they were both exciting and daunting. Trained as an engineer and scientist, I spent the first 15 years of my career in a traditional teaching and research role. In retrospect, it was great preparation for my current position as chancellor. Teaching is, by its nature, a leadership position where conflicts and challenges are handled daily. In addition, as the leader of research projects covering public policy issues, I worked with policymakers and social scientists and discovered the fine art of shaping conversations in order to reframe problems and issues and to define actions, a critical skill for any leader.

My experience as a Kellogg Fellow in the mid-1980s was pivotal in my transition from faculty to administrative leadership. Through the Kellogg program, I was exposed to different cultures, broader conceptual frameworks on the truth, formal leadership theories, and opportunities to hone my personal leadership practices. Following the fellowship, I chose a deliberate focus on leadership for my career, a track that developed first through a position as the director of a research center, then as a dean, vice president, provost and—today—chancellor. My career took me to different universities, ranging from a large land grant university, to a private research university, and now to a public urban university. This diverse exposure to different academic cultures and practices is today a great strength; it feeds my passionate belief that leadership, at its best, is an opportunity to access the collective wisdom of others and move it to action for social progress.

GREAT CITIES HAVE GREAT UNIVERSITIES

By 1999, my dream to serve a public research university was a powerful force in my personal goals. I was looking for a university that wanted who I was—a university interested in my vision. I was clearly focused on the shift of organizational management from predictable, incremental outcomes to the opportunities found in *un*predictability, the more natural experience of our times. I believed that a successful organization—and especially a successful university—must celebrate ideas emerging in many places throughout the organization and bring them forward. I knew my deepest commitment as a leader was to produce a work environment that supported bold actions and quantum change. I knew this would have to happen in an urban university; I hoped for one that was already strong in its foundations, but one that recognized the ultimate advantage of shifting the culture to accommodate a quantum leap forward in its educational and service accomplishments. I came to the conclusion that an urban university was the best place for an educator looking to make a real difference for mainstream America.

Thus, the urban university that I sought would be located in a city that clearly understood the copartnership of university to civic agenda, a community that valued the university's ideas, training, and expertise to fuel its vision. Such a sustained copartnership needed to include an active school of education community serving the public schools at all levels with exemplary leadership.

Reform in public education has been both a battleground and battle cry for our country's major urban areas. Countless millions of dollars have been poured into these reform efforts, and Kansas City's schools are no exception. Although there are success stories in our city as well as other urban areas across the country, too often these attempts at K–12 reform have been dismal, transitory, or nonexistent. While I had not been in a faculty or a leadership role relative to a school of education in my own career, I felt these schools had one of the most critical roles to play in our society. Like many scientists, I also felt that faculty in schools of education had abrogated that responsibility in favor of ivory tower studies about education. Until I moved into administrative roles in the 1980s, I had not considered that I, as a scientist, might be abrogating my responsibilities also. I have come to believe that the faculty in the colleges of arts and sciences also carry responsibility for K–12 educational viability. At UMKC, it is gratifying to witness faculty in several academic units across campus stepping forward to join the active deliberations about how we can foster a renaissance in our schools.

For me, UMKC was the right place, at the right time, in the right city. Kansas City knows it needs a great university to be a successful competitor in a twenty-first-century economy. While the jury is still out, both the city and the University have focused and are making remarkable progress together. We are ready to take a quantum leap forward. I feel blessed to be here.

That said, all is not rosy. Kansas City is geographically and racially divided. As I discovered in my early drives through the community, the metropolitan area is literally defined by State Line Road, a thoroughfare that delineates Kansas and Missouri. Johnson County, one of the wealthiest counties per capita in America, is situated on the Kansas side of State Line. Kansas City itself is divided further by Troost Avenue. Go east of Troost, and you are in the black part of town, often viewed as a landscape of compromised neighborhoods and expectations. This geographical divide defines everything from governmental services to educational and socioeconomic opportunities.

Sitting right in the middle of this estranged urban landscape, two miles from State Line Road and bounded on its east side by Troost Avenue, is UMKC. To my mind, UMKC is in the perfect position for an urban university. Our campus vision of "a community of learners making the world a better place" opens the door for us to take the full complement of urban challenges—race, economic development through research and business growth, opportunities to build a quality public education system, social infrastructure needs focused in neighborhoods, and the cultural amenities to sustain our spirit—and create "new standards in higher education." (Our Emerging Future, 2003, para. 1, online). What better or more fertile ground for the leadership principles I have studied and honed to be put into action?

LEARNING TO LEAD: PRINCIPLES FOR TRANSFORMATION

> Access the creativity, ideas and energy of the people toward actions for social progress.

As I reflect over the past 15 years and the formal leadership roles in my experience, 10 principles emerge as essential to my own effectiveness and my ability to drive change. Each of these principles, in turn, shares relationships with three organizational change goals: (1) access the collective wisdom of others; (2) inspire others to show up and claim the vision; and (3) produce an organization that is joyful, manifests a spirit of community, and performs at a high level of accomplishment.

The following narrative outlines these 10 leadership principles. Later in the chapter, I will illustrate how the foundation formed by such leadership guidelines, and the actions prescribed, are changing the UMKC School of Education and the university's capacity and desire to assist the public schools in Kansas City, Missouri.

1. Lead the conversation about the university's vision all the time

Leading the development and implementation of a vision for our university means talking about it all the time and holding the vice chancellors, deans, and everyone in administrative roles accountable for talking about it all the time. It means making decisions from the perspective of the vision, including all personnel decisions. This, in my experience, is extraordinarily difficult and usually results in changes in leadership positions. However, if the chancellor doesn't hold the vision as context for the accountability of every administrator, including herself, nothing ever happens. The vision sits on a piece of paper, becoming yet one more plan in the archives.

2. Model the university's values

Together with talking about the vision, nothing is more important for a leader than to model the values. UMKC's values were determined in a highly participatory process marked by open and candid communication. They are clear directives for my leadership. As chancellor, I must openly communicate good news, bad news, ambiguities, mistakes, and successes—and all other administrators must follow my lead. The payoff for such candor, however, is rich. There is no access to the collective wisdom without trust, and trust requires openness even when it hurts. That openness must start at the top. I work hard to make all personnel decisions values-based, especially the hiring (and possible firing) of administrators. Many ivory tower decisions are made outside such values guidelines, and many ubiquitous university practices (e.g., the pay scale for part-time faculty) are inconsistent with stated institutional values. At UMKC, our principle calls for acknowledging the historical or habitual practices that are inconsistent with our values and supporting a plan to work toward clarity and consistency.

3. Listen all the time

I was once given the advice, "if you are dying to say something, it probably means you shouldn't say it." It is good advice. I've also learned that talking without listening—by all involved parties—is wasted energy. How do you get others to listen to you? Listen to them. People listen when they feel heard. Moreover, by listening, I normally find out my colleagues already know what I was going to say—and more. Again, there is no access to the collective wisdom without listening.

4. Set the context for every issue

I spend a great deal of time, as does my executive cabinet, reframing issues, constantly setting the context for growth, change, and progress. In every discussion, we consider: What is the real question? Why do we want to talk about or care about this issue? The answer to those questions is the context for an issue. The issue will never be effectively addressed if the context is not agreed upon first.

5. Work to impact the network of conversations

Essentially everything in an organization happens in the context of conversations between people throughout the organization. People always have a choice in a conversation. Should I have this conversation in the context of blame, complaint, resignation, or cynicism (often the dominant context for conversations in universities), or can I convert the framework into a conversation about possibilities and opportunities? Might I even have the discussion in the context of some small action that could offer the possibility of a solution? The culture of the organization exists in the context of our conversations. From the philosopher Heidegger I have learned that "language is the house of being" (1977, p. 193). Our language determines who we are.[1]

6. Make promises and keep them; be accountable

Being accountable for results that have measurable outcomes and measurable timetables engenders trust as well as a high level of performance in an organization. Installing that principle as the norm for a leadership team is extraordinarily difficult. It is risky and requires constant vigilance. Missed deadlines happen, but when they are acknowledged as having been missed, trust emerges. Specific timetables for progress not only focus results, they also are foundations for building momentum and inspiring organizational achievement.

7. Say out loud what is normally left unsaid

Most meetings, in my experience, are inefficient because they leave the real issue unsaid. A context for the meeting exists which is not dealt with

openly—perhaps a turf battle, a performance problem, a personality conflict, a feeling of stress, loss of dignity, failure, or fear. Saying what is so out
loud, without making it wrong, just what is so, takes all the power out of
the perceived issue and allows everyone involved to deal with the real issue
at hand.

8. Do not operate out of fear

In any leadership position, but especially during times of organizational
change, breakdowns occur that are unexpected. Not knowing how they
will be interpreted externally or how to handle them internally evokes fear
in any leader. I have learned that when fear begins to take hold, I can recognize it by the myriad "what-if" questions that occupy my mind—especially in the middle of the night. That is a sure sign to simply stop and go
to the vision and values for guidance. With that step, the stand that must
be taken is clear. Declaring the stand nearly always clears out the morass
of indecision and stalemate and a breakthrough occurs.

9. Know myself and take time for reflection

I have learned the meaning of the phrase "keep good company with
yourself." Whatever is the most effective way for you to stay centered and
balanced, do it every day—exercise, journaling, whatever it is for a leader—
the disciplined practice is essential. My own disciplines, when I adhere to
them, free me from frustration and anxiety, creating room for creativity
and humor.

10. Acknowledge mistakes

In any complex and fast-moving organization, leaders make mistakes.
In fact, most leaders, when they are judged great by historians, indicate
that their mistakes and successes are positively correlated. The leadership
preamble, however, is: the success doesn't occur if the mistake is not acknowledged. For me, the admonition is clear—clean up my mistakes
openly.

THE UNIVERSITY OF MISSOURI-KANSAS CITY

The University of Missouri-Kansas City is well positioned to take on the
processes necessary for quantum change. We know as a university community that this city, our state, and our constituents are seeking the lead-

ership and opportunity historically fueled by institutions of higher education. We understand that the current unsettled economic climate and forces demanding educational change can and will engulf the institution with or without our influence or planning. We are choosing to lead rather than only respond to this environment. In my view, UMKC and the emerging new economy, based in ideas and a highly skilled, problem-solving workforce are perfect partners to meet the remarkable challenges ahead. Rather than settle for the more traditional and incremental improvement methodologies to keep pace with these challenges, we can deliberately link our progress as a university directly to the community and region we serve and respond quickly and effectively to both internal and external needs. This is a view of a quantum future that is invigorating the people of UMKC and our civic partners in Kansas City.

My own leadership to effect this alignment, however, must clearly confront and support both the unique areas of strength and possibility within UMKC and the historical fact of diminished returns and relationships that are indicative of the less successful areas of our campus. The School of Education and its influence with the deeply problematic K–12 issues of Kansas City, together with the corresponding lack of success in building strong bridges from our campus to local ethnic communities, are two particular examples of challenges ahead that we examine in this case study.

To build a context for UMKC and its future, three special features of historical and current position must be noted. First, location and geography. UMKC is located in two of the most vibrant areas of Kansas City and at the divide between the major white/black ethnic groups. The main Volker campus is on the Country Club Plaza, one of the premier tourist and shopping areas of the city. The health sciences campus is located on "Hospital Hill" near Crown Center, the Hallmark Corporation and the city's old downtown. The Plaza area is home to a vibrant cultural/intellectual hub including the Nelson-Atkins Museum of Art, the Stowers Medical Research Institute, the Ewing M. Kauffman Foundation, and Midwest Research Institute. Hospital Hill is home base for Children's Mercy Hospital, Truman Medical Center (our city's respected indigent care facility), Western Missouri Mental Health Center, and the Kansas City Public Health Department. Both the Plaza and Hospital Hill/Crown Center are areas of substantial urban energy and growth. However, both campuses are also bounded on their east sides by Troost Avenue, the divide between black and white Kansas City.

Second, UMKC's history provides an unusual context for monetary support from both the public and private sectors. The university began in 1929 as the University of Kansas City. This private institution, spawned and driven to fruition by the vision of the Kansas City Chamber of Commerce, recognized the city's need for a university to serve its citizens. A board of trustees comprised of leading businessmen was established and a charter was granted. Raising a large endowment during the Great Depression seemed an impossible goal, but the board persisted and on October 2, 1933, the first classes were held at the University of Kansas City.

Although the people and responsibilities have changed, the UKC Board of Trustees still exists today, tying the university to business and industry and providing the network for fundraising, legislative connections, and overall expertise. The board's impact is critical. The work of the trustees, in combination with a special state match program, has led to the establishment of 47 endowed chairs and professorships at UMKC, and the professors who hold these positions play an essential role in the quantum changes now underway.

A major change in the university's history occurred on July 25, 1963, when UKC joined the University of Missouri System with a corresponding name change to the University of Missouri-Kansas City. Today we are the University of Missouri System's designated campus for the visual and performing arts, health sciences, and urban affairs.

Third, UMKC is uniquely dominated by professional schools. The university has 11 academic units, including a health sciences combination that few universities can match: schools of medicine, dentistry, pharmacy, nursing, and biological sciences.

Because some of the schools with separate and rich histories merged with UKC, much like a conglomerate, the university functions somewhat like a loose federation. The Dental School and the Conservatory of Music in particular have their own reputations and identities, both stronger than UMKC's identity nationally. This has positive impacts in some domains and negative impacts in others. I sometimes feel the whole of UMKC is less than the sum of the parts.

In addition to the Dental School and the Conservatory of Music, other areas that attract quality faculty and students include the University's six-year program in the School of Medicine, the brand of the Bloch School of Business and Public Administration (endowed by Henry Bloch, cofounder of H&R Block), an interdisciplinary Ph.D. program, and fast-track and combined degree programs that allow students to obtain a degree at an accelerated pace.

Forty-three percent of UMKC's 13,800 students are graduate and professional students, pursuing postbaccalaureate degrees. This is a high percentage for a public research university and gives us a powerful strength. The professional programs also place us in a wonderful position to provide a highly skilled work force for the city and to partner with the civic development agenda. UMKC is also a significant employer in Kansas City, with 2,300 full-time employees, including 557 tenured and tenure-track faculty, and 1,400 part-time employees.

Intermixed within this strong university profile is our School of Education, a program with almost 50 years of history, 43 tenured or tenure-track faculty, and direct access to the urban and suburban public education microcosm. Though located in a community of national prominence with regard to desegregation and urban education conversations, I have not experienced it as a major force on campus or in K–12 issues. Of the total student body at UMKC, 22 percent report their ethnic origin as persons of color; half of this group is African-American. Yet our School of Education does not enjoy corresponding enrollment levels of African-Americans preparing to serve the educational needs of their community. The School of Education offers all degree levels: bachelor's, master's, specialist, and doctoral. In fiscal year 2002, 328 students obtained degrees from the UMKC School of Education.

Gayle Holliday, president of G & H Consulting LLC and a Kansas City community leader, is a participant in an informal advisory group designed to increase the University's performance and reputation with the African-American community. She has told me that African-American students specifically "do not think of UMKC as a first choice school for them, because the outreach has not been there" (personal communication, October 28, 2002).

During one of the initial meetings with my documenter for this project, it became clear to me that she had her own "already listening" viewpoints about Kansas City, race relations, and UMKC. She is a Ph.D. student in the UMKC School of Education and a 53-year-old African-American female who is native to Kansas City. She tells me that she began her education in the Kansas City public schools, but was transferred to parochial schools by her parents after several racial incidents in largely all-white schools. Pressing her to be frank with me, I asked how people responded to her decision to begin doctoral studies at UMKC. In a matter-of-fact tone of voice, she replied, "Every black person I talked to told me to stay *away* from UMKC. The comments ranged from 'those folks will never let you get that piece of paper' to 'all that place does is suck the life out of black folks and they still don't get those initials behind their name.' " Having been raised east of Troost and to this day hesitant about venturing into Johnson County, she told me her initial supporters and contacts at UMKC were so different than her past experiences with the institution, that she "went with her gut" and began her doctoral studies in our interdisciplinary program. "It was the best decision I've made in a long time," she said. "My classes have been wonderful and my committee has opened my mind to new ways of thinking I never dreamed possible. Without UMKC I doubt if I would have ever recognized my calling to teach."

THE UNSPOKEN CONVERSATION

This is a very polite town; one of the statements often made about the area is how nice the people are and how civil they are in conversations. This civility, however, is not without a cost. As Sherry Lamb Schirmer observes in her book *A City Divided: The Racial Landscape of Kansas City, 1900—1960*, defining an absence of racial conflict as harmony only produces denial about true race relations (2002). This is harsh, but no doubt real to many. It also points to the importance of one of my key leadership principles: Say out loud what is normally left unsaid.

Oddly enough, the differences in perceptions and conversations about race and class roughly parallel the two streets that bisect Kansas City North to South—Troost Avenue and State Line Road. UMKC is in the middle— geographically, politically, and demographically. It is an absolutely amazing spot from which to listen and shape a conversation. The conversations I had with people to the east of the campus were polite most of the time, but a wait-and-see attitude prevailed. I could sense I had to prove myself in some ways. Later, I would learn that these residents viewed UMKC in fairly negative terms. Many of the people I talked to felt as if they were not welcome on the campus. At best, they did not feel UMKC could bring any meaningful change to their lives or to students in their neighborhoods. Some were outright hostile and let me know it.

To the west, the landscape was certainly prettier—and definitely whiter. Many Kansas City civic and business leaders live in Kansas. My conversations with these people were often more comfortable on a personal level, however, I still came away feeling as though UMKC was somehow found wanting. Not until later would I realize that UMKC was not necessarily seen as Kansas City's university by many of these people. Their attitude was not necessarily hostile; they simply didn't view our campus as a catalyst for change, a site for innovation, or a place where leadership for the city could emerge.

UMKC AND THE PUBLIC SCHOOLS

Considering this marked racial division, it is not surprising that Kansas City did not embrace the 1954 *Brown vs. Topeka Board of Education* decision with enthusiasm. Initial efforts had black and white students in the same school, but on different floors. After this was challenged, floors no longer segregated blacks and whites, but integration still did not flourish. White flight began with an exodus to the nearby suburbs in Missouri and Kansas. As more and more whites moved out, followed by middle-class minorities, the Kansas City Missouri Public School District faced new financial and other challenges.

The problems led to what I've heard described as one of the most expensive desegregation experiment in public education. UMKC was active in that experiment. Two professors at the university, Dan Levine and Eugene Eubanks, were profoundly involved in the school desegregation case in the 1970s and early 1980s. With help from their colleagues, these UMKC leaders played a huge role in everything from the development of an educational improvement plan to designing the magnet school plan. Gene Eubanks, who became dean of the UMKC School of Education, led the desegregation monitoring committee for more than 10 years.

As part of the case, a court-ordered increase in property taxes produced a massive improvement program, bringing with it new or renovated facilities, state-of-the-art equipment, smaller class sizes and innovative magnet themes. Parents were allowed to have their children taken to and from school in private taxis.

Nevertheless, many white parents, especially those who had moved across State Line Road to Johnson County, Kansas, would not allow their children to be part of what they deemed a racial experiment. Black parents were also unhappy. Because a 40 percent white racial quota was imposed by the judge, many seats sat empty in the more desirable magnets, while black students were forced to attend crowded neighborhood schools. Today, only a few magnet schools remain. Most schools have reverted back to the neighborhood school concept, since the state of Missouri was removed from the case, which resulted in a massive loss of dollars for the district.

In the years since the desegregation lawsuit was filed in 1977, the Kansas City Missouri School District (KCMO) enrollment has dropped by more than 13,000 students and minority student enrollment increased by 13 percent. More specifically, enrollment dropped from 45,700 in 1977 to 32,000 in 2000, while minority student enrollment increased from 68 percent to 82 percent. In 2000, the average ACT score of those KCMO students who took the exam was 17.8, compared with a Missouri average of 21.5 and a national average of 21.0 (Williams, 2000).

For perspective, today the population for the metropolitan Kansas City area (which includes suburbs in both Missouri and Kansas) is 1.8 million. Of that population, 13.4 percent is African American. In contrast, of the 441,000 people within the limits of Kansas City, Missouri, one-third is

African American; nearly 40 percent are minority (2000 U.S. Census). Enrollment of African Americans at UMKC is 11 percent, mirroring the metropolitan area. Within the School of Education, African- merican enrollment is 20 percent, however only 8 percent of the undergraduates in the School of Education are African American. The contrast between the inner city and the suburbs and between Missouri and Kansas is dramatic.

The profile of minority students and staff in the schools is equally interesting. According to an article in *The Kansas City Star* (White, 1999), about half of the students in the Kansas City, Kansas, school district are minority (with 22% minority staff), while almost 75 percent of the students are minority in the Kansas City, Missouri, district (with 43% minority staff). This compares with an average of only 4 percent to 18 percent minority students in the 22 suburban school districts (and only 1% to 5% minority staff). The contrast between the inner city and the suburbs and between Missouri and Kansas is dramatic.

Charter schools are now also emerging. In 1999, UMKC began to sponsor charter schools; we now sponsor seven. According to a story in *The Kansas City Star* on October 10, 2002, one in five public school students within the Kansas City Missouri Public School District's boundaries was enrolled at a charter school in the fall of 2002. Since charters began enrolling students in 1999, the number of these schools has grown from 15 to 18; enrollment has passed 6,000 (Franey, 2002). While the jury is still out on the overall effectiveness of charter schools, it is clear to me that these schools are extremely popular with African American parents in the district, whose children make up close to 85 percent of the student population.

While much attention is paid to what goes on in the classroom, the Kansas City Missouri Public School District has also been challenged by what goes on downtown with district and school board leaders. The district has had a seemingly never-ending succession of new superintendents; in 30 years, the district has had 20 superintendents.

When I arrived, the superintendent was Dr. Benjamin Demps (as this goes to press in 2004, the current superintendent is Dr. Bernard Taylor). I visited with Dr. Demps and asked him what UMKC could do to help him and the district. He had no immediate response, but clearly appreciated the question. Later, I would realize why the question may have caught Dr. Demps off guard. Despite the intense involvement of some faculty from the School of Education, the university overall was not known for its involvement in the community or the school district. Alan DuBois is the longtime executive director of Genesis School, a haven for *last-chance* students from the public schools. He says professors at the university continually turned away from his partnering requests: "Some of the professors were concerned about their status—and what working with kids who are poor and in trouble would do to that status. The rationale used to be, 'We were never intended to solve urban issues.' But, in my mind, if you are dependent on public dollars, it is not a separate thing. If you are an urban university, you have to address urban problems" (personal communication, September 16, 2002).

My lack of previous experience with a School of Education provided me no safe haven when it came to accepting responsibility for our university's less-than-stellar record in producing results for the children of our urban community. How to turn this around was clearly a new challenge for me—and one for which there appeared to be no simple solutions.

THE UMKC SCHOOL OF EDUCATION

I began looking for the solutions by putting my third leadership principle into action. I listened all the time. What I discovered was that virtually no one was neutral when it came to the UMKC School of Education. The school suffered from low esteem within the community as a whole, and especially within the minority community. Within the university community, the school was perceived to be at war with itself. Faculty and staff blamed central administration for imposing deans with little or no consultation—the prior dean had suffered a short and unpleasant tenure marred by allegations of racism. Restructuring of the school's academic programs had not gone well; nationally recruited chairs withdrew their applications in the face of the conflicts they encountered. School of Education faculty resented allegations of low morale and insisted they were involved in multiple, urban-centered reform and educational initiatives. Finally, the current dean felt she had not been given the institutional support needed to bring order to the chaos. I could go on, but the point is, it seemed obvious that solutions to the problems of the School of Education were not likely to come from within the school without significant changes being made.

The interim provost and I spent time with faculty, staff, and administrators seeking to redirect the energies of the school toward the urgent business of educational reform in Kansas City. We felt that our efforts largely were being ignored by the School of Education and our efforts to find a middle ground between the faculty and the dean were not effective. I would have considered phasing out the school if not for my strong and unrelenting belief that an urban university in the twenty-first century cannot aspire to greatness without a great School of Education engaged in the reform of education in the region.

The incumbent dean, brilliant and energetic, but lacking prior administrative experience, reached the point where she felt she could no longer be effective. I did not ask for her resignation, but neither was I completely surprised when it was offered in the Spring of 2001. Her frustration was obvious to all.

My frustration was eased in early summer 2001, when new leadership emerged for the School of Education. Dr. John Cleek was one of those key leaders who showed up for the vision; in a clear demonstration of the leadership principles, he wanted to help lead the conversation about the vision and model the values. He had demonstrated this shortly after my arrival at UMKC, when he stopped by to see me and said: "I like what you are saying and doing; I think I see what you want to do. Your vision is one that higher education needs, and I want to help you, Martha. What can I do?"

At the time, Cleek was a faculty member in the Bloch School of Business and Public Administration with a doctorate in Foundations of Education. He had been president of two community colleges before coming to UMKC and had vast experience as a leader. I immediately asked him to develop UMKC's first enrollment management plan and to develop it in collaboration with the academic deans and the admissions office. We both saw that the outcome of the development of the plan had to be: "Enrollment is Everyone's Business."

In the summer of 2001, as that project was winding down and was clearly on the path to success, I shocked Cleek by asking him to consider being interim dean of the School of Education. He indicated that any affirmative answer from him would depend on faculty acceptance of him. I introduced Cleek to the School of Education faculty and staff. I told them of my strong commitment to making our School of Education a centerpiece of the new UMKC. I also told them I believed the School of Education deserved a chance to prove what was possible if the faculty and administration worked together to develop an intentional future worthy of the best all of us could contribute.

Cleek told them he was ready to accept my challenge, but only if he was assured that they were willing to make a fresh start. He pledged to work with them in finding common ground and challenged them to share with him their personal commitment. His challenge to them was very direct, "Tell me what vision for the future would cause you to be willing to work harder than you have ever worked before." The response from the faculty and staff was immediate and mostly positive.

The response from the community to changes within the School of Education has been more cautious—more in line with Missouri's famous "Show Me" attitude. As Gwen Grant, president and CEO of the Urban League of Greater Kansas City says, "The quality of public education in Kansas City is in a horrible state. So, the outcome is indicative of the (university's) involvement. However, you don't just place the blame on UMKC; the whole community has accountability" (personal communication, September 16, 2002).

Cleek and I have had many long conversations about what it will take to focus the School of Education on the issues of teachers and principals in the schools. We both know it will not be easy. We also know we must engage faculty from other schools within the University. And, we know we have a moral obligation to future generations of children in Kansas City to give this effort our very best.

Again, Gwen Grant: "I know the chancellor is trying to make changes. But dealing with faculty and resistance to change, the commitment has to be there, or they will just stay the course." The commitment is here. What results we can produce remains to be seen.

PLANNING FOR THE FUTURE AT UMKC

In May 2000, I launched a change process at UMKC—a process that I believe will bring value to the University and the entire community, including the public schools in Kansas City, Missouri. The process is grounded in theories about the role of language and conversations in changing cultures, living systems, quantum organizations, and quantum human intelligence.[2] I am of the opinion that traditional strategic planning processes lead to planning documents that find their way quickly into university archives, making only a modest difference, if any. Engaging in traditional strategic planning was, for me, tantamount to "doing the same thing and expecting a different result."

Rather than do that, we began something quite different with a small group of UMKC leaders working together for three days to discuss what was possible for UMKC. That led to additional faculty, staff, and student retreats throughout the summer of 2000, with each group contributing to the design of UMKC's future. To date, roughly 2,000 people have been engaged in this process, several hundred intensively.

I refer to this as UMKC's transformation process, drawing from the substantial literature on higher education transformation. Many faculty, it turns out, find the term *transformation* highly distasteful. Nevertheless, for our purposes, transformation is defined in two domains: as outcomes and as a shift in the culture of the institution.

As outcomes, the transformation is intended to produce a *constituency that is highly engaged* in the vision and an *organization that is highly accomplished*, performing at levels previously unknown, qualitatively and quantitatively. I have a constituency in Kansas City and within UMKC that has accepted responsibility for specific accountabilities and actions. For example, I work formally and directly with an executive cabinet of six people, a cabinet of 36 people that includes the deans and others, an extended cabinet that includes 150 faculty and staff as well as a few students and community leaders, and a set of trustees that includes 60 people from the private sector in Kansas City. All together, we have 12 specific projects and four specific focus areas in which we are attempting to perform at new levels of accomplishment. These are aimed at demonstrating results and assuring that our time and resources are focused.

In the American Council on Education series on institutional transformation, Madeleine Green writes: "A crucial step in implementing institution-wide change is expanding the group of supporters from the few (the president or administrative and faculty leaders) to the many (a critical mass of faculty, administrators, staff, students and other interested groups). Through the process of informed and energetic conversation, a change permeates a campus by getting others excited about and moving toward change" (1999, p. 43). As a shift in the culture of the institution, transformation refers to the process of moving from a Cartesian to a quantum internal culture; for example, a hierarchical approach moves to relational, a determinate culture moves to a more unpredictable one (Kilman, 2001).

As we strive to become a quantum organization, we are designing policies and promoting a culture in which the institution accepts unpredictability as opportunity; celebrates the fact that great ideas can emerge in many places; encourages responses to be brought forward from the bottom to the top of the organization; embraces entangled relationships, putting them to work for the whole; and searches for the solutions that are "both/and" rather than singular. The process is deliberate in its design to access the creativity and imagination of participants and, by its very nature, is therefore messy, unpredictable, and dynamic. In theory, it should be well suited to take advantage of the university's tradition of shared governance, a tradition I view as valuable, important to our future, and currently ineffective.

We remain in the early stages of this process. As Green writes, "[transformation]...is not accomplished overnight; change that is sufficiently pervasive and deep to qualify as transformational change requires changing processes, values, rewards, and structures throughout an institution, all of which take time" (1998, p. 6).

THE TRANSFORMATION PROCESS AT UMKC

A key element of our process was a set of workshops open to people across the strata and hierarchy of the university. Three-day workshops were designed with four intended outcomes: (1) to access the creativity, ideas and energy of people across the institution in shaping the vision; (2) to produce a cadre of people at every level of the institution who saw themselves individually as vital elements of making the vision real and saw actions they could take individually that would cause the vision to become real; (3) to support the development of new relationships, projects, and solutions not available before; and (4) to provide the support for these people to become leaders in conversations throughout the university aimed at transforming the culture.

Recall from my list of leadership principles that "culture exists in conversations." The people who attended the workshops learned to recognize the conversations of cynicism and saw how to shift them. Participation was by choice, with workshops filled on a first-come, first-served basis. Seven hundred faculty, staff, students, and community members participated in 10 workshops.

Equal in importance to the workshops was—and is—the extended cabinet created in January 2001. These 150 people, all of whom have taken the workshop, are charged to provide and model leadership, to create and model the UMKC core values, and to generate the new UMKC culture through their conversations. Again, participation on the extended cabinet is by choice.

By the summer of 2001, the School of Education was notable for its limited, almost non-existent, participation in the retreats of the year 2000, in subsequent workshops, and in the extended cabinet. John Cleek changed that. After taking the reins as interim dean in the late summer of 2001, John immediately introduced two of the three-day workshops, specifically for the School of Education. While the workshops were again by choice, participation was high. Why? I believe most faculty was highly concerned about the future of the School of Education, given the turnover of deans. I believe they had begun to see their own role in causing that destructive turnover and were willing to give this interim dean and these workshops a chance. More than 65 percent of the faculty and staff in the School of Education participated in one of the workshops.

After this, the focus of the school began to shift to the UMKC vision and, more specifically, to UMKC's role with K–12 education in Kansas City. That role is clearly a part of the university's vision, values, and goals. The jury is still out on the success of this shift in the School of Education.

UMKC 2006: VISION, VALUES AND GOALS

From the workshops and retreats emerged the UMKC vision, mission, values, and goals. Our vision—A Community of Learners Making the

World a Better Place: creating new standards in higher education, including

- Academic excellence
- Campus without borders
- Unleashing human potential is manifested through our mission, including:

  - Lead in life and health sciences
  - Deepen and expand strength in the visual and performing arts
  - Develop a professional work force; collaborate in urban issues and education

- Create a vibrant learning and campus life experience through processes that have us living our values, including:

  - Education first
  - Discovery and innovation
  - Integrity and accountability
  - Diversity, inclusiveness, and respect
  - Energized, collaborative communities

We have developed measures for our five goals.[3] By 2006:

- We are a national leader in scholarship and creative activity.
- We attract, nurture, and develop responsible community leaders.
- We are an essential community partner and resource.
- We are a workplace of choice.
- We have the resources to fuel our vision.

HERE AND NOW—RISING TO THE CHALLENGE

A reading of some of the history of the public schools in Kansas City and conversations with participants in that history led me to conclude that the origins of the problems with teacher education and with urban public schools—that is, the current problems with both of our products, namely teachers in the case of UMKC and educated young people in the case of the schools—are extraordinarily deep and complex. I also hear blame everywhere. My conclusions are undoubtedly the conclusions made by most chancellors of most urban universities in America today. The issues are embedded in the history of our nation, especially in the history of slavery and civil rights; in long struggles with bilingual education; in a long, frustrating, and expensive effort by the courts to produce racial balance;

and in the inability of UMKC and other Missouri and Kansas public universities to train and support teachers and principals successfully.

Today, Kansas City finds itself in the same situation as most cities in the country. We have a teacher shortage driven by high rates of attrition and migration, coupled with problems attracting people of color to the teaching profession. As in most cities, although many of UMKC's graduating teachers stay in this area geographically, they do not necessarily start or remain teachers in urban schools. And, teachers, principals, and counselors are provided little assistance in their career development and career support.

Gwen Grant of the Urban League, states, "Based on academic achievement, UMKC has not done a good job in terms of preparing teachers to teach in an urban environment. Their teachers don't come out prepared to teach urban youth. Research shows that teacher quality is the number one indicator for either low or high student achievement. If the University has a role in preparing teachers, and if we have poor education outcomes in our district, that is obviously something we need to look at" (personal communication, September 6, 2002).

I agree, but what to do now? I expect the next two and a half years to be challenging as the University and especially the UMKC School of Education work to be the educational reform partner in Kansas City that drives positive results. The challenges are both internal and external to the university. I summarize them in four categories, indicating where we stand in each, identifying next steps and delineating my role as chancellor in each.

1. Establishing Partners

On April 29, 2002, I was pleased to convene an Educational Showcase on campus attended by some 200 area educational, business, and civic leaders. Interim Dean Cleek and the faculty of the School of Education challenged everyone in attendance to join us in a Partnership for the Educational Future of Kansas City. Partners were asked to commit to two accomplishments: By 2006, every child in our region would have access to a highly qualified, competent, and caring teacher and every school would have a transformative educational leader in charge. UMKC will not proceed without key partners from the school districts of Kansas City, the teacher organizations in these schools, the private foundations of Kansas City, technology providers, and some representation from the business, civic, political, and religious leadership of Kansas City. Those who wished to partner signed an agreement and most participants did sign up.

As of this writing, the Partnership for the Educational Future of Kansas City is moving forward. A planning grant has allowed us to hire a director and open an office. Working groups representing faculty, the school district, and community are addressing issues of collaboration in curriculum development and outlining the governance, operating, and funding structures for the Partnership. We have proposed the establishment of Professional Development Academies as clinical laboratories for teacher education and a virtual network to link all teachers, especially those who can mentor new educators. Our timetable is aggressive and we know that much of our learning will be achieved through trial and error.

My role as chancellor now is five-fold: (1) continue to raise money from private foundations and individuals for the effort; (2) find one or more technology providers interested in applications of broadband technology in training teachers and in the public schools; (3) show my support internally for the UMKC leaders that are working to change the internal culture, procedures, policies, and curriculum; (4) provide access to the UMKC leaders to civic, business, and religious leaders where my role as chancellor opens doors not available to them; and (5) talk about this effort all the time internally and externally as one of UMKC's top priorities.

2. Addressing the Internal Culture and Actions of UMKC

As we proceed with or without external funding, I believe at least two problems with the internal culture of UMKC must be addressed for a successful effort. The work we have done over the last two years at UMKC is a good start and is essential. First, teacher and principal preparation cannot be the responsibility of the School of Education alone. At UMKC, we must make this a serious issue for the College of Arts and Sciences and some professional schools. In the formal degree programs for both teachers and educational leaders, both content and methodology must be excellent and must be coordinated and that will involve numerous schools. Secondly, the faculty reward system must support faculty who engage in teacher education and in partnerships, and it does not currently do so.

Dealing with these internal issues, which are across schools and colleges, means that the provost to whom these deans report must have the leadership role. My first priority as chancellor had to be to find a provost who agreed with the commitment and held the value of partnering. I hired Provost Steve Ballard in the Spring of 2001; like John Cleek, I believe he was attracted to the emerging vision and values of UMKC, and, he is committed to partnerships. My role now is to give him my full support as he works to make this a university-wide priority internally. He currently is working on two fronts: (1) to develop the partnerships among the College of Arts and Sciences, some professional schools, the School of Biological Sciences, and the School of Education; and (2) to change the faculty reward system so that faculty will be rewarded for participation in this priority.

The provost took the most important step when he hired deans for the College of Arts and Sciences and the School of Business and Public Administration, both of whom are committed to partnerships and hold a set of personal values that make UMKC's engagement with K–12 issues a natural priority. Interestingly, since my arrival as chancellor, new deans are present in all of the schools that will be involved in this effort. Any project of this level of importance and priority requires committed leaders at all levels. The provost has made it clear to these deans that, even in these extremely difficult budgetary times, this priority will be supported. Changing the faculty reward system is proving to be more difficult; however, both the provost and I are confident that many faculty are naturally interested and it is those with whom we will work.

In addition to the partnerships across schools and the reward system changes, the deans and faculty in the School of Education and College of Arts and Sciences are working on revisions in the lower-division curriculum to include one course in each of the first two years built around the theme of Cultures and Community. I am told this course will also include a service-learning component aimed at having our preeducation students in the schools during their first two years. The provost is also working with the deans to make joint appointments for content area faculty, including those who teach content-specific pedagogy across schools at UMKC.

3. Changing the Internal Culture and Actions of the School of Education

Within the School of Education, Dean Cleek has numerous initiatives underway. He has installed a new chair of the Division of Curriculum and Instruction and a newly established position of director of teacher education. Both of these leaders were drawn from the ranks of senior faculty within the School of Education, providing some validation that our faculty would rise to the occasion.

The dean and faculty are currently exploring the possibility of preadmitting preeducation students to the School of Education in order to give the faculty a head start on preparing them for successful entry into the teaching profession. A Turning Point Academy is planned to assist minority high school students prepare for college and funding is being sought to increase the diversity of teachers by developing a program for recruiting from other professions. A redesign of teacher preparation curriculum to align better with competences is under way.

In addition a two-way exchange program is under discussion. University faculty from the School of Education will spend a semester in residence in the schools with a parallel teacher-, counselor-, and administrator-in-residence program planned at UMKC. Program support for existing and emerging education leaders—especially principals—is a priority and the School of Education is also studying the creation of a virtual network of support for all teachers in the district.

4. Establishing a Teacher Preparation Academy

As this goes to press in 2004, planning-grant money has been acquired from two private foundations for a Teacher Preparation Academy to be developed in partnership by the School of Education and College of Arts and Sciences. The Academy has three features that, in my view, are vital to its success.

First, it takes a clinical approach to education. I am told that the Teacher Academy model is similar to the way we educate health professionals at UMKC. For example, the clinical, onsite experience of prospective teachers will start early and be integrated with theory through practice in the schools. A network of local schools has verbally committed to partner with UMKC in this effort. In each school, UMKC will have clinical professors, master teachers, teaching fellows, and teaching interns working as teams. This is similar to the docent team approach we use in the School of Medicine that includes physicians, residents, interns, and medical students from each year of medical school training.

The second feature of the Academy is a focus on technology. Our technology goal is to link the professional development schools, the academy site, and the homes of the students with broadband technology to take advantage of a curriculum that fully utilizes the network in teaching teachers, leaders, and the students. Broadband providers nationally indicate that what is missing for "broadband to take off" in America is a "killer application." The education of students in public schools is viewed widely as one of several potential killer applications.

The third element crucial to the Academy's success is its advisory board of partners. I will take the lead inviting external constituents to serve on an advisory board chaired by Provost Ballard. The board will include the deans, several K–12 superintendents and representatives from teacher leadership organizations, religious organizations, the technology company, and funding sources. The advisory board will be expected to take overall responsibility for improving Kansas City schools as evidenced by the performance of the students in these schools. To join the board, each partner will be asked to take personal accountability for a specific outcome. Again, the willingness of people to engage at such a high level of accountability remains to be seen.

We know what we must do. Do we have the political will to accomplish the needed changes? I am not sure but I am optimistic. This is not only an educational issue. It is a public policy issue that will require a powerful con-centration of political will to overcome the barriers of politics, bureaucratic inertia, and conflicting public opinion, and to ensure the necessary in-vestments of time and money.

These are significant barriers, to be sure. Success will require the com-mitment of all the partners. It will require that commitment be sustained both through the successes and through the breakdowns when outcomes do not proceed as planned. I now believe we have the right plan and peo-ple at UMKC. Some early successes and evidence of committed partners are the next steps in achieving the dream.

NOTES

1. For further development of the role of background conversations in main-taining or changing an organization's culture, see: Ford, 1999, and Ford, Ford, & McNamara, 2002.

2. The references listed at the end of the chapter are useful. For information on the role of language in changing cultures see: Heidegger, 1962; Ford, 1999; and Ford, Ford, & McNamara, 2002. Wheatley, 1992, describes living systems and Kil-mann quantum organizations. Theories of quantum human intelligence are ex-plored by Zohar, 1996 & 1997 and Marshall, 1996.

3. For a list of the measurements against which we evaluate progress of our goals for 2006, see our Web site at http://www.umkc.edu/thevision/goals.html. Click on each goal to view the specific measures.

Martha W. Gilliland was named chancellor of the University of Missouri-Kansas City in 2000 after serving as provost at Tulane University in New Or-leans and in leadership positions at the University of Arizona in Tucson, the Uni-versity of Nebraska in Lincoln, and the University of Oklahoma in Norman. She holds undergraduate and master's science degrees from Catawba College and Rice University and a doctorate in environmental engineering/systems ecology from the University of Florida. In 2001 she was appointed to the President's Council of Advisors on Science and Technology, a panel of 22 leaders from the public and private sector who advise the White House on science and technology issues. The following year she was awarded the Policy Studies Organization Hubert H. Humphrey Award as the nation's "top public policy practitioner." Dr. Gilliland serves on numerous boards in Kansas City, including the Kansas City Area De-velopment Council and the Kansas City Area Life Sciences Institute, Inc.

BIBLIOGRAPHY

Ford, J. D. (1999). Organizational change as shifting conversations, *Journal of Organizational Change Management, 12* (6), 480–500.

Ford, J. D., Ford, L. W., & McNamara, R. T. (2002) Resistance and the background conversations of change, *Journal of Organizational Change Management, 15* (2), 105–121.

Franey, L. (2002, October 10). For charter schools, the numbers rise but supporters and doubters differ on reasons. *The Kansas City Star,* p. A1.

Green, M., Eckel, P., & Hill, B. (1998). *On change: En route to transformation,* (An occasional paper series, ACE Project on Leadership and Institutional Transformation). Washington, DC: American Council on Education.

Green, M., Eckel, P., Hill, B., & Mallon, W. (1999). *On change III. Taking charge of change: A primer for colleges and universities.* Washington, DC: American Council on Education.

Heidegger, M. (1962). *Being and time.* New York: Harper and Row Publishers, Inc.

Heidegger, M. (1977). *Basic writings.* New York: Harper and Row Publishers, Inc.

Kilmann, R. H. (2001). *Quantum organizations: A new paradigm for achieving organizational success and personal meaning.* Palo Alto, CA: Davies-Black Publishing.

Marshall, I. N. (1996). Three kinds of thinking. In S. R. Hameroff, A. W. Kazniak, & A. C. Scott (Eds.), *Towards a science of consciousness, the first Tucson discussions and debates* (pp. 729–738). Boston: The MIT Press.

Schirmer, S. L. (2002). *A city divided: The racial landscape of Kansas City 1900–1960.* Columbia, MO: University of Missouri Press.

Stulman, J. (1972). Quantum jump. *Fields within fields . . . within fields,* 5(1). New York: The World Institute Council.

U.S. Census. (2000). *Profiles of general demographic characteristics: 2000 census of population and housing, Kansas City, MSA.* (pp. 16 & 81). Mid-American Regional Council.

Wheatley, M. J. (1992). *Leadership and the new science.* San Francisco: Barrett-Koehler Publishers, Inc.

White, T. (1999, August 22). Students offer lessons in harmony, and problems at top tarnish image of KC district. *The Kansas City Star,* pp. A22, A23.

Williams, M. R. (2000, August 19). More taking ACT: Kansas scores rise slightly to tie with Missouri's. *The Kansas City Star,* p. B1.

Zohar, D. (1996). Consciousness and Bose-Einstein condensates. In S. R. Hameroff, A. W. Kazniak, & A. C. Scott (Eds.), *Towards a science of consciousness, the first Tucson discussions and debates* (pp. 439–450). Boston: The MIT Press.

Zohar, D. (1997). *Rewiring the corporate brain.* San Francisco: Berrett-Koehler Publishers, Inc.

CHAPTER

Partnerships, Accountability, and Results in Educational Reform in Georgia

Carl V. Patton

Creating a collective purpose involves institutionalizing the vision through effective and frequent communication. In essence, this is how I have encouraged urban educational reform in Georgia. I came to Georgia State with a vision that was consistent with the needs of the university. I aimed to expand our relationship with the community, establish accountability mechanisms, and then show our results. Georgia State has accomplished this, and, in turn, we have strengthened the community of which we are a part.

Georgia State University is a leading urban research university located in the heart of Atlanta. It is the second largest institution in the University System of Georgia, with more than 40,000 degree-seeking students as well as a large population of students enrolled in nondegree educational programs. Of the total student population, 27,500 students are enrolled on campus each semester. The university offers 52 undergraduate and graduate degree programs in more than 250 fields of study. Thirty percent of our students are pursuing graduate degrees. Involvement in the community, being accountable for our academic and fiscal decisions, and producing measurable results, characterize Georgia State University today.

Georgia State is also the most diverse campus in Georgia, reflecting the composition of our state with more than 45 percent minority and multicultural representation in our student body. The university draws students from every county in Georgia, every state in the nation, and more than 145 other countries, but 75 percent of the students attending our downtown campus and north metro center come from the 20-county Atlanta metropolitan area.

Our location in a metropolitan area provides a rich opportunity for enhancing traditional methods of learning. Most of our educational programs offer learning experiences that are conducted in and meet the wide-ranging needs of our community. These opportunities enable students to develop a lifelong connection with the community and to gain an understanding of civic responsibility.

One of our greatest institutional strengths is also one of the advantages of being an urban university: the diversity of the students and faculty the university recruits. Student and faculty diversity benefits all students since it challenges stereotypes, broadens perspectives, and sharpens critical thinking skills.

This chapter chronicles my leadership at Georgia State and my direct and indirect involvement in various projects, initiatives, and policies to support schools, teachers, and students in Atlanta. Throughout the last 10 years, I have worked to become an even more valuable community player through my involvement in the community and leadership of local initiatives. Support for the local public schools is a key component of these efforts. In most cases, these relationships required active solicitation, substantial time and energy commitments, and patience. However, these investments have been valuable as they garnered passionate and dedicated supporters who have helped to advance our initiatives in many other areas.

Besides the direct ways I have become involved in educational initiatives, I have also learned the importance of broadening the university's leadership base by placing qualified individuals in key positions and then empowering them to achieve success. This has required me to push decision-making down the organizational chart and relinquish control to those who have expertise in education reform.

This chapter also examines the complexities endemic to creating meaningful change in a dynamic urban educational system with a variety of educational constituents. Although this chapter does not describe every enterprise in which Georgia State is involved, it cites initiatives that illustrate the essence of our engagement with local school districts and the community at large to support urban education.

My presidency at Georgia State began in 1992. The University System of Georgia's Board of Regents felt that my experience with urban and university campus planning, economic development, and academic leadership made me a good fit for the university. From the outset, I was aware that the university could capitalize better on its existing institutional strengths, improve its academic reputation, engage more fully in the life of the community, and implement policies to provide greater accountability. During the past 10 years, the Georgia State University community has made significant progress working toward each of these goals with the help of an outstanding provost, strong deans, and energetic department chairs.

Early in my tenure at Georgia State, we created a strategic plan that included annual action plans and budgets. In addition, I became directly involved in urban planning and development projects in Atlanta and at the university. The outcomes of these initiatives have had a positive impact on our institutional profile and national reputation. As a result of a concentrated team effort, Georgia State has become a first-choice university among students. Today our student body is the best qualified in our history.

Although Georgia State has always been conscious of its connection to the community, during the past decade the university became more active in finding solutions to urban issues. Today our students, faculty, and staff are deeply connected with urban Atlanta. Later in the chapter, I will elaborate on my involvement with the community. Before I continue, however, I would like to introduce our university perspective on teacher education and our College of Education as well as provide a contextual description of the university's urban environment.

THE IMPORTANCE OF TEACHER EDUCATION

During the past 30 years, Georgia State has been a major producer of teachers for the state of Georgia and the southeast. Although enrollments in our College of Education declined in recent years, primarily due to increasing opportunities for women in other career fields and a heightening of our entrance requirements, we have taken action to strengthen recruiting to meet the growing need for teachers. At the same time, we have attempted to increase the quality of the teachers we produce in order to serve society better. We recognized that the perception of low-quality teaching in the Atlanta schools directly reflected on us because of the large number of the system's teachers that we prepare. This concern was not restricted to our College of Education but also involved our College of Arts and Sciences, which provides many of the courses our education students take toward their degrees.

We have made education reform a *university-wide priority* at Georgia State. One example of this can be seen in the formation of our Professional Education Faculty (PEF), a formal structure of the Colleges of Education and Arts and Sciences faculty that is responsible for educator preparation programs at the undergraduate and master's levels. The operational arm of this body is the Professional Education Council (PEC) and its standing committees. Recognizing that change initially requires a critical mass of committed faculty, we set up separate disciplinary task forces to work on program alignment with P–12 standards. Fully aware that we cannot affect education reform alone, the PEF has been expanded to include teachers and administrators from five local Atlanta school districts.

THE COLLEGE OF EDUCATION

Georgia State's College of Education was created in 1967 in response to a variety of social, political, and economic factors. In that post-Sputnik era, schools across the country were under greater public scrutiny to implement more rigorous academic standards. In addition, the civil rights movement directed more attention toward issues of equality and balanced educational opportunities. In both cases, schools were seen as the method for alleviating these problems.

Another circumstance that favored the emergence of the College of Education was the severe shortage of teachers in Georgia at the time—much as we are experiencing today. School administrators responded to this need in September 1967 by adopting a resolution to establish Georgia State's College of Education and, thus, marked the beginning of what would become one of the country's largest teacher education institutions (Hall, 1988).

Today, the College of Education serves 5,000 students—two-thirds at the graduate level—and graduates 500 new teachers each year.

The college's commitment to prepare individuals to work in school, clinical, government, and industrial educational settings and to advance knowledge while engaging in the life of the community reflects the university's broader institutional mission. The college collaborates with local schools and other agencies to prepare early childhood, middle school, and secondary teachers, as well as principals, special educators and school counselors, and psychologists grounded in theory and practice. Today, there are more than 22,000 teachers in Georgia who graduated from our College of Education.

ATLANTA PUBLIC SCHOOLS

Atlanta Public Schools (APS) is the primary school system serving the metro Atlanta community with 97 schools and an enrollment of 57,000 students in grades K–12. Eighty-nine percent of APS students are black, 7 percent are white, and 4 percent are members of other racial and ethnic groups.

Similar to many other urban districts, students in APS underperform in critical areas. For example, on the 2000–2001 Stanford 9 Tests for grades 3, 5, and 8, the APS falls below the state average on every test. On the 2000–2001 Grade 8 writing assessment, 27 percent of the APS students were not on target, compared with 17 percent statewide. The high school completion rate for the graduating class of 2001 was 53.6 percent compared to the state rate of 71.1 percent, and the APS total SAT score of 856 for these students compares poorly with the state average of 973 and the national average of 1012 (*2000–2001 Georgia Public Education Report Card: Atlanta City*, 2001).

Even in light of these sobering data, the community has high hopes for APS. But these hopes exist along with continuing concerns about the quality of education, engendered, in part, by personal experiences with APS graduates or through its poor reputation as reported in the media. This disenchantment with the system also has a historical basis. In the 1960s, APS experienced a highly contentious desegregation process. Desegregation caused many whites and members of middle- and upper-class families of all races to abandon metro schools. The significance of this urban flight cannot be understated; during this time the system lost many key stakeholders and influential advocates, both white and black. Today, APS continues to experience shrinking enrollment in contrast with Atlanta's surrounding suburban districts, which are experiencing unconstrained growth.

Poverty is, of course, related to the issue of urban flight. As members of more affluent groups evacuated, greater percentages of impoverished individuals remained and concentrated in the metro urban area. This legacy continues today; four out of five APS students are eligible for the free/reduced price lunch program. Certainly, the consequences of urban poverty and a chronically underfunded school system are closely linked and have affected not only the quality of instruction in metro schools but also have contributed to problems in attracting and retaining quality teachers. Intense competition for new teacher graduates in Atlanta's expanding suburbs results in ample job opportunities and attractive incentives without requiring teachers to deal with the challenges facing urban schools.

APS will experience more than 3,330 vacancies during the next five years, a figure that represents more than 85 percent of its current teaching staff. High attrition rates for new teachers contribute to this figure. For example, by January 2001, of the 519 teachers hired in 1998, 37 percent had left the district; and of the 643 teachers hired in 1999, 27 percent were gone—rates higher than the national average for teacher turnover (Coburn, 2001).

Retirement also contributes to vacancies. More than one-third of the current teaching force is age 50 or older. Some researchers estimate that the system should anticipate 600 to 700 retirements during the next five years. It is expected that the system will require more than 750 new teachers for the 2006 academic year. Recent reports have encouraged APS to, "develop a 'Compelling Package' that not only attracts new talent, but also provides new teachers with the induction, mentoring and professional development they desire...and to make the system a truly attractive place to work" (Coburn, 2001, p. 5).

All of these challenges facing APS pose both opportunities and risks for the school system and for Georgia State's College of Education. The school system has the opportunity to recruit qualified individuals with a vision and commitment to bring about dynamic change and renewal while the college has the opportunity to act as an architect of this "Compelling Package." To avoid offering quick-fix or short-term solutions for some of these complex challenges, the college needs to focus on long-term investments that will enhance APS.

To be successful, urban school reform requires a deeply rooted commitment to the community; it must engage every constituent from student to superintendent and it must occur on multiple organizational levels. It also requires the fostering of long-term institutional initiatives to build partnerships and restore relationships.

Moreover, as I suggested earlier, the College of Education needs to look inward when assessing some of the challenges facing Atlanta's schools, with the recognition that Georgia State is implicated in a number of these challenges. Since many of the teachers in Atlanta earned their degrees from Georgia State, the quality of teaching in the city's schools can be held to be a reflection of the quality of instruction at the university. Furthermore, the quality of instruction, educational opportunities, and academic success experienced by students in APS directly affects the quality of future applicants for admission to Georgia State.

ENGAGEMENT WITH THE COMMUNITY

I came to Georgia State in 1992 with a vision of strengthening the university's relationships with key constituents and a desire to become more involved with the city. At Georgia State, this new direction required transformational change; altering the culture of the institution by changing underlying assumptions, behaviors, processes, and products. Such change must be intentional, deep, and pervasive and it has to occur institutionwide (Eckel, Hill, and Green, 1998). At Georgia State, insulation was a deeply imbedded component of institutional culture. Previous administrations had not embraced the diversity and opportunities that Atlanta's urban environment provided. I knew that for the university to be successful in advancing and fostering an inclusive culture with its local environment, we would need to change our inward focus and develop better connections with the community.

Since I am educated as an urban planner, I will provide a physical illustration. At Georgia State, separation from the life of the city took its most obvious form in our campus environment. Historically, administrators tried to separate the university from the city with platforms and catwalks. Under my administration, the university has engaged in an aggressive physical development program. A few years ago, we unveiled the university's 10-year blueprint for growth called the "Main Street Master Plan." This plan has been guiding our strategic development decisions. It focuses on creating a vibrant, inviting campus that expands our current potential to engage more fully in the life of our community. The plan contains physical expressions of this engagement: placing large windows in existing and new buildings to open them to the street, creating a walkable main street through campus, and taking down some of the platforms and catwalks. Although all the plans are not yet implemented, the completed projects have been successful in creating a university-community link and have been welcomed by the community.

I also realize that physical planning decisions mirror the educational mission of a university and reflect the institution's level of support for the local community. Therefore, much of my energy has been dedicated to implementing academic decisions that enhance the potential of the local community. I believe that our urban location provides more than a place to gain experience; it is a platform for prospective urban educators to address complex urban problems. I also believe that Georgia State's involvement in efforts that strengthen the community also strengthen the university. So, if Georgia State can make sound academic decisions that benefit the community of which we are a part, then we should make them.

My role in fostering community partnerships has been predominantly in the area of urban planning and revitalization. I believe that my involvement in these strategies has helped Georgia State assume a more public and influential role and has allowed the university to position itself among a more diverse set of stakeholders.

In recent years, we have involved community leaders and neighbors in developing our campus physical plan in order to enhance its chance for success. We have even worked with a community advisory group to ensure that our building designs fit with the character of the neighborhood. In addition, a group of concerned alumni helps advance our agenda in the state legislature.

After arriving in Atlanta, I quickly moved into active leadership roles with a number of community organizations, allowing me to use my expertise to reshape a large portion of the downtown environment. I have served as chair of Centennial Olympic Park Area, Inc. (COPA), a private nonprofit organization that is developing the area around the 1996 Olympic Park. As chair of the group, I helped to create plans for the redevelopment of the area around the park, including the construction of several hundred units of new condominiums and apartments.

I also serve as chair of Central Atlanta Progress (CAP), a coalition of business members concerned about the downtown environment. CAP is working to make Atlanta a more livable, workable, and safe environment for the entire community, including our students. CAP has led the effort to create solutions to safety issues in the downtown community through the Downtown Ambassador Force. This force is a 54-person team that patrols the 120-block district.

The Ambassador Force is based on the notion that a visible, authoritative, yet friendly, group of people assigned to patrol downtown can make the district safer, cleaner, and more hospitable. The initiative is working: crime is down for the third straight year, the sidewalks are cleaner, and surveys show that the people who live, work, and are educated downtown feel better about their neighborhood. As a member of CAP, I worked to get the initial district formed and approved by the property owners in the district, even going door-to-door asking the landowners to vote for the new taxing district.

Our university involvement in another community initiative also underscores the importance of engaging in community-wide efforts. The Metropolitan Atlanta P–16 Council is a comprehensive community initiative aimed at raising expectations and ensuring student achievement. It is housed at Georgia State under the guidance of Provost Ron Henry and has my complete support. The council is comprised of parents, citizens, and business representatives who, together, discuss and implement initiatives to further urban reform efforts. Because members of the council are also metro community members, the group has a more thorough understanding of the complexities of urban educational reform. This results in the implementation of more tangible measures for improvement.

The Council recognizes that qualified teachers have the greatest impact on improving student achievement in Georgia. The group, therefore, decided to focus on the issue of teacher recruitment by establishing the Advanced Academy for Future Teachers in an effort to attract bright, talented, and diverse individuals into the teaching profession. Each year talented high school students are recruited and provided with opportunities to participate in the education process and gain skills, knowledge, and an understanding of the educational environment. Selected students are provided with teaching experiences, training seminars, and opportunities for collaboration with teachers and other educators in Georgia and the nation. In addition, opportunities for speaking engagements at high schools and future teachers clubs provide leadership experience for the participants.

Edi Guyton, associate dean of the College of Education, has put the Council's ideas into action. She believes that the Council's vision, guidance, and commitment to supporting teachers and enhancing teacher quality is critical to the success of the program. She acknowledges that it requires extra effort to organize and include so many stakeholders who are pressed for time and represent a wide range of constituent groups. But she also affirms that these partnerships are essential and they ultimately enhance reform efforts. Likewise, I believe that universities represent sources of limitless potential that can be unleashed through a clear understanding of how we generate lasting value to our public schools, our city, our state, and the nation.

I have learned a number of lessons regarding urban partnerships. Many of these lessons can also be applied to developing critical partnerships necessary for urban school reform. For example, through strengthening our bond with the community, we can forge personal relationships that often prove to be decisive in future opportunities. Reformers operating in isolation run the risk of becoming spectators in the educational reform process or lose support due to their renegade reputation. Neither outcome is profitable when numerous educational reform agendas compete for the backing of educational stakeholders (McAdams, 1997; Unseem and Nield, 1995).

Being part of the community also makes good economic sense. Georgia State is only partially supported by state funding; therefore, we need to acquire resources from a variety of sources: the private sector, foundations, grants, and contracts. Engagement in the community helps us leverage these resources. Moreover, most members of the local community understand that their own economic viability is dependent on quality education. Parents, community members, teachers, principals, school boards, corporate sponsors, and policymakers are powerful voices within school communities (Fullen, 2000). With such a diverse constituent group, it is essential that they understand the issues collectively.

For Georgia State, building partnerships with these constituent groups is both good politics and good policy. Many of the educational successes we see today resulted from innovations created through university research and initiatives. Establishing an appropriate climate to support and expand this kind of research requires more than just state and federal dollars; it requires effective partnerships among academe, local schools, and at times, private agencies. Such partnerships have the potential for generating the resources, innovations, political allies, and essential advocates needed to create necessary changes in the schools.

Finally, I have learned that being involved in communities requires an understanding of the historical, political, and social characteristics of the culture. It further necessitates including and strengthening all constituents of the educational community, including students. This need to be inclusive became clearer from my experience with the Communities In Schools of Atlanta (CISA) organization.

COMMUNITIES IN SCHOOLS

Eight years ago, I was approached with an opportunity to serve on the CISA board. I was attracted to the program because of its dedication to helping urban children achieve success in schools through traditional or alternative methods of instruction. In addition, the program was committed to determining why students were leaving urban schools at such high rates. I also was impressed with the program's focus on maintaining a high degree of local autonomy. Although it is affiliated with the national Communities in Schools (CIS) organization, CISA seeks to understand and respond to the unique needs of its own urban community. CISA's organizational goals were consistent with my own commitment to elementary and secondary education.

Helping children stay in school is fundamental to any reform initiative, but the prospects for many children in Atlanta are desperate. The *2002 Kids Count Factbook,* produced by The Annie E. Casey Foundation, ranks Georgia 44th among the 50 states in terms of child well-being. Additionally, nearly a quarter of Georgia's children live in poverty, and even these rates do not accurately portray the breadth of poverty as federal formulas for calculating poverty levels are almost 40 years old (Harman and Upchurch, 1995). Nor do these statistics speak to the concentration of poverty as it relates to urban areas.

Although these statistics appear bleak, I believe that all children can succeed in schools with the appropriate support. All too often, high-risk and urban students do not receive adequate resources and guidance to mitigate these conditions successfully. In the concerted effort to address the needs of high-risk students, both universities and community organizations such as CIS have important roles to play.

CIS believes that supporting children is fundamental to all community renewal efforts, and that student success is essential to improving the social and economic future of the community. To this end, the program unites local leaders, citizens, parents, and students and provides schoolwide support and individual services to students. Students at risk are given personal attention and placed in a one-on-one relationship with an interested adult. The students receive tutoring, career mentoring, mental health counseling, leadership training, cultural enrichment, and life skills training. Essentially CIS determines what children at risk need to succeed and finds a way to provide it to them.

Currently, Atlanta is one of 49 local CIS programs in Georgia where 53 school systems and more than 67,000 students are served. CISA is run by a nonprofit organization funded primarily by contracts with school districts, grants, and private contributions from the community. CISA was launched to quell the high student dropout rate, which had reached 40 percent and surpassed the national rate.

Having exceeded the term limits for membership on the board of directors, I moved on to chair the community advisory committee of CISA. In retrospect, my board leadership came at a critical time for the organization. When I assumed that role, CISA was in the midst of a fiscal crisis, and its relationship with APS was less than ideal. At that time the organization had a single program strategy—running high school academies, an alternative educational option for at-risk students. APS reform was moving in a very different direction that did not coincide with the services CISA could offer.

I knew that one of my first tasks was to communicate the urgency of the organization's problems to the CISA board. I provided the board with two options: change the way they conducted business or go out of business. I also realized that, to remain viable, CISA needed to engage in strategic coalition building, expand its organizational mission, and develop key alliances.

The most pressing issue was securing finances for the coming year. CISA's financial trouble primarily stemmed from a change in its executive leadership and a failure to execute a contract with APS, which had been funding a major component of the organization's previous budget. I needed to convince the board to act quickly in developing significant relationships with community advocates and with other CIS organizations. We decided to bring back a former executive director and influential advocate, Patty Pflum, to assist us in getting back on track, help foster relationships with the state's CIS organization, and nurture relationships with APS. Eventually these relationships helped the board create a viable budget. The board decided that, because of the political differences with APS, CISA needed to expand its outreach and begin offering services to nearby DeKalb County. If APS saw CISA's success in DeKalb, they would perhaps realize that CISA was an essential player in urban school reform. The strategy worked, and within a short time—and after the arrival of a new superintendent—CISA was invited back to APS.

Beverly Hall, the new superintendent of APS, had successfully used a concept called Project GRAD (Graduation Really Achieves Dreams) in her previous superintendent position. Project GRAD contained a social services component that was similar to the support services provided by CISA, and we proposed to Hall that CISA could offer these services through a contract to APS. This relationship took on a personal meaning, not only because I was involved in program development, but also because it was CISA's first new contract with APS apart from the high school academies. Today, I believe that Project GRAD is one of the most important new school reform initiatives for APS, and CISA is an integral component of the success. The CISA component now serves close to 10,000 students and is a collaborative effort between schools and the community to address the educational needs of the inner-city school system. Project GRAD has raised reading proficiency scores in the APS, with 62 percent of elementary students now reading at or above grade level, up from only 28.6 percent before GRAD was implemented.

CISA is stronger today than ever before, and I believe that my role in the program can account for a substantial portion of its success. Just a few years ago, CISA was on the verge of financial devastation, with 15 staff and only three academies. Today, CIS has more than 70 staff and serves 40 schools. The program is helping schools experience success in attendance, discipline, achievement, and high school completion. While I do not claim credit for the full impact CIS has had, I am proud of our results: nearly 70 percent of students touched by CIS have improved attendance and fewer discipline problems, and the average high school completion rate has increased 6.6 percentage points from 1997 to 2000.

I attribute the revitalization of CISA to a variety of factors. First, I decided to remain as chair for a longer period than was typical to provide a constant figure during a difficult transition. I also believed that by initiating the program in DeKalb County, our positive results would provide the organization with the credibility and time needed to reestablish a relationship with APS.

The eventual support of the new APS superintendent, Beverly Hall, proved to be critical. We garnered her backing in several ways: we used board members who had credibility with APS to present CISA credentials to her; we encouraged her staff members who were friendly to CISA to recount our good work; and we asked members of the state-level CIS organization to reinforce CISA achievements with her. Our task was made easier since Superintendent Hall was already familiar with CIS from her experiences elsewhere and could understand how the organization's presence was needed in Atlanta.

My experiences with CISA reaffirmed the resistance that exists to educational reform efforts that are perceived to be risky and involve new stakeholders with innovative ideas. Essentially, our ideas threatened the former APS culture by offering an alternative approach to educational reform. Research has shown widespread concern about the repercussions of advocating change in schools. Connel and Klem (2000) write about the conundrum of threatening the existing culture. They assert that advocates for change must create a culture that nurtures change efforts. This meant showing APS that CISA was a significant player in educational reform; tangibly this involved fostering significant relationships and demonstrating our results.

It is also difficult to move a change agenda forward in a highly bureaucratic and political system. CISA did not have the political clout to engage at the most important level of the change process. In this situation, I recognized that my position as a visible university president would be critical to the organization's success. Early on, much of my energy with CISA was dedicated to developing advocates and key alliances within the educational community. After many months of hard work and proven results, CISA finally earned the respect of the local educational community.

Through the experiences of strengthening the CISA coalition and building alliances, I also learned that our educational reform effort would have failed had the board not been acutely aware of the historical, political, and social characteristics of the school-community culture. Although reform efforts must draw upon best practices and proven research, they must also be crafted with the specific needs of the community in mind. This involved investigating the successes and failures of other reform efforts, so that CISA could anticipate how the community would respond to another attempt at educational reform.

Discouraged by the empty rhetoric of educational reform and ongoing racial tensions, many parents lack the energy or interest to participate in any new reform effort. In addition, administrators, teachers, counselors, and others in the school community lack the confidence and knowledge to engage reform. Consequently, it was critical for CISA to create a *shared* vision, which earned the organization the trust needed to be a credible member of the reform movement.

There was a critical decision point in the early days of my chairmanship of CISA when I realized the organization was in deep financial trouble, was losing active supporters, and was disenchanted with the new executive director. Believing in the purpose of CISA, along with a friend who served on the state CIS board, I invited several longtime financial supporters and key members of CIS of Georgia to a breakfast meeting. I basically laid out the problem and asked for their help, and I unabashedly told them that if we could not get the help we needed, I would take steps to close down the organization.

To their credit, there was an outpouring of good will and personal support as well as an offer to help provide financial and staff resources. With this backing, I was able to reenergize the board, bring back Patty Pflum, and reestablish the credibility of CISA, and, with the board's help, balance the budget and resume fundraising. Frankly, my near-decade of successful, visible involvement in the Atlanta volunteer community allowed me to call upon friends who forgave the recent CISA problems because of my involvement in its rehabilitation plan.

ACCOUNTABILITY AND RESULTS

Although my participation in CISA is a visible example of presidential leadership, I also believe that I demonstrate my commitment to education in several other ways, such as helping to create effective institutional policies. As previously mentioned, I am committed to accountability mechanisms that lead to measurable results. Basically this means spelling out how academic policies and fiscal decisions will be evaluated so that we can measure and publicly report progress toward our goals. This commitment is reflected in academic policies such as posttenure review and the triennial evaluation of administrators and regular program review. It is also substantiated by my involvement in the conceptualization and implementation of "The Georgia State University Quality Assurance Guarantee for Educators" policy. I strongly affirm that as a state-supported institution, the university is accountable to the state legislature, the university system's Regents, and the communities where Georgia State graduates teach. Furthermore, the public increasingly demands financial and educational accountability from elementary, secondary, and higher education institutions.

I first began to guarantee our results in my public speaking engagements and Rotary Club tours. I boldly told audiences that if they hired any Georgia State graduate who could not do what he or she was educated to do, the university would reeducate the employee free of charge. I saw this as a matter of building credibility. What better way than this, I felt, to show that we are serious about providing quality education. I continue to use the campuswide theme of accountability and results to demonstrate that Georgia State is committed to quality education and academic excellence. Georgia State even enjoyed national attention with our basketball win-guarantee policy. The university promised to refund the cost of a game ticket to our season ticket holders for any home losses.

I particularly understand the urgency of our accountability and results commitment as it relates to urban educational issues. Researchers describe that the climate for teacher accountability is upon us and must be addressed (Schalock, 1998). My commitment to accountability and results has taken on a unique approach in our College of Education. Under the direction of Dean Ron Colarusso, the college has substantiated this commitment by creating a guarantee for the quality of any educator that it recommends for initial certification in Georgia. The college takes measures to fulfill this guarantee even after the student's education at Georgia State is completed. Along with each quality assurance guarantee is also a promise to work with school districts, teachers, and principals through additional support services if our graduates are not able to perform satisfactorily.

Our policy, put in place in 1999, is described in a straightforward, three-page document that says we will guarantee for two years from graduation or initial certification the quality of any educator we recommend for initial certification in Georgia. We guarantee that the graduate has completed an accredited educator preparation program, has passed or exempted PRAXIS I and PRAXIS II, and has met several other standards such as completing a capstone experience, demonstrating subject-matter knowledge in a specialization, demonstrating effectiveness in teaching students from diverse backgrounds, and using technological teaching tools.

We provide a warranty on the graduates' teaching effectiveness, provided they are teaching within state guidelines a reasonable number of subjects in their field, have been given an induction to the school and district, and have been assigned a mentor who provides guidance and support. The retraining will involve an individualized plan with specified learning outcomes. The policy statement even includes a step-by-step procedure and list of documentation to be provided by principals who wish to have us honor the warranty.

It is exciting to see how this policy has gained community support and statewide acceptance. The university system's Regents followed our example, in part as a result of the leadership of our provost in P–12 initiatives, and today a Quality Assurance Guarantee is being implemented across all state system colleges and universities. It is also fulfilling to see how this policy has enhanced our capacity to initiate other innovations.

The Quality Assurance Policy has reinforced the college's stance on supporting teachers even after graduation. According to Associate Dean Guyton, it has also assisted the college in reevaluating the ways students are prepared to be effective teachers in the urban environment. The policy further encouraged the college to make sure there is a meaningful connection between the classroom and the teaching environment.

One program that directly emanated from this policy is the Metro Atlanta Beginning Teacher Support and Induction Consortium, another successful project under the guidance of Associate Dean Guyton. The goal of the Consortium is to increase student achievement by supporting, developing, and retaining committed and effective beginning teachers for our schools. The underlying theme for the consortium is that induction communities are more powerful than relying on a single mentor for beginning teachers. The induction community for a beginning teacher includes all school personnel, teachers, parents, students, and others in the school. Consortium members include representatives from APS, three other metro school systems, and the Georgia Association of Educators.

The Consortium is based on key research findings that document the relationship between teacher effectiveness and student learning (Sanders and Horn, 1998). Guiding principles of the consortium include the idea that supporting new graduates is a shared responsibility and that key persons and agencies all must work to support, develop, and retain beginning teachers. Intervention begins during a teacher's preservice experience and continues until the teacher can act independently and effectively to assume the full scope of professional responsibilities. The program focuses on the beginning needs of teachers and provides new teachers with resources, training, support, and communication.

Using the Consortium as an ongoing mechanism to integrate the work of its members in the area of teacher support and induction, the College of Education has developed the Teacher Education Graduate Induction Program. Although many school systems have their own induction and mentoring programs, Georgia State recognized a need for continued involvement in the initial years of a graduate's professional teaching career. In Guyton's words, "the purpose of Georgia State's program is not to duplicate or interfere with existing programs, but to complement them" (personal communication, July, 2002). The college's two-year induction plan for teacher education graduates involves various support components including personal, group, and technological contact, professional development, and teacher assessment. It is funded by Georgia State, reflecting our commitment to this vital component of teacher education.

Although our quality assurance guarantee for educators only applies to Georgia State graduates, the college realizes that urban reform must involve all teachers, regardless of where they received their educational training. Therefore, the Consortium is committed to providing assistance to any teacher who requests involvement. The Consortium's involvement in schools not only underscores the importance of institutional policies that can directly support educational innovation, it also demonstrates the ongoing necessity to look for creative and research-based methods to support schools, teachers, and students.

The Consortium's work also depicts how the urban environment defines many of the challenges teachers encounter in the area of educational reform. As previously discussed, Atlanta schools face many challenges: teacher shortages (attributed in part to high teacher drop-out rates), teacher retirements, and recent reform mandates that demand smaller class sizes. Additionally, many of our public school students deal with multiple socioeconomic and family issues. Invariably, this causes Georgia State to change the way problems are addressed, looking for creative solutions that not only fit with the goals of the institution but are also consistent with the goals of the community.

ALTERNATIVE CERTIFICATION

Like the Consortium, one outcome of alternative teacher preparation programs has been to rethink the nature of teacher education as well as visualizing new approaches to teacher education. I realize that many contest the efficacy of these programs and criticize them for not offering a valuable contribution to educational reform. At Georgia State, however, we have found that these programs can be effective. I concur with College of Education Dean Colarusso when he states that nontraditional programs can become a viable solution in urban reform initiatives. At the same time, the college needs to ensure that these programs maintain professional standards and produce highly qualified teachers. The alternative programs must ensure that students meet the same standards that are required in our traditional training programs.

Our alternative programs have experienced substantial success. Although we offer several different programs, ours typically involve more time and effort than others. The TEEMS (Teacher Education Environment in English, Mathematics and Social Studies) program, an alternative preparation program, for example, involves career-changing students in intensive summer coursework in pedagogy, then two supervised classroom teaching experiences during the academic year, followed by another summer of coursework.

Since 1994–95, of the 143 students who have graduated from our TEEMS program and entered teaching, 129 are still teaching—a 90 percent success rate. As part of our Induction Consortium, the College of Education has hired a full-time coordinator of education affairs who will collect similar data for all of our alternative and traditional education programs.

Frankly, we need all the qualified teachers who can be prepared through regular or alternative programs. In Georgia, of the 10,176 teachers hired in 2000, more than 7,400 were hired to meet the replacement demand, while only 2,700 were hired to fill the growth demand (Borello, 2002). Furthermore, the number of new teachers from traditional teacher preparation programs has declined dramatically in the past several years. For example, in 2000, 21.8 percent of all new teachers came from traditional programs, a figure that represents a 6 percent decline from 1997 (Borello, 2002). Regrettably, our College of Education graduated 329 new teachers from traditional four-year programs in 2000, approximately 300 fewer than it did three years earlier.

During the past several years, our College of Education has partnered with the Haberman Educational Foundation, a not-for-profit organization that houses the National Center for Alternative Teacher Certification Information. I have served on that board for a number of years to advocate on behalf of alternative certification programs as a way to get more qualified individuals in the classroom.

As a Haberman Foundation board member, I have become familiar with the alternative certification literature, in particular the research results of various forms of alternative certification. This allowed me to speak definitively on the topic when it was debated in Georgia in recent years. Moreover, the Haberman Foundation has developed the Star Teacher and Star Principal interview techniques for selecting individuals who will be successful teachers and principals in urban settings. Since my professional work has taken place in urban settings, this data set has allowed me to speak strongly and convincingly about the need to select the right individuals for the tasks involved in urban education.

THE SUPPORTIVE LEADER

It has been said that, "a vision without the voice of a prophet can neither inspire nor guide" (Deetz, Tracy, and Simpson, 2000, p. 45). Although I can only sometimes be part of creating the vision, it is always possible for me to be the "prophet's voice." While I cannot be personally involved in every reform initiative, I have accepted that most of my time should be spent creating conditions for *others* to enact change.

Although this chapter is primarily devoted to the direct role I play in supporting educational initiatives, most of my energies are devoted to indirect methods: articulating a vision, placing effective individuals in key positions, and offering my continued support to various initiatives. I am drawn to Clawson's notion of distributed leadership in evaluating my own role. Clawson defines distributed leadership, as a "comfortable process whereby those who have the perspective, the skills, and the motivation to deal with the situation of the moment step to the fore and assume—and are granted—influence on the group" (Clawson, 1998, p. 128). For this to happen, everyone must be comfortable with the institution's collective purpose and their individual role in achieving this. I would like to say that in the past decade I have been able to establish a collective purpose at Georgia State.

Creating a collective purpose involves institutionalizing the vision through effective and frequent communication. Today, if you look at our academic, strategic, and fiscal plans, you will see that they all share similar goals of being *a part* of the community, not *apart from it,* stressing accountability, and showing our results. Although various projects and plans emerge, Georgia State's vision remains consistent to these three principles and to its primary goal: to be the leading urban research university educating tomorrow's leaders, performing hands-on service in our urban region, and conducting research that finds solutions to real problems. Going forward, we must balance our expanding role with our desire to serve the needs of our primary community, namely Georgia State students, faculty, and alumni.

Fullen (2000) writes that not only is it important to express ideas that you value, but also, as a leader you must extend what you value, listening to the ideas of others. Once I articulated a clear institutional direction, it became essential for me to delegate program improvements and specific strategies to other individuals and departments. I very rarely tell people what to do; however, at the same time, I hope they will buy into what I consider good ideas. In doing this I am able to broaden and strengthen the university's leadership base. I am convinced that a university president can empower more individuals and allow them to take the most effective approach by pushing decision-making authority down the organizational chart.

I am comfortable relinquishing this control because I have put together a team of individuals who have a keen sense of, and can work toward, our shared institutional vision. It is through the leadership of Georgia State's provost, Ron Henry, and our deans, that we are able to move our challenging agenda forward. Moreover, in a large institution that requires substantial private support, there is a limit to the time I can spend on campus in hands-on activities. As our provost likes to tell students, the difference between his job and that of the president is simple: the president's job is to get money and the provost's job is to spend it. This is how we split up the job at Georgia State.

Throughout my tenure, Georgia State has hired people who are experts in their fields. As the president, I let them do their jobs in the best way they know how. This approach does not remove me from the process entirely since I must keep generating and sharing ideas in the hope that my colleagues will adopt some of them. I have learned to trust the way gifted people choose to solve problems.

Another aspect of my leadership is ensuring that the College of Education is financially supported and represented at the institutional decision-making level. I am committed to putting resources into the College of Education and then letting the dean make the critical decisions. This benefits the university, the college, and the community. The college identifies and implements the programs that best meet the needs of urban educators rather than being coerced into buying mine.

I have also learned that although evaluation is a difficult process when outcomes are not easily quantified, it must become a critical component of any reform effort. My involvement in CISA, the Haberman Foundation, and the community underscores the importance of engaging in a process of evaluation for the sake of continuous improvement. Management guru Peter Drucker believes that change agents are often unwilling to critically evaluate the outcomes of change efforts, however, evaluation is essential because future successes are dependent on documenting and communicating effective changes. He writes:

> One of the tasks of leaders is to make sure that we constantly put our scarce resources (people and money) where they do most good. We have to be results-focused and opportunity-focused. Good intentions are no longer enough... [this] means being willing and able to abandon efforts that don't get results—either because we don't know how to produce results or are misdirecting our efforts, or providing remedial services. (1999, p. 34)

I believe that when Georgia State takes on community service projects, we need to show results. We publish an easily understood annual report of accountability that shows the results of our efforts beyond the university. This also assists in developing strategic relationships with key stakeholders in the educational community. Developing trusting relationships is essential to the viability of a project, and trust is strengthened when others are aware of results and can see a history of successes.

As a public university, we must also show state leaders and budget officers what we do with our public funds and how our research has a statewide economic impact. Our presence directly contributes more than $2 million per day to the state economy; our graduates work in every county of the state; and, our widely distributed brochure, "Serving All of Georgia," clearly illustrates our statewide impact. Through greater accountability and by displaying our results, we can show that Georgia State is a viable and essential member of the community.

While some people may say I'm too focused on dollars, I like to believe I am fiscally alert. And fiscally alert we must be if we are to succeed at educational reform. The dollars are just not there for failed experiments. We need to know what we are doing, we must focus on results, and we must be accountable for our actions.

FINAL THOUGHTS

University presidents can certainly make an impact on school reform if they wish. Early in my tenure at Georgia State, I found that the Atlanta community welcomed my involvement in community service. The credibility associated with the presidency of a large, public institution allowed me to speak up on important issues and accept leadership positions in visible community organizations. It was clear to me that Atlantans would embrace a university president who was willing to roll up his sleeves and work on community problems.

My initial involvement was in urban development, my professional discipline. With early visibility and success in this area, I gained the opportunity to be heard on other community topics, including elementary and secondary education. As an urban planner, I have always held that community renewal and revitalization are essential to school renewal. Flight from the central city led in great part to the decline of our school systems, so conversely, renewal of the city will be needed to repopulate our neighborhoods and rebuild community support for our schools.

As a university president, I have tried to have an impact on both community renewal and school reform. We university presidents certainly have a stake in community renewal and local educational reform, if only to assure the quality of the students we are expected to admit to our institutions in the future. Beyond this, however, I truly believe that university presidents should aid school change directly through personal involvement as well as indirectly through support and guidance.

Using both strategies, I have helped the Atlanta community address critical problems and mobilize resources. Our ongoing university involvement underscores the importance of commitment, persistence, and establishing credibility.

I like the quote widely attributed to Teddy Roosevelt: "Do what you can, with what you have, where you are." I think that sums up the challenge for leaders in educational reform today. Each leader must ask: "What can I do? What do I have to give?" While each of our answers may vary, we must recognize that our engagement efforts today will shape our communities tomorrow. And, if our efforts are successful, we should be able to increase the supply of excellent teachers, provide better and more satisfying careers for teachers, and, ultimately and of utmost importance, offer students a higher quality academic experience.

Carl V. Patton *was named president and professor of Public Administration and Urban Studies and of Geography at Georgia State University in 1992. He previously served in administrative positions at the University of Toledo and University of Wisconsin–Milwaukee, and as a visiting professor to Huazhong University of Science and Technology in the People's Republic of China and Gadjah Mada University in Indonesia. Dr. Patton is currently the chair of Central Atlanta Progress and serves on the board of directors of the Centennial Olympic Park Area Inc., the Metro Atlanta Chamber of Commerce, the Georgia Research Alliance, and The Haberman Foundation. He is also on the executive committee of the Atlanta Regional Consortium for Higher Education. The recipient of numerous awards, Dr. Patton was named one of the "100 Most Influential Georgians" from 1997 through 2002, and was awarded the Ivan Allen J. Community Service Award from the Metropolitan Atlanta Crime Commission.*

BIBLIOGRAPHY

2000–2001 Georgia Public Education Report Card: Atlanta City. (2001). Atlanta: The Georgia Department of Education. Retrieved May 6, 2003, from http://accountability.doe.k12.ga.us?Report01/Educ/761.pdf.

The Annie E. Casey Foundation. (2002). *Kids count databook: State profiles of child well-being.* Baltimore, MD. Retrieved March 31, 2003, from http://www.aecf.org/publications/data/entire_book.pdf.

Atlanta Public Schools 2001–2002 System Report. (2002). Atlanta, GA: Department of Research Planning and Accountability, Atlanta Public Schools. Retrieved March 31, 2003, from http://www.atlanta.k12.ga.us/our_schools/system_overview/system_report/apsreport2001–2002.pdf.

Borello, L. (2002, Spring). Multiple choice: Are alternative preparation programs the answer to Georgia's teacher shortage? *Georgia State Magazine, 1*(2), 14–19.

Clawson, J. (1998). *Leading teams: Getting below the surface*. Upper Saddle River, NJ: Prentice Hall.

Coburn, R. (2001). *Saving the starfish: Recruiting and retaining qualified teachers and principals*. Atlanta, GA: A Report for the Atlanta Public School System.

Connel, J. P. & Klem, A. M. (2000). You can get there from here: Using a theory of change approach to plan urban education reform. *Journal of Educational and Psychological Consultation, 11*(1), 93–120.

Deetz, S. A., Tracy, S. J., & Simpson, S. L. (2000). *Leading organizations through transition*. Thousand Oaks, CA: Sage Publications.

Drucker, P. F. (1999). The discipline of innovation. *Fund Raising Management, 30* (3), 34–36.

Eckel, P., Hill, B., & Green, M. (1998). *On change: En route to transformation*. Washington, DC: American Council on Education.

Fullen, M. (2000). Three stories of education reform. *Phi Delta Kappan, 81*(5), 581–584.

Hall, J. (1988). Origin and history of the college of education, Georgia State University, 1967–1987. Unpublished Ph.D. dissertation, Georgia State University.

Harman & Upchurch. (1995). *Education improvement in Georgia*. (Available from Georgia Partnership for Excellence in Education, 233 Peachtree Street, Suite, 200, Atlanta, GA, 30300.)

McAdams, R. P. (1997). A systems approach to school reform. *Phi Delta Kappan, 79*(2), 138–143.

Sanders S. & Horn, S. (1998). Research findings from the Tennessee value-added assessment system (TVASS) database: Implications for educational evaluation and research. *Journal of Personnel Evaluation in Education, 12*(3), 247–256.

Schalock, H. D. (1998). Student progress in learning: Teacher responsibility, accountability, and reality. *Journal of Personnel Evaluation in Education, 12* (3), 237–246.

Unseem, E. L. & Nield, R. C. (1995). A place at the table: The changing role of urban public education funds. *Urban Education, 30*(2), 175–195.

CHAPTER 10

Passionate Connections, Informed Decisions, Executive Leadership

Shirley C. Raines

Through strategic planning and specific actions, I am helping to create the passionate connections that I believe are necessary for the University of Memphis to excel. This vision involves investing in people, creating interdisciplinary initiatives, and building partnerships.

Anyone who knows me understands that I am passionate about the importance of education. I value the many roles the University of Memphis plays in the lives of individuals and the community by promoting the ever-widening pursuit of learning throughout our lifetimes. I believe, as Peter Drucker has often written, that knowledge is the key resource not only for the strength of nations but also for the success of individuals. I believe that, especially in urban environments such as Memphis, this knowledge must be acquired through schooling.

I am a teacher and I value my career choice. My first position after college graduation was teaching second grade in Louisville, Kentucky. Later, before pursuing doctoral studies in teacher education, I coordinated a project to prepare teaching assistants and served as the director for 14 Head Start centers. Prior to accepting the presidency of the University of Memphis, all of my positions in higher education (professorships, department chairs, and dean) were in Colleges of Education (COE). I have dedicated my life to teaching and to teachers.

Knowledge of schooling in Tennessee was also the key to my consideration of the presidency of the University of Memphis, and the search committee's consideration of me. I had knowledge of the state, the issues, the challenges, and had enjoyed some measure of success in working with urban school districts in Fairfax, Virginia and Tampa, Florida. Since the University of Memphis prepares more of the teachers for Memphis and Shelby County than any other college or university, our stake in the success of the surrounding school districts is key to how we are perceived as a College of Education and, indeed, as a university.

When the position of president of the University of Memphis was announced in 2000, I was a vice chancellor of Academic Services and dean of the College of Education at the University of Kentucky. Simultaneously holding two key positions in a university certainly placed me in the arena of interactions with presidents and was good preparation for the intensity and organization needed in the presidency. While the search firms found me soon after becoming a vice-chancellor, it was not until a confidante, a former president, suggested that I should be considering presidencies that I seriously entertained the idea.

As a native Tennessean, I have been grateful to the citizens of my state for a public education from elementary through graduate school. I have also been grateful to donors for the scholarships that enabled me to pursue higher education. At some point in one's career, the urge to give back becomes strong. My decision to accept the presidency was cemented while reading newspaper accounts of Tennessee's intense interest in improving P–12 education, the desperate straits of schools in jeopardy of being taken over by the state, and the tremendous need of a state with a severely undereducated population in terms of college degrees.

In an article entitled "The Leader's Greatest Gift," Chip R. Bell asks, "Why are you here, in this role, at this time? What difference will you being here make? What legacy will you leave behind? Will you be forgotten for what you maintained or remembered for what you added?" (1996, p. 13). These questions are particularly salient for me, as an educator, when I consider my potential impact on teacher education at the University of Memphis. Leadership, Bell contends, is fundamentally about influencing others through passionate connections. For me, this starts with selecting leaders for the university and for our initiatives who have a deep knowledge about their field combined with a passion for the importance of their work to the university and to society in general. I believe this is the essence of effective leadership in higher education.

THE UNIVERSITY OF MEMPHIS: POSITIONED FOR POSITIVE CHANGE IN TEACHER EDUCATION

Within a 100 mile radius of the center of Memphis, across two state lines, is a population of more than two million people. The 18th largest city in the nation, Memphis is a major medical, transportation, communication, and distribution center for the nation. It is also an urban center with all the social, economic, and educational issues typically associated with metropolitan life. For a lifelong educator from Tennessee, Memphis presents an irresistible challenge.

I became president of the University of Memphis in July 2001. The University of Memphis, an urban research institution founded as West Tennessee Normal School in 1912, is the largest local university and the flagship of the Tennessee Board of Regents system. We have approximately 20,000 students (approximately three-quarters undergraduates and one-quarter graduate or law students), more than 2,500 full-time employees, and, according to the Memphis Area Chamber of Commerce, pump more than $1 billion into the local economy annually.

The university's student body is diverse, with a 40 percent minority population (35% American, 5% international). We meet the needs of this diverse population through more than 129 areas of study. New degrees in fields such as health care administration, bioinformatics, and hotel and resort management ensure that our graduates can obtain the educational foundation necessary to succeed in our rapidly changing world.

Several characteristics distinguish the University of Memphis from other urban institutions of similar size and create a unique context for teacher preparation here. First, and most obvious, is the fact that approximately 80 percent of our student body comes from Memphis and Shelby County. Many of these students are the products of Memphis City or Shelby County Schools; in fact, Fall 2001 statistics reported that approximately one-third of our undergraduate population came from Memphis City Schools (MCS).

Second, the University of Memphis has a large number of nontraditional and transfer students. In recent years, first-time freshmen made up only one-tenth of our total student population. Although most graduating seniors in Shelby County are typical in their desire to go away to school, the percentage of those who return after a year or two to complete their education with us is greater than one would expect. As our director of Admissions says, many students can't wait to get away from Memphis, but then a lot of them come back home.

Third, graduates of the University of Memphis tend to stay in Memphis. A conservative estimate of the number of alumni currently living and working in the Memphis area is about 100,000. This figure includes a majority of the teachers in the Memphis City and Shelby County Schools, as well as those in the surrounding counties in Northern Mississippi and Eastern Arkansas. Given this pattern of alumni remaining in the area, the opportunity to graduate and place highly qualified teachers who are familiar with the culture of our region not only benefits the region's schools and their students, but also contributes to our success at the University of Memphis. Our university is truly a central segment of the lifelong learning cycle in Memphis. The products of K–12 schools become our students. The graduates of our programs become the parents and teachers of children in the K–12 schools...and the cycle continues.

As I have come to know the city and the university—and appreciate our interconnectedness—I have begun to envision a level of public engagement that I believe will become my legacy. I see the University of Memphis as a living laboratory for government, industry, and, of course, for education that will help to shape the future for our city. I believe that both the university and the city have attained a level of readiness for such engagement and both will benefit from the impetus of committed executive leadership at the university, working with our partners in the community.

Three themes have directed my approach to education and my vision for a publicly engaged university. Through strategic planning and specific actions, I am helping to create the passionate connections that I believe are necessary for the University of Memphis to excel. This vision involves (1) investing in people, (2) creating interdisciplinary initiatives, and (3) building productive partnerships.

These three themes are best illustrated in my response to one of the first challenges I faced as a new president: launching two simultaneous searches for deans of both the College of Education and the College of Arts and Sciences. The searches gave me a unique opportunity to find outstanding leadership, to emphasize my expectations that educating teachers was the interdisciplinary job of both colleges, and to foster new partnerships, both on campus and with the educational community.

Investing in more good people to join our university's dedicated faculty and staff was key to the College of Education, as well as other university initiatives. The investment in people is congruent with my concerns for P–12 education and is seminal to our success at the University of Memphis.

Encouraging interdisciplinary relationships is also vital. Representatives from both colleges served on each other's search committees. Chairs of the search committees met with me and accepted the challenge for dynamic leadership to recruit and aggressively engage the academic community and the community-at-large in review of the finalists.

Any search process for a new dean is characterized by many twists and turns, but the guiding principle that the search committee clearly understood was the need for deans who would be engaged with the public schools. The Provost and I met together with the search committee to set the charge from the beginning: select leaders who were passionate about interdisciplinary initiatives and community partnerships. As the first indicator of our shared concerns, I appointed to the College of Education search committee one of the members of the Board of Education and two associate superintendents. They served enthusiastically and without reservation, from the early tasks of writing the position description to the final hiring. As a result, the selected dean had contacts and support within the school systems even before he arrived on campus. He now holds appointments to the two school superintendents' staffs and began working closely with P–12 administrators as soon as he came to Memphis.

Provost Ralph Faudree and I shared the vision of the University of Memphis with all of the finalists and tested their stated values of diversity and engagement with the community through intensive questioning and examination of their past experiences. Thoroughness and concrete examples of their past leadership led to the selection of Ric Hovda as dean of the College of Education, an external candidate, and Henry Kurtz, dean of Arts and Sciences, an internal candidate. Our commitment to interdisciplinary partnerships has already born fruit. Both deans are coprincipal investigators in grants with both the Memphis City Schools and the Shelby County Schools. They have become partners on campus and industriously work for the improvement of teacher education.

Such partnerships will be important as we move forward with positive change in teacher education in Memphis. Teacher education and P–12 schools in Memphis are at a pivotal juncture, a point we've heard repeatedly at the more than 200 community speeches and forum meetings we have held. It is a time during which many of the major players have changed, and powerful economic and political forces are at work. While my work as a new president is just beginning, we now have in place the people who share a passion for education and the partnerships that can make change possible.

MEMPHIS AND OUR REGION

Memphis is located in Shelby County in the southwest corner of Tennessee. It is bordered on the west by the Mississippi River and the state of Arkansas, and on the south by the state of Mississippi. Population in the Metropolitan Service Area recorded in the 2000 census was 1.1 million. Memphis and Shelby County have separate governments and separate school systems.

The second largest port on the nation's inland waterway system, Memphis has a rich rivertown history, which includes playing a pivotal role in the Civil War and enduring the yellow fever epidemics in the mid-1800s that killed or chased away two-thirds of the population, causing the city to declare bankruptcy. For more than a century, cotton has been the dominant agricultural product of the region, and King Cotton is still celebrated here in annual carnivals.

Today, Memphis may be best known for its rich musical heritage. With Graceland, home of Elvis Presley, and Beale Street, home of the blues, the city attracts tourists from across the nation and the world. From opera to rhythm and blues, rock and roll, and jazz, Memphis and music are synonymous.

No less well-known are the major business enterprises that call Memphis home. FedEx Corporation, founded here in 1972 by Frederick Smith, is by far the city's largest employer with nearly 30,000 employees. FedEx is known worldwide for logistics and supply chain management.

Kemmons Wilson opened his first Holiday Inn in Memphis in 1952, and he remained one of the city's most prominent citizens and benefactors until his death in February 2003. Mr. Wilson provided funding for the new Kemmons Wilson School of Hospitality and Resort Management at the University of Memphis, which houses an operating, full-service hotel franchise.

The city is also known for its quality health care, and is the location of St. Jude's Children's Research Hospital and the University of Tennessee Health Sciences Center. The biomedical field is also beginning to attain prominence. Through medical device industries such as Medtronics, Smith-Nephew, and Wright Medical, Memphis is becoming known for research and distribution in the field of health care.

The University of Memphis has historically maintained relationships with these three major industries. To be truly engaged, however, requires stronger, more proactive partnerships than this university has ever known. We are seeking and creating those partnerships now.

One of our new partnerships is the FedEx Technology Institute being constructed on the University of Memphis campus. Underwritten by a $25 million public-private partnership, the institute will provide an information technology infrastructure for multiple centers and academic programs. Basic funding for the Institute was obtained before I arrived at the university; however, plans for its integration with the community and existing programs on campus, and especially with education, were unclear. Since the outcomes of our existing partnerships will be the benchmarks for developing new ones, I knew it was critical for an executive director to be named who could clearly understand and articulate the Institute's vision both on campus and in the community, and who could forge and nurture relationships with corporate, foundation, and university partners to ensure that the FedEx Technology Institute reaches its potential. I convinced Jim Phillips, a former executive at Skytel, Motorola, and iPIX, and distinguished University of Memphis alumnus, to bring his unique combination of technological and entrepreneurial expertise to the university. He and I meet weekly to discuss progress and I have made clear the importance of encouraging initiatives that will link teacher education with the technical resources of the Institute.

Engagement with the public schools in effective uses of instructional technology will be one of the programs of the Institute. A consortium of seven universities providing teachers to the Memphis City Schools— which includes the University of Memphis—has received one of IBM's $1.5 million Reinventing Education grants for a technology-based initiative to help prepare high-quality teachers. I met with the IBM team to assure them of our university's commitment to finding bold new ways of putting technology to work to prepare teachers, as exemplified by our commitment to the Institute. The teacher education program at the University of Memphis will incorporate the technologies of Learning Village software into our methods classes and field experiences.

MEMPHIS CITY AND SHELBY COUNTY SCHOOLS

The University of Memphis partners with two very different school districts. The largest school system in the state and the 20th largest metropolitan system in the nation, Memphis City Schools serve approximately 118,000 K–12 students in 175 facilities. The Shelby County Schools system administers 45 public schools in the county outside the Memphis City limits, serving more than 45,000 students.

Although schools within each system differ greatly from each other, the Memphis City Schools system generally can be characterized as urban, while Shelby County's schools are primarily suburban in nature. The State of Tennessee Department of Education's most recent Report Card awarded D's and F's in all subject areas except writing to Memphis schools, and A's and B's to Shelby County schools (2002).

Systemwide, approximately 70 percent of students in the city qualify for free or reduced-priced lunches, and 25 of the city's schools are designated "Priority 3" with poverty indices of 100 percent. Memphis City Schools students are 87 percent African American and slightly more than 9 percent white. The statistics are almost reversed for Shelby County, where three-quarters of the students are white and 22.3 percent African American. Overall, Shelby County's poverty index is 15 percent. Populations of Asian and Hispanic children, as well as children of other ethnicities, are low in both systems (Research Departments, Memphis City Schools and Shelby County Schools, personal communication, September 2002).

According to a study recently released by the Education Trust, 36 percent of Tennessee teachers are teaching classes out of their field, compared with the national average of 24 percent (Jerald, 2002). Although exact figures are not available from the school systems, we know that in the city approximately 800 teachers are teaching on provisional certificates or teaching classes for which they have not been certified. Clearly, the educational challenges in our region are great, as is the university's responsibility to assist in meeting them.

One of the major challenges the Memphis City Schools has faced recently is a period of change—in leadership and direction. In 1995, under the leadership of then-superintendent Jerry House, Memphis City Schools became a New American Schools (NAS) jurisdiction and began implementing the whole-school reform models endorsed by NAS. The initiative began with 34 pilot schools and, by the year 2000 every school in the district was expected to be engaged in whole-school reform using one of the NAS designs or another model approved by the district. Although initially viewed as vehicles for positive change and implemented with some enthusiasm in the early years, whole-school reform became unpopular across the district as implementation ceased to be voluntary.

The Center for Research in Educational Policy at the University of Memphis worked closely with Memphis City Schools to evaluate implementation of national whole-school reform models during the House administration. Steven Ross, Center director, describes in detail the Memphis school reform story and provides insight into the status of this large urban system at the time I became president:

> The expansion of the restructuring in 1998–99 from 70 to 161 schools put Memphis on the map as the only New American Schools jurisdiction to implement full systemic reform. It also introduced some policy decisions that appeared to increasingly weaken the reform initiative over time. First, the obviously large number of restructuring schools and the multiple models being used appeared to dilute the district's already stretched ability to support individual schools' efforts. Second, the district requirement that all schools adopt reforms unavoidably included relatively high-performing schools that didn't want to change their approaches, as well as very low performing schools with high teacher mobility and limited capacity for making substantive changes.... In the fall of 1999, Superintendent House...announced plans to leave the district. Concomitantly, during the 1999–2000 school year, commitment to the reform efforts at many schools diminished.... According to district staff members (including former design facilitators) who were interviewed, one apparent result of these actions was reduced quality in the implementation of the designs in many schools. Another was more vocal

opposition to the reforms.... Achievement gains plummeted in 2000 for schools in their fifth year of reform.... Comparable dips also occurred that year for the other reform cohorts and for the district overall (2001, p. 7).

Johnny B. Watson, a longtime Memphis educator and well respected in the community, succeeded House as interim superintendent and, following active recruitment and direct invitation by the School Board, assumed the position on a permanent basis. In the spring of 2001, the five-year districtwide comprehensive school reform initiative was discontinued.

With 73 of its schools identified by the state last year as "low performing," the system and its current superintendent are actively seeking successful strategies for these urban schools. As of August 2002, 32 of these struggling schools improved enough to avoid probation and are now classified as "on notice but improving." The remaining 46 risk state takeover if acceptable progress is not made during the coming school year.

The Shelby County School System also has undergone a recent superintendent change, however it is not confronted with the reform challenges that face the Memphis City Schools. None of the schools in Shelby County appear on Tennessee's list of low performing schools.

Periods of change can cause stress for university-community partnerships, especially when leadership also changes. I believe it is important that the University of Memphis continue to remain a constant partner with our school systems, and so, following the changes in superintendents, Center researchers continue to help school personnel document teaching and learning strategies in low performing schools. They also are conducting formative evaluation of new initiatives begun by Superintendent Watson. Fortunately for both the school system and the Center for Research in Educational Policy, the shared goal of helping to improve the city's schools has enabled this partnership to continue as district leadership has changed. I have also been active in speaking publicly in support of the districts and of our current superintendents, with the sincere message that the University of Memphis is a supportive partner involved in work for which there are no easy solutions or quick fixes.

THE COLLEGE OF EDUCATION AT THE UNIVERSITY OF MEMPHIS

Partnering with Memphis schools is not a new idea at the College of Education, which has been preparing teachers since 1912. Today the college enrolls 2,700 students in more than 60 undergraduate and graduate degree programs. Initial teacher education programs are offered in 27 licensure areas across five departments. The college also operates a campus elementary lab school, an early childhood education lab school, and two centers: The Center for Research in Educational Policy and the Center for the Study of Higher Education.

The students in our teacher preparation programs mirror in many ways the overall student characteristics of our university. A large percentage of our teacher education majors transfer to the College of Education from other colleges and majors. Many more are older, second career students; this is especially the case during times of economic downturn. Of the 406 Masters of Arts in Teaching students enrolled in a typical fall semester, more than half (57%) were age 30 or older, and 21 percent were in the 40 or older age bracket.

Approximately 40 percent of our teacher education graduates are employed by Memphis City Schools, and many more begin working in Shelby County each year. The systems' personnel departments cannot provide us with actual numbers of our graduates in their employment at a given time, and follow-up survey efforts from our college are not 100 percent successful, but any meeting of teachers in Shelby County will include a large percentage of University of Memphis graduates. When I spoke to more than 150 Memphis City Schools principals recently and asked how many held degrees from the University of Memphis, it appeared as though every hand was raised.

When I arrived at the University of Memphis two years ago, I found a teacher education program that I would characterize as solid, although not stellar. The college was celebrating NCATE accreditation and proud of the fact that no weaknesses were identified by the visiting team. Leadership at the College of Education is emerging from a lengthy period of transition. Before my arrival the former COE dean was tapped by the Tennessee Board of Regents to lead the complex project of combining two local community colleges, serving as interim president of the new institution for several months before assuming the position permanently. During this lengthy time period, the former associate dean served as interim for two years, postponing his retirement until the deanship was filled in 2002.

Fortunately, there has been stability in the office of Teacher Education. The current assistant dean worked in that office as the coordinator of student teaching and has developed and maintained strong working relationships with the city and county school systems as well as with some of the more rural systems in the surrounding area. She has been in place long enough to refine existing practices so that the department works smoothly and she is working with the new dean to explore ways to improve the teacher education program.

Existing partnerships between the College and the community and with other colleges and schools on campus, however, need to be strengthened. This was made clear to me when, as an introduction to the city, I spent a day with the superintendent of Memphis City Schools and visited four schools with him. During that time, which was very pleasant and cordial, I did not get a sense of common purpose or enthusiastic support for the improvement of teacher education. I was also concerned that, although we have 16 schools identified as Professional Development Schools (PDS), these sites were not highlighted as a part of the system's improvement efforts. It is important that the superintendent and I become partners in education, openly sharing common goals and concerns. To support our partnership and to symbolize it publicly, I have made a point to accept every public speaking invitation from the schools. Over the past two years I have given speeches in support of the schools and superintendent at everything from NEA banquets to a parent involvement conference.

The stage is set to positively impact teacher education and improve educational opportunities for all our citizens. My first steps as president to fulfill this potential are being taken by focusing on my three leadership themes to create passionate connections by investing in people, increasing interdisciplinary work, and building productive partnerships.

INVESTING IN PEOPLE

Investing in people first involves creating an exceptional leadership team that shares a unified vision and then helping to create an environment in which all faculty and staff can flourish. The first step in investing in people at the presidential level is recruiting the most highly qualified individuals possible. In terms of teacher education, that means ensuring that the decision makers at the University of Memphis have an understanding of the importance of preparing quality teachers for our nation's schools, of the relationship between studies in the content area and professional studies, and of the long-term impact of the teachers we prepare here on the students who will eventually come to us as freshmen. Our commitment to engagement and interdisciplinary initiatives must first be embraced by administrators at both the university and college levels if it is to be realized at the program development and classroom instruction levels. To use Phil Schlechty's often-repeated mantra, faculty will only *respect* and engage in cross-college collaboration when we continually make clear what we *expect* and back it up with our rewards systems—what we *inspect*.

I began by assembling a leadership team that understands my commitment to engagement and to education. Many new presidents rush to create their staff soon after they arrive. I found that it takes time to get to know the strengths of the people at the university and for them to understand their new leader. I have observed that it takes about a year for people to realize that the ideas and vision a new leader has are not just rhetoric. By the end of my first year, I had a team that believed in our vision and was eager to work to make it happen.

Our provost is an internationally respected mathematics scholar. A professor of mathematics and former dean of the College of Arts and Sciences, he is better prepared than most top-level administrators to provide the needed support for our College of Education.

My executive assistant has her doctorate in Educational Psychology and Research. I deliberately sought someone with a terminal degree because I wanted this individual to have credibility with the academic units. In terms of building a strong teacher education program for urban schools, her experience is invaluable. She directed the city schools' Teaching and Learning Academy before returning to the university, and spent the last five years engaged in school reform research through our Center for Research in Educational Policy.

As described earlier, in the past year, both the College of Education and the College of Arts and Sciences have appointed permanent deans after more than a year of interim leadership. The search for and selection of deans on a university campus is an extensive process involving college faculty and staff, college and university administrators, and students. The role of the president in the official search process is almost tangential; however, the culture of any campus is very much impacted by the priorities set by the president and the actions that follow those priorities. When an individual applies for a leadership position such as dean, he or she looks for evidence of a compatible environment. Therefore, my investment in the people who have become deans since my arrival began as soon as my belief system and priorities began to influence the culture of the University of Memphis. I have made it clear that we are seeking deans who are enthusiastic about high levels of engagement with our communities.

For teacher education at the University of Memphis to move forward, all barriers between the College of Education and the College of Arts and Sciences must come down. Faculty in the College of Arts and Sciences must see content-area preparation of teachers as an important mission. Under the leadership of the new dean, Henry Kurtz, I believe this will happen. His philosophy is clearly expressed in the following quote from the dean's page of the Arts and Sciences newsletter, published shortly after he arrived at the university: "Forget the ivory-tower image: this university is in the community, and of the community, and therefore we need you to help us build the first-rate programs our students and this community deserve" (2002, Spring, online).

Ric Hovda, the dean of our College of Education, says openly that he was not seeking a new position when approached by a colleague about the search at our university. He changed his mind after spending some time learning about Memphis and its university. In his interview session with College faculty, he stated, "I think there is tremendous potential here for redefining the role of higher education in community engagement and the legitimacy of teacher education." In his early stages as dean, Hovda has taken some critical steps. Building on the theme of investment in people, one of his first decisions was to identify an individual whose primary responsibility is faculty professional development. This person occupies an assistant dean position, which underscores the value now being placed on investing in the quality faculty who will lead the future University of Memphis.

Another early decision was the designation of a director of accreditation to assist departments with ensuring that program standards are met and that units receive and maintain accredited status. Since preparing application materials and arranging for accreditation site visits are usually added duties for faculty and administrators, the presence of a knowledgeable individual whose defined role is to assist with this important work is another kind of investment in the people who make up the College of Education.

We know that high-quality faculty and staff are not attracted to a college or university by salary alone. We also know that, given Tennessee's current financial situation, we may not be able to offer the most competitive salaries. Now more than ever, we must work to create an attractive work environment in which people feel valued, energized, and engaged. One way in which I have tried to energize faculty and staff at the University of Memphis is by using project teams to tackle individual challenges and initiatives. I especially like to create teams around inventive projects that can distinguish our university and that offer members of the team the opportunity to work creatively. Recently, for example, we renovated a building for student and academic services. It involved a lot of hard work for the project team but it also encouraged team building and creative problem solving.

Building a team of outstanding people is important, but as a leader, I must also hold them accountable for results. Accountability for results in improved teaching education is only possible when everyone has the right kind of data to make informed decisions—data that more often than not must come from research and practice. Our College of Education has a wealth of expertise that can be directed toward improved teacher education. One of Tennessee's four principal investigators for the Student Teacher Achievement Ratio (STAR) project is John Johnston. The STAR study provided evidence that class size affects student achievement (smaller classes really are better!) and was foundational to Tennessee's Basic Education Program funding plan.

As mentioned previously, the College houses one of Tennessee's Centers of Excellence, the Center for Research in Educational Policy, directed by Steven Ross. The center has become nationally known for its expertise in research and evaluation related to teacher education and comprehensive school reform. In cooperation with William Sanders of the University of Tennessee, the center conducted longitudinal research to determine the achievement effects of implementing comprehensive school reform models. Center researchers are actively involved in Tennessee and nationally in school-based research and formative and summative evaluation.

INCREASING INTERDISCIPLINARY WORK

The most immediate and obvious way in which teacher education is benefiting from our emphasis on increasing interdisciplinary work is the improving relationship between the College of Education and the College of Arts and Sciences. Eliminating silos among various academic and administrative units on campus and developing a collaborative culture in which territoriality is minimized is a major challenge. With deans in both of these colleges who are determined to work cooperatively, we are moving toward interdisciplinary success.

In terms of P–16 education, interdisciplinary initiatives can be defined as those that have systemic impact—that cross barriers among schools as well as among disciplines. Many of our faculty members have worked diligently and successfully with small programs or individual schools. However, their impact is negligible in the face of the number of schools and the amount of need unless the program or model can be taken to scale and institutionalized. It is significant that of 14 outreach programs for K–12 students, 12 examples of faculty involvement in teacher training and curriculum reform initiatives, and 27 basic or applied research projects listed by faculty of the College of Arts and Sciences for 2002, not one involved faculty from the College of Education. Faculty from both colleges have regularly partnered with groups of students and/or teachers, individual schools, or local school systems—but they have not formed partnerships with each other.

As president, I found this situation to be unacceptable. Working through the provost, I have communicated to both the College of Education and the College of Arts and Sciences that a strong partnership between the colleges is critical to the success of both. Both deans have approached their college leadership roles believing that collaborative efforts are not only beneficial but also necessary, and have engaged in planning to achieve that goal. Eventually, they expect faculty in their respective colleges to work cooperatively to examine and redesign teacher education programs. However, their first challenge is to jointly design and champion a major cultural shift.

The first step in preparing for new ways of working together was a simple act with a strong message. The dean of the College of Education met with Arts and Sciences Faculty, and the dean of Arts and Sciences met with faculty of the College of Education. They discussed areas of common interest and responsibility, highlighting areas in which outreach, professional development, and research would benefit from shared expertise. As a result, at the Fall 2002 College of Education faculty meeting, one of the year's priorities was described as "establishing and/or examining existing partnerships with key stakeholders and university units to ensure viable, valued, visible, and vital collaborative relations with mutually accepted goals, outcomes, and accountability measures."

The recently obtained "Teaching American History" grant for nearly $1 million from the U.S. Department of Education is indicative of major steps in the right direction for these two colleges. The goal of the project is to improve the achievement of American history students in low-performing schools. The grant was collaboratively written, and the interdisciplinary program will be collaboratively implemented, by faculty from the Political Science and History departments from the College of Arts and Sciences; faculty from the Department of Instruction and Curriculum Leadership from the College of Education; and Memphis City Schools personnel.

The colleges have also made plans for an Institute for Excellence in Teaching and Learning, the purpose of which is to develop a comprehensive approach to improving and sustaining the highest levels of teaching and learning in the Memphis region. They plan to collaborate in the areas of recruitment, formal teacher preparation, and continuous professional development for teachers, capacity building at school sites, and research and development.

BUILDING PRODUCTIVE PARTNERSHIPS

Nurturing old partnerships and forging new ones is not the sole responsibility of the university president. But it is my responsibility to encourage my leadership team—and their faculty and staffs—actively to cultivate community relationships. Before deciding to come to Memphis, the COE dean met with the city schools superintendent to ensure that a stronger partnership between the College of Education and Memphis City Schools could be built and sustained. As a result of his early contacts, the dean was invited to go to Harvard to attend a leadership academy with Memphis City Schools executive staff. Participation in this high-level professional development session, which occurred before he moved to Memphis and assumed his responsibilities as dean, quickly established a partnership that is critical for moving forward. "It's all about relationships," says this new college leader, and he is moving quickly to establish those relationships.

The new partnership with Memphis City Schools greatly increases our opportunities for systemic influence. The dean's presence in MCS Executive Council meetings allows him to keep his finger on the pulse of the district and to stay abreast of changing priorities and concerns. He can gather information to take back to the college that can be used to guide decision making for programmatic and research priorities.

At the same time, the dean will have a forum for discussing College of Education initiatives and garnering understanding of and support for those initiatives within the district. If a strategy, approach, program, or initiative is shown to produce the desired outcomes on a small scale, a case can be made at the highest level of the district for marshaling resources and expanding to similar schools so that more children can benefit. Essentially, the bureaucratic structures of both the university and the school system that have blocked open communication and prevented timely and efficient action are being circumvented by the action of a dean who understands how large urban school systems and large urban universities work.

Facilitating greater communication between campus and community is central to building effective partnerships. While the role of the dean is essential in keeping the channels open, as president, I have definite responsibilities as well. In addition to encouraging the deans to find their public voice, I can add the voice of the university when needed. It can be a difficult line to draw, but it is important to choose those occasions and opportunities at which I join the deans in endorsing their efforts to the community and adding the imprimatur of the university.

I can also assist campus leaders in making sure that the partnerships they create are productive ones. I can help remove barriers to partnerships by accessing resources, helping to reprioritize projects or assembling people. It is my responsibility to learn about initiatives, commend individuals for their efforts and, with my provost and vice presidents, offer support to the deans and their faculty. Passionate connections are forged when great ideas become breakthrough initiatives. We in universities are often very good at generating those great new ideas, but we're not always as good at following up with results, especially when our ideas involve the hard work of collaborating on community-led initiatives. To help the university with our partnership efforts I appointed David Cox from the School of Urban Affairs and Public Policy to my office to oversee our community efforts. His responsibility is to make sure that when we launch a new partnership we have the requisite planning and follow up in place to assure success. If we are to be credible partners with our communities they must be able to count on us to deliver results as well as ideas. Universities are complex places and it is important for me as president to be aware of the multitude of projects and their progress so that I, too, can be accountable for their success.

There are a number of recently launched partnerships that hold promise for significant results. The dean is restructuring the College of Education Advisory Board to ensure that all members understand and are committed to the university's goals for teacher education and other programs in the College. He, as well as the deans of other colleges, is involving the advisory board in development initiatives in addition to other support activities.

Professional Development Schools currently in place are being evaluated to determine their effects on and value to all partners. To be successful, PDS's must serve as an incubator for teaching and learning strategies. It is important that the children and adults in each individual school receive the educational benefits of the partnership; however, it is essential that the entire school system, as well as our teacher education curriculum, is positively influenced—that the concentration of resources in these few schools produce outcomes that have positive impact on a much larger scale.

Although the earliest and most focused efforts at college-school partnerships occurred with Memphis City Schools, relationships are also being nurtured with the large Shelby County School system and with smaller, more rural systems in west Tennessee to ensure rural student teacher placements.

A new major partnership initiative already beginning is the design and implementation of a new Leadership Academy. We do not have enough qualified individuals to lead our urban schools, and high-quality administrators are necessary for school improvement. Our administrative certification program needs comprehensive revision. Together with the Memphis City Schools superintendent, the dean is gathering a group of outstanding principals and other leadership experts to work with the College and Memphis City Schools to design this Academy.

One powerful addition to the Leadership Academy task force that further strengthens the tie between education and practice is the creation of a new "School Leader in Residence" position. James B. Mitchell, Jr., the recently retired and highly respected superintendent of Shelby County Schools, has agreed to accept this challenge. His experience and insight will be an invaluable resource, as he works with students, teaches in the college, serves on planning teams, develops initiatives, and assists in networking with school superintendents throughout west Tennessee.

One cross-functional initiative underway with a central role for the College of Education is the Advanced Learning Center. Organized and supported by the Offices of the Provost and Information Systems, the Center receives additional support from the FedEx Technology Institute. Its focus is on quality teaching, deep thinking, and the effective application of advanced technology tools and methodologies to achieve the best possible learning experience for every student. The Advanced Learning Center will be a major vehicle for improving the FITness (Fluency with Information Technology) of all our faculty and students and will help us prepare teachers who are technology users.

LOOKING AHEAD WITH HOPE AND CONFIDENCE

As I close this chapter, I am entering my second year as president of the University of Memphis. We have much to accomplish here, and the need is great, but the foundation we are building is strong. We are investing in the right people and those people are investing in each other and in P–16 education through strong partnerships. We are working across disciplines to break down traditional barriers in the interest of systemic change. We are searching for measurable solutions to the challenges that face us—solutions that can help our community by improving teaching and learning at all levels. We are becoming a university more engaged in all aspects of the community in which we live and work—the community that provides the majority of our students and for which we educate the majority of teachers and, directly or indirectly, the majority of citizens.

We are fortunate to have individuals and foundations in Memphis with the improvement of education as a central mission. As we move forward with the P–16 concept, as we make strides in the improvement of teaching and learning at all levels, we know we can count on their help and support.

This is just the first chapter of what I hope and believe will be an urban education success story. I believe that I am meant to be here, in this role, at this time. Because of my background as a teacher and my own passionate belief in the importance of education, I feel able to "influence others through passionate connections," to use Chip Bell's phrase, through this position as president of an urban research university. I am confident that we are positioned for positive change in teacher education and for ever-increasing levels of public engagement. I look forward to the chapters ahead.

Shirley C. Raines *is the 11th president of the University of Memphis and the first woman to hold the office. Previously she was vice chancellor for academic services and dean of the College of Education at the University of Kentucky in Lexington; she has also held academic appointments in education at numerous institutions throughout the Midwest and Southeast and early in her career was a teacher in Kentucky and Indiana. She holds a doctorate in education from the University of Tennessee in Knoxville and has also completed the Management Development Program from the Harvard Graduate School of Education. She was also selected for the Knight Foundation's Higher Education Executive Training Program at the Wharton School of the University of Pennsylvania. Widely regarded as an expert in early childhood and teacher education, Dr. Raines is immediate past president of the Association for Childhood Education International, an organization more than 100 years old with members in 72 different nations. She has received two distinguished research awards from the Eastern Educational Research Association as well as the Phi Delta Kappa Chapter Award for Distinguished Service to Education.*

BIBLIOGRAPHY

Bell, C. R. (1996, October). The leader's greatest gift. *Executive Excellence*, 13–14.

Jerald, C. D. (2002). *All talk, no action: Putting an end to out-of-field teaching.* The Education Trust. Retrieved March 11, 2003, from http://www.edtrust. org/main/main/reports.asp.

Kurtz, H. (2002, Spring). From the Dean. *Profiles, 1*(1), 2. College of Arts & Sciences, The University of Memphis. Retrieved March 31, 2003, from http://cas.memphis.edu/profiles_spr_02/kurtz.html.

Ross, Steven. (2001, December). *Creating critical mass for restructuring: What we can learn from Memphis.* AEL Policy Briefs. Charleston, WV: AEL.

State of Tennessee Department of Education. (2002). *Tennessee School System 2002 Report Card.* Retrieved March 31, 2003, from http://www.k-12.state.tn. us/rptcrd02/.

CHAPTER 11

Filling in the Moat: A Case Study of Presidential Leadership in Recruiting, Preparing, and Retaining Urban Educators

Michael Schwartz

Building relationships requires reaching out to district officials at all levels: counselors, teachers, administrators, and the superintendent and her chief academic officer. At another level, it requires that I paint a new portrait of who we are at Cleveland State, one that both my university colleagues and those colleagues in the schools can recognize, believe in, and live out.

I arrived at Cleveland State University (CSU) in April 2001 as interim president. I had previously returned to teaching at neighboring Kent State University, where I had enjoyed an eight-and-a-half year tenure as president. I accepted the position of interim president, assuming I would hold down the fort for what I imagined would be a short term of no more than 16 months. Being from a nearby institution, I thought I had a good understanding of the terrain and, I reasoned, I could use my experiences at CSU when I returned to teaching higher education classes at Kent State. Little did I know I would fall in love with the place and the people who work and study here. CSU got under my skin when I saw the university's potential, solved a few problems, talked to students who were seeking a more meaningful future and wanted our help getting there, and worked with good people who really cared about the institution, want to be of service, and get better at what they do. I guess I got under CSU's skin as well, for on November 13, 2001, the Board of Trustees voted unanimously to appoint me as the institution's fifth president in 38 years.

As I began my explorations of the university—getting to know the university and its community—I found the institution to be in some fiscal and administrative turmoil. Many administrators had the word *interim* in front of their titles and budget cutting was the order of the day. More troubling, I also perceived an invisible chasm between the university and its surrounding city. It was a kind of social moat I vowed to fill. That moat aptly serves as a metaphor for the challenges of creating partnerships for recruiting, preparing, and retaining urban educators. And, to fill the moat, I believe academics—university presidents and their faculties—must increasingly take on the role of "the public intellectual." By public intellectual I mean an individual within the academy who focuses research efforts *outward*, rather than inward, who conducts and shares scholarship beyond the academic community with communities that can benefit from the results and theoretical implications of that research. Many intellectuals within the university community tend to focus their work inward, publishing and sharing the results of their research with other academics in their particular fields and disciplines. They attend conferences and contribute to publications that reach like-minded academics. Public intellectuals, however, turn outward, working within the community to solve problems through the knowledge they generate and use in their academic endeavors.

I believe that, as public intellectuals, we need to participate more fully in agenda setting for urban communities and then become part of the solution to urban problems. In my role as president, I have begun to forge the groundwork for senior faculty, like me, to take our ideas out into the community to address real problems and engage real people in the intellectual dialogues that not only fill the moat but forge relationships that are binding, politically and economically reinforcing our efforts to build a stronger local and global economy.

A UNIVERSITY AND COMMUNITY PROFILE

CSU is the most diverse public institution in Ohio, serving 15,746 students in 2001, of whom 17.6 percent were African American and 2.4 percent Hispanic. Our College of Education serves 2,788 students, of whom almost 20 percent are African American and 2.4 percent Hispanic. Academically the university is dedicated to strong faculty research, large graduate enrollments, accessibility, and an urban focus. CSU has built a strong technological platform for classroom instruction over the past decade and today offers compressed video instruction at 10 remote locations in the region with interactive connections available worldwide. We currently partner with more than 100 civic, nonprofit, and corporate entities in the region including more than 60 education and social service agencies.

CSU serves our student community at a relatively modest cost to students and accepts students who are willing to work hard, strive, and achieve often in spite of disadvantaged backgrounds. CSU's students generally come to the university with the firm intention of changing their lives and the life of the whole community for the better—and they do it: 85 percent of CSU's graduates remain in northeast Ohio to live and work. The faculty is the instrument of that change; I learned early in my experiences on this campus that the faculty takes responsibility for the success of our students' futures very seriously. The shared goal of our faculty and staff is for CSU to be a student-focused center of scholarly excellence where teaching and research feed off each other for the benefit of students. I have learned that CSU is perfectly positioned and capable of making wonderful changes in the lives of people in the community. CSU changes lives, one student at a time.

The city of Cleveland and the entire region need a strong public university. Cleveland, similar to most other major urban centers, faces increasing problems of poverty. Unemployment is high and there is a critical need for workforce development. The Cleveland Municipal School District (CMSD) serves about 73,000 students, 71 percent of whom are black, 8 percent Hispanic, and 20 percent white (2000–2001 Annual Report).

Unlike many urban districts, the administrative leaders of the CMSD—that is, the school board and the chief academic officer (rather than the superintendent)—are appointed by the mayor. This current form of governance followed a 20-year revolving door period of 10 different superintendents appointed by an elected school board and resulted from a federal judicial decision that transferred the control from the school board to the Ohio State Superintendent of Education. In 1995 the state superintendent appointed a deputy state superintendent, responsible solely for the Cleveland Municipal Schools, who turned to then-mayor Michael White for assistance. In 1996 they created a Strategy Council to engage the broader community to help create a plan for district governance and responsibility. Together, civic leaders, parents, philanthropic leaders, and politicians created a plan to improve public education that placed primary responsibility for the district in the mayor's hands. In 1998, Mayor Michael White appointed the first chief executive officer of the CMSD—Barbara Byrd-Bennett, a New York City veteran administrator with a reputation for making a difference in student achievement in the schools under her tutelage.

As the new CEO, Byrd-Bennett redesigned the central administration of the district and, to assure fiscal and educational responsibilities were being met, reinforced newly negotiated Academic Achievement Plans that were cocreated by teachers and administrators at every school. In her four-year tenure, she developed a positive reputation for creating changes that would result in higher levels of student achievement, better attendance, and the retention of high quality teachers.

I serve as an ex officio member of the CMSD School Board and have made a habit of visiting local schools not only to identify needs and offer service but also to engage local political and economic leaders in the community in dialogue about our most pressing educational issues. During my visits I learned that the district is one of four in Ohio rated by the State Department of Education as in "academic emergency" for meeting only three of the 22 standards on which the statewide rating is based. While there has been improvement in scores over the past three years, less than a quarter of sixth-grade students, for example, can pass the reading, science, or math proficiency tests (*District Level Performance*, 2002). Only about 35 percent of ninth-grade students will graduate from high school—and that low figure does not include the large number of children who never become ninth graders.

This dropout rate is an indicator of an even more serious problem: urban educators' sheer despair over their inability to impact the achievement gap and increase students' abilities to pass state-mandated proficiency examinations. Given this tragic situation, I believe it is an ethical responsibility of CSU and those who work in it to serve as public intellectuals, using what they know about their disciplines to participate in community-wide partnerships to address these serious concerns. This has become the focus of much of my work and our university's work with the urban district and our community.

DEVELOPING A VISION

Creating a vision for a large, urban university is essential and yet it is the day-to-day work, creating the conditions that allow us to accomplish the elements of that vision, that are most important and key to presidential leadership. One of the most obvious conditions that faced me as I sought to define CSU's future was its isolation from the community—physically, symbolically, intellectually, and economically.

Perched close to the shore of Lake Erie and close to the halls of the city government, the public schools, world-renowned museums, and the symphony, the CSU campus is central to the life of the city, however, the campus could not easily be identified as Cleveland State University. Although we house our administrative offices in one of the tallest buildings in the city, nowhere could anyone easily see our name—not from the sidewalk, the highway, or the air. One could literally walk the campus without finding any identifying traces of our name except on official publications and stationery. While we might be at the decision-making table, CSU appeared invisible in the city and was often confused with a local community college. I learned quickly that distinguishing ourselves as an urban university wasn't enough to sustain partnerships with the district and other local institutions and to secure continued funding from our distinguished foundations. I decided to establish an identity for CSU—first, physically, by ensuring that our name and the location of colleges and offices were prominently displayed near sidewalks and walkways and posted atop our tallest building for all of Cleveland to see, and second, with a strong, well defined and publicly understood vision statement.

As I met with members of the CSU community, I gained a sense of who we are and what we hope for, redefining my own perception of the University. With input from the faculty, staff, students, administrators, and other community members, we drafted this initial vision statement, which reflects not only my beliefs but also what I heard from my community:

> We will be recognized as a student-focused center of scholarly excellence that provides an accessible and exceptional education to all. We will be a place of opportunity for those who seek truth, strive toward excellence and seek a better life for themselves and for their fellow citizens. As a leader in innovative collaboration—both internally and externally—with business, industry, government, educational institutions and the community, the University will be a critical force in the region's economic development. We will be at the forefront of moral, ethical, social, artistic, and economic leadership for the future and embrace the vitality that comes with risk. We will be the strongest public university in the region and be known for our scholarship in service to students and to our community.

Inherent in this vision statement are not only my commitment to our role as public intellectuals contributing to the well-being and prosperity of our community but also my belief that CSU must be recognized for its moral, ethical, social, artistic, and economic leadership by using scholarship to serve both students and the broader community. Such intentions require considerable risk on our part, risks that require intellectual, emotional, and economic support. Realizing such a vision requires integrity and some courage.

Our need for courage calls to mind a recent visit I made to a local elementary school as "principal for a day." I had the pleasant task of reading to the kindergarten class. After I finished, I asked the children what the story was about. Literal-minded as they were, they replied, "fish." I smiled, "this is really about courage," I told them. "It's about doing the right thing even when it's hard." That's what being an academic, what being a university president, is all about. As I told these youngsters, "it's all about opportunity. We can give you the chance. If you can take advantage of it, the whole world opens up to you." In these words are reflected my own father's wisdom, "learn as much as you can about as many things as you can, and you'll find your way in the world." My way is to pave the ground for others to walk along with me while making their own way.

ACTING THROUGH DEMOCRACY

Public education is the foundation of our democracy, a democracy that becomes more complex and more threatened every day. I believe that higher education helps people defend their own personal liberty while protecting the democracy that binds and protects us. The words inscribed on the May 4 Memorial at Kent State University inform all who read them of the business of higher education: "Inquire, Learn, Reflect." To those words, I add, "Act." Education that does not lead to action is education that has been wasted.

If we don't provide every child with an environment in which achievement is possible and expected, we will pay a heavy price, one that will stifle the economic development of our urban communities and encourage a "brain-drain" of educated citizens away from the metropolitan areas that need them most. This reality both creates fear and stimulates the courage that local citizens—educators, politicians, entrepreneurs, philanthropists, and clergy—must muster to keep our children in school and to provide them with the high-quality education that can stimulate intellectual, social, personal, civic, and economic growth and initiative.

The prevailing and simplistic public and legislative view in Ohio (and many other states)—that higher education is nothing more than job training—is unacceptable. Students need to *learn how to learn*, because their first job will most certainly not be their last. They must understand that there is life after work. They need to know the place of the arts and humanities in their lives. They need to have some understanding of human culture. And, especially now, they need to understand the complexities of citizenship in a rapidly changing and complex democracy, threatened as it is by antidemocratic forces. Education is about living a life and coming together as a community; as an urban university we should try to act upon this Deweyan ideal. Therefore, during my first year as president I spent many hours getting to know the community, the schools, the university, and their various intersections. My aim was simple: heal the divisions between CSU and the community, form coherent partnerships, and help develop secondary education with the clear understanding of CSU's importance to the community.

During my first year, not only did I serve as ex officio member of the appointed Cleveland Municipal School Board, I visited *every* Cleveland Municipal high school, making students more aware of their opportunities at CSU. I met with principals and counselors and listened to what they needed from CSU. I met with students and encouraged them to do good work, have courage, accept the challenge, and join us at the university. Every school I visited—and every principal, counselor, teacher, and student I met—taught me something new. It is a humbling thing to know that after 40 years of teaching, I am still learning new things every day.

I learned that some schools need simple things from the university: teachers need someone to talk to about mathematics or science education, how to set up a new lab, and how to motivate students. Also, I learned that some schools need big things from the university, for example, a place to house 400 displaced seniors whose high school was scheduled for renovation. I realized students might not even be aware that the university is here to serve them and many don't know how they can go about pursuing a university education. Helping them understand life's possibilities is a responsibility that weighs heavily on our collective shoulders.

I also learned that one of the greatest forces at work in the lives of Cleveland children is the faith community. In our case, it is represented by the Cleveland United Pastors in Mission, a group of about 70 local African American pastors who directly impact the spiritual, economic, and political lives of many in our community.

My new understanding of the schools, their governing board, and the United Pastors led me to take a relational stance to my work. I learned in my travels that a deep distrust of CSU, rooted in a fear of racism, was undermining my attempts to fill in the moat between the Cleveland Municipal Schools and the university. I heard rumblings—30-year-old stories that characterized CSU in a grim manner. I learned that the African American community often saw our university as racist. At the same time, whites in the first ring of suburbs viewed our university as "a black school."

I sought to meet head on that challenge of conflicting and erroneous impressions by hosting a series of dinner parties where I could meet with principals, counselors, and other members of the community to discuss how we might build bridges, reinforce each others' efforts, and lend support by providing the kind of educational experiences that would keep our youth in school and also provide them with high-quality experiences that will lead to their individual success and our community's further development.

Through our informal gatherings we got to know each other, trust each other, and share each other's concerns for quality education such as the re-cruitment and retention of highly qualified teachers, the recruitment and preparation of highly competent school administrators, and the role of the family and extended family in helping keep children in school. In addition, on two occasions, I invited all members of the United Pastors in Mission and their partners to the CSU campus for dinner. Almost all came. The first meeting was a meeting of the minds to discuss our interdependence and need to rely more on each other for support. At the next dinner meeting, we ate, we small talked, and then we frankly discussed key issues. We agreed that a 35 percent high school graduation rate—which was news to some of the pastors—was unacceptable. We discussed the role of family support in making a dent in this statistic and we discussed the fact that, in many re-spects, the church is family for many children. The schools cannot make a difference without family support, that is, the support of the black pastors and their congregations. The result of the second dinner was plans for an education summit, where black pastors, CSU administrators and faculty, the chief academic officer of the CMSD, and other Cleveland teachers and parents would discuss what we could collectively do to improve the lives of our city's children and provide them with better opportunities.

I believe this is a clear example of my assuming the role of the public in-tellectual—by balancing the private and public nature of my work as an academic and bringing this work to a public audience determined to make a difference in our community. Too often, our work as academicians turns us inside toward other academics rather than toward public service or ad-dressing the social conditions that bind us and which can also threaten our freedom and democracy. It is through this activity of involving the public and playing critical roles in social and economic renewal that I see the greatest impact of my leadership as president. Reinforced by an institu-tional and civic environment that is supported by long-standing, respon-sive partnerships, my ability to provide leadership by addressing critical economic and educational issues is enhanced. A concomitant responsi-bility is to create an environment that both positions CSU as a civic leader and supports partnerships that address civic concerns.

RESPONDING TO A CALL(ING): A HISTORY OF INDIVIDUALS

CSU has a long history of partnering with the CMSD to recruit, pre-pare, and retain urban educators. The College of Education provides at least half of the teachers currently employed in CMSD and is educating all of CMSD teachers working toward alternative licensure. Many of our collaborative programs focused on high-need areas such as the preparation of competent teachers of special education, mathematics, and science. Beginning in the mid-1970s, for example, two dedicated faculty members in special education and science education began career-long efforts to provide the district with knowledgeable, skilled urban teachers. Over the combined 58 years of their teaching careers at CSU, these two individuals focused on improving pedagogical content and were responsible for directing more than 25 projects that attracted more than $20 million in funding, which provided for the professional development of more than 900 urban teachers. One might characterize each of these individuals as having a calling for urban teacher preparation; their work exemplifies a dedication to partnering with CMSD that is unsurpassed locally.

As with many university-school partnerships, however, many CSU collaborative programs were generally funded with soft money from grants and foundations and were not *systematically* designed to address local needs. Typically, CSU/CMSD partnerships, driven by a call for proposals or foundation requests, addressed an immediate need. While this built a temporary so-called bridge across the moat separating CSU from the surrounding community, over time, without sustained support, many of these bridges crumbled, their purpose served and initial goals met. Most CSU collaborations, in retrospect, were much the work of individual faculty members; their calling, more than any other impetus, fueled their efforts to sustain a partnership, which was difficult at best. All programs to support students' academic and classroom success faced the challenges of highly bureaucratic systems (both the university and the school district) and the difficulty of building relationships with ever-changing district supervisors, directors, and principals. As a new president, I was struck by the zeal, creativity, and professionalism with which individual faculty members built bridges but at the same time I was struck by their feelings of isolation from both CSU and CMSD.

Other College of Education faculty members have created a string of programs to assist the district in filling vacant teaching positions with qualified educators, to address the reform of schools and of professional practices, to retain new teachers through complex mentoring systems, and to provide professional development that leads to deeper understandings, stronger pedagogy, and better test scores. However, very few of the programs engaged a college other than the College of Education in efforts to prepare and retain highly qualified teachers. Less than a handful of more than 50 programs developed during the past 20 years engaged three or more colleges. Those programs that did involve the Colleges of Education and of Arts and Sciences defined the roles of faculty in ways that inhibited on-going interdisciplinary interactions about broader educational and economic concerns.

In recent years, the College of Education has worked more diligently to build on its partnerships, taking the lead in the state on alternative licensure in special education, mathematics, and science education, and in creating a 13-month master's program for the initial licensure of urban secondary teachers. Funded locally by foundations and by state and federal grants targeting alternative routes to teaching, especially for minority candidates and in high need areas, these programs have built on the long-standing partnerships with the CMSD.

Although these more recent activities are laudable, they have been mea-gerly supported by both the university and the school district. They exist largely because of a talented, dedicated faculty determined to prepare highly competent urban teachers. They exist in isolation, as bridges *across* the moat but not as groundswells that *fill* the moat, that link our institutions *structurally*.

Thus among my first tasks as president was to link CSU more closely to the city, its schools, its government, and to economic development and prosperity. I saw CSU as the place where solutions, resources, abundant energy, and social capital lay untapped. My job was to begin to build new, stronger, and longer-lasting bridges with an identity that linked us sub-stantively to the community.

To begin this work, I met with leaders across institutions, city govern-ment, business, foundations, and schools. I worked with foundation exec-utives and program directors and listened carefully as they and other com-munity members shared their concerns, their dreams, and their hopes. I found a distinct need, in a city ravaged by monthly closings of industries and the flight of the middle class to the suburbs, to create an identity for CSU as a metropolitan leader in economic growth and development. I learned that rarely had anyone in CSU's previous administrations been a vocal advocate for CSU and for our potential to be a strong community partner. Virtually no one had advocated both for image and the financial support that could help the university figuratively take its chin off its chest and roll up its sleeves to make a difference.

I determined, with the unanimous support of my vice presidents and ad-ministrative council, to focus our efforts on improving K–12 education. To do this, I tried to provide an example of a university officer that continu-ally engaged in community activities geared toward learning what and how to improve our children's achievement. I also focused on creating the con-ditions necessary to support the interdisciplinary work of faculty who chose to follow my lead. Such conditions include developing strong leadership that supports shared, ethical decision making; engaging the university community to identify and solve community problems; and, importantly, finding financial support for innovative solutions. The President's Initiative Fund is an example of these conditions coming together to engage our university community in more public roles where we can put our minds, hearts, and hands to work on solving significant problems through democratic means.

THE PRESIDENT'S INITIATIVE AS A CALL TO PUBLIC INTELLECTUALISM

Locally funded for $1.9 million by the Cleveland and Gund Foundations and matched with university funds, the President's Initiative was developed to engage faculty in community-based projects that would have significant economic impact. My work in creating this initiative included not only securing the support of local foundations but also developing institutional support for its success by engaging academic leadership and communicating the initiative's benefits to faculty and staff. The idea was to seed community partnerships that would engage interdisciplinary teams of faculty with community constituents to have a positive economic impact while at the same time increasing the visibility of CSU.

Ultimately, I hope that these projects will develop into signature programs that distinguish CSU through their significant contributions to urban growth and development. In accord with my notion of the role of the public intellectual, the President's Initiative called for faculty to turn outwards—to focus their instruction, research, and service on community-based needs through collaborative work that would strengthen our mutual relationships, our university image, and our collective economic development.

The initial call for proposals stressed five areas: (1) biomedical and health sciences; (2) urban planning and development; (3) education; (4) arts, humanities, and social science; and (5) engineering, business, and law. A total of seven proposals were funded: four of the seven partner CSU faculty with CMSD schools to improve mathematics, science, and literacy proficiency; five of the seven also focus directly on educational outcomes in high-need areas such as mathematics, science, writing, and reading; and two also focus on arts education in the broader community.

These projects are just the beginning as other initiatives will follow. The focus of other internally funded grants encourages individuals to use their intellectual capital to refine our community through the democratic processes and institutions that exist for dialogue and action and that make a difference in our cultural, political, and economic advancement. My intention is to support efforts that engage members of our community in civic activities that can define CSU as a major force for change and development.

FACING OBSTACLES

Two obstacles stand in our way of making a difference in the broader community and, more specifically, in our urban schools. The first is our image of ourselves and the negative perception of CSU by the communities around us, especially the African American community. I have taken seriously my job as president to create and promote a positive image and to confront with facts and a clear vision those who are misinformed—both inside and outside the university. As I have already described, we are working to create a more visible and positive presence and, through the President's Initiative, will reach out in substantive ways to become a more significant community partner.

The second, equally challenging obstacle facing CSU right now is a lack of funds. Ohio has always been a state that has not invested heavily in public higher education and tuition rates have been relatively high as a consequence. The state budget was cut by 6 percent during my first year at the university and finances have only gotten worse since then. I believe the president's job is to get his/her hands on every dime he/she can and spend it wisely on behalf of the students and faculty. Getting the money we need to realize our vision is, at best, difficult in these economic times. However, my role in creating structures to support our economic growth has been multifaceted, raising public awareness of the problems with our legislated financial support to higher education, securing local support for community-based initiatives, and ultimately filling the moat with a positive image of CSU as a vital contributor to the educational and economic security of the community.

When I arrived at CSU, the institution was in fiscal disarray. Through more stringent financial planning and accountability the university is still poor but at least it is no longer declining financially. Prior to my arrival, the university suffered significant losses because of ongoing problems with the installation of a new computer system for institutional management. Unexpected costs of implementation and design of the system drained both the operating budget and a significant portion of the reserves. My term as president began with a thorough review of the fiscal terrain and accountability systems that assured our fiscal responsibility and prosperity. We initiated a budgetary system that provided local (college-based) control of and accountability for economic stability and ensured that we were not spending beyond our means. Though painful and time consuming, collectively we were able to come into balance by engaging the Colleges to determine where and how to cut costs while maximizing service. In most cases, we were able to secure existing tenure-track positions while consolidating services.

I soon learned that an important role I must play was that of the educator—making local business leaders and the public more aware of our plight for state and private dollars. Everywhere I went, I discussed the issues of our state's system for funding higher education. I spoke at regular civic events about the issues of public higher education and the relationship of those issues to K–12 matters. Over time, business leaders and politicians echoed my concern. The local newspaper, *The Plain Dealer*, among other state papers, ran a series of editorials calling for more equitable, substantive support for higher education. In his quest for re-election, the governor promised to increase funding for higher education.

Initially, when I interacted with leaders in education, business, and private philanthropic foundations, I was surprised that this simple behavior—serving as an ambassador for the good work we do at CSU—was uncommon in our institutional history. As I visited schools, I asked what they needed from CSU. School administrators responded with simple requests and I connected them with the departments and resources that could help. Not only did educators seem surprised that I would ask them what we could do to help, they seemed even more surprised to get a response. As I visited with business leaders, I found a general lack of information about our accomplishments and a residual belief that we "just weren't good enough." Soon, I prepared myself with a litany of the recent grant acquisitions and honors bestowed upon our university community, sharing these wherever I went—a meeting of local superintendents, a City Club speech, and at my inauguration. Friends in leadership positions of the local foundations reinforced my fear that locally, CSU was viewed, at best, as inconsistent in responding to community needs and sparking economic development and, at worst, inadequate in its responses. Sometimes, I learned, we were our own worst enemies in reinforcing these beliefs with comments, attitudes, and absences from decision-making arenas where we ought to sit and be active. I endeavored to put us at the table—every education, business, and foundation table—where community action began and took place. After a year of such endeavors, I encouraged the dean of the College of Education to engage in similar activities, meeting regularly with school leaders and foundation directors to identify ways in which the university could respond to local needs and secure the support necessary to do so.

In my ambassadorial role, I am helping to fill the moat by building a strong foundation of relationships and structures that support the university and school district's mutual efforts to provide high-quality education to all and to improve the local economy. At one level, this is a personal task, for building relationships requires my reaching out to district officials at all levels: counselors, teachers, administrators, and the superintendent and her chief academic officer. At another level, it requires my painting a new portrait of who we are at CSU, one that both my university colleagues and those colleagues in the schools can recognize, believe in, and live out. Despite rather heroic, ongoing efforts to assist the district in recruiting, preparing, and retaining high quality urban educators, I found that CSU was not always viewed as the most responsive, highly qualified teacher education center in the area.

For instance, while writing this case study, I learned of a major National Science Foundation grant being developed by CMSD in collaboration with a small, private Jesuit college and a prestigious private university that does not have a teacher education program. Despite the numerous partnerships we've developed and the joint grants we've attracted for CMSD, the district moved far down the block to partner with other institutions. Many district leaders remain unaware of our growing national reputation. Needless to say, I was concerned and did not hesitate to contact the CEO of the district not only to find out why this had occurred but also to insist upon our participation in the project. These contacts resulted in our receiving a substantial piece of the grant, providing mathematics and science coursework to middle-school teachers who have elementary certification that does not meet national content standards.

There have been successes as well. Recently the district's CEO called me for help with a space problem. In rebuilding and refurbishing many schools each year—a major initiative supported by the public and the state—the district needed classrooms in which to house displaced programs. With just a few phone calls, we were able to negotiate the CMSD's rental of an old and vacant classroom building on campus that, although scheduled for demolition, was easily refurbished for the two-year interim home of two district programs. In addition to benefiting CMSD, we now have schoolchildren and their classrooms on our campus with easy access to university resources as well as teacher educators and prospective teachers who can use these classrooms for required urban field experiences.

FILLING THE MOAT WITH RELATIONSHIPS, RESPECT, ETHICS, AND ACTIONS

Through increased and enhanced relationships, Cleveland State University is beginning to forge new ground and fill the moat that separates us from the community. But this is just a beginning. These examples remind me that I must play an even more visible role in my relationship with the CMSD. "Look to us," I must say through my words and actions with the schools. The chief executive officer and I have spoken frankly about our relationship in the hope that we can be even more reciprocally responsive. CSU really needs to be seen not simply as the solution to some problems but as the local *leader* in preparing high-quality urban educators.

It is even more important to strengthen our ties to the community through our efforts to become a vital, powerful force in this region. We need business and industry as spokespersons and advocates for higher education in the legislature and beyond. Our responsibility is to connect to the rest of the city and to do so we must forge alliances with business, industry, public schools, health care organizations, and everyone else with whom we can make common cause. By doing so, we can demonstrate to our legislators that we do not stand alone in our desire to develop a better life for all citizens. When the university needs some friends, as it surely did in the last session of the legislature, for example, it has somewhere to turn for allies.

During my brief tenure at CSU I have learned that the university is perfectly positioned and capable of making important changes in the lives of people in the community. I am resolved that by the time I leave, this university is going to be reaching out. When people say "the university," they will mean CSU, their *public* university. I see my term as president as a real opportunity for renewal and for CSU to become a student-focused center of scholarly excellence and service. To this end, I regularly ask my colleagues to lead ethically, willingly, and with the conviction that we can make the world a better place. I ask them to act civically, using democratic structures to apply what they know in changing the world for the better.

By working together we can make such change happen here. That is my goal.

Michael Schwartz became the fifth president of Cleveland State University in 2002 after serving as president of Kent State University from 1982 to 1991. He began his academic career at Wayne State University and also held leadership positions at Indiana University at Bloomington and Florida Atlantic University, where he served as dean of the College of Social Science. He is a member of the North Central Association of Colleges and Schools consultant-evaluator corps and a member of its Accreditation Review Council. He has served on the Association of Governing Boards' Commission on Strengthening the Academic Presidency and has published papers on higher education issues. President Schwartz has served as a trustee of the Northeastern Ohio Universities College of Medicine and of Central State University. He was awarded an Honorary Doctor of Laws degree by Youngstown State University and a Distinguished Service Award by the American Association of State Colleges and Universities.

BIBLIOGRAPHY

2000–2001 Annual Report. (2000–2001). Cleveland, OH: Cleveland Municipal School District. Retrieved March 31, 2003, from http://www.cmsdnet. net/administration/2000annualreport.htm.

District level performance indicators. (2002). Columbus, OH: Ohio Department of Education. Retrieved March 31, 2003, from http://webapp1.ode.state. oh.us/district_rating/detail.asp?id = 31.

CHAPTER 12

Building on Strength: Portland State University's Educational Partnerships for Diversity

Daniel O. Bernstine

I am convinced that the most effective change in an institution occurs when we make a deliberate effort to build on already existing strengths and values. Therefore, a vision should not be created without first knowing the institution.

As I began to think about writing this account of my presidential leadership and its influence on Portland State University's recruitment, preparation, and retention of teachers, I felt somewhat unsure about the extent of that influence. After all, faculty and other campus administrators are the major players. I continue to believe that their special expertise and experience uniquely prepare them to take the lead. After five years as president, however, I also know that presidential actions do have the potential to enhance individual efforts. In my case, I took action by identifying several presidential initiatives that could provide a supportive environment and framework for focusing our activities at Portland State University (PSU). I believe our story at PSU may help inform the work of other institutions where faculty and their teacher colleagues are tackling together the difficult issues faced by our school systems. By focusing on the successful endeavors and challenges of our campus initiative on diversity I hope to contribute ideas for others to consider.

PORTLAND STATE UNIVERSITY: "LET KNOWLEDGE SERVE THE CITY"

Portland State University is a comprehensive public university with seven colleges and professional schools of growing distinction, located at the center of a dynamic urban community of more than 2 million people. The university has 22,000 enrolled students (a number that is growing annually) and serves 40,000 individuals in credit or noncredit classes each year, including nearly one-third of the Oregon University System's enrolled graduate students. With 60 percent of Oregonians within commuting distance of our campus, PSU is one of our state's primary vehicles for meeting higher education, research, and public service needs, now and in the decades to come. Our institution serves the Portland metropolitan area—one of the nation's most livable cities and the state's population and commercial center—through academic program flexibility, intellectual creativity, and dedication to lifelong learning. The university's 49-acre campus merges seamlessly with downtown Portland; a bridge that links PSU to the city proclaims our motto: "Let Knowledge Serve the City." This motto is reflected in our mission, vision, values, and especially in our actions.

The university's mission is to enhance the intellectual, social, cultural, and economic qualities of urban life by providing access throughout the life span to a quality liberal education for undergraduates and to an array of professional and graduate programs especially relevant to metropolitan areas. The university conducts research and community service that support a high-quality educational environment and reflect issues important to the region. It actively promotes the development of a network of educational institutions to serve the community. And we look to our community to provide us with learning environments outside the traditional classroom that bring the knowledge of the community into the curriculum.

I arrived at PSU in 1997 from the deanship of the University of Wisconsin Law School. In addition to serving as General Counsel of Howard University I also worked for the U.S. Department of Labor. I must admit that as PSU's new president, teacher education was not my highest priority as I settled into my new role as president. I knew that the university's evolving place in the Oregon University System, its new enrollment-driven budget model, and the cultivation of a growing number of alumni and friends of the university would take up most of my time and efforts. In balancing my time and priorities, I viewed the more than 1,000 education students as an important component of 16,000 then enrolled on campus but they were not my major focus.

I soon learned, from positive feedback received as I met with people in the community, of the impact our graduates have on the local school districts. The Graduate School of Education (GSE) has been preparing and graduating excellent teachers since 1956. Our GSE has the respect of the K–12 community because of long-standing partnerships between the university and the schools. I knew I could trust the competency and commitment of the faculty, especially under the leadership of Dean Phyllis Edmundson, who began her tenure shortly after I began mine.

I believe the influence of my education in law has made me a careful listener and observer. My leadership style is one of facilitator, a role that I continue to strive for with each of our academic units. I want to help the deans and their faculty to be successful not by mandating particular initiatives but by encouraging them to think strategically about how they can engage the community and support our students. As a new president, I didn't want to "rock the boat" when major and significant initiatives already were abundantly evident throughout the campus. I was attracted to the institution because entrepreneurial and innovative faculty members were already in place and active in positioning PSU locally and nationally. My challenge was to continue to enhance the academic climate not chart a brand new course. I was determined to first listen carefully to the campus community.

LEADERSHIP THROUGH PRESIDENTIAL INITIATIVES

Through my work with other university presidents and my participation in the Kellogg Project on Institutional Change, I have seen how various leadership styles can effectively guide an institution. I am convinced that the most effective change in an institution occurs when we make a deliberate effort to build on already existing strengths and values. Therefore, a vision should not be created without first knowing the institution. I identify with Michael Fullan's concept of an evolving *shared vision from collective action*.

> Visions are necessary for success but few concepts are as misunderstood and misapplied in the change process. Visions come later for two reasons. First, under conditions of dynamic complexity one needs a good deal of reflective experience before one can form a plausible vision. Vision emerges from, more than it precedes action.... Second, *shared* vision, which is essential for success, must evolve through the dynamic interaction of organizational members and leaders. This takes time and will not succeed unless the vision-building process is somewhat open-ended. (Fullan, 1993, p. 28)

One of my early actions as president was to appoint a Commission on Campus Climate and Life. I wanted to learn what we valued as our strengths as well as discover what we perceived as our weaknesses. My Web site, the President's Corner, posted the results of a year of consultations, reviews, and recommendations by the commission. The report was comprehensive and helped me, as a new president, to understand the core values, the pride, and the concerns of faculty, staff and students.

Starting with the Campus Climate and Life project, I began to learn about this campus community and the values it holds. This reflective experience helped me understand what new initiatives were likely to be successful. Based on my expanded understanding of the campus and with the recommendations of the commission and an ad hoc group of advisers, I decided to launch three initiatives that would have the potential to affect every student and program at the university. The initiatives I chose were student advising, assessment, and diversity. Each of these presidential initiatives is led by an action council composed of faculty, staff, and students. Professor Devorah Lieberman was appointed as vice provost and special assistant to the president to provide direction and continuity to the initiatives. As president it is important not only to identify the strengths of the institution, but also to find leaders who are able to expand and develop them further. I look for effective individuals who will be accountable to me for results.

I am proud of the accomplishments of our action councils and have recently added a fourth concurrent initiative: internationalization of the university. In keeping with the original intent and tone of the commission's report that emphasized better communication, the campus community is well represented on the councils. Updates on our hard-won accomplishments are found on the President's Corner Web site.

Portland State University had a well-established stage from which I launched these initiatives, especially the diversity one. It is an institution that values its work with a diverse community and the clear benefits of community-based learning for students. Faculty, staff, and students reflect an institutional resolve to be responsive to all its communities. This resolve includes finding ways to partner with the K–12 community to work together in finding resolutions to the problems faced in the schools.

It is the diversity initiative that provides me with a platform from which I can address some of the ways that my administration has helped expand our thinking on the recruitment, preparation, and retention of teachers for high need urban areas as well as for the new diversity of students across the state. Although K–12 was not necessarily my target when I selected diversity as a focus, the initiative has helped raise our consciousness on this topic in whatever work we engage, including work with K–12 education.

The PSU Graduate School of Education actively is implementing many of the goals of the Diversity Action Council by creating recruitment plans and allocating resources for diversity initiatives. Our initiatives build on the consistent message of community engagement and "Let Knowledge Serve the City."

DIVERSITY AND THE GRADUATE SCHOOL OF EDUCATION

Portland State University was fortunate when Graduate School of Education Dean Phyllis Edmundson accepted the appointment as cochair of the campus Diversity Action Council. Her personal commitment to providing a campus climate that truly reflected the diversity of our community has guided her effective leadership of the council as well as the school. At a 1999–2000 GSE retreat, the faculty engaged in long- and short-term strategic planning that included an action agenda for diversity and equity. The dean spoke to the need to connect firmly to a moral purpose, to prepare people to work with students who are typically underserved, to work toward elimination of the achievement gap for students of color and poverty, to ground their work in schools and communities, and to commit to conversation and dialogue as a foundation for action. She acknowledged the need at that time to set aside nonessential committee work in order to make time for work on the diversity agenda. Each faculty and staff member was invited to serve on at least one working group dedicated to some aspect of the equity and diversity agenda, from community engagement and asset mapping to creating culturally responsive pedagogy, course design, and assessment.

It was an audacious and potentially troublesome challenge to the GSE—audacious because of its span and troublesome because faculty were already working hard to achieve many of these goals in addition to numerous others. Echoing my university-wide call to action, Dean Edmundson was asking a conscientious faculty to do more.

Before looking at some of the ways this challenge has created new responses, as well as supported and encouraged ongoing successes in areas affecting K–12 teachers, I want to review PSU's relationship with its communities, especially between the K–12 community and the programs in the GSE.

PSU, THE PUBLIC SCHOOLS, AND THE COMMUNITY

Connections with K–12 education have long been important to Portland State University. The first dean of what would become the Graduate

School of Education was a former superintendent of the Portland Public Schools. A number of faculty members throughout the university started their careers as teachers and administrators in the school systems in the region. The institution's mission of access and serving the community is a meaningful part of daily work and is expressed as values that are held strongly by faculty and staff, as evidenced most recently in a campus survey that revealed that 80 percent of our departments—across all schools and colleges, not just education—have one or more existing partnerships currently in place with Portland area schools.

Portland Public Schools is the largest school district in Oregon, with more than 54,000 students enrolled (we also interact with more than 20 school districts in the tri-county metropolitan area). The district includes 100 schools and 50 special-needs and contract programs. Forty-three percent of students qualify for free and reduced-cost lunches. With 16 percent African American, 9 percent Latino/Hispanic, 9 percent Asian, 2 percent American Indian, and 64 percent European American students, the district is becoming increasingly diverse, especially compared to the state of Oregon as a whole, which has a 13 percent minority population (Leadership Advisory Committee, 2001).

State testing results from the state's 2001 Report Card show that 79 percent of third grade students meet or exceed the challenging state standards in reading and 74 percent meet or exceed the standards for mathematics. By tenth grade, 54 percent of students meet or exceed the reading standards and 43 percent meet or exceed the mathematics standards. As in other school districts, the academic achievement of students of color, students who are poor, and students who are learning English is substantially lower than for European American students who frequently come from more economically secure families (Oregon Department of Education, 2001).

Portland Public Schools has faced serious financial and leadership challenges over the past decade. While costs escalate, resources have not kept pace, and the district has made deep cuts in programs while continuing to struggle to meet the needs of an increasingly diverse and high-need student population. The community has a deep and abiding interest in the public schools as a resource augmenting the livability of the city, but the struggles the district has had over the past years have eroded confidence in the quality of education that can be provided.

One testimony to the community's concern for the schools is the Leaders' Roundtable, a group of individuals from K–20 education, business, and city and county government, which focuses on improving educational opportunities and strengthening collaboration around educational issues affecting Multnomah County (downtown Portland). As president of PSU,

I serve as a member of the Leaders' Roundtable. Currently, the Leaders' Roundtable and the Multnomah County Commission on Children and Families have a three-part agenda for improving learning opportunities for children and young people: to ensure that all children read at grade level by the end of third grade, to provide effective education for young children, and to strengthen learning opportunities for adolescents. Clear benchmarks, specific commitments by all partners, and regular assessment and reporting distinguish the work on this ambitious agenda. I am proud to be a member of the Roundtable, but after a year I convinced the group that the addition of Dean Edmundson would add important experience and leadership. We both participate in activities on the Roundtable; she serves as a member of the steering committee for a third grade reading initiative and my role is to be diligent in making sure that the work of the Roundtable and its goals are known and understood by individuals who may have resources to help us be successful. As president, I can also offer the community connections to talented individuals from the university who add their considerable expertise.

As a manifestation of PSU's motto "Let Knowledge Serve the City," the campus has focused during the past several years on an initiative we call Great City-Great University. This initiative grew out of our deep convictions that every great city needs a great university and that Portland deserves a university that is not just in the city but also of the city and that contributes to the vibrancy and success of the region. One of the areas of emphasis in the initiative has been K–12 education. We are exploring how the university and the schools in the area are currently partnering and what potential collaborations are possible.

I personally host faculty roundtable dinners and invite the community to public forums convened to share ideas and strengthen our relationships. One of these forums featured President Diana Natalicio and Dean Arturo Pacheco from the University of Texas, El Paso who spoke both to an audience of teachers, staff, students, and educational leaders in the community about working together to make high-quality educational experiences accessible to all students. We invited Diane and Arturo because of their leadership of the El Paso Collaborative for Academic Excellence. The collaborative successfully brings together the city's education, community, business, and civic leaders around a common goal of high academic standards and achievement for students at all educational levels. Their work has been nationally recognized for contributing to the improvement of academic achievement in the region. Schools in El Paso have provided convincing evidence that poverty and diversity need not be barriers to high achievement. Our invitation to have them on our campus and to invite K–12 community members gave a clear message that we were reinvigorating our efforts to take responsibility in this area.

THE GRADUATE SCHOOL OF EDUCATION

The preparation of professionals for roles in public schools is an important part of the Portland State portfolio. Portland State University has a vested interest in maintaining strong public schools in the region. We have a commitment to providing cohorts of excellent teachers who develop teaching skills in local elementary and secondary schools.

As the most comprehensive school of education in the state, we prepare the largest number of teachers, school counselors, and school administrators—about 250 general and special education teachers a year in post baccalaureate/graduate programs. More than half of the school administrators in the Portland metropolitan region have earned their licenses through programs at PSU and more than three quarters of the graduates of the Graduate Teacher Education Program (GTEP) take positions in schools in the area.

During the 1999–2000 academic year, the GSE had 64 full- and part-time faculty. Of those 64, 11 percent represented diversity in terms of ethnicity. In addition, faculty across the campus are involved in teacher education through activities that include participating actively on the faculty senate's Teacher Education Committee, identifying prospective GTEP students, advising students, providing opportunities to try out teaching as mentors in University Studies and science classes, and developing and implementing research projects and courses designed with prospective teachers' needs in mind.

I strongly advocate for and support the GSE's mission of challenging itself and others to meet our diverse community's lifelong educational needs. The GSE's mission is described in three guiding principles that echo our university-wide diversity efforts. The principles are to build programs on the human and cultural richness of the university's urban settling; develop programs to promote social justice, especially for groups that have been historically disenfranchised; and strive to understand the relationship among culture, curriculum, and practice and the long-term implications for ecological sustainability.

Such a mission is possible only when it is championed not only by me, as president, but also by the dean, faculty, and staff as well. To that end, the GSE has established criteria for recruiting and promoting faculty colleagues that include commitment to teaching as a moral endeavor and to promoting justice and equity in schools. Faculty has experience working in culturally diverse settings and preparation in the content they will be teaching. In addition to successful pre-K–12 classroom experience (three year requirement) faculty must demonstrate an interest in working in schools doing collaborative research and in assisting in school renewal efforts.

Tenure-track faculty must be able to provide evidence of their ability to establish and sustain an agenda of scholarly work that exemplifies knowledge in service to the city. They must demonstrate excellence in teaching, advising, and supervision of diverse students; scholarly contributions to knowledge in education; and community outreach, including work in and with schools. Such a commitment by our faculty pays off in national recognition for PSU and exemplary community partnerships. Faculty from the GSE have created collaborative action research projects with schools; offered in-service workshops throughout the state, region, and country; and attracted numerous grants in support of improving instruction, assessment, and use of technology, including a state-wide, federally funded Title II Oregon Quality Assurance in Teaching grant.

Teacher education is a university-wide commitment at PSU, even though the professional licensure program is offered only at the graduate level. Prospective teachers complete undergraduate majors at Portland State or other institutions, complete prerequisite courses and compete for admission to the program. The average GPA for students admitted to the GSE is 3.4, their average age is 27, and more than 40 percent come from PSU undergraduate programs. Approximately 17 percent of the students are from underrepresented ethnic groups. Candidates are required to present evidence of successful experience working with children and young people from various cultures, socioeconomic levels, and diverse communities. They must have knowledge of a foreign language, complete a set of prerequisite courses, and pass national examinations verifying their competence in both basic skills and subject matter knowledge. We admit approximately 75 percent of the qualified applicants to our programs.

THE UNIVERSITY STUDIES ADVANTAGE

Students who enter the Graduate School of Education from any one of Portland State University's undergraduate programs have a distinct advantage: their participation in our award-winning general education program: University Studies. The four-year curriculum is designed to provide a cohesive program of integrated learning throughout the baccalaureate experience. This program translates well for a teacher education program that is designed to prepare teachers for the economic, cultural, racial, and other forms of diversity found in today's urban classroom. Graduate School of Education students who begin their studies as freshmen at PSU in our Freshman Inquiry, team-taught, interdisciplinary courses have the opportunity to become teachers who are better prepared for a diverse teaching environment because of University Studies' strategic learning goals.

The inclusion of diversity and multicultural themes across the curriculum is coupled with learning experiences about the variety of human experience. Course titles such as Faith and Reason, Knowledge, Art and Power, Metamorphosis, Popular Culture, and Cyborg provide clues to the span of possible cross-disciplinary learning elicited by the themes and their teams of teachers. The ultimate goal of University Studies is to enable graduates to develop the appropriate attitudes and skills needed to pursue lifelong learning. The program specifically endeavors to include diversity and multicultural themes in the curriculum and to enhance student capacity for understanding and appreciating the rich complexity of the human experience.

To ensure that more students are given an opportunity to gain this Freshman Inquiry experience, we recently began collaborating with several area high schools and a community college to offer the first-year program on their campuses. This required significant collaboration on course development and faculty development activities. High school teachers attend the PSU summer retreats and participate in the same activities as our University Studies faculty. High school teachers meet with their university and community college colleagues on topics that include assessment, creative pedagogies, collaborative teaching and learning models, the scholarship of teaching and learning, and diversity in the classroom and the community. They share experiences on the production of student learning portfolios.

In 2002, in addition to our on-campus offerings, we began to offer Freshman Inquiry at four high schools and one community college. Our newest additions highlight our ongoing goal to create a seamless web of instructional opportunities across a diverse student population. This is especially evident at one of our newest schools, Vocational Village. Students who attend Vocational Village have been unsuccessful in at least two traditional high school environments. Vocational Village is a program that gives students a special opportunity to work in a classroom environment with their peers to achieve a high school diploma. When we began few of the students there were considering higher education. We now are seeing Vocational Village students who are preparing for advanced study; they will be able to apply their Freshman Inquiry credits toward application to area community colleges, PSU, or other institutions. While I hope that these students will consider PSU, our real goal is to open doors for students who have never before thought about higher education as an option.

DIRECT INVOLVEMENT IN THE SCHOOLS

Faculty and students participate in a wide variety of activities in and with public schools, thanks to the community-focused research and scholarship of our faculty and students. I continue to be impressed by the range and variety of ways that students and faculty from across the campus are connected with public education. I strongly support this all-university approach, which is manifested in many ways, including:

- The dean and faculty in education participated in the Portland Public Schools strategic planning efforts as members of the core planning team and action teams.
- Undergraduate students engage with faculty in capstone courses that focus on problems identified by schools including improved safety at schools by changing traffic patterns, community surveys, studies of teacher attrition, and parental involvement.
- Geographers offer professional development opportunities for teachers.
- Population researchers conduct studies for school districts to predict enrollments and aid planning.
- The School of Fine and Performing Arts faculty offer opportunities for young people to experience and participate in arts activities.
- Action research teams from many academic departments help schools assess the availability of technology learning opportunities in the community.
- The National Science Foundation (NSF)-supported Center for Learning and Teaching works to improve the preparation of science teachers and builds on earlier NSF-supported work to strengthen the preparation of teachers in science and mathematics.
- Students preparing to be teachers spend more than 100,000 hours annually working in schools helping young people learn.

DYNAMIC INTERACTION AND DIVERSITY AS A FOCUS FOR EDUCATIONAL INITIATIVES

Portland State University's initiative in support of a diverse learning environment and its long and productive history of community engagement have not only shaped my agenda as president and the message I carry to our community, our students, and our funders, but it is also an enduring foundation from which the GSE has focused its priorities. As president, I have helped to frame the priorities for our institution, but it is the participation by university leaders, faculty, and staff in a dynamic interaction that has produced the successful models emerging from our diversity initiative and other collaborative efforts.

It is the faculty and staff at the GSE who have used the lens of diversity to focus programs on recruitment of minority teachers, digital equity, and specially designed curricula in both the teacher and general education programs. Their efforts are worth describing in more detail as they illustrate the range of creative approaches that results from the open-ended vision-building process that I encourage.

PORTLAND TEACHERS PROGRAM AND BILINGUAL TEACHERS PATHWAYS

Although almost 40 percent of public school enrollment in Oregon is composed of minority students, minority teachers and administrators, who should reflect the backgrounds of the underrepresented population, make up only 4 percent of faculty employed by school districts and education service districts (*Minority Teacher Report, 2001*). The Portland Teachers Program (PTP) is designed to continue to reduce this gap.

PTP is a 13-year partnership comprised of PSU, Portland Community College, and the Portland Public Schools. Undergraduate students from historically unrepresented groups who agree to teach in Portland Public Schools receive scholarships. In 2001 the Northwest Education Regional Lab reported that "PTP is one of the oldest of a number of programs throughout the northwest designed to pull nontraditional candidates into the teacher-preparation pipeline. The need for new teachers over the next decade is critical. The need for minority teachers who reflect the growing diversity of America's student population is perhaps even more acute" (Sherman, 2001). The collaborative program has grown from about 15 students in 1989 to 53 students with active scholarships in 1999. More than 50 students have graduated from the program, the majority of whom are working in the Portland Public Schools.

As I learned more about PTP through this writing project, I better understood its real and potential impact on bridging the gap between the numbers of minority teachers and the numbers of minority students. Even during fiscally lean years, I have supported PSU's continued expansion of its financial commitment to this partnership for program support and full student scholarships.

The Bilingual Teacher Pathways (BTP) program is designed to prepare bilingual, bicultural educational assistants to become fully licensed teachers. In partnership with area community colleges and 20 local school districts, the program recruits these paraprofessionals for a seamless program of coursework and field experience. Mt. Hood, Clackamas, and Portland Community Colleges were all part of the original grant proposal and have been active partners in the implementation of the program. Students can begin the program at one of the community colleges and transfer to PSU after the first two years of the undergraduate experience. Faculty from the community colleges have worked closely with GSE faculty and BTP staff to develop and refine the program. Students who hold baccalaureate degrees (sometimes from other countries) can enter at the post-baccalaureate level.

With the support of Title VII dollars, the program is designed to create a teacher licensure and degree program with an English-as-a-second-language endorsement, as well as providing individualized advising, assessment, student services, financial support, mentors, and community building. Graduates of this program create a critical pool of teachers who will bring special skills to the classroom and be mentors to a growing mix of multiethnic and multicultural students in our schools.

PREPARING TOMORROW'S TEACHERS TO USE TECHNOLOGY (PT3)

An enterprising group of faculty and teachers, led by Professor Lois Cohen in the GSE, is working on ways to engage teachers in the use of technology in order to enhance student learning and decrease the digital divide that separates many urban students from academic success. The project, Preparing Tomorrow's Teachers to Use Technology (PT3), not only expands on the vision of my diversity initiative but also prepares future teachers to understand the potential use of technology to support learning and to integrate it into their teaching day. The project also identifies and provides resources to continue to help them teach effectively using technology as an educational tool. The grant also provides resources to support faculty development, create partnerships, and purchase equipment.

The project's partners include two community colleges, statewide and regional educational organizations, Oregon Public Broadcasting, and K–12 schools including the Portland Public Schools and the private sector. Internal partners include the GSE, the College of Engineering and Computer Science, the Graduate School of Social Work, the College of Urban and Public Affairs, the Office of Information Technology, the library, and the Center for Academic Excellence.

Along with these activities, the project hosted a symposium on digital equity for all the Oregon PT3 grantees and community/business partners. I welcomed the participants and emphasized our institution's continued commitment to the goals of the project and to continued collaboration with a broad range of community partners.

The enthusiasm and expertise generated by this project is invigorating faculty work. The grant is helping to create an asset map that will communicate sources beyond the schools from which students can gain knowledge about the availability and use of technology for learning. The community capacity mapping has a geographic focus in lower-income Portland areas with research being conducted by students in the GSE. In addition to creating an information resource for the community, students themselves will be rich sources of information for their future students. While creating the asset map, students and participating educators are able to offer field-based teaching methods, evaluation, and assessment suggestions to the community. The goals of the mapping project include developing a dynamic inventory of community-based educational resources, improving the quality of educational experiences for children, and strengthening and expanding school/community ties. Faculty members expect that this project will result in the creation of a template for future projects in the PSU Graduate Teacher Education Program.

As part of the project's work, a Teacher Education Continuum Committee was created. It includes representatives from PSU, Portland Community College, and Clackamas Community College. The committee has been working to develop an across-the-board alignment of education class offerings among the three institutions and incorporate national technology standards throughout their education courses.

ADVANCING CROSS CULTURAL EDUCATION SKILLS

As former Secretary of Commerce William M. Daley has noted, the emerging digital economy has become a major driving force in our nation's future. "We must ensure that all Americans have the information tools and skills that are critical to their participation. Access to such tools is an important step to ensure that our economy grows strongly and that in the future no one is left behind" (U.S. Department of Commerce, 1999).

Portland State University, in partnership with the Northwest Indian College (NWIC) in Bellingham, Washington, and the University of Texas (UT), is piloting a program that may serve as a building block for future programs among educational institutions as well as a model for other programs. When I met with the faculty from this project, I saw how they were combining many of the values that the PSU community had identified as congruent with our mission: serving the community, increasing diversity, and providing greater access to education.

The Advancing Cross Cultural Education Skills project will provide, through a distance-learning format, modules created for the purpose of increasing usage and knowledge about distributed educational technology for NWIC education faculty. Distributed education modules are currently being developed as a part of PSU's current PT3 grant, and those modules will be modified to more effectively serve the needs of the education faculty at NWIC. UT will assist with the modification of these modules, based on its extensive experience with both distance learning and culturally responsive curricula. A virtual library was created for the NWIC to reflect the sensibilities of the Native community generally and the Lummi Tribe specifically. Currently, PSU Computer Science students are creating a Web site for the NWIC as part of their senior capstone project.

THE IMPORTANCE OF PROGRAMS FROM ACROSS THE CAMPUS

In the American Council on Education report, *To Touch the Future: Transforming the Way Teachers are Taught* (1999), college and university presidents are given an action agenda. It calls for presidents to ensure that education faculty and courses are coordinated with arts and sciences faculty and courses. I was pleased to learn that interdisciplinary partnerships were already in place at PSU when I arrived, largely because of the initiative of the faculties themselves and with the encouragement of Marvin Kaiser, dean of the College of Liberal Arts and Sciences, and Dean Edmundson. Early in Dean Edmundson's tenure she says she remembers meeting with a group of science faculty at their request who wanted to know how the two schools could enhance their work together. She was encouraged by their initiative and collaborative approach.

The PSU Center for Science Education (CSE) is a good example of such collaboration. The CSE has been a vibrant part of the College of Liberal Arts and Sciences since 1993. The center prides itself on its ability to be responsive to the needs of community partners, students, and faculty colleagues from all disciplines of science. The mission of the CSE, directed by professor William Becker, is to enhance science teaching and learning through innovative education, research, and community outreach programs. The center provides undergraduate general education courses in the sciences for all majors, a Master of Science Teaching program, and professional development opportunities for current science educators. The center also supports community partnerships that involve citizens and community institutions in activities that employ the inquiry practices of science.

An example of one of their activities is the creation of the Twenty-First Century Community Learning Centers (CLC) in the Portland Public Schools. The CLC program helps four north and northeast Portland middle schools and their communities connect the school curriculum with the local community and issues of concern. CSE staff and graduate students do this by offering professional development workshops for teachers, administrators, and community members on various aspects of community building through youth projects. They also run after-school clubs, with the help of PSU University Studies Capstone students, which extend the school day in a community context.

The CSE is active in supporting and retaining current teachers by engaging them in scholarly activities that help them become more knowledgeable and confident in teaching science as an inquiry activity. The center does this in a manner in which students and teachers participate as investigators in projects that use a scientific approach to creating and defending knowledge claims. Meaningful project opportunities for students and teachers are created by establishing partnerships with community groups, businesses, agencies, and special interest groups.

Many of our programs are directed at and serve students and teachers in high-needs settings but we do not believe that teaching and learning via science inquiry is effective only for gifted students. In fact we have begun to gather evidence that project-based instruction is more effective for at-risk students than traditional classroom teaching and learning environments. Several faculty in CSE are interested in documenting this claim. One will be working with a group of Jefferson High School students as part of a University Studies partnership. Another has been examining gender preferences to various learning styles.

REFLECTIONS ON THIS PROJECT AND ADMINISTRATIVE LEADERSHIP

In this chapter I have looked at how a presidential, campus-wide initiative on diversity has helped focus and influence the goals and priorities of various programs and special projects in the GSE and across the campus. I have described programs that have addressed diversity in terms of digital equity, recruitment of minority students, work in schools with high percentages of minority students, recruitment of bilingual education students, and specially designed curricula in teacher education and general education programs.

By engaging in the diversity initiative, we also are taking part in an important national agenda. I look forward to expanding our initiative by reviewing recent national research findings such as those from *The Changing Face of America's Children*, a two-year national project by the National Association of State Boards of Education and the Joyce Foundation. It explores the role of state policies in the creation of a culturally competent education system, one that "prepares students for a diverse society and workforce; educates a culturally diverse population to high standards of achievement; and fosters national unity while respecting and honoring diversity" (*The Changing Face*, 2002). Through local efforts like our own, each national initiative will gain momentum and we, in turn, will benefit from the work of other institutions.

The Urban Educators Corps President's Initiative, from which this book project emerged, is both an all-university and a partnership endeavor. It focuses on activities undertaken in partnership with local urban school districts. Again this work fits well with PSU's strong commitment to the community. At PSU, K–12 is one part of that community.

As president, I must keep a balanced perspective on the various demands placed on me and the university, especially the community expectations for our responsiveness in many arenas. As a result of writing this chapter and reading the accounts of my colleagues, I have discovered additional ways of enhancing my advocacy of K–12 education, and I plan to explore these ways, including having a greater presence at program events. But my span of responsibilities demands that I continue to rely on the effective shared leadership that emerges from an institutionally shared vision. I trust those most directly engaged to let me know when my personal involvement is most critical.

This commitment to shared leadership was well established at PSU before I arrived, and I have, as president, had the wonderful opportunity to build on that strength. I have tried to do this by encouraging campus leaders, faculty, and staff to take action in ways that best suit their own unique abilities and the needs of our students and community. Our shared values are now further articulated and established in a recent report from a cluster of focus groups conducted as part of our 2002 planning and visioning activities. Participation in this dynamic interaction characterizes what I do as a university president and what our faculty and staff do so well. Together we have challenged ourselves to find new ways to express existing values. In a similar way, we are building a vision of K–12 education together with our communities.

Creating what I call a nurturing climate for an independent and entrepreneurial campus is not easy, however. It requires flexibility and a willingness to allow the process to be at times open-ended. It requires many leaders taking action. But together, these actions build a vision that is created by participants and guided by a clear institutional agenda. I am sufficiently encouraged by the focus of the work described in this chapter to think that our diversity initiative helped provide such an agenda. Together, we continue to "Let Knowledge Serve the City" and beyond.

NOTE

I would like to thank Donna Bergh, documenter for this chapter and those who contributed to this project, including Mary Kay Tetreault, Phyllis Edmundson, Carol Mack, Lois Cohen, William Becker, and Jusy Patton at Portland State University, and Deborah Cochrans at Portland Community College.

Daniel O. Bernstine *was appointed the seventh president of Portland State University in 1997 after serving as dean of the University of Wisconsin Law School for seven years. Previous appointments include general counsel of Howard University, staff attorney with the Office of the Solicitor at the U.S. Department of Labor, and the William H. Hastie Teaching Fellow at the University of Wisconsin Law School. President Bernstine has also been a visiting professor at the Inter-American Comparative Law Institute at the University of Havana Law School in Cuba and at Justus-Liebig-Universität in Giessen, Germany. A former chair of the board of directors of the Urban League of Portland, he is also a member of the board of the Portland Metropolitan Chamber of Commerce, the United Way of Columbia-Willamette, and the Council on Legal Education Opportunity. He currently serves on the Leaders' Roundtable, a group of leaders in K–20 education, business, and city and county government that focuses on improving educational opportunities in Portland.*

BIBLIOGRAPHY

American Council on Education. (1999). *To touch the future: Transforming the way teachers are taught.* Washington, DC.
The changing face of America's children. (2002). Alexandria, VA: National Association of State Boards of Education. Retrieved March 31, 2003, from http://www.nasbe.org/Research_Projects/Changing_Face.html.
Fullan, Michael. (1993). *Change forces.* New York: The Falmer Press.
Leadership Advisory Committee, Portland Public Schools Board of Education. (2001, October 22). *Letter to the Portland Public School Board.* Portland, OR: Portland Public School District. Retrieved March 31, 2003, from http://www.pps.k12.or.us/projects-c/lac/part1.php.

Minority teacher report: A ten-year perspective. (2001, February). Salem, OR: Governor's Office of Education and Workforce Policy.

Oregon Department of Education. (2001). *District report card: Portland School District*. Salem, OR: Oregon Department of Education. Retrieved March 31, 2003, from http://www.pps.k12.or.us/schools-c/progress.php.

Sherman, L. (2001, Winter). "Pipeline to tomorrow." *Northwest Education Magazine*, 7(1). Retrieved March 31, 2003, from www.nwrel.org/nwedu/2001/pipe.html.

U.S. Department of Commerce. (1999, Revised November). *Falling through the net: Defining the digital divide*. Third report in the Falling Through the Net series on the telecommunications and information technology gap in America. Retrieved March 31, 2003, from http://www.ntia.doc.gov/ntia home/fttn99/contents.html.

RECOMMENDED READING

Ratcliffe, J. (Ed.) (1999). "The Portland State University Studies Initiative: General education for the new century." *Journal of General Education*, 48 (Special Issues), 1–215.

Tetreault, M.K., & Rhodes, T. (2002). *Institutional change as scholarly work: The case of Portland State University*. Unpublished manuscript. Portland, OR: Portland State University.

White, C.R. (1994). "A model for comprehensive reform in general education: Portland State University." *Journal of General Education*, 43, 168–229.

CHAPTER

The Des Lee Collaborative Vision: Institutionalizing Community Engagement at the University of Missouri–St. Louis

Blanche M. Touhill

Through the Des Lee Collaborative, the University of Missouri–St. Louis has institutionalized its partnership with the St. Louis region. No longer is community engagement dependent on individual faculty members. It is now a visible and defining feature of our university mission. In a recent strategic planning process, the university added a fourth component to its mission—partnerships. Henceforth, the campus is committed to research, teaching, service, and partnership.

If I had to name one of the most important attributes for leaders in higher education, I would say it is the ability to form relationships—to connect individuals, ideas, and opportunities to produce results. Relationships certainly have been at the foundation of one of the most exciting and successful initiatives of my tenure as chancellor of the University of Missouri–St. Louis—the Des Lee Collaborative Vision. Thanks to a partnership with a visionary business leader, E. Desmond Lee, a supportive community, and creative and talented faculty and staff, the University of Missouri–St. Louis (UM–St. Louis) has been able to create 35 endowed professorships that have linked our university with our urban community, fostered interdisciplinary collaboration on campus, enriched our campus offerings, and energized our partnerships with the St. Louis schools.

The endowed chairs that are the focus of the Des Lee Collaborative Vision did not happen overnight or appear spontaneously. They grew out of a university history of urban engagement, my personal commitment to community involvement and leadership, and with the assistance of community leaders who are equally committed to UM–St. Louis and to the future of our urban schools.

UM–ST. LOUIS AND OUR LAND-GRANT HERITAGE

I began my career at UM–St. Louis in 1965 as an assistant professor just two years after the university opened its doors. Our institutional roots, however, go back to 1839 when the University of Missouri was established in Columbus, in the center of the state. In 1870 the Missouri School of Mines in Rolla was added as a second campus with an engineering focus. By the 1960s, in response to increased public demand for educational opportunities for urban residents, the University of Missouri established two additional campuses, one in St. Louis and one in Kansas City (UMKC). As part of the University of Missouri system, these two new campuses had the same fundamental mission as the campuses in Columbia and Rolla; that is, research, teaching, and service. All four were considered public, land grant, research universities with a focus on baccalaureate, masters, doctoral, and professional programs. That history and mission continues to define UM–St. Louis and it informed my own approach to leading the institution.

There were, however, differences among the campuses. Both of the newer campuses were formed to serve their local urban communities but while UMKC grew from an older private university (the University of Kansas City), UM–St. Louis was built from the ground up on land vacated by a country club. It also drew more of its students from the local St. Louis area and from the beginning enrolled a higher percentage of nontraditional students. This commitment to local learners of all ages quickly put the St. Louis campus on the path to acknowledging its urban identity. The decisions made early on about the university's relationship to our region have set the pace for our current interactions.

One of the first questions facing the UM–St. Louis faculty was whether the university's methodology and delivery systems would be traditional or nontraditional. The faculty decided to use traditional methodology to teach nontraditional students but class hours and locations would fit the needs of the nontraditional student. Initially this led us to schedule classes in the morning and the early afternoon and soon thereafter to create an evening college. This college had no faculty of its own but used the regular faculty, curriculum, and standards of the programs offered during the daytime. There was an evening college dean who organized and administered the program offered after 5:00 P.M.

Another adjustment was the operation of campus extension. As a land-grant university, the St. Louis campus anticipated reaching out to the community to help solve problems as well as offer credit and noncredit programs to enrich the lives of the citizenry. Very little of the state-level cooperative extension funds were allocated to the St. Louis campus, however, so our university created a program of outreach to the community funded by the campus, student fees, grants, and contracts. This campus extension program proved successful, eventually becoming one of the top-five programs in the country for total annual enrollment.

Research on a land grant campus—both basic and applied—was always an important part of faculty activity. To support the development of our doctoral programs, our first chancellor, James Bugg, stressed the research priority. In the early days, grants and contracts were mainly the purview of the sciences and gifts were virtually nonexistent. Faculty members interested in viewing the urban area as their laboratory did so on an individual basis, often struggling to convince their department, school, or campus appointment, tenure, and promotion committee that their activity in the community could count toward their progress in their professional advancement. As a result, individuals chose their urban activity carefully or else had a clear understanding from their administration and peers that their urban agenda was part of their assignment. There was no school or college that was out in the community working on urban problems in a focused or dedicated way and there was no institutionalized commitment to the community other than to teach the citizens of St. Louis.

When I became chancellor in 1990, the vision for our university was beginning to change. My two immediate predecessors, Chancellors Arnold Grobman and Marguerite Ross Barnett, had clearly articulated our university's urban mission and began to advance the idea of partnerships with the community. Their ideas fit well with what I believed our university could and should be and with my own conviction that UM–St. Louis needed the assistance of our community if it was to grow and thrive. I concluded if the campus could reach out to the community and, in turn, the community would respond and support the campus, then the growth and recognition that the campus deserved would come sooner rather than later.

As chancellor I used every opportunity to speak on and off campus about our current linkages to the community and to encourage others to make whatever connections they could. As a native St. Louisan, I knew the area and the people and had already developed a broad network of relationships with organizations, businesses, and leaders. When I first became chancellor, several of my advisors cautioned me about serving on advisory boards, especially for nonprofit organizations that did not have powerful business connections. They were concerned that I would overextend myself with little benefit accruing to the campus. They recommended, instead, that I accept only one or two nonprofit board appointments of major organizations—such as the St. Louis Symphony or the Regional Commerce and Growth Association—whose boards could link me to leaders in large companies.

I knew, however, that connections with the community were crucial for campus growth and recognition so I deliberately did not discriminate between large or small boards or between boards with powerful business connections or ordinary citizens. Eventually I was serving on 25 to 30 boards. I made it clear that I could not attend every meeting but I did support the organizations' benefit galas and was available when my assistance or expertise was needed. As a result, I was increasingly sought out by the local citizenry as well as by CEOs for assistance in a variety of projects, becoming the connecting link to faculty and staff. Whenever we could find a win-win match between the university and the community, partnerships were formed.

During those early partnership endeavors it was necessary to find faculty who were willing to get involved. Many faculty members worked in earnest to connect to various aspects of the community but the connections, for the most part, rested on individual relationships. This meant that when faculty members changed on the campus side or the leaders in the partnering organization changed on the community side, the connections were challenged. Although outreach was still not institutionalized—and where it existed it was still in a silo of its own—nevertheless a foundational network of connections to the community, beginning in my chancellor's office, had been established.

THE BEGINNING: DES LEE AND URBAN SCHOOLS

Like many urban school districts across the country, the St. Louis Public Schools (SLPS) faces monumental challenges. Of the 42,000 students at its 112 schools more than 80 percent are eligible for the free or reduced lunch program. Demographically 78 percent of the students are black and 17 percent white. While the graduation rate is improving, in 2002 it stood at only 53.3 percent. The state's Missouri Assessment Program documents improved performance by all grade levels on state tests in math, communication arts, social studies, and science but the challenges are great: in 2002 only 2.5 percent of the 10th and 11th graders tested as proficient or advanced in math and almost 75 percent were only at "step one" or "progressing" in the communication arts of reading and writing (Missouri Department of Elementary and Secondary Education, 2002).

Helping to meet the challenges of educating St. Louis students has been an all-university priority for UM–St. Louis from the beginning. Our first chancellor created joint appointments between the College of Arts and Sciences and the College of Education. Most departments in arts and sciences had faculty members who taught methods of teaching in their content area and also supervised student teachers in that specialty. Today, our College of Education is the largest supplier of educators in the state and educates a major portion of the teachers, principals, and counselors for the St. Louis metropolitan area. The success of the SLPS is a responsibility we take seriously.

My predecessor, Chancellor Marguerite Ross Barnett, created important relationships with the business community which reflected our concern for the loss of human potential and our desire to create a highly educated workforce for St. Louis. Together we established a number of pre-collegiate programs for disadvantaged students that involved a myriad of activities such as after-school mathematics and science clubs, Saturday academies, and summer programs on campus. As vice chancellor for academic affairs under Chancellor Barnett, I was intimately involved with the creation of these programs. I worked directly with the superintendents of the public schools and their staffs and also chaired a committee made up of other higher education institutions in St. Louis to help SLPS obtain a major National Science Foundation (NSF) grant designed to make substantive changes in mathematics education.

When I succeeded Chancellor Barnett, I wanted to continue our school partnerships and also expand them beyond pre-collegiate initiatives to enhance teacher education. The stage for more systemic change was set by a visit from Charles Granger, a faculty member in the Department of Biology who had spent much of his professional career instructing student teachers in science education and in helping high school teachers to upgrade their teaching skills. He and Monti Throdahl, a retired businessman, met with me to discuss improving science literacy for teachers and students. In the course of our conversation, Throdahl told me he was a friend of an unnamed philanthropist who was interested in promoting science literacy. The philanthropist had just made large contributions to a number of cultural institutions in St. Louis that had programs for children interested in science, including the Missouri Botanical Garden, the St. Louis Zoo, and the St. Louis Science Center. Throdahl mentioned that his philanthropic friend wanted to know if the UM–St. Louis would like to be involved in coordinating this movement to make science literacy a force in St. Louis.

I unhesitatingly replied that we would. I already had strong personal relationships with the named cultural institutions and I knew we had the ac-

ademic resources on campus to be an effective partner. And so I was introduced to the philanthropist, E. Desmond Lee.

Des Lee has an interesting history. Born in rural Sikeston, in southwest
Missouri, he moved as a young boy to Columbia, Missouri, where his father,
Edgar Lee, served as president of Columbia College, a two-year school for
women. Late in his teens, the family moved to St. Louis and just before graduating from Washington University, Lee convinced his father to go into business with him and a friend, Jim Rowen, and Rowen's father, John. The four
men formed the Lee Rowen Company to produce pant creasers and hangers.

At the beginning of World War II, Lee entered the military where he
became an officer with a company of African American soldiers in his
command. Lee eventually took part in four different landings in Europe,
one of which was at Anzio. Lee vowed that if he ever got out of the war
alive and made money from the new company he had just helped to start,
he would become a philanthropist. His money would be spent on education, particularly for disadvantaged African Americans. Lee wanted to
provide these students with a more level playing field in elementary and
secondary education so they could take advantage of higher education.

When I met Des Lee, we had an immediate rapport. Lee's belief that education is the key to all our hope and our progress became the animating
ideal behind our goals; a mutual plan for meeting them was soon agreed
on. I proposed to take advantage of a new program within the University
of Missouri whereby the state would match the donation for an endowed
professor or chair. The goal of the program was to recruit exceptional faculty who could bring to the university additional grants and contracts, enhancing our reputation as a research institution. The first endowed professorship at UM–St. Louis was in the College of Nursing—a traditional
endowment that was narrowly focused on research. Lee endorsed the program but he had several important conditions that I agreed would fit well
into the mission of UM–St. Louis. He wanted his endowed professors to
have an outreach component to their work to ensure that they would collaborate not only with each other but also with the partnering organizations in St. Louis that he also funded.

Together we created the template that would define what eventually became 35 endowed professorships (and still growing). There are several key
elements to the success of the endowed professorships. Lee astutely established advisory groups for most partnerships, which widened the circle of
individuals who were willing to help, either with advice or money. And he
convened social events and annual meetings where the professors and their
partnering organizations would get to know one another and report on
their activities reinforcing important interdisciplinary connections.

THE DES LEE COLLABORATIVE VISION

Our first two Des Lee professorships, established in 1996, were designated for science education with a particular emphasis on science literacy. Because the professorships involved national searches for individuals who were leaders in their field, the search committee included not only relevant department faculty but also faculty from other departments who might partner on interdisciplinary initiatives, as well as a representative from the community and from Des Lee's office. The endowed professors were required to perform half of their work on the campus, teaching at least one course a semester, maintaining their scholarly obligations, and applying for grants and contracts, while working the other half of their time in the community with their partnering organization. My role was to support the vice chancellor of academic affairs, the deans, and department heads as they defined the parameters of the professorship and built faculty support. I made a point of following the recommendations of the search committee in appointing their preferred candidate. While I gave faculty and administrators free rein to implement the professorships, it was clearly understood that if my assistance was needed, I was supportive and available. The deans also understood that they could refuse to accept a Des Lee professorship in their school or college but if they did so, it—and the dollars that went with it—would go to another dean.

The creation of the first Des Lee Professorship in Science Education marked a distinctive change in the partnership between UM–St. Louis and the public schools. Our focus moved from programs predominantly for precollegiate students to programs for teachers and/or parents and caregivers. This is not to say that student programs were phased out. On the contrary, the student programs remained in place and many new student-focused programs were created. But the overall emphasis shifted dramatically to programs for teachers and/or parents and caregivers. For this shift to take place, internal changes needed to happen first. UM–St. Louis had for many years been one of the leaders of science education in the St. Louis area. Arts and sciences faculty in biology, physics, chemistry, and mathematics held joint appointments with the College of Education, teaching specialized methods courses and supervising student teachers. They were also engaged in the schools, working with both teachers and students in specialized programs. But the activities of the faculty did not link with one another.

Because Des Lee insisted that the newly endowed professor in science education not only engage in outreach but also actively collaborate within the university, it was important to reinforce our campus networks. All of the disparate activities in science education across the campus were reorganized into a new unit, the Regional Institute for Science Education (RISE). This was not an easy task because faculty had ownership of their individual programs and were at first hesitant to collaborate. Part of the leadership task in higher education is to work patiently within the system. I supported the dean of the College of Education who was able to take advantage of some voluntary employee changes to build support for RISE.

The first Des Lee Professor was William Kyle who also became the director of RISE. Dr. Kyle actively encouraged collaboration within a collegial atmosphere, an approach that facilitated faculty involvement. To improve scientific literacy he focused on professional development for teachers by presenting workshops to enrich the pedagogical skills and scientific knowledge of the teachers. He collaborated with the St. Louis Science Center to develop curriculum materials for early childhood centers that not only helped childcare workers teach scientific concepts to children but also increased parental involvement.

He also developed a student-centered, inquiry-based model for middle school science teachers, Enhancing Leadership for Middle School Science, which was funded by the NSF. The program involved two other campuses in the University of Missouri System and four school districts adjacent to those campuses.

Another project, Linking Food and the Environment: An Inquiry-Based Science and Nutrition Education Program, funded by the National Institutes for Health, focused on fourth- through sixth-grade students. This program engaged teachers and parents and caregivers in helping students understand the relationship between food and biology, the impact of food on health, and how technology affects the movement of food around the world. This program was a collaboration with Teachers College, Columbia University, and two collar-county school districts in St. Louis—Normandy and Maplewood-Richmond Heights.

The second Des Lee professor in science was James Shymansky who partnered with the St. Louis Science Center, the St. Louis Zoo, and the Missouri Botanical Garden on a project called GTE Passports to Science Literacy. Based on a NSF project called PALS (Performance Assessment Links in Science), the science educators at each of these institutions used Aesop's fable "The Crow and the Pitcher" as a basis for preschool and primary-age students to examine the basic principles of water displacement. As part of the program, the students also received a "passport," which they could take on future visits to the Zoo, Botanical Garden, and Science Center where additional learning could take place. Dr. Shymansky's main efforts were on science education curriculum changes for prospective teachers seeking the bachelor's and master's degrees. That curriculum stressed a more inquiry-based, child-centered approach and hands-on activity.

These two endowed professors began what soon came to be called the Des Lee Collaborative Vision, a project that Lee says is "the greatest thing in my life." It has also enhanced the mission of UM–St. Louis, becoming the instrument to institutionalize partnerships between UM–St. Louis and the St. Louis community. As cofounder of the collaborative, I worked closely with Lee as he identified new opportunities to link community organizations to professorships at the university. Our partnership worked because we shared the same vision for community engagement and the importance of education for the youth of our region. As chancellor I raised awareness of the potential of the professorships with my deans. When there was an opportunity to appoint a new dean of the College of Education I specifically chose Charles Schmitz because his vision for the college matched mine and that of the collaborative. He has helped the college expand on the opportunities for engagement that the professorships encourage.

THE IMPACT OF A PHONE CALL

After two science education professors were in place, Lee focused on tying the campus to some of the outstanding organizations in St. Louis such as the Missouri Botanical Garden, Missouri Historical Society, Opera Theater of St. Louis, St. Louis Art Museum, St. Louis Symphony Orchestra, and the St. Louis Zoo. These organizations found their way into the collaborative through unusual circumstances. While at a Board of Curators meeting at the UMKC one Friday afternoon, I received a call from Lee. He asked if UM–St. Louis would be interested in having endowed professors collaborate with each of the previously named St. Louis organizations. I could confidently answer yes because I had established strong relationships with each of those organizations through my board and community involvement and, in fact, had recently taken faculty to meet with all of them about current or new partnerships.

Lee then asked me to verify agreements for endowed professorships linking UM–St. Louis to the appropriate organizations as soon as possible. I quickly called all of them and, except for one organization, I was able to receive an affirmative answer over the phone. The one exception gave an affirmation several days later. I called Lee back to tell him the mission was accomplished and then I rushed to make the plane back to St. Louis.

The result of my afternoon making phone calls in the airport was six endowed professorships for UM–St. Louis, which have helped to garner additional funding and research grants for the university, added exceptional faculty, enriched our campus offerings, improved our efforts to address educational challenges in the schools, and linked us to the community. This was possible not only because of Lee's vision and generosity but also because we already had a foundation of relationships with the community organizations in place. I could get a prompt verbal agreement to a partnership because the directors of the organizations knew me, trusted my leadership, and understood the university's commitment to the community. Community trust is an invaluable asset and essential to the success of the collaborative.

THE VISION IN ACTION

The six professorships that resulted from my airport conversation with Des Lee illustrate well the interdisciplinary benefits as well as the community partnerships that have resulted.

Two of the six professorships enhanced the research capability of UM–St. Louis through partnerships with the St. Louis Zoo, Missouri Botanical Garden, and the university's Center for Tropical Ecology. The two new professors hired in molecular biology and avian conservation developed a specialized lab for undergraduate and graduate students and they partnered with scientists from the zoo and botanical garden. Their work also helped the university's ongoing efforts to foster scientific literacy for area school children.

The remaining four of the six professorships were directly connected to elementary and secondary education through partnerships with the St. Louis Art Museum, the St. Louis Symphony, the Opera Theatre of St. Louis, and the Missouri Historical Society. The Des Lee Professors of Art and Music specialize in education for elementary and secondary school children as well as professional development for the teachers. In addition, they plan many programs for teachers that weave music and art together. The art professor has an office in the St. Louis Art Museum, works with the education department there, and helps them prepare materials for teachers and children planning to visit the museum. Des Lee, as part of his effort to create a more level playing field through education, provides for 10,000 tickets to the St. Louis Art Museum to be available annually for school children from disadvantaged backgrounds and half-priced tickets for all other students when special exhibits are on display.

The music professor brings musicians from the St. Louis Symphony and the Opera Theater to the classrooms of SLPS and surrounding county to enrich the lives of children with music. The program is currently active in 53 public and private schools. Sometimes the musicians play or sing, some-

times they teach, sometimes they talk about the history of a musical instrument or the story line of an opera. The Opera Theater staff, on occasion, teaches the students to write and perform their own operas. Once a
year, 300 young singers perform at the E. Desmond Lee Music Collaborative Choral Festival accompanied by musicians from the St. Louis Symphony and the Youth Orchestra and conducted by a faculty member from
UM–St. Louis. The endowed professor also works with the teacher in
preparing lesson plans for music education that can be used when the visitors have left. Endowment funds also are available to provide discounted
tickets for performances at the St. Louis Symphony, the Opera Theatre,
and the St. Louis campus.

Collaboration with the Missouri Historical Society resulted in the development of a museum studies program. The endowed professor and graduate students work throughout the community preparing displays, taking
part in archeological digs with middle and high school students, and working on grants to restore historical sites.

EXPANDING THE VISION

As Des Lee began to develop the collaborative, several of his colleagues
and friends who liked the idea of outreach and collaboration on behalf of
disadvantaged children, also funded endowed professorships. The first contribution of this kind came from William Orthwein. He had a particular
interest in the St. Louis Science Center and endowed a professor who
would work for both institutions. Professor Patricia Simmons works with
the members of the education department at the Science Center to prepare materials for students and teachers who visit the center. She has also
been successful in bringing together representatives from other higher education institutions to partner on grants to help middle and high school
students as well as their parents prepare academically for college. Dr. Simmons was the leader in obtaining a $5 million GEAR UP grant to prepare
almost 1,000 students for college entrance by 2006. Many of these students
also have been involved in a project fostered by the museum studies program to prepare the history of the Greenwood Cemetery founded in 1874,
where 30,000 African Americans from the St. Louis community are buried.

Another friend of Lee's, Sandy McDonnell, already sponsored an active
program in character education. The addition of a UM–St. Louis endowed
professorship, however, brought to his program intellectual coherence and
national visibility. Professor Marvin Berkowitz works with the Principals
Academy, which helps educate 30 elementary and secondary principals
each year on ways to bring character education into the classroom setting.

Berkowitz also works with faculty in the College of Education on character education curriculum for future teachers.

Another professorship designed to stimulate citizenship education was sponsored by philanthropist Theresa Fischer. The resulting Kids Voting program encourages middle-school students to learn about local and national elections and to accompany parents to the polls where their "votes" are compared with actual results. Many parents comment they had never voted until their children insisted they vote with them on election day.

As so often happens, attracting new donors for the Des Lee Collaborative Vision was less a case of active recruiting than building on existing relationships. Developing partnerships involves getting to know people and spending time with them. When you spend time with people, they give you ideas and sometimes those ideas can lead to donations to the university. On occasion individuals who had heard about the collaborative would approach me with an idea for a partnership and ask if Des Lee would be interested in funding it. I would arrange for a meeting with Lee where we could all discuss how the idea would benefit the university and the community. There were times when we agreed the idea was a good one, but Lee would suggest that the nominator fund the professorship. Lee is a persuasive individual and despite some protests, that is how some new donors came to fund the collaborative.

It was both Des Lee and his wife Mary Ann who brought the next endowed professor to the collaborative. Mary Ann Lee had served on the board of Springboard for Learning, an organization that identified and trained individuals to work part-time in SLPS to bring the children special lessons. Most of the Springboard teachers were individuals from other countries who talked about their native land and customs. There had long been a connection between the Center for International Studies at the UM–St. Louis and Springboard and so a professorship to link us even more directly to SLPS was a logical next step. Mary Ann Lee encouraged Alan and Helen Shopmaker to agree to endow a professor to help St. Louis students learn with a global perspective.

Another colleague of Des Lee's was Chuck Knight who contributed funds for an endowed professor in the field of technology and learning. But he did not stop there. Knight teamed up with friends Jack Taylor and Des Lee to build a technology learning center where student teachers and elementary and secondary school teachers come to learn computer skills for more effective teaching. The professorship partners with Ranken College, which specializes in technical training, and UM–St. Louis offers courses at Ranken for St. Louis area schoolteachers. In 2001–2002, almost 67,000 teachers used the center.

Other philanthropists who later joined the collaborative were Adam and Judith Aronson who funded a professor in modern art who organized elementary and high school visits to the Laumier Sculpture Park. Des Lee also funded a professorship to encourage families to use Forest Park as a natural laboratory.

The collaborative also spawned other giving opportunities. In addition to the professorships, Lee endowed several graduate scholarships to provide graduate students with funds enabling them to work with partnering organizations. The awarding of those stipends is open to any member of the collaborative regardless of whether Lee funded the particular professorship.

As chancellor, not only did I work to develop relationships that produced supporters, ideas, and donors for the university but I also used my leadership position to communicate to the campus and the community about the impact the endowed professorships were having on our community partnerships. Each year I had the opportunity to make two major speeches: one on campus to faculty, staff, and students at which I reported on the state of the university; and one downtown to St. Louis business and civic leaders—The "Chancellor's Report to the Community." This speech is a tradition started by Chancellor Grobman, whose first address was to a group of 16 St. Louis citizens; the audience now numbers more than 1,200. It is an ideal forum for me to stress the work of the collaborative, celebrate our partners, and garner more support for UM–St. Louis. Through the years I have used the address to announce many of Des Lee's endowed professorships.

Since the collaborative began in 1996, it has grown to include Des Lee professors in:

- Criminology and criminal justice (to study ways to control child violence);
- Tutorial education;
- Contemporary art education;
- Women leaders and entrepreneurship; and
- Disabilities education.

It did not take Des Lee or me long to realize that community collaboration required sound public policy decisions. In an effort to help the community, Lee endowed a professorship in public policy, which led to a research center to develop and implement public policies for livable communities in partnership with numerous public, private, and governmental agencies. One important project of the center focuses on work force development; it outlines staffing needs in the St. Louis area for the next 20 years as they relate to elementary, secondary, and higher education capabilities.

St. Louis is a regional medical and scientific center. Just as the endowed professorships connect the campus to the cultural institutions, we are now also connected to the medical and scientific community through an endowed professorship in nursing oncology with the Siteman Cancer Center and an endowed professorship with the Danforth Plant Science Center.

Lee and I are also interested in the multicultural aspect of American life. Because a great percentage of the children in SLPS are African American, Des Lee funded a professorship to help children establish an identity with their heritage. The professorship works closely with the Center for International Studies at UM–St. Louis, which is connected to 14 ethnic communities in St. Louis. The center, and its endowed professors in Irish, Greek, Chinese, and Japanese studies, have helped to internationalize the campus and open doors to overseas study for our students, as well as to offer opportunities for foreign students to study with us.

THE ST. LOUIS SCHOOLS PARTNERSHIP

As the collaborative expanded at UM–St. Louis, Des Lee's focus remained on education, particularly for the disadvantaged. Under the leadership of Charles Schmitz, dean of the College of Education, the university was working ever more cooperatively with SLPS. Dean Schmitz had started a steady stream of student teachers into the schools to take part in observations as sophomores and to do their practicum as seniors. As those students graduated they took jobs as teachers with SLPS. Dean Schmitz also carried on the work of the previous dean to sponsor two professional development schools in the district. Also, I had worked with several of the superintendents in a variety of partnerships, building a foundation for a strong relationship with the current superintendent, Dr. Cleveland Hammonds. Both he and I wanted to find ways to institutionalize our relationship and a Des Lee endowed professor linking the campus directly to the superintendent seemed an ideal solution.

Lee agreed and endowed an urban educator who would follow the collaborative model and who would, in addition to his work at UM–St. Louis, report directly to the superintendent and serve on his cabinet. Ric Hovda was selected and as one of his first projects implemented the Career Transition Certification Program to address teacher shortages in math, science, technology, music, and art. Individuals were recruited who had college degrees in those areas of need and who wanted to make a career change to teaching but could not do so because they lacked a certificate to teach. As part of the program, the teacher recruits taught in the SLPS, were mentored by experienced teachers, and took courses from UM–St. Louis. The Missouri Department of Elementary and Secondary Education was a partner in this experiment. The program was experience-driven and standards based. At the end of two years the mid-career transition teachers receive certificates to teach in the St. Louis Public Schools.

As a result of this initiative, during the 2000–2001 school year, there was no middle or high school classroom in SLPS that was not filled by a teacher who held an appropriate specialized degree and was at least provisionally certified to teach. In addition, the national average for retaining new teachers in urban districts is approximately 50 percent. The retention rate of Career Transition Teachers is more than 80 percent.

Dr. Hovda also led a $1.3 million Title II Teacher Quality Enhancement Grant for urban teacher recruitment and retention. Working with eight regional universities, the community colleges, and the St. Louis and East St. Louis Public Schools, this group has laid plans to provide 450 high-quality teachers for urban schools over a period of three years. Hovda also cochaired a district-wide task force to examine professional development in the district. The report was approved by the Board of Education and became policy in February 2000. The new program requires professional development for all employees, all of whom have to submit an annual personal development plan based on standards outlined by the National Staff Development Council. And finally the school board established a Professional Development Academy as both a physical site for professional development and as a concept that commits the district to the study of and development of high-quality professional development.

The partnership between the university and the superintendent of schools proved highly successful. In January 2000 Hovda was appointed director of the Office of Professional Development for SLPS in addition to his duties as professor at UM–St. Louis. As director he was responsible for coordinating, facilitating, and evaluating professional development throughout the district.

One of the projects of the Office of Professional Development was to focus on 10 schools in the JeffVanderLou District located in the mid-town area of the City of St. Louis. This geographic area was the focus of major community assistance initiatives in social services, economic development, housing, and education. Hovda's office was responsible for the professional development of the teachers and administrators in the 10 schools, specifically working to upgrade the science and technology curriculum. Hovda also worked on a special mentoring program and a state-of-the-art analysis of research on best practices in providing professional development for at-risk students.

STILL GROWING

As of this writing, the Des Lee Collaborative Vision is still growing. The collaborative has linked UM–St. Louis with the community, especially in the field of education for elementary and secondary school children, as well as in a wide variety of other areas from entrepreneurship to contemporary art. All of the professors in the Des Lee Collaborative are committed to collaboration with each other, with other faculty, and with St. Louis institutions. The total number of members in the Des Lee Collaborative Vision is now 35 with endowments of more than $20 million. Thanks in large measure to the collaborative, UM–St. Louis grants and contracts recently reached $97 million. The range of programs, courses, and research opportunities for our students has expanded. Thanks to Lee's commitment to education, our relationship with SLPS is growing and we are finding new ways to link our teaching, research, and service.

Most important, however, through the Des Lee Collaborative, UM–St. Louis has institutionalized its partnership with the St. Louis region. No longer is community engagement dependent on individual faculty members. It is now a visible and defining feature of our university mission. In a recent strategic planning process, the university added a fourth component to its mission—partnerships. Henceforth the campus is committed to research, teaching, service, and partnership.

Little did I realize when I first met with Charles Granger and Monte Throdahl to discuss Des Lee's idea for a professorship that it would have such a profound effect on St. Louis, on the campus, and on me. I know this partnership will do nothing but grow.

Blanche M. Touhill is chancellor emerita and professor emerita of history and education at the University of Missouri–St. Louis. She joined the university as an assistant professor in 1965 and was the first women to complete the tenure process. During her career she served as associate dean of faculties, associate vice chancellor for academic affairs, and vice chancellor for academic affairs before being named interim chancellor in 1990 and chancellor in 1991. She served UM–St. Louis as chancellor for 11 years. Dr. Touhill is or has been a member of more than 33 professional and community associations and boards including the American Association of State Colleges and Universities, Trans World Air-

lines, the Urban League of Metropolitan St. Louis, and many St. Louis cultural organizations. Her commitment to collaboration and diversity has earned recognition from the Urban League, the Ethical Society, the Dr. Martin Luther King Jr. State Celebrations Commission, and the Conference of Christians and Jews. In 1997 Dr. Touhill became the first woman to receive the St. Louis Citizen of the Year Award. She currently serves as secretary for the Great Cities' Universities.

BIBLIOGRAPHY

Missouri Department of Elementary and Secondary Education. (2002). *St. Louis City: School data and statistics*. Retrieved March 31, 2003, from http://www.dese.state.mo.us/schooldata/.

CHAPTER 14

The Initiative for Teacher Education: A Journey to Shape the Future

Joseph A. Steger

Our journey to change the way we educate teachers came to be emblematic of larger transformations on our campus. Not only did change force us to seek out community collaborations but it also taught us to be a strategic friend and partner in urban renewal, economic transformation, and civic and social responsibility.

The University of Cincinnati and its Cincinnati Initiative for Teacher Education is a case study not only in transforming the preparation of schoolteachers but also in creating new conditions of leadership, partnership, and collaboration. By cultivating new growth, alliances, and forms of accountability for our collective educational endeavors, the University of Cincinnati (UC) has discovered fresh insight into the diversity of our students, the challenges they face, and the responses we can make to serve them better.

FINDING OUR TRUE CHARACTER

As president of the University of Cincinnati from 1984 to 2003 and provost prior to that, I have experienced three economic recessions—the early 1980s, 1990, and the present challenge—so I fully understand Ohio's conservative approach to funding higher education. During my 20 years at UC, state funding has fallen from nearly 40 percent of its operating funds to less than 25 percent, resulting in yearly budget cuts and reallocation of resources for the university.

When I came to UC, entrepreneurship, business, and management experience framed my outlook based on my work at Prudential Life Insurance, the State University of New York–Albany, Rensselaer Polytechnic Institute, and Colt Industries, where I had been director of organization development and human resources. My ongoing research had focused on the management of technology, technology transfer, the identification of management talent, and the role of public education in economic development.

Financial viability, I knew, was absolutely necessary at the university in order to transform it into a national leader in teaching and research. The University of Cincinnati already has a distinguished history: founded in 1819 it has been the source of innovative change and discovery, including co-op education, the oral polio vaccine, the electronic organ, and the first antihistamine. Today the university serves almost 33,000 students, the majority from the state of Ohio. To facilitate our ongoing growth, UC has continued to serve as a public institution, yet has budgeted as a private one. Before the stock market declined in late 2001, we had built our endowment from $300 million to $1 billion, cut operating costs by more than $100 million, and increased research support to more than $260 million.

Through the years I have witnessed how excellence in fiscal viability, infrastructure investments, faculty, research, and high-performing academic programs has been the backbone of the university. Nevertheless, I have also believed its true character lies elsewhere—in the quality of what we give our students, our campus, and our city. This story is really about how we came to understand that being an authentic solution for public education meant walking in the shoes of students and teachers in the overcrowded hallways of neighborhood schools.

Our journey to change the way we educate teachers came to be emblematic of larger transformations on our campus. Not only did change force us to seek out community collaborations, it taught us to be a strategic friend and partner in urban renewal, economic transformation, and civic and social responsibility.

THE UNIVERSITY OF CINCINNATI

Throughout the 1990s, the University of Cincinnati advanced strategically with a focus on nine initiatives: pedagogy; faculty development; the convergence of knowledge; innovative research, and scholarship; new analytical and technological tools; global perspectives; shaping an environment for learning; financial viability; and return on investment. As we identified those needs we came to discover striking parallels in the simultaneous calls to transform public education and the preparation of teachers. Calls for renewed investments in school infrastructure, new research-based instruction, pedagogy, and lifelong learning echoed in both the schoolhouse and the academy.

The fact that higher education and public education shared the same challenges, however, came as a new realization to many. My own awareness of our shared destiny came from participation during the 1990s to the present in the Metropolitan Growth Alliance Planning Committee in which I joined other business and higher education leaders to study the City of Cincinnati's economic development. We soon realized, of course, that the quality of our public education was a critical component of our region's future success, and so I became a leading member of the Buenger Commission, formed specifically to address educational issues and opportunities.

In the late 1980s, UC was an exception in the university community in the way we heeded various calls for redesigning teacher education. After deans and provosts had aligned us with the 1986 report of the Holmes Group (a consortium of research universities dedicated to partnering with schools to improve teacher education, see Holmes Group, 1986), our faculty and university leaders forged a partnership with Cincinnati Public Schools (CPS) and the Cincinnati Federation of Teachers (CFT), both also engaged in comprehensive reforms. On the surface, the university and the school district appeared to have disparate goals but at the center of both institutions was a new understanding of a learner-centered environment. As our organizations continued to meet, we found enough common interest to move forward in the implementation of new Professional Development Schools and internship-based teacher education.

If in the past 10 years we have learned anything, it is that an education program must adapt *continuously*. As the 1990s turned to the new millennium, answers previously formed for teacher education no longer fit as they had originally. Leadership changed as school superintendents, deans, and presidents moved on. Economic realities began challenging the financial feasibility of the one-year teacher internship model that we had developed. In a world of mandatory proficiency testing, schools have an even greater need for content-area expertise and pedagogical excellence. Fortunately our collaboration habits forged in the 1990s and the sustaining investment in meeting the imperatives of change have allowed us to find new ways to move forward.

The UC College of Education itself has been affected by the dominant trend toward more comprehensive models of accreditation, as codified in the National Coucil for Accreditation of Teacher Education (NCATE) 2000 Standards, and the relatively new requirements of Federal Title II Reporting. To meet these challenges, we are applying 20 years of research toward developing valid benchmarks and a hallmark set of identifiable characteristics for high-performing and sustainable teacher education programs.

UC COLLEGE OF EDUCATION AND TEACHER PREPARATION

The UC College of Education's mission is to prepare teachers to address the *urban* educational needs of our community using research-based practices in diverse environments. While teacher education is the college's largest program, its 3,000 students can explore a variety of school and community service programs, including school psychology, counseling, health promotion, and school administration. The college graduates between 300 and 350 students a year with many of those graduates accepting employment with CPS.

In the late 1980s and early 1990s, the university began reforming its teacher education programs by addressing challenges such as the rising tide of mediocrity in public schools, as reported in *A Nation at Risk* (National Commission of Excellence in Education, 1983). We set out to develop rigorous teacher education programs grounded in three foundations:

- extensive content area preparation,
- intensive preparation for making content accessible to P–12 pupils, and
- heavily-mentored, field-based experiences in public classrooms.

We titled this reform effort the Cincinnati Initiative for Teacher Education (CITE). To ensure deep content knowledge, all students were required to earn two baccalaureate degrees, one in education and another in a content area from another college, predominantly from the McMicken College of Arts and Sciences. Students also participated in paid, yearlong internships in public schools to gain proficiency and experience.

CITE adopted an ambitious set of plans that paralleled the goals outlined in several national reports including:

- Tomorrow's Teachers: A Report of the Holmes Group (1986)
- *A Nation Prepared: Teachers for the 21st Century* (Carnegie Forum on Education and the Economy, 1986)
- *What Matters Most: Teaching for America's Future* (NCTAF, 1996)

These plans aligned with CPS' new Master Plan, which established a career ladder for teachers, site-based management, and 13 new Professional

Development Schools where UC interns would gain field experience. The results have been so successful that the CITE program has been featured in the PBS documentary "Only a Teacher" and received recognition from the National Commission on Teaching and America's Future, the American Association of Colleges of Teacher Education, the American Federation of Teachers, the Ohio Business Roundtable, NBC Nightly News, *Time* magazine, and *U.S. News & World Report*. A model of continuous improvement modifies the program to meet new needs and challenges particularly in the areas of assessment, accountability, and accreditation.

CINCINNATI PUBLIC SCHOOLS

As an urban district, CPS has been experiencing a steady decline in student population as well as increasing racial and socioeconomic isolation. CPS has lost more than 7,000 students in the last decade falling from a 1991–1992 enrollment of 50,000 to a 2001–2002 enrollment of 42,700. District-wide, CPS has demographics reflecting 71 percent African American (compared to the city's 44%) and 24 percent Caucasian. Almost 75 percent of the district's students participate in the free or reduced-cost lunch program and there is a high school dropout rate of 49 percent (statistics are not kept for elementary and middle schools) (*Overview of Cincinnati Public Schools*, 2002).

Furthermore, CPS is demographically separated into two systems, one of high-performing magnet schools and another of low-achieving neighborhood schools. At the high-performing end is Walnut Hills High School, a widely respected college preparatory program, which last year achieved a 99 percent graduation rate and a 99 percent passage rate for its 1,241 students who took the ninth grade proficiency test. Similarly, the School for the Creative and Performing Arts is a nationally known, inner-city magnet program with a 90 percent passage rate on the ninth grade proficiency test. At the low-achieving end of the spectrum are CPS neighborhood high schools where an average class of 700 students will see more than 500 drop out before graduation (*Committed to Success for All*, 2002).

Nevertheless, CPS is poised to disprove the current realities of schooling for minority and low-income students. To date, the district has been the only one of eight large urban districts throughout Ohio to pull itself out of academic emergency, the lowest of accountability classifications, and move up to academic watch. Accomplishing this feat required implementing a strategic plan that articulated performance expectations, provided schools with clear data for making decisions, helped them make critical financial decisions through student-based budgeting, trained parents and community members to be involved in the schools' daily operations, and encouraged school partnerships with identified lead agencies. The university functions as the lead agency in several CPS school locations including Western Hills High School.

Results are encouraging. In 1998, only 9 percent of the district's fourth graders passed the state's fourth-grade proficiency test but by 2002, the rate more than doubled with 19.5 percent passing all five sections of the test. In addition, remarkable improvement was shown in the individual sections with writing and mathematics scores doubling and reading and science scores up by more than 60 percent (*Committed to Success for All*, 2002).

Furthermore, schools with the district's most disadvantaged students have made significant gains. Parham Elementary School provides a dramatic example. With demographics of 95 percent minorities and an 88 percent poverty rate—figures that have remained constant over the last five years—Parham had *no* fourth grader in 1998 pass all parts of the fourth-grade proficiency test and, worse yet, not one passed either the mathematics or the science section. Yet, as one of the district's first schools to be reconstituted under the new plan, Parham has exceeded its annual improvement targets for student performance every year and remained in the top five of the most-improving schools (*About Parham*, 2003). To support families and students, Parham has several core partnerships including a U.S. Department of Education-funded GEAR UP program with the university. Now in its fourth year and designed to pave a way to college for students, that program also involves the high schools into which the students matriculate.

HISTORY OF THE CINCINNATI INITIATIVE FOR TEACHER EDUCATION

During the nearly 10 years of CITE's existence, the program's unique quality has been the college's development of partnerships among a wide variety of schools, Cincinnati businesses, and community leaders. One example of this kind of successful collaboration was the relationship between the former superintendent of Cincinnati schools and the university. I was able to assist in establishing funding for a faculty position for the superintendent from the business community. His involvement on our faculty helped to enhance our communication and strengthen our school partnerships.

One of the key reasons for CITE's success is its foundation in a multi-disciplinary focus, which was an important component of the university's strategic agenda. I believe that interdisciplinary relationships are critical to the future of higher education—we cannot let the walls of our schools and colleges bump into one another or our scholarship will suffer; fortunately, forming interdisciplinary relationships is a goal that the university has adopted enthusiastically. Now, when a university community sets its strategic agenda, a president has three jobs: (1) sell the idea university-wide; (2) move money around; and (3) recognize those who are doing the work. I made it my task to make sure everyone at UC knew about our interdisciplinary focus. The campus has responded and today, for example, we have engineering faculty teaching calculus in the high schools and opening their labs to high-school students during the summer. I then made sure that there were university funds available to support collaborative efforts (and defended them from those who did not qualify for them) and was active in winning state funding as well. And, perhaps most important, as president I celebrated and recognized individuals and departments who were successfully creating and implementing the collaborations that continue to distinguish our university and community partnerships.

While partnership building between the campus and community has not always been smooth, all parties have come to share a new language and a common set of concerns, enabling us to move forward to increase program quality and student retention. Fortunately, this successful collaboration has spread beyond the College of Education and has moved university-wide.

The nature of teacher education has needed to change, especially in content areas of high need such as mathematics and science. While developing programs for teachers already in the classroom, we paid particular attention to the national mandate for professional teaching standards. Key efforts included: preparing teachers for National Board for Professional Teaching Standards certification; assisting teachers in fulfilling heightened requirements for Ohio state licensure; widening access to the master's degree for working teachers; instituting programs to increase diversity within the teaching force; and creating a new doctorate in Urban Educational Leadership to foster a new generation of leaders.

National Board for Professional Teaching Standards

The National Board for Professional Teaching Standards (NBPTS) is a benchmark indicator of teaching excellence and a credential that recognizes an already-licensed teacher's knowledge, skills, and accomplishments as defined by the board. The College of Education, the McMicken College of Arts and Sciences, and the College of Engineering, in partnership with the Mayerson Academy for Professional Development, have developed and provided new content-based courses for CPS teachers preparing for NBPTS certification.

As of this writing, almost 300 CPS teachers have been trained through the professional study program developed with the Mayerson Academy, a

CPS Professional Development training center, and offered under the auspices of the NBPTS. A parallel track to the NBPTS program was also developed to prepare teachers for entry into the NBPTS candidacy program. Giving precandidates a year of preparatory professional courses maximizes the rate of matriculation through this rigorous professional development and review process. Nationally, NBPTS programs matriculate only 42 percent of teacher participants within a year. In Cincinnati, 72 percent of participants became nationally certified within a year.

Standards in Practice

Standards in Practice (SIP) is a coaching and mentoring process that helps align teaching and student learning with the proficiency and promotion standards established by CPS and the Ohio Department of Education. UC's College of Education and CPS developed the program and implemented it at multiple school sites to mentor teachers in the alignment of standards-based curricula and high-stakes testing with pedagogy and content. Funded by the University Partnerships Program of the Martha Holden Jennings Foundation and the Procter & Gamble Company, the SIP model includes the following goals:

- build a school environment focused on standards,
- accelerate gains made by low-income children and minorities,
- ensure regular, structured conversations among teachers and provide structured coaching and mentoring on the content and goals of assignments as well as the relationship of those goals to the proficiency and promotion standards, and
- effectively incorporate best practices and the appropriate pedagogy into each school setting.

A key element of SIP is the group of professional coaches who mentor teachers to consistently analyze student work in relationship to the district's promotion standards, rubrics, and portfolios. At present, five full-time SIP coaches work at 16 CPS training sites and the College of Education teaches the SIP processes to its prospective teachers so that novice teachers entering the district can effectively participate.

Teacher Recruitment in High Need Content Areas

CPS and CFT have been key partners in developing master's degree programs with teacher licensure in areas of high need including mathematics, science, and special education. The initial programs, Middle School Master's with Certification and Special Education Master's with Licensure, enhanced teacher diversity through nontraditional recruitment and by offering licensure paths for selected groups of individuals including CPS paraprofessionals. Furthermore, the shortage of special education teachers has caused the College of Education to begin work on reinstating an undergraduate special education with licensure program.

In addition, Cincinnati Transitions to Teaching (CT[3]) is a collaborative effort among Cincinnati Public Schools, the UC College of Education, Procter & Gamble, the Cincinnati Business Committee, and multiple community agencies to recruit, prepare, and retain mathematics and science teachers committed to urban students. Funded with a $1 million U.S. Department of Education grant that runs for two years, CT[3] will recruit and train up to 50 new mathematics and science teachers for CPS.

More recently, a National Science Foundation (NSF) program in mathematics and science education was funded to join the efforts of the College of Education and the College of Arts and Science in recruiting teachers for high-needs urban school districts. Often these teachers are nontraditional recruits placed in alternative licensure cohorts with a school district that promises future employment on successful completion of the program.

Educational Leadership in Urban Schools

UC College of Education faculty and national experts designed the college's Urban Education Leadership (UEL) doctoral program to prepare educational leaders for urban schools. The innovative, interdisciplinary, practitioner-oriented program aggressively recruits candidates from PK–16 schools, social service agencies, and community-based organizations for a comprehensive academic and professional program in leadership development. The program's third cohort of students includes school administrators, a past school board member, community-based organizers, and distinguished teachers.

Closely linked with cutting-edge school and community-based programs that function as partnership sites for joint learning and research, UEL is well positioned to produce graduates who can create and facilitate high quality, successful learning environments for children and families in urban communities. Participants have urban internships that offer significant opportunities to use newly acquired research and leadership skills. The UEL program seeks to foster partnerships among urban schools, community agencies, and state and regional governmental institutions.

The College of Education has also partnered with CPS and the state to implement the program, Diversifying the Teaching Force, which will train and place more minority teachers in local schools. High levels of collaboration and trust are at the heart of these programs to support alternative routes to teacher licensure. In a real sense, the lessons of partnership support this culture of crafting leveraged solutions that make a difference.

These selected programs illustrate that through collaboration we have created a practical model not only for *what* can be done but also for *how* to do it. I believe, however, that raising the standard of teaching is only part of the answer to education's problems. New, wide-ranging liaisons and partnerships must also address issues of diversity, parenting, family, and community—issues that enter the classroom with each child. Recruiting, supporting, and retaining teachers from under-represented groups continues to be core to the college's traditional mission. Likewise, creating new, research-trained leaders for urban schools and agencies through UEL is central to the college's *renewed* mission.

WORKING TOWARD CONTINUOUS IMPROVEMENT

In Cincinnati, we have crafted a local solution to a national problem forged in a new spirit of collaboration. Over time, the College of Education has continued to modify the CITE program in response to the needs of schools, feedback from our students, and follow-up data from graduates, while attending to Title II Reporting, Ohio Licensure Standards, Academic Content standards, accreditation guidelines, and standards from professional organizations. Consequently, programs have become more flexible and diverse.

For example, although we maintained a heavy emphasis on content preparation, the requirements of completing two degrees became an unreasonable burden. We found that we could ensure content expertise without asking students to complete dual-degree requirements. Because we have also come to understand that teaching is a developmental process, we have placed greater emphasis on supporting teachers throughout their careers. As a result, the demands of lifelong learning have meant an increasing number of colleges from Arts and Science to Engineering and University College have developed substantial collaborations with PK–16 partners to meet the increased content and pedagogy needs.

I am proud to have played an early role in empowering our education faculty and administration as they worked hard to shape a comprehensive response to national and local demands on the profession. The lessons learned though research and reflection, multiple partnerships, and the adoption of best practices and standards-based education are built around the following propositions, which I have supported and helped to articulate throughout the university:

- Rich content knowledge. Teacher education is the responsibility of the whole university. It is critical that teacher candidates have strong content knowledge in the subjects they are to teach (Monk & King, 1994).

- Effective instructional practices. Content knowledge alone is not enough. Teacher candidates must be proficient in using research-based strategies to make the content accessible to all students (Fetler, 1999; National Reading Panel, 2000).

- Extensive clinical experience. Teacher candidates must have well-designed and extensive clinical practice with experienced mentors who can provide feedback, coaching, and help in continuing to develop instructional practices (Borko & Mayfield, 1995).

- Rich experiences with diverse populations. Because our nation's rich cultural and ethnic diversity provides abundant perspectives that make us stronger, teacher candidates must embrace this diversity and have the skills to facilitate teaching all students (Ladson-Billings, 1994). Although our schools have a notable heritage working with diverse cultures and races, this history is not without mistakes and tragedies. Too often children with special needs have not received the services they needed to succeed. We can and must remedy this (Merseth, Elmore, & Schorr, 2000).

- Technology expertise. Teacher candidates must be able to integrate technology into their instructional practices and use it to bring resources into under-funded schools and classrooms (Cuneo & Harnish, 2002).

- Ongoing support and professional development for teachers. Lack of support is one of the leading reasons teachers leave the profession (Bolich, 2001). Therefore, carefully structured, supportive experiences such as mentoring and ongoing professional development are critical for teachers. Targeted professional development programs linked to standards and outcomes can dramatically improve student achievement.

- Rigorous accountability. Teacher education programs must have a multi-tiered system of accountability, measuring graduates in content areas, pedagogical knowledge, and classroom performance (Delandshere & Petrosky, 1998), as well as a continuous improvement process linked to accreditation to aid ongoing development of programs.

PK–16 PARTNERSHIPS

By seeking new collaborations, the university has continued to form productive partnerships in the community. The UC Institute for Community

Partnerships (UCICP) is an alliance for forging and supporting urban initiatives. A joint effort of the Ohio Board of Regents, the College of Education, the McMicken College of Arts and Sciences, the Division of Student Affairs, and the College of Design, Architecture, Art, and Planning, the UCICP collaborative hosted a 2001 conference at which 350 community, school, and university representatives focused on partnerships to enhance both institutions.

After a request for seed proposals was announced at the conference, several new urban initiatives with schools were implemented. Part of a larger, ongoing initiative originating in the Office of the Provost to expand, strengthen, and better coordinate colleges' PK–16 partnerships, the conference concentrated on identifying in-service and degree options for teachers in high need content areas and creating pipelines to encourage students to pursue higher education. The conference also addressed other campus issues such as exploring the potential to create community learning centers in neighborhood schools, developing technology and Web-based resources for students and teachers, and connecting health and social services to the schools.

As a result of the conference, new PK–16 partnerships were funded with UC, CPS, and community agency partners. Projects include the following:

- Development of a comprehensive health and wellness program for students of the East End Community Cultural Heritage School
- Integration of distance-learning technology into environmental science at Walnut Hills, Hughes Center, and Clark Montessori schools
- Expansion of mental health services at Rockdale Academy
- Expansion of information literacy for social studies and science concepts beyond the current Hughes Center and Clark Montessori programs
- Providing on-site, college-level studies at Western Hills High School starting with English courses delivered by UC's University College
- Development of a Summer Academy for Information Technology at Taft High School
- Professional development for middle school math teachers with the College of Education
- Development of a master of arts degree at McMicken College of Arts and Sciences for CPS language arts teachers

Of these projects, the Western Hills High School is now fully organized as a university school in partnership with University College. Taft High School has reorganized as a technology magnate school with substantive partnerships with industry and a co-op program that leads to industry standard certifications in technology and full preparation for college-bound students.

Although the College of Education counts many active PK–16 partnerships with schools, community groups, and agencies, the number of such partnerships in all UC colleges has grown exponentially in the past five years and has become an active component in the annual goals of the provost and deans. This is important because although my recognition of collaborative initiatives, as president, is important, it is equally important that such efforts are rewarded within each school and college. We have come to value—and I continued to encourage—PK–16 partnerships as fundamental to our mission, essential to our research and outreach agenda, and crucial to our program of collaboration for student success.

CHALLENGES AND COMMITMENTS

I am keenly aware that serious challenges face teachers today. The unfortunate increase in violence and unrest in many schools is not limited to our urban core. Likewise, the ravages of poverty continue to intensify, creating an ever-increasing number of students who come to school hungry. In addition, more students live in single-parent homes and a growing number of seductive traps continue to lure students into trouble. Drugs, alcohol, early sexual experimentation, and other disastrous distractions that can undermine a student's potential always lurk in the shadows.

Unfortunately, the achievement gap between students from challenged environments and those from more affluent environments continues to grow. This is no surprise given research showing that the most challenged schools are likely to have a disproportionately high rate of teachers who are brand new, under-prepared, and/or teaching outside of their field. These schools also have high teacher turnover rates, further exacerbating the difficulty of attracting and retaining a qualified teaching force.

Also, we have an increasing shortage of teachers in mathematics, science, and special education. These shortages are even more acute in our most rural and urban centers.

These contextual factors create not only a series of challenges but also opportunities for teacher education. While teacher education cannot fix these problems alone, the provision of caring, qualified, and competent teachers is a lynchpin to improving the quality of this nation's education. In conclusion, I share seven observations that might help to provide guidance to others facing these same challenges with the same commitment to change:

1. Handling Teacher Education Correctly Is Difficult

Providing teacher candidates with the knowledge, skills, and dispositions to be effective teachers is extremely complex. Like all worthwhile activities, teacher preparation requires a great deal of effort and commitment. Simple solutions are likely to fail and our children will bear the brunt of these experiments. One of the strongest leadership lessons I have learned is the importance of endurance. It takes a long time to get a lot done and as leaders we must be willing to be involved for the long haul. Commitment must be at the core of what we do in order that we stay the course.

2. Handling Teacher Education Correctly Is Expensive

Teacher education candidates must have a significant amount of practice in real settings to develop their teaching skills. Clinical practice takes a significant amount of resources to supervise and mentor candidates. But these are dollars well spent and as president I could help to advocate for and protect needed dollars for teacher education.

3. Teacher Education Is the Responsibility of the Whole Institution

Teacher education programs cannot and will not be the cash cows for the institution, therefore everyone across the institution must take the education of teachers seriously—and contribute in real ways. Sister colleges and schools have important resources that can provide future teachers with content knowledge and facilitate their understanding of the diversity of our multicultural urban environments.

4. We Must Create a Seamless PK–16 Educational System

Education is the key to opportunity and opportunity is the fuel that has made this country great. Students from the early ages must believe that college is a real option for them. Our colleges of education are portals for universities to forge effective university-school partnerships. Such partnerships need the recognition of the university president and constant communication both on and off campus.

5. We Must Take Advantage of the Growing Diversity in Schools

The growing diversity in schools provides a rich set of perspectives that can make our nation stronger. Our teacher education programs must enable teacher candidates to embrace and celebrate this diversity. As leaders, we encourage this through our own staffing decisions and by encouraging interdisciplinary efforts in support of courses that focus on multicultural understanding.

6. We Must Understand the Technological Revolution

Every aspect of our lives, from buying groceries to getting a medical diagnosis, is impacted by technology. Similarly, technology is having a dramatic impact on the way students learn and access information. Technology can be a positive tool or it can be another factor that widens the gap between affluent students and those from low-income and challenged settings.

7. We Must Create Alternate Pathways to Becoming a Teacher That Embrace Rigor

As president I was committed to challenging UC to set the highest academic and research standards. This must be a guiding principal for our teacher education programs as well. With increasing shortages in teaching, the need for alternative pathways to become a teacher is evident. In developing these alternatives, we must remember that our children and their families are entitled to caring, qualified, and competent teachers. Literature clearly documents that teachers play an important role in their students' learning and teachers mature and improve over time (NCTAF, 1996).

Research on several alternative licensure programs suggests that teachers who choose these alternative routes leave the profession at an alarming rate, much higher than those who choose a more traditional path (NCTAF, 1996). As a result, teacher turnover is compounded. We must be diligent in developing alternative pathways with the same accountability components as standard teacher education programs. Our most distressed school systems, that is, schools in our urban core and our most rural areas, are the ones most likely to hire teachers who choose an alternative approach. Consequently, these schools face the most serious challenges and their students cannot afford another burden that could contribute to an ever-increasing achievement gap.

The University of Cincinnati is a microcosm of the challenges facing public education. In a real sense, its challenges mirror those of PK–16 education. The quality and longevity of the university's commitment to excellence and partnership will characterize the next decade of its journey.

The daily business of sustaining our long journey requires a commitment to knowing our partners, trusting a common mission, and sharing a vital vision for the equity of all students. Our ability to sustain joint responsibility for the priorities of public education is the very quality that will determine the character of our institution, the commitments of faculty and staff, the success of our students, and our integrity as a great urban university.

The common language of the Cincinnati educational endeavor may have its roots in national reports and manifestos, in the metaphors of architecture and master planning, and in the stark demographics of students and families challenged and failed by our educational systems, but it is in the more human dimensions of partnership and collaboration that we are finding new local leadership and new directions.

Joseph A. Steger retired as president of the University of Cincinnati in 2003 after serving for 19 years. He previously held management positions in both industrial and academic organizations such as Colt Industries, Prudential, and Rensselaer Polytechnic Institute. He has also consulted worldwide with both government and private organizations including the People's Republic of China, New York City Police and Tax Department, General Electric, the National Science Foundation, and Texaco. He currently serves as vice chairman of TechSolve (formerly the Institute of Advanced Manufacturing Sciences), as chair of the Board of Drake Center, and chair of the Ohio Supercomputer Center Governing Board. He is also a member of the National Collegiate Athletic Association Board of Directors, the Ohio Aerospace Institute Board of Trustee, and the National Commission on Cooperative Education.

BIBLIOGRAPHY

About Parham. (2003). Retrieved March 31, 2003, http://parham.cps-k12.org/index.html.

Bolich, A. M. (2001). *Reducing your losses: Help new teachers become veteran teachers.* Atlanta, GA: Southern Region Education Board.

Borko, H., & Mayfield, V. (1995). "The roles of the cooperating teachers and university supervisor in learning to teach." *Teaching and Teacher Education, 11* (5), 501–518.

Carnegie Forum on Education and the Economy. (1986). *A nation prepared: Teachers for the 21st Century.* The Report of the Task Force on Teaching as a Profession. New York: Carnegie Corporation of New York.

Committed to success for all. (2002). Columbus, OH: Ohio Department of Education. Retrieved March 31, 2003, from http://www.ode.state.oh.us/reportcard/.

Cuneo, C. J., & Harnish, D. (2002). *Approaches to online learning.* Paper presented at the Annual Meeting of the American Educational Research Association, New Orleans, LA.

Delandshere, G., & Petrosky, A. R. (1998). "Assessment of complex performances: Limitations of key measurement assumptions." *Educational Researcher, 28* (7), 14–24.

Fetler, M. (1999). "High school staff characteristics and mathematical results." *Education Policy Analysis Archives, 7* (9). Retrieved March 31, 2003, http://www.epaa.asu.edu/epaa/v7n9.hmtl.

The Holmes Group. (1986). *Tomorrow's teachers: A report of the Holmes Group.* East Lansing, MI: The Holmes Group.

Ladson-Billings, G. (1994). *The dreamkeepers: Successful teachers of African American children.* San Francisco: Jossey-Bass.

Merseth, K. K., Elmore, R. F., & Schorr, L. B. (2000). "Schools, community-based, interventions, and children's learning and development: What's the connect?" In M. C. Wang & W. L. Boyd (Eds.), *Improving results for children and families: Linking collaborative services with school reform efforts.* Greenwich, CT: Information Age Publishers.

Monk, D. H., & King, J. A. (1994). "Multi-level teacher resources effects in pupil performance in secondary mathematics and science: The case of teacher subject matter preparation." In R. G. Ehrenberg (Ed.), *Choices and consequences: Contemporary policy issues in education* (pp. 29–58). Ithaca, New York: ILR Press.

National Commission of Excellence in Education. (1983). *A nation at risk: The imperative for educational reform.* Washington, DC: U.S. Government Printing Office.

NCTAF (National Commission of Teaching and America's Future). (1996). *What matters most: Teaching for America's future.* New York: National Commission on Teaching and America's Future.

National Reading Panel. (2000). *Teaching children to read: An evidence-based assessment of the scientific research literature on reading and its implications for reading instruction.* Washington, D.C.: National Institute of Child Health and Human Development.

Overview of Cincinnati Public Schools. (2002). Cincinnati, OH: Cincinnati Public Schools. Retrieved March 31, 2003, from http://www.cps-k12.org/general/Overview/overview.html.

CHAPTER

A "Metroversity" for a New Millennium

Eugene P. Trani

Presidents of the new "metroversities" of the twenty first century must look outside the traditional relationships that institutions have with the community into arenas in which they can become full partners. Influencing the quality of local schools is perhaps one of the most important roles that presidents and their institutions can assume. It is one thing to serve on a board of a civic organization. It is another to lead it and to work with its members and constituencies to set the agenda. In other words, if universities of the future are to have the impact that they are capable of, presidents have to change.

Since my appointment as president in 1990, Virginia Commonwealth University (VCU) has become a dynamic collaborator in economic growth and development in metropolitan Richmond, the capital of Virginia. As president of a major urban university and chairman of Richmond Renaissance—a collaboration of leaders from business, city government, and the African American community—I have had a unique opportunity to join other leaders in reshaping the future of economic revitalization in Richmond. And, improving the educational achievement of our public school children is fundamental to that future.

University leadership is now compelled to take an active role in addressing community problems and in forging public policy that will lead to effective plans and programs. Leading change has to include a vision that is consistent with the aspirations of a variety of constituencies. All the key stakeholders of the community—from the institution's faculty and administration to neighborhood residents, local government, and civic leaders—must assume ownership in any shared idea of the future, especially with regard to city public schools. The business community, in particular, has a direct stake in the quality of the city's schools because of the economic stimulation that a well-educated workforce creates. The business community, in turn, can offer important links to the university. Through my chairmanship of Richmond Renaissance, I have been able to bring both sectors together on behalf of the education of our community's children.

Indeed, this kind of synergy is perhaps the most important factor in achieving community-based revitalization. Partnerships can do more to effect change than any one person or organization. From those synergies come realistic action plans that include methods of evaluating progress and, ultimately, a long-term commitment on the part of all stakeholders to their shared idea of the future, in this case the importance of sustaining quality public schools.

VIRGINIA COMMONWEALTH UNIVERSITY: A "METROVERSITY" FOR THE TWENTY FIRST CENTURY

When I came to VCU in 1990, it was clear that to effect the kind of change that would allow VCU to more directly influence the future of the community, from the economy to health care to K–12 education, a long-range planning process would be the most important first step. The process had to involve a broad spectrum of faculty, student, staff, and administrative leaders and it had to result in initiatives that would ultimately secure the financial future of our academic and medical missions during the turbulent 1990s and early twenty first century. That process led to A Strategic Plan for the Future of Virginia Commonwealth University (1998), which was adopted by the Board of Visitors in 1993 and revised in 1998.

At its most fundamental level, VCU's strategic plan recognized that we had a unique opportunity to redefine the identity of the university beyond the notion of *urban*—which, similar to *residential*, describes institutions of higher education primarily in terms of their location—to a more complex *metropolitan* idea that describes our interconnectedness with the community both locally and globally. In other words, it was time for us to imagine VCU as a "metroversity" (Pulley, 2001), characterized by a central commitment to a global, multidisciplinary approach to teaching, research, service, and patient care in the context of the local environment. Several major highlights of VCU during the last 13 years of my tenure help explain the comprehensiveness with which we could and did undertake the achievement of this new concept.

VCU is not only Virginia's largest university located in an urban center but also one of only three institutions in the state ranked among the top

100 research universities in the country as a Carnegie Doctoral/Research University-Extensive. VCU's annual revenues of $1.4 billion include more than $180 million in research funding. Our 1,600 full-time faculty are nationally and internationally recognized for excellence in their fields. VCU also supports 16 interdisciplinary centers and institutes of excellence that engage faculty from across our campuses in public policy research, health research, and such high technology research applications as biotechnology and biomedical engineering.

VCU enrolls more than 26,000 students on our academic campus and at the VCU Medical Center. It offers 164 undergraduate, graduate, professional, doctorate, and postgraduate certificate degree programs through the College of Humanities and Sciences and the schools of Allied Health Professions, the Arts, Business, Dentistry, Education, Engineering, Mass Communications, Medicine, Nursing, Pharmacy, and Social Work. VCU students can pursue their educational goals through day classes as well as an extensive selection of evening courses and off-site programs. Twenty VCU graduate programs are ranked by *U.S. News & World Report* among the best of their kind in the nation with two ranking number one in their disciplines. Many other programs enjoy national rankings for excellence from their respective professional organizations and societies.

Since its introduction in 1993, VCU's strategic plan has taken advantage of its scope in education, research, public service, and patient care to develop a framework in which the faculty and administration can engage in a mutually beneficial exchange of ideas, experiences, activities, and initiatives that provide resources and opportunities for VCU, the communities of Richmond, and beyond. The role of the president within the metroversity concept is to facilitate this kind of collaboration among diverse leaders, disciplines, and sectors.

Before assessing the impact of institutions on their communities, however, it is essential that presidents identify exactly how their institutions will benefit by extending their academic mission into the community. What is the value of that community linkage for student learning and faculty scholarship? Will it provide greater hands-on experiences for students, expand fieldwork sites, or lead to credit courses that support a real-world educational experience? How can this new vision of the mission support faculty roles and rewards beyond traditional teaching and publication expectations? The community-based initiatives that VCU developed over the past 13 years, including our School of Education's development of customized student programs, which are embedded in the metropolitan region's school divisions, adequately answer these essential questions.

RICHMOND PUBLIC SCHOOLS

Richmond's public schools serve more than 26,000 students at 31 elementary, 10 middle, and 9 high schools. Ninety percent of students are African American, with 7 percent white and 2 percent Hispanic. Almost 92 percent of students qualify for free or reduced-cost lunch (Richmond Public Schools, 2003). The strong relationship between low-income and historically weak performance on standardized tests is obvious in the performance of public school children. Thirty-four schools in Virginia are identified as failing under the No Child Left Behind legislation; half of these schools are in Richmond (Virginia Department of Education, 2003).

With a School of Education ranked thirty-ninth in the country by U.S. News & World Report and a goal to strengthen our partnership with the area's school divisions, VCU will continue to have a critically important role in the enhancement of public schools by working within the collaborative framework established by our strategic plan. Leading that effort is Dr. William C. Bosher Jr., who was appointed in July 2002 as the new dean of the VCU School of Education.

Dr. Bosher previously served as superintendent of two of the Richmond area's four metropolitan school districts and as the superintendent of public instruction for the Commonwealth of Virginia. Because he was also on the Board of Directors of the Richmond Metropolitan Chamber of Commerce and the Board of Trustees of the University of Richmond, he brought significant experience to the deanship in the public, private, and civic sectors that would strengthen the strategic bridges between our School of Education and its communities.

Indeed, I believed that it was critically important to appoint someone with a high level of public school experience and expertise that had been gathered from years of working within the school systems and at the state level. It signaled a major commitment on the part of the university to be very serious about our relationship between our School of Education and K–12 education in Richmond and throughout the Commonwealth. Thanks to significant enhancements in the collaborative work of the university, the school board, and the school administration as a result of the appointment of Dr. Bosher, there already have been major increases in 2002 in the number of schools accredited under the state's new Standards of Learning program. This state initiative, which has received national recognition, provides an annual assessment of students in grades 3, 5, 8, and 11. The areas of English, math, science, and the social sciences are tested against rigorous and specific academic expectations.

THE VCU STRATEGIC PLAN: A FRAMEWORK FOR CONNECTIONS

Consistent with the metroversity concept, a broad framework of connections in which both VCU and the community would realize benefits from partnership was essential to the success of our strategic plan, which would, among other things, set the stage for enhancing the involvement of the School of Education in area schools. That framework included implementing key priorities that I established at the beginning of my tenure at VCU, which formed the foundation for the vision of our strategic plan.

One of these priorities was a master-site building plan, developed in concert with neighborhood organizations, which would expand the university into underused corridors next to campus. This expansion would provide much-needed facilities for students. And for Broad Street, Richmond's major thruway adjacent to campus, it would start a revitalization process that would evolve into a much broader vision of downtown revitalization under the auspices of Richmond Renaissance. VCU's construction in this corridor, currently worth more than $84 million, has already attracted a large regional lumber and hardware supply store, a supermarket, and upscale apartments. VCU's master-site plan also incorporates guidelines that integrate the design of new buildings with the native architecture of their surroundings, thus further underscoring VCU's vision of its interconnectedness with the city.

Another step that would develop VCU's connection to community revitalization involved the development of programs that would depend directly on the expertise of VCU administrators and faculty. Among the new programs established within this broader framework were community advisory boards for the campuses that maintain neighborhood involvement and interest in university planning and promote the sharing of jurisdictions between VCU police and Richmond City police to facilitate community policing—which has had a measurable impact on the reduction of crime in these jurisdictions while also significantly improving VCU's image among its neighbors. Another new program, the Community Service Associates Program, brings VCU learning and scholarship directly into the community.

The latter program is designed to allow VCU faculty, through a reduced teaching load, to take a semester to work intensively with community organizations on projects that will benefit from their expertise. Thus, programs are selected on the basis of mutual interests on the part of the faculty member and the organization's mission. Through the Community Service Associates Program, faculty have not only had a direct impact on an identified community need but also have enhanced the real-world dimensions of their scholarship and teaching and, thus, furthered the educational priorities of VCU. In fact, the program has spawned the development of service-learning courses for students, which engage them directly in the community along with their faculty, in disciplines ranging from art education to nursing to urban planning. Since the program's inception in 1990, faculty from 50 different academic units at VCU have contributed to 255 community-based projects in partnership with 167 different organizations.

In the context of collaboration, VCU's strategic plan also sought to develop the university's potential to influence economic development in Richmond and the state. That idea of our influence, in fact, grew out of the community, which recognized the tremendous potential of VCU's faculty to have a material impact on developing the workforce and research for the high-technology era.

At about the time of my arrival at VCU, the Greater Richmond Chamber of Commerce put together a broad-based group of city and county leaders in a long-range planning process that led, in 1991, to the publication of the strategic plan, "Focus on Our Future." That plan identified the development of a biotechnology research park and an engineering school as vital to the entire region's future and it named VCU as the lead partner in that effort. These initiatives became key elements of VCU's strategic plan and led to the establishment of the Virginia Biotechnology Research Park and the VCU School of Engineering, the latter unique in its focus on manufacturing in new technology industries and the relatively new field of biomedical engineering. Within these priorities opportunities for engineering, business, and medical faculty to collaborate in interdisciplinary teaching and research have dramatically increased.

Considering the historically prominent role of VCU's medical center in health care education, research, and patient care, it also was clear that VCU should be a forerunner in responding to the challenges brought about by health-care reform. This role was reflected in Building a Health Care Delivery System, a strategy that grew out of the larger strategic plan for the entire university. It, too, sought to develop mutually beneficial relationships with different sectors of the community concerned with the delivery of health care. Some of these strategies include establishing primary care and specialty care satellite centers throughout Richmond; a Medicaid HMO; enhanced relationships with area physicians in a variety of specialties, insurance providers, businesses, and corporations; and, most importantly, the VCU Health System, one of the most significant organizational changes in our institution's history. All these new directions have

led to better quality and delivery of health care to diverse patient populations while helping to secure the financial future of the teaching, research,
and patient care mission of the VCU Medical Center and its responsibilities as the leading state provider of indigent care.

UNIVERSITY-SCHOOL PARTNERSHIPS

As important as the Virginia Biotechnology Research Park and the
School of Engineering have been to Richmond's and Virginia's economic
development, it was clear that a more aggressive, broad-based initiative on
behalf of neighborhoods, which would incorporate an emphasis on public
schooling, would be equally vital to the region's economic infrastructure.
And, in fact, VCU already had some experience in this regard through its
relationship with the Carver neighborhood adjacent to campus.

Early in my tenure, VCU and the Carver community, a predominately
low- to middle-income African American neighborhood and the location
of the largest urban elementary school in Richmond, began working together informally to provide educational experiences for VCU students
and educational opportunity for Carver residents. Steps to formalize the
Carver-VCU relationship began intensively in 1997 when a Carver-VCU
Partnership Steering Committee was assembled, composed of a team of
VCU faculty from different disciplines, Carver residents, and representatives from the school and city agencies. Out of that committee came the
Carver-VCU Partnership with the goal to improve neighborhood safety,
education, community and economic development, health, and social services. Eventually supported by a Community Outreach Partnership Center (COPC) Housing and Urban Development (HUD) grant, the Carver-
VCU Partnership has become a model university-neighborhood program
not only for Richmond but for HUD as well.

Among the priorities of the Carver-VCU Partnership is educational
achievement of children and adults alike. The partnership's services include a Parent Resource Center equipped with computers where residents
can have access to and receive assistance with computer and Internet
classes as well as other services such as workshops on job preparation, effective parenting, and mentoring. Carver School students also receive intensive tutoring through America Reads and the AmeriCorps program
based in our Office of Community Programs, tutoring from VCU students
enrolled in service-learning courses, and enrichment opportunities through
after-school programs.

In addition to educational services, VCU's nursing faculty and students
provide children with health screenings each fall and our dentistry faculty

and students provide weekly screenings and treatment through the school's mobile dental van. Graduate students in the Department of Psychology and the School of Social Work also provide psychological assessments, individualized behavior plans, and small group sessions for students and families.

In all, more than 30 academic and administrative units contribute their time and talents to the Carver-VCU Partnership. Now in its sixth year, the program has garnered more than $1 million in external funding, led to a reduction in crime, and even inspired the production of a play on the Carver community's history that received widespread local acclaim.

Other partnerships with the city's schools in which VCU is involved include the Better the Odds program targeted to enhancing Richmond schoolteachers' computer expertise through access to software, specialized workshops, and technology training. The School of Education also is working with city schools to improve services for special education students.

Another School of Education project established in 1991, the Metropolitan Educational Research Consortium (MERC), brings VCU faculty together with teachers and administrators on research projects on issues and challenges confronting practicing professional educators. The consortium includes the school districts of Chesterfield, Hanover, Henrico, and Powhatan counties and the cities of Colonial Heights, Hopewell, and Richmond. A major benefit of MERC is that members can position themselves to compete for grants requiring a school-university partnership. MERC currently provides services to more than 12,000 teachers and administrators and 150,000 school children.

Other VCU schools and programs, such as the School of Engineering, the College of Humanities and Sciences, and VCU Life Sciences, have built excellent relationships with city schools that are helping students train to become teachers and administrators in their respective disciplines. VCU Life Sciences has, in fact, developed a science-teacher preparation track as part of its undergraduate and graduate programming.

More recently, VCU education faculty have been working on developing doctoral training focused on urban issues and civic engagement and designed to prepare principals and other educational leaders for the city's public schools. And in recognition of the growing diversity of the surrounding counties, the Henrico County Public School System, whose 43,000 students are 47 percent minority, has joined with the VCU School of Education to create three master's tracks and one doctoral track focused on developing educational leaders for the county.

These partnerships, along with our strategic initiatives that facilitate faculty and student involvement directly in the community and support economic development in the Richmond area, show how VCU is integrating engagement across disciplines and across different community sectors. In fact, VCU is now a national model of the impact of higher education on urban and economic development. In a commissioned multi-site study, the Department of Housing and Urban Development ranked VCU at the highest level for institutionalizing outreach and community partnerships, a ranking VCU shares with only seven other colleges and universities in the country (U.S. Department of Housing and Urban Development, 1998).

VCU also was one of two case studies, along with Columbia University, in the spring 2002 report, *Leveraging Colleges and Universities for Urban Economic Revitalization: An Action Agenda,* published jointly by CEOs for Cities, an alliance of mayors, corporate executives, and university presidents, and the Initiative for a Competitive Inner City, which is focused on inner-city development. VCU was chosen as a case study because of its value in exploring the little understood role of universities in urban areas and economically distressed inner cities. For example, the study applauded the Carver-VCU Partnership as a demonstration of an institution that has assumed local and regional leadership on multiple levels to achieve mutual objectives. The report states that "by all accounts, the VCU-Carver relationship has been a success. The university has expanded its real estate without alienating the neighborhood most affected by the expansion." Moreover, "VCU now has formal structures in place to connect the community with the university" (CEOs for Cities, 2002, p. 51–52).

RICHMOND RENAISSANCE AND THE SCHOOLS

The major result of implementing a community-based strategic vision during the 1990s and at the beginning of this decade is that VCU is now seen as a legitimate community leader. In order for institutions to reach such a position of influence, presidents of the new metroversities of the twenty first century must look outside the traditional relationships that institutions have with the community into arenas in which they can become full partners. Influencing the quality of local schools is perhaps one of the most important roles that presidents and their institutions can assume. It is one thing to serve on a board of a civic organization. It is another to lead it and to work with its members and constituencies to set the agenda. In other words, if universities of the future are to have the impact that they are capable of, presidents have to change.

I began my own process in this regard by first seeking to become more involved with the Greater Richmond Chamber of Commerce. That involvement, which began early in my tenure in relation to the 1991 report "Focus on Our Future," eventually led to my appointment as chair of the

Richmond Chamber for the 1997–1998 term—a recognition, really, of VCU's achievement of its strategic vision to link its mission to broad community priorities. In 2001, I was then asked to serve as chair of Richmond Renaissance, an organization with a focus on bringing diverse leaders together to work for economic development and the revitalization of downtown Richmond—again, a result of the position of community leadership that VCU had attained through its strategic plan.

Through my chairmanship of Richmond Renaissance, I have been able to bring our faculty directly in touch with a diverse spectrum of community and business leaders who have come together around revitalizing downtown Richmond and, as part of that objective, embraced the idea of broad-based community involvement in transforming local public schools. For example, I have invited faculty from VCU's College of Humanities and Sciences to Richmond Renaissance meetings to discuss the kinds of courses and experiences that future teachers will require within the dramatic changes occurring in the workplace of the twenty first century, particularly in the life sciences. I also have encouraged members of Richmond Renaissance to collaborate with VCU education faculty to seek grants for math and science programs in the schools.

Through linking university leadership with community leadership, I have been able to expand the foundation for collaboration beyond a specific project between a university faculty member and an organization or a university education school and a school system, to one that is concerned broadly with the improvement of the local public schools. The coming together of diverse sectors within a major civic organization has inspired their leaders' long-term commitment to sustaining institutions and industries. And there is now an across-the-board recognition that no institution is more important than the schools.

One of the most important benefits of the metroversity perspective within this broader context is its unique ability to foster greater understanding between businesses and schools. Too often, business leaders blame schools for an inadequately prepared workforce while school leaders believe that business has only a weak grasp of the realities of urban education. When they are brought together, they can begin to appreciate the other's challenges and, more importantly, their mutual stake in having vibrant, high-quality public schools.

The involvement of Richmond Renaissance at this more comprehensive level of collaboration, in fact, was crucial for encouraging the Richmond business community to become more active in school reform. Business leaders know that importing a skilled and well-educated workforce to Richmond can take the local economy only so far. Attracting new business and business expansion depends as much on a high-quality public education system as on favorable tax rates or access to an effective transportation network. New industries will attract corporate headquarters to Richmond but good schools will keep them here. Thus, good schools and thriving industries are both essential to a region's economy. In this way, a consensus has emerged among business owners around the priority of improving city schools through Richmond Renaissance.

As we began to engage in the strategic thinking necessary for changing public schools, it was important that we not dictate the nature of school reform but rather work with school leaders on an agenda of ways that Richmond Renaissance members, through the new Education Committee, could support the school system's goals. Some very effective, early results from this approach have been workshops sponsored by local businesses for principals, who increasingly are asked to be managers as well as educators. Corporations also have developed a resource list of companies willing to provide grants and volunteers to schools.

Through the relationship between Richmond Renaissance and the city's schools, VCU and the business community have also become more involved in the recruitment and retention of effective and dedicated teachers for the city's schools. Although a teacher shortage plagues the entire nation, it is particularly worse in urban environments where the challenges of working with diverse student populations can seem daunting to even the most intrepid teachers.

Business leaders, through Richmond Renaissance, have joined the human resources staff of Richmond schools in recruiting promising new educators at job fairs around the country. Jim Ukrop, a member of Richmond Renaissance's Education Committee, heads up this effort. Each year, Mr. Ukrop leads a group composed of members of Richmond Public Schools, representatives from the business community, and representatives from VCU and the University of Richmond on teacher recruitment trips to New York, Boston, and Pittsburgh. Companies lend their corporate jets to fly these volunteer teams to these locations to recruit the best and brightest. A month after the recruitment trips, prospective teachers are invited to Richmond for a weekend of activities and interviews with principals, a tour of Richmond, a reception, and other activities. The purpose of the weekend is to encourage these teachers to take teaching positions in public schools in Richmond. If out-of-state teachers accept positions here, VCU allows them to pay only in-state tuition and fees for graduate-level courses.

This collaborative recruitment effort under the auspices of Richmond Renaissance has been so successful that over the last three years, 800 teachers have been recruited to the Richmond Public School System.

STRATEGIES FOR REINVENTING SCHOOLS

It was additionally obvious to Richmond Renaissance's Education Committee that improved schools would require a fundamental change in the relationship between Richmond's public schools and the Richmond community. Clearly, public urban school systems cannot undertake reform alone. They have neither the control nor the resources necessary to make big differences across the board in student achievement. Richmond Renaissance, therefore, began to help when Civic Strategies, Inc., a consulting firm, agreed to work with Richmond's school board, superintendent, and Richmond Renaissance to develop a strategic plan for Richmond Public Schools.

At the outset, it was agreed that the partners in the strategic planning process would represent all sectors: the schools and their leadership, the business community, Richmond Renaissance (through its Education Committee), VCU, the faith-based community, parents, local citizens, and community agencies. The plan would be founded on the concept of reinventing the relationship between school and community. The collaborators agreed that to be enduring, the strategic plan for improving local public schools also had to reflect what the people of Richmond's communities believe should be their future direction. Prolonged success depends on the extent to which community stakeholders are equal partners in the process, from inception to implementation. As research activists in the community—collecting useful information and sharing experiences about the schools—their influence in the ultimate outcome would be genuine.

FIRST STEPS

To implement a new idea of schools in the city, a strategic planning committee was established with 24 individuals representing all sectors of the community. The committee took up the following questions:

- What should a strategic plan endeavor to achieve on behalf of public schools?
- What would the committee's priorities be?
- How would the plan redefine roles, responsibilities, and relationships among the sectors represented on the strategic planning committee?
- Where would support and resources come from?
- How could the plan maintain the long-term involvement of the community stakeholders in the schools?

The most important initial challenge that the strategic planning committee faced was generating public interest in its goals. That required a public relations effort to educate the public about the important role of Richmond's public schools in the community and in society as a whole. While there are several outstanding and, in fact, model schools in the city, highly publicized failings often overshadow the achievements of these schools. Thus, public relations planning called for developing multiple opportunities to talk about the committee, its purpose, and the achievements of Richmond's public schools while describing the many challenges facing public urban education in Richmond.

The strategic planning committee members' next task was to meet with community leaders to talk about the new concept of schools as extensions of, rather than islands in, the community—that the community depended on the schools for its social and economic future just as the schools depended on the community for their future. It was important to seek these leaders' guidance in developing new ideas for reinventing the role of schools in the community as well as their suggestions for other collaborators and resources.

Throughout the process of identifying the steps needed to develop a strategic plan, the strategic planning committee knew that teacher and parent representation and support as well as strengthened school leadership were vital to any effort to transform Richmond's public schools. Thus, city- and school-based parent teacher associations (PTAs) would be central to the strategic planning process by providing a conduit for parental involvement in the schools and serving as a link between schools and families. School principals also would become more active in community relations so that the basis for the ongoing recruitment of community stakeholders could be established to sustain quality schools.

CENTERS OF COMMUNITY LEARNING AND ACTIVITY

From these first steps came the plan, Community-Wide Vision for the Future of the Richmond Public School System. The plan essentially called for the transformation of schools as places for classrooms to schools as comprehensive centers of student learning and community engagement. Richmond Renaissance enthusiastically adopted this approach and incorporated it into our larger vision of a revitalized city.

It is important to us at Richmond Renaissance that in the process of expanding the role of schools in the community, we ensure that the academic mission of schools drive every strategic consideration taken up by the strategic planning committee. In other words, how can the community engage in schools as *learning* centers? Investigating creative ways to achieve this objective was essential in order to overcome the absence of parents' involvement in their children's schools because of their own negative or limited experiences in school. Schools as community activity and learning centers would draw parents and residents to schools in a nonthreatening way while furthering the committee's efforts to publicize what the schools were doing well. If parents, community and business leaders, and neighborhood residents could experience for themselves the positive effects of a school's mission, they could become more amenable to involvement in developing and implementing strategies for school improvements.

In addition to facilitating the work of the strategic planning committee, it was important that I, in my role as university president, ensure that VCU faculty and administrators were continuing to work directly with the strategic planning committee, Richmond Renaissance, and other organizations to support the implementation of this new vision of our local public schools as *schools-within-community*.

PROGRAM AND IMPLEMENTATION DEVELOPMENT

Along with the excitement of a new vision for the schools came the more mundane and more challenging issue of how to translate that vision into reality. The members of the strategic planning committee had to think about the practical requirements that would come with schools as community activity and learning centers. Extending school hours, for example, raised such cost issues as extra cleaning and upkeep of facilities, after-school compensation for staff, daycare for children while parents participated in activities, providing those without transportation the means to come to the schools, insurance, and the myriad other legal and practical considerations that accompany the kind of transformation envisioned for Richmond's public schools. The committee realized that working closely with the school's teachers, staff, and the parents would be the most effective way to address these contingencies while also guaranteeing the all-important buy-in among these key constituents in the concept of schools as community activity and learning centers.

It was equally important that the needs of all the participants in schools as community activity and learning centers—students, parents, and residents—be clearly defined so that programs would be relevant to them. This consideration, again, included developing services and programs that would be unique to the school mission not duplicative of services provided by churches and other community agencies. That would preclude offering services such as summer day care, for example, while developing programs that would enhance computer skills, career development, and many other remedial and skill-building needs identified by the stakeholders.

This approach additionally offered one of several ways in which businesses, VCU, and many other sectors could become directly involved in the schools. For example, businesses could offer to upgrade a school's computer lab so that students, parents, and residents would have access to state-of-the-art hardware and software. Similarly, programs could involve business and university mentors in math and science, arts, crafts, music, and reading. Field trips to corporate and other sites could be organized with the goal to involve all the participants, not just students.

For families and neighborhood residents, additional services along the lines of those offered through the Carver-VCU Partnership, such as health and dental screenings, counseling and career services, and Internet access, would be invaluable. Speakers from the business, civic, and university communities also could be identified to lead parenting skills workshops, support groups, and financial management seminars, and the schools could be used for meetings and gatherings of community organizations and for recreational activities. In this way, families and residents would have a new experience with the schools, further strengthening their sense of responsibility for and pride in them.

The overall objective, then, would be to motivate everyone in the community to become the primary stakeholders in their neighborhoods' schools. Ongoing recruitment and training of collaborators and accountability processes would be integral to the success of schools as community activity and learning centers. The most important take-home lesson would be that learning is both a function of the formal classroom and a function of the community as a whole in which everyone has a stake and from which everyone can benefit.

CHOOSING A MODEL SCHOOL

To pursue the vision of schools as community activity and learning centers, Richmond Renaissance's Education Committee chose a model elementary school as our guide and Mr. Ukrop as our leader. As one of the heads of Richmond's leading family-owned and -operated community and regional grocery stores, he is himself a model of community and business leadership.

Mr. Ukrop first brought Swansboro Elementary School, located in south side Richmond, to our attention as a possible regional model for a community activity and learning center. He had pleasant memories of his days as a student at Swansboro and was involved in the school's efforts to improve student academic achievement through an adopt-a-school mentoring and tutoring program. As a result of that involvement and his growing admiration for the school's development and implementation of community programs, Mr. Ukrop suggested to us that we take a field trip to the school, coordinated by a Swansboro school consultant and volunteer, to see for ourselves how a school can be a successful community activity and learning center and an enticing environment for a partnership between a business and a school.

After visiting the school and speaking to the students, teachers, principal, and the school's community liaison, we decided to use Swansboro as our Richmond model. In fact, Swansboro Elementary School's mission statement could not have been more reflective of our own philosophy for developing schools as community and learning centers: "Our mission at Swansboro Elementary School is to provide an educational setting where students acquire the skills necessary to become responsible, productive members of our global society. We believe these skills can best be obtained in an environment where parents, staff, and members of the community continue to learn and work together to motivate, encourage, and nurture our students."

True to its mission statement, Swansboro Elementary School is open 16 hours a day with each day focused on a different theme for students, parents, and community residents. For example, the Technoblast Workshop is offered on one of the evenings to students who need to enhance their computer skills for Virginia's standardized achievement tests. Students attend the workshop with their parents or guardians who also use the computers to develop and practice their own computer skills. Other evening themes include a career night, parenting skills, and health and nutrition. Classes are also offered five days a week to help interested adults prepare for the Graduate Equivalency Diploma (GED).

The key benefit of Swansboro Elementary School's program is that it was developed at the grass-roots community level, a platform that is integral to our vision of schools as community activity and learning centers. The school and its programs also are well managed by the administrators, faculty, and staff, making it relatively easy for businesses to step in and become a part of the total school mission.

TOWARD A MANUAL OF BEST PRACTICES

The strategic planning committee's next step was to determine exactly how to engage businesses in the transformation of the schools. After some considerable brainstorming, Richmond Renaissance's Education Committee, the strategic planning committee, and other VCU experts and Richmond community parent and teacher groups decided to undertake the creation of a best practices manual for an adopt-a-school program along the lines of the Swansboro model.

It was important from my perspective that the strategic planning team create a model specifically designed for Richmond rather than using other community models. Although there are general principles common to all models, local businesses and other collaborators know their own schools and the environment in which they operate. Richmond's model, therefore, had to incorporate that familiarity if it were to succeed in engaging businesses in the way that all of us were envisioning for our city's public schools.

As part of that process, the strategic planning committee had to consider these questions: What does it mean to say your business wants to adopt a school? Is it just a mechanism to provide goods, services, or both— or something entirely different? What will businesses derive from partnering with a school?

The answers would obviously come from individual business owners but within the context of the mission of Richmond Renaissance—that we all have a stake in helping to provide good schools for our city's children if they are to raise their own expectations for themselves and, in the process, become citizens committed to the well-being of their communities as well as workers with the skills and education required for the twenty-first century workplace. In other words, dividends for businesses in these collaborations are not in short-term financial gains—and businesses know this. Their payoff is down the road when, in large part because of their engagement in the schools, Richmond can more effectively grow its own workforce as well as nurture the development of the city's future leaders.

To facilitate the connection between businesses and the schools within the adopt-a-school model, the strategic planning committee members decided that it would be helpful for schools to develop statements of need describing their challenges, goals, the steps needed to achieve them, and the benchmarks they would use to measure success. A manual of best practices would assist the schools in developing these statements and, as such, make it easier for businesses to understand how to tie their involvement to the schools' objectives. Designing the best practices manual also would include: (1) developing and writing guidelines and mechanisms for adopting schools; (2) determining which schools have a management system in place sufficient for sustaining the program; and (3) clarifying Richmond Renaissance's role as that of match-maker between businesses and suitable schools.

Although we at Richmond Renaissance considered a best practices manual critical to facilitating business involvement in the schools, the representative from the Richmond Education Association suggested that rather than presenting principals and teachers with a so-called business plan as a fait accompli, the best practices manual would describe preconditions—that is, the environment needed to facilitate collaboration—as well as partnership roles for everyone involved with the school assuming the role of managing the process of forming partnerships. Following this process, a project manager was appointed to recruit business sponsors and work with the appropriate school personnel to get the project and the collaboration rolling.

IN THE END

During the past two years, the Swansboro School has moved from a provisional rating by the Virginia Department of Education to full accreditation, the highest distinction available from the state. While statewide budget constraints have prevented the strategic planning team from expanding the community activity and learning center model to additional schools, everyone involved in the process thus far is optimistic that it holds promise to increase community involvement in the schools and, importantly, develop a greater understanding in the community of how children learn.

For Virginia Commonwealth University, the process of imagining schools as community activity and learning centers and participating in the development of a best practices manual have provided tremendous opportunities for faculty and administrators from many disciplines, including education, to deepen their relationships with the schools. These opportunities have continued to transform our own institution and, from the perspective of VCU's strategic plan, that is very much to the point of becoming a metroversity.

The groundwork for getting university-wide involvement in this project evolved from VCU's strategic plan and VCU's commitment to a careful assessment of the university's unique character and strengths. VCU, a university of the twenty first century, is now one whose borders are open to the community not as a public service add-on but as a function of its entire mission. VCU's involvement with Richmond City Schools, therefore, is intrinsic to the metroversity concept, no different from opening the doors of faculty laboratories to the commercialization process through a research park or engaging the industrial community in the development of a unique interdisciplinary engineering school.

Pursuing this new idea of the twenty-first century university—the metroversity—is, in fact, critical if the role of our nation's cities as the engines of future economic prosperity is to be sustained. That is why presidents must join mayors, school superintendents, and business and community leaders at the community-wide planning table. That is why they must be not only academic leaders but also community leaders.

VCU is making real and lasting contributions to the economy, communities, health care, and public education in the Richmond region and the entire state. In the process, we have incorporated a significant real-world dimension into the learning, scholarship, and research opportunities that we offer our faculty and students. We have, in other words, learned from our community. As a result, our faculty and students are engaged in the community not simply for extra credit or to do the right thing but as the essential foundation for university learning, scholarship, and research in the twenty first century.

Eugene P. Trani has served as president of Virginia Commonwealth University and president and chair of the Board of Directors of VCU Health System since 1990. Previously, he was vice president for academic affairs and professor of history at the University of Wisconsin System. At VCU, he developed a strategic plan founded on establishing community partnerships and has led VCU's efforts to internationalize its campuses, most recently through the development of the VCU School of the Arts in Doha, Qatar. He also has established a new, comprehensive teaching, research, and public education program called VCU Life Sciences, which involves faculty from medicine, health sciences, basic sciences, the humanities, business, engineering, and education in the new field of biological complexity. In addition to community service, Dr. Trani is a nationally recognized scholar of history, foreign affairs, and the role of higher education in community and economic development, both in the United States and other countries.

BIBLIOGRAPHY

CEOs for Cities & Initiative for a Competitive Inner City (ICIC). (2002). *Leveraging colleges and universities for urban economic revitalization: An action agenda.* Retrieved February 28, 2004, from http://www.ceosforcities.org/research/2002/leveraging_colleges/.

Pulley, J. L. (July 20, 2001). "Brick by brick, an urban university rebuilds its campus alumni ties." *The Chronicle of Higher Education*, Money and Management Section, p. 24.

Richmond Public Schools. (2003). *Statistics.* Retrieved March 31, 2003, from http://www.richmond.k12.va.us/statistics/statistics2.htm.

Strategic plan for the future of Virginia Commonwealth University VCU. (1998). Retrieved March 31, 2003, from http://www.vcu.edu/provost/plan.

U.S. Department of Housing and Urban Development. (1998). *Colleges and communities: Partners in urban revitalization—A report on the Community Outreach Partnership Centers program.* Retrieved March 31, 2003, from http://www.oup.org/pubs/annrpt.html.

Virginia Department of Education. (2003). "Schools identified for improvement under the No Child Left Behind Act of 2001." *VA School Report Card.* Retrieved March 31, 2003, from http://www.pen.k12.va.us/VDOE/src/vasrc-nclb.shtml.

CHAPTER 16

The President's Role in Educational Reform: Concluding Observations

Nancy L. Zimpher and Kenneth R. Howey

Leadership, especially in service to K–12 education, requires individuals deeply committed to a vision of community-university engagement and exceptionally accomplished in managing complexity.... All of the presidents and chancellors who have contributed to this volume have committed their lives to this demanding task for one simple reason: They cannot imagine a calling more important or a challenge more rewarding.

The primary focus of this book has been the leadership of university presidents in connecting their campuses and communities to urban school renewal. We are interested in how presidents have brought their leadership skills to bear on the education of our cities' youth. In the first chapter we provided a comprehensive review of the challenges inherent in teacher education reform and urban school renewal. Further, we described what presidents can and are doing to improve teacher quality, through a variety of strategies, both internal and external to the university.

Efforts to reform teacher education and enable school renewal in urban settings do not exist in a vacuum. They are part of the larger context in which presidents serve. To that end, this project also sought to understand better two specific aspects of presidential leadership and institutional context. First, how does the president's understanding of university engagement provide context for teacher education reform and urban school renewal? And second, what steps have these institutional leaders taken to promote understanding within the university so that the education of teachers and school renewal has a central place in a campus's community engagement?

We are indebted to our contributing chapter authors, the 14 presidential members of the Great Cities' Universities (GCU), who have freely and, we believe, provocatively shared their stories with us. This concluding chapter seeks to further contextualize the individual presidential accounts through a cross-case analysis of the leadership issues facing these presidents and a survey of some of the distinctive strategies that these presidents are using to make engagement in school-university collaboration a reality. Sources for this summary reside both in the chapters presented in this text and in interviews we conducted during 2002–2003 with each of the contributing authors about leadership in general. We were interested in their candid reflections about conceptions of presidential leadership generally and, more specifically, in the ways in which they arrived at engagement strategies specific to urban educational reform.

THE CONTEXT OF ENGAGEMENT

Ernest Boyer's clarion call for the "engaged university" launched a generation of discourse that continues to this day. In his examination of the nature of scholarship in the academy, Boyer observed: "As we move toward a new century, profound changes stir the nation and the world. The contours of a new order—and the dimensions of new challenges—loom large on the horizon. It is a moment for boldness in higher education" (Boyer, 1990, p. 75). While the cyclical debates within higher education focus on issues of core curriculum, the quality of campus life, roles and responsibilities of the professoriate, and the economics of higher education, no debate in our recent history has resonated more than the discussion of what constitutes the engaged university. Most notably, the Kellogg Commission's investment in the future of state and land-grant colleges and universities resulted in a multidimensional self-study of how higher learning could enter a new era with an eye toward "one irreducible idea: that we exist to advance the common good; the covenant between public universities and the American people." (Kellogg Commission, 2000, p. 9).

What would the engaged university look like? Here is one view:

> Engaged institutions will produce graduates who will be ready to move along a path of self-directed learning and growth. These graduates will understand the connection between what they have learned in the classroom and the strategies that are necessary to apply these concepts to problems they will face in their careers and in their communities. They will be products of "interactive universities" which have developed partnerships with civic, business and political leaders to build better communities. Yesterday's "ivory

tower" institutions which were designed to be separate from society cannot possibly prepare today's graduates to help solve the problems of tomorrow. (Kellogg Commission, 1999, p. 3)

This vision of the future, this moment for boldness, has never been more pressing than in the problem-rich urban context in which the Great Cities' Universities' presidents and chancellors find themselves today. Presidential leaders face a unique opportunity to impact not only their universities but also their communities. As Gregory O'Brien, former chancellor of the University of New Orleans (UNO), observed, "the urban university really is a different kind of institution that we lead. As a president, I think you have to be very, very committed to changing the prospects for urban America. And it's got to go beyond what we do on our campus to include the community. I may have reinvented my job several times, but I never changed my vision of what we were supposed to do. It really is about changing the destiny of the city and of the metropolitan area." Such a personal commitment to engagement is reflected in how Gerald Bepko, now retired from Indiana University–Purdue University Indianapolis (IUPUI), defines the urban president as "a champion for the value of university engagement," a commitment to service that he believes can dramatically improve quality of life and personal fulfillment.

While the presidents and chancellors of public urban research institutions face unique leadership challenges based on the varying size, demographic profile, history, and academic specialties of their respective universities, all of the 14 leaders interviewed for this book are united by a passionate belief in a mission of community engagement as a defining focus of higher education's teaching, research, and service. Because of this commitment to the communities in which they reside, urban presidents face two unique leadership challenges: (1) the additional responsibility to communicate to the community the mission, vision, and expertise of the university to benefit the region the institution serves, especially in regard to its commitment to urban education reform; and, (2) the reality of connecting to and working with a wide range of constituents with a multiplicity of agendas that can be both invigorating and daunting.

This challenge confronts Chancellor Martha Gilliland of the University of Missouri–Kansas City (UMKC), who began her tenure with the conviction that engagement is fundamental to her vision for the university: "The basic mission of a public research university is to educate mainstream America and enhance the economic and social well being of a region/state. In my role as chancellor, it was clear to me that placing our university as a central resource for both economic development and the personal development of our citizens was a top priority and an incredibly complex challenge." For Cleveland State University's president Michael Schwartz, engagement is an ethical matter: "I believe it is an ethical responsibility of the university and those who work in it, to serve as public intellectuals, using what they know about their disciplines to participate in community-wide partnerships to address these serious concerns. This has become the focus of much of my work and our university's work with the urban school district and our community." University presidents have the opportunity to fulfill this ethical responsibility when they lead their institutions toward what Bepko calls "exemplary civic engagement."

One of the primary ways in which presidents define their civic engagement leadership is through their partnerships with public education. Urban presidents understand the importance of K–12 education to the mission of the university because they are part of the urban community and its problems and because they rely on public education for qualified, competent students. As Chancellor Jo Ann Gora of the University of Massachusetts Boston (UMass Boston) observes, "the university plays such an important role in the community, and one of the most visible roles we play in the community is through the Boston Public Schools. What we are doing is such a priority; promoting our involvement in the community is part of the larger image." Gilliland corroborates this commitment. "My strong and unrelenting belief is that an urban university in the twenty-first century cannot aspire to greatness without a great School of Education, engaged in the reform of education in the region."

For Bepko, engagement in elementary and secondary education is the way in which universities can help people advance themselves. "Urban campuses have to measure themselves by the success of their constituencies. That is why year by year I've gotten more and more involved in K–16 education." Nancy Zimpher, former chancellor of the University of Wisconsin–Milwaukee (UWM), concurs. "You can't have a brighter workforce if you don't have a strong K–16 pipeline, and you can't have a diverse workforce if you don't have a pipeline through which the majority of students can successfully advance. I don't know how we can do more important work for a productive and economically viable community than to produce an educated populace."

Even as presidents and chancellors recognize the importance of K–12 education to their own institutional mission, they are equally aware of the challenges such engagement entails. As Joseph Steger, retired president of the University of Cincinnati admits, "conducting teacher education the right way is difficult. Providing teacher candidates with the knowledge, skills, and dispositions to be effective teachers is extremely complex. Like all worthwhile activities, teacher preparation requires a great deal of effort and commitment. Simple solutions are likely to fail, and our children will bear the brunt of these experiments." Georgia State's President Carl Patton knows well the costs of such commitment. "In most cases, these relationships require active solicitation, substantial time and energy commitments, and patience. However, my investments have garnered passionate and dedicated supporters who have helped to advance our initiatives in many other areas."

One of the reasons that K–16 partnerships can be challenging is because urban universities often face a skeptical—or worse, unaware—public that must first be educated about the strengths the university can bring to the table. Portland State's President Daniel Bernstine faced such an obstacle. "Our basic challenge is to get the perception of the institution to catch up with the reality of what we are doing," he admits. "That's not uncommon for an urban school because historically 'urban' meant 'inferior' to many people who were unfamiliar with us. And the fact that we have an access mission is interpreted to mean that our students cannot go someplace else; although, the reason they cannot go someplace else is usually for geographic or economic reasons, not because of inferior credentials." Still, solidifying connections with the community can be challenging. "UMKC was not necessarily seen as 'Kansas City's University' by many people," says Gilliland. "The attitude was not necessarily hostile; they simply did not view our campus as a catalyst for change, a site for innovation, and a place where leadership for the city would emerge." Schwartz agrees: "People know we're here, they just don't know what we do for a living. I found a distinct need to create an identity for CSU as a metropolitan leader in economic growth and development, an unsung and sleeping giant in a city ravaged by monthly closings of industries and the flight of the middle class to the suburbs."

President Eugene Trani, of Virginia Commonwealth University, also faced a "vast separation from our community" and made bridging that divide a major part of his agenda. He did this by communicating the advantages VCU offered as an urban institution. Getting the message out takes more than a good public relations department, however. All the presidents emphasized the leadership commitment necessary to be a visible and vocal presence in their communities. "I'm all over the place, often from 7 A.M. to 10 o'clock at night and every weekend," says Trani. "The police keep tabs and radio signal each other: 'He's back and driving around campus again.'"

Blanche Touhill, chancellor emerita of the University of Missouri–St. Louis, believes the president needs a widespread community presence, which in her case meant she was involved in everything. "I'm on the civic progress committee, which is a group of the big corporations in St. Louis. I'm on three of the major women's groups in St. Louis. I'm on the nonprofits. I probably am listed on 25 to 30 different boards. Now, I don't go to 25 or 30 board meetings every month, but I do go when they need me. Our university is always represented." Despite the demands, these presidents speak of the rightness of this agenda—for the university, the community, and the schools. Touhill says it this way, "I think it is very easy to step back from the vision. You know, the right vision is just filled with fight and it is filled with tension. But I think that that's what this job is, and you have to just keep pushing the vision forward."

THE COMPLEXITY OF LEADERSHIP IN PRACTICE

As the presidents and chancellors talked about their personal approaches to leading public research institutions committed to urban education, they identified a range of strategies that address the unique challenges of serving the community as well as the university—and meeting the multiplicity of demands from both. Repeatedly these presidents use terms like complexity, unpredictability, a swirling and eddying of forces. They talk about the variety of constituencies served, all with compelling—and sometimes competing—agendas. This kind of environment calls for creative approaches to leadership. Sylvia Manning, chancellor of the University of Illinois at Chicago (UIC), uses the image of a cascade of leadership that flows from the chancellor to the provost and deans to department heads and faculty and outward to the schools and community.

Another way of looking at this dynamic process of directing the complex relationships that entwine urban campuses with their communities is to see leadership in terms of six practices that build on and mutually reinforce and enhance each other.

Six Leadership Practices

1. Creating a vision
2. Engaging the university
3. Engaging the community
4. Taking action
5. Being accountable
6. Committing to long-term change

Taken together, these six practices form a framework for presidential leadership that simultaneously connects university to community, action to results, and accountability to long-term change in a growing and ongoing spiral of interaction. And at the core of these leadership practices is the vision of the engaged university that both anchors and inspires its growth.

Following are examples of how our author-presidents reflect on this interactive and recursive spiral of leadership practices.

CREATING A VISION

A public urban research university cannot be all things to all people. If it is to serve its students and its community it must understand its strengths, its responsibilities, its resources, and the opportunities it can fulfill. The first duty of urban leaders is to understand and help to create a vision for the institution that is true, that will inspire, and that can be accomplished. As former president of Connecticut College, Claire Gaudiani, has noted, "one of the keys to a successful presidency is understanding how little power you have over people, yet what enormous power you have over their imagination. The role of the vision is to connect the knowledge and skills of the president and the community so powerfully that an outcome well beyond what anyone could have imagined actually results" (Gaudiani, 1996, p. 61). This vision varied for each of our presidents but for all of them, creating and supporting the vision is their first and ongoing concern as leaders. Bepko saw his role as "keeper of the values of the university"—he defines the president's job as shaping and reinforcing the vision and values of the university community so that over time people will embrace them and be energized to apply their creative talents.

In this sense, a president has to know the university and its traditions—the "unique landscape" of each institution, as Wayne State University's president Irvin Reid describes it. New leaders have to be students of the university because "all universities are not created for the same purpose," says Zimpher. "You have to talk to a lot of people and get the lay of the land. What you decide to do has to be very indigenous to the institution." As Manning sees it, "leadership is a self-conscious examination of the context, an understanding of the individuals within that context, and a willingness to suit one's leadership to that context and those individuals." Some presidents actually become institutional "historians in residence," as was the case with Touhill. She spent two years writing the history of UM–St. Louis before becoming chancellor, a process that helped her think deeply about the institution and internalize its values. "What I believe in is really what this campus believes in," she says.

Sometimes the university's vision is not self-evident or may be fractured by competing perceptions. In such cases, as Trani learned at VCU, identifying a unifying and authentic vision is imperative. "When I arrived in 1990, I did not have a university. I had a group of individuals united by paychecks and disagreements over parking," recalls Trani. "I had to build a sense of the university." Trani capitalized on the strength of his medical campus by "capturing it academically" and making it a part of the university. "Putting the two institutions together and building a sense of the university, no question about it, is the most important thing I've done. Now we're thinking like a university." Such vision building is not incremental and not for the faint of heart. Patton takes his inspiration from the architect, Daniel Burnham, who advised in 1893: "Make no little plans; they have no magic to stir people's blood. Make only big plans for a noble concept once recorded shall live forever" (Larsen, 2003, epigraph). Noble visions are the first task of the urban university president.

ENGAGING THE UNIVERSITY

One synonym for public leadership in a complex environment is *involvedness*. If a compelling vision for the engaged university is essential to presidential leadership, it is possible only through the involvedness of both campus and community in creating it, refining it, and living it. It begins first through campus engagement.

Gilliland at UMKC led a visionary process of faculty, staff, and student retreats that ultimately involved about 2,000 people in discussing what was possible for the university, a process that was intended to "produce a constituency that is highly engaged in the vision and an organization that is highly accomplished." Similar to Gilliland, Zimpher also launched a campus engagement effort at UWM called The Milwaukee Idea. It ultimately involved more than 500 people from campus and community in creating a new vision and a series of initiatives focused on education, the economy, and the environment. Essential to the process was linking the new vision to ideas already familiar to both campus and community. "The Milwaukee Idea grew out of a 100-year tradition called the 'Wisconsin Idea' that had animated the University of Wisconsin since its founding," says Zimpher. "It was an idea of community/university partnership that was already a part of this state. I think every university has its 'Wisconsin Idea'—you just have to find it. It is what means something to people; it is a part of their tradition and their love for their place and their history."

Once the vision is determined, it needs advocates. Repeatedly, urban presidents talked about the importance of forming a team—a group within the university that shares the vision and that works together to implement it. In educational reform that team typically includes the provost and dean of education as well as deans of other partner colleges. President Shirley Raines of the University of Memphis had the unique opportunity to fill the deanships for both the colleges of Arts and Sciences and Education at the same time. She used this opportunity to lobby for increased interdisciplinary engagement across both colleges.

As important as academic leaders are to the vision, the vision also requires the involvement of faculty and staff at all levels, on a temporary or full-time basis, who help to connect the vision internally to the campus as well as externally to the education community. Several strategies for team building emerge from our presidents' observations: find leaders who are effective, accountable, and committed to the vision; use existing staff when possible; create new structures to support innovation; create temporary teams to build relationships and skills.

Bernstine, for example, uses existing university structures to reinforce the vision and reach out.

> I try to involve faculty in as many ways as possible, sometimes through the existing governance structure [the university and faculty senates] and through the President's Advisory Council [a group of six or seven appointed by the faculty senate]. If I'm not comfortable that the current structure will work to solve the problem, I'll deploy a special committee that represents a broad cross-section of the university. And then I make sure I appoint someone in whom I have confidence in to actually move the initiative along— not necessarily a *powerful* person, but a person who gets things done, who knows how to use the existing structure to get people to buy into the initiative and move it along.

Manning talks about the power of "distributed leadership" and the power of other leaders on down the line. A "continuum of committed leadership" is required she says because faculty and department heads are able to act on their commitments to education only to the extent that their dean will support them. Not only do presidents lead through teamwork, as O'Brien suggests, they should also look to contrarians—those who bring alternative perspectives to the table. "You should surround yourself with people who really do think differently than you do. You need to have people who are not afraid to tell you that you're wrong. I always try to recruit opposites to my weaknesses," says O'Brien.

Each president interviewed found ways to involve individuals from the staff inherited from the previous president and also to use the transition as an opportunity to attract people who can bring new talents and energy to the vision. Steger suggests that "hiring good people is half of the secret to leadership—and firing bad ones is the other half." He was not afraid to suggest to people who did not want to engage in the vision that they would be happier working someplace else. "I turned over nine deans and four officers when I got here," Steger admits. "And then we rebuilt the team. As a team, we generated where we wanted to go." Presidents must be mindful, however, as Trani cautions, that transitions have consequences. "There are presidents who come in and they throw half the crowd out. And half the crowd leaves friends who then spend the next five years waging a guerilla war against the president." To counter transition problems, Reid fits the team to the vision, not the vision to the team. "I don't start with an organization chart. I start with a mission, a vision, and a set of goals. Then I say 'what kind of organization do I need to help me do this?' I want to empower very strong vice presidents and I want them to take responsibility for their actions." For most presidents, effective university engagement boils down to Patton's guiding principle for leadership: "Hire good people. This involves making sure to form good search committees and refusing to hire second best."

To diversify leadership, Zimpher created a matrix structure. She identified key people at the outset that could take the lead and who had been under-recognized—consistent with what some change leaders in higher education call the positional faculty or the impellers. This put people in different positions who were given the authority and resources to run oppositionally to the traditional organization. She also created Deans Councils around major institutional initiatives. So, for example, in UWM's education partnership, the dean of education meets regularly with about five other deans and together they provide leadership for the partnership. Raines followed a similar path, creating short-term teams around individual projects. "I bring different divisions of the university together to create the team. The style is team problem solving, with the goal of working together and then moving on to another team."

As soon as a unified leadership team is in place (and it can take time to identify, recruit, and unify an effective team), presidential leaders seek to broaden the circle for collective action. There will always be faculty and staff who reject the vision, however, it is more important to target the majority who need only to find the connection between the vision and their own work. Leaders expand involvement through several strategies: they communicate the vision; support those who follow the vision; provide incentives for involvement; create conditions under which individuals can succeed—early; and foster interdisciplinary connections.

Many of the presidents interviewed cited the power of persuasion as critical to engaging the university. As Patton observes, "creating a collective purpose involves institutionalizing the vision through effective and frequent communication. I believe in the power of talking, talking, talking."

Reid uses the example of his technology park for how he involved faculty and staff. He went to every single department and every school and college within the university talking about the project—"imbuing them with my excitement." Gora also spends a lot of time using her so-called bully pulpit as chancellor to emphasize the importance of public education to the institution. "When the chancellor or president says something is important, all of a sudden everybody says 'okay,'" she observes. "So you can do a great benefit by saying to the whole institution that public education matters."

Once presidents have created their team and raised campus awareness, they must support those who follow the vision and who are working to change the internal culture, procedures, policies, and curriculum. Steger did this by resisting the temptation to "over-manage." He encouraged his deans, vice provosts, and provosts to "run their shops;" the only time he intervened was "if they went astray from where the rest of the institution was going." Allowing others the freedom to interpret and implement the vision changes the nature of presidential leadership. As Manning observes:

> Leadership is a role that requires a desire to be of *service* to those one leads. What in truth we all do is—by whatever means we can—get other people to do good work. You move from *doing* to creating the conditions under which *other people* can do it. You're always asking 'what do I need to do to the environment or to the external relationships that will allow this group or this whole institution to keep moving forward?' So that means that you've got to get all the other people who are doing it to feel recognized and valued and so you try to push them to the front for that reason.

Bepko agrees. He focused on recruiting quality people to be responsible for the major work of the institution, blending them into a teamwork environment. "And then I got out of their way and encouraged them to pursue their subsidiary vision once they bought into the larger sense of what we were trying to achieve. My task as president was to facilitate what these action-level people were doing within the framework of our larger vision."

Obviously, reinforcing and rewarding are also necessary tools. Raines publicly says that education is important and then follows up with rewards for the faculty who do the work. "I need to let them know that their efforts are valued and recognized." One important way that presidents can reward faculty and academic leaders is by protecting the vision—especially during times of financial cutbacks. "When you have a conceptual framework of a vision that fits into the mission of the institution, it should not suffer in the face of cutbacks," says Reid. He works to find ways to enhance and retain programs that are essential to the university's vision.

ENGAGING THE COMMUNITY

If engagement—especially with urban schools—is a measure of institutional success, presidents agree that fostering involvedness with external constituents is also vital. Being an outside president is an essential part of the job description in order for leaders to know and be plugged into the complex network of community relationships that facilitate increased engagement. Urban presidential leaders also seek wide civic involvement and establish relationships with key community leaders, they establish or build on joint and reciprocal leadership partnerships, and they use their influence to gain community support. To the greatest extent possible, presidents reflect the balance needed to leverage internal activity with their desire to engage the broader community in the university's mission.

As Bepko recalls, he was expected, as president, to be "outside" because "that is what the public expects of urban university chancellors and presidents." These public expectations demand a significant investment from the president as O'Brien can attest. "You have to get yourself into the city," he says. "I attended every cocktail party, every event; I was busy every night of every week for the first five years. But that's how you get credibility in the community. It's just so important." Zimpher concurs:

> People in the community want to see the institution physically and personally represented by someone who will be visible. Woody Allen is often quoted as saying that 80 percent of success is showing up. I showed up and I showed up and I showed up—at UWM I had more than 200 engagements annually. But you not only have to show up, you have to be articulate and you need a message. I had a message. I knew what UWM was about. My community presence was not just a marketing ploy; it was a reflection of my institution's fundamental belief system and my passion about UWM and The Milwaukee Idea.

With presidential leadership also comes the responsibility for reciprocal involvement. Being in the community is important and so is inviting people into the president's house. Steger knew that it can be "a big deal" to go to the president's house. Being a good host is an important way to create good relationships with people, relationships that often result in increased involvement with the university. Michael Schwartz, who writes in his chapter about his efforts to "fill the moat" between the Cleveland Municipal Schools and the university, found the intimacy of a presidential dinner the ideal vehicle for solidifying relationships.

A number of our presidents who were new to their communities also learned early on the wisdom of engaging the community through existing university-community relationships. When Gora arrived at UMass Boston she found a mayor and superintendent already supportive of K–16 education. "I walked in, scanned the horizon and I saw the alignment. And I'm not walking away from it!" Steger was able to build on a long institutional history of co-op education in Cincinnati. He realized the co-op tradition already set the university apart in the public's perception, so one of his first steps was to upgrade this perception. Raines took advantage of the retirement of a popular and successful county school superintendent and brought him into the university as a temporary faculty member to lead efforts in improving leadership for principals. Bernstine reengaged with Portland State alumni, an often ignored but valuable community network for urban universities. Reid found productive partnerships with so-called competitors, the University of Michigan and Michigan State. These universities realized that none of them could become a leader in the life sciences alone and they agreed to a joint effort that has paid off in significant state financial support for all three. Reid is also using partnerships that have developed around his technology park to create new relationships with a charter school and his engineering school.

Once accepted in the community, presidents constantly acknowledged the public expectations of their role. University presidents lead by congealing public opinion and by encouraging, not by mandating or making arbitrary decisions. New presidents were careful not to appear publicly as "know-it-alls" telling the community what to do. All agreed that credibility and trust with the community is essential because community support is vital for public urban universities. Without it, the university remains under-funded, under-appreciated, and under-respected.

The presidents spent a good amount of time sharing their views on the concept of the convening power of university presidents. The common view is that, for whatever reason, university presidents seem to possess a degree of neutrality typically not assigned to elected officials in particular, nor even to corporate leaders. As a consequence, they have gathering power; if they call a meeting of key community leaders, they will come! Accordingly, we heard of many examples of presidents doing just that: Schwartz hosted dinners at his home wherein he invited guests for public discourse about school reform; Touhill brought together community organizations, faculty, and potential funders to discuss endowed professorships; and Manning convened a state-wide P–16 leadership summit at UIC to help position the university, internally and externally, in its commitment to partnership with urban schools.

Many of the presidents talked about how they have extended their convening activities to active civic leadership. Trani, for example, serves as president of Richmond's downtown renewal initiative, Richmond Renaissance. Bernstine chaired the board of directors of the Urban League of Portland.

And Zimpher played a catalytic role in convening the seven partners, and ultimately forty board members, of The Milwaukee Partnership Academy.

TAKING ACTION

As author and change agent Michael Fullan notes, vision emerges from, more than it precedes, action (Fullan, 1993). Reflective experience—especially amid the complexity of urban education and earned through dynamic interaction among university, community, and school district—is essential. Presidents model the ideal of action and also foster engagement by others to move the vision forward. Gora speaks of the challenges of getting others to act on the vision and to move forward in an academic culture that likes to "discuss, debate, deliberate, talk, not do." She is clear that action is required:

> I try to say "here's an idea" and then I listen really closely to what people say. If they are enthusiastic, I go forward full steam ahead. And if they say "there's a problem" I suggest alternatives or urge others to do so. In the end we have something that most people can agree with. I try to give others the credit for the final product. Then, I push hard to implement. Because if you don't, nothing happens.

One way in which vision becomes action is through a clear strategic plan that defines goals and tactics and provides the discipline and accountability for action. Raines says it's all in the launch and monitoring process. "When we form a partnership we make sure that there is a plan, and we make sure we keep track of it because we in universities are very good with ideas but not always great with follow up."

BEING ACCOUNTABLE

The challenge of urban education reform requires not only passionate community-university partnerships but also effective partnerships that make a real difference in how children learn. The community is often wary of new ideas and programs because too frequently change has not produced results. Urban research universities can bring unique resources to the challenge of measuring and evaluating the change they help to create. In a world of reduced state funding, demonstrated results can also lead to alternative funding opportunities. Presidents in this study achieved accountability through multiple routes.

"In addition to my strong belief in using data to make decisions, with deep knowledge from research and practice for guidance, I also believe in placing authority with quality leaders for accountability for results," says

Raines. Bernstine ensures accountability through his appointments and their achievements. "I appoint chairs to campus-wide initiatives who are committed to an action agenda with measurable outcomes," he says. "We value assessment as a tool for accountability." Gora follows a similar approach by involving individuals with a clear timeframe for reporting back results. "I really hold people accountable and then I praise them and give them public recognition so they feel rewarded because what I'm trying to do is change behavior. I am trying to get them to realize that what is important is not *thinking* about things, but *doing* things."

Holding an institution to new standards is a key strategy, says Gilliland. In 2000, when she became chancellor of the University of Missouri–Kansas City, she committed to an ongoing process to help university faculty and staff conduct serious self examinations of the standards to which they held themselves accountable. These self examinations were inclusive, accessed the wisdom of faculty, staff, students, and constituents; involved creative dialogue, not solely intellectual debate; and resulted in new ways of measuring and new standards. Annual accountability reports work well too, says Patton. "I demonstrate my commitment to education by creating effective institutional policies," he says. "I am highly committed to accountability mechanisms that lead to measurable results. Basically this means spelling out how academic policies and fiscal decisions will be evaluated in order that we can measure and publicly report progress toward our goals." As several of the presidents and chancellors noted, it is their responsibility to set institutional expectations for accountability, to encourage use of benchmarks for all initiatives, and to ask—relentlessly—for results.

COMMITTING TO LONG-TERM CHANGE

The average tenure of a university president currently hovers around five to six years. The group of 14 urban research university presidents assembled for this study range from newly appointed leaders to those with 20 years' experience at the same university. Six of the 14 logged more than 10 years at their current institution and, according to them, it was for good reason. The challenges of leadership and of addressing what are truly long-term urban problems—such as education, economic development, and health care—cannot be addressed through a few short-term initiatives or quick-fix solutions. The hard realities of partnership—often difficult to maintain and grow over time—are echoed in the need for sustained and persistent leadership. And so, the advice from those who have stayed the course is: commit to the long haul.

As Bepko notes, "the relationships between universities and the schools in their states may be viewed best in terms of how they will be shaped and formed over long periods of time with many experiments, many efforts by many people, and accumulated experience." The long view is important. O'Brien agrees that there is a real value to staying at an institution. "There is a certain calling to leadership of these urban universities.... [Presidents] are more engaged at a frontline level and must be very, very committed." O'Brien admits that presidents will go through cycles during their tenure—he suggests that the best opportunity to make a difference may come after the initial honeymoon. After 19 years of service as a university president, Steger learned that endurance is important to leadership. "There are not enough hours in a day to get your job done and so commitment has got to be a real big part of your life. It takes a long time to get things done—to build a power base and a donor base takes years."

Committing to long-term institutional leadership requires ongoing change and adaptation as well as endurance. Throughout a cycle of leadership, and especially if a president stays for a decade or more, there are important lessons to be learned, says Reid. No matter what organization the president puts in place, it needs to be renewed frequently, about every five years. "If you are a dynamic president, if you're going to be a president that doesn't just sit and ride on what you did in the first five years, you can't do it with the same people," says Reid. "You've got to completely tear down the organization and start over. You don't reset the vision because the vision evolves. But the people don't necessarily evolve and that's why organizational change is necessary. As the leader, you're always ahead. I didn't go into this job as a shrinking violet and the board did not hire me to maintain the status quo, even when that status quo is one that I've created." Furthermore, Reid observes, the president needs constant self-examination. "Never close your mind to the idea that something you thought was a great idea yesterday may no longer be a great idea!"

CONCLUSION

As these reflections reveal, today's public urban university presidents are pivotal links between the rich resources of dynamic institutions of higher education and the energy and potential of our metropolitan centers, with all their challenges and opportunities. Leadership, especially in service to K–12 education, requires individuals deeply committed to a vision of community-university engagement and exceptionally accomplished in managing complexity. They must engage both campus and community in the difficult tasks of creating responsive institutions in successful cities and they must use the power of their position to convene, inspire, and produce results. All of the presidents and chancellors who have contributed to this book have committed their lives to this demanding task for one simple reason: they cannot imagine a calling more important or a challenge more rewarding.

The 14 stories described herein are testament to the good work that is being done to help the youth of our cities learn. But there is still much to be done. The problems and challenges in our urban school districts are long-standing and pervasive. Tens of thousands of youngsters continue to fail in school. Historically, universities have limited their role in redressing these problems primarily to the preparation of educational personnel. Nonetheless, even when done extremely well this has proven to be an inadequate response. Regardless of the quality of teachers or school district leaders, only nominal improvements in school achievement have been made by youth—and especially minority youth—enrolled in these urban schools. Teacher renewal and retention cannot occur over time without major changes in schools and school districts as well. School organizational patterns and cultures have to be structured to enable *teacher* as well as student learning. But the problems obviously go beyond schools. High quality, largely self-renewing schools are needed in a variety of neighborhoods and communities, especially in neighborhoods defined by pockets of urban poverty. These urban presidents and chancellors have exerted leadership at all levels; community renewal, changes at the district level, individual school reform, and improved preparation for the individuals within these schools.

Clearly urban university presidents are in a position to exert influence in all these areas. They can leverage resources wisely within their institutions and mobilize key stakeholders outside their walls to address the big picture. They understand the nested or layered nature of reforms, which are needed to improve learning for all youngsters.

While we readily admit that there is yet much to learn about how universities might best proceed in helping to advance needed reforms in P–12 education, we believe that the stories shared herein provide important stepping-stones to further progress.

Nancy L. Zimpher *became the twenty-fifth president of the University of Cincinnati in 2003 and its first woman president. She previously served as the chancellor of the University of Wisconsin–Milwaukee. A teacher and educator, she also served as Dean of the College of Education and executive dean of the*

Professional Colleges at The Ohio State University in Columbus, Ohio. She was president of the Holmes Partnership from 1996–2001 and co-coordinator in 2000 of the U.S. Secretary of Education's National Summit on Teacher Quality. She is the recipient of the American Association of Colleges for Teacher Education's Edward C. Pomeroy Award for Outstanding Contributions to Teacher Education.

Kenneth R. Howey *is a research professor in the College of Education, Criminal Justice and Human Services at the University of Cincinnati. Previously he held faculty and administrative appointments at the University of Minnesota, The Ohio State University, and the University of Wisconsin–Madison and the University of Wisconsin–Milwaukee. He was the principle investigator for the longest-running study of teacher education in the United States and for several years directed the national reform consortium, the Urban Network to Improve Teacher Education, UNITE. He is the author of several books and articles on teacher education. Dr. Howey is the recipient of the American Association of Colleges for Teacher Education's highest award for distinguished contributions to teacher education throughout a career.*

BIBLIOGRAPHY

Boyer, E. (1990). *Scholarship reconsidered: Priorities of the professoriate.* San Francisco: Jossey-Bass.

Fullan, M. (1993). *Change forces.* New York: The Falmer Press.

Gaudiani, C. (Spring, 1996). "Developing a vision." In J. Block McLaughlin, (Ed.), *Leadership transitions: The new college president.* (pp. 59–70). New Directions in Higher Education Series, No. 93. San Francisco: Jossey Bass.

Kellogg Commission on the Future of State and Land-Grant Universities. (1999). *Engaged institutions: A commitment to service. Profiles and data.* Third working paper. Washington, D.C.: National Association of State Universities and Land-Grant Colleges. Retrieved September 18, 2003 from http://www.nasulgc.org/publications/kellogg/profiles.pdf.

———. (2000). *Renewing the covenant: Learning, discovery, and engagement in a new age and different world.* (Sixth report). Washington, D.C.: National Association of State Universities and Land-Grant Colleges. Retrieved September 18, 2003 from http://www.nasulgc.org/Kellogg/kellogg.htm.

Larsen, E. (2003, February). *The devil in the white city: Murder, magic, and madness at the fair that changed America.* (Epigraph, 1st edition). Crown Publications.

Index